Gender in Scotland, 1200–1800

Place, Faith and Politics

Edited by
JANAY NUGENT, CATHRYN SPENCE
AND MAIRI COWAN

EDINBURGH
University Press

Edinburgh University Press is one of the leading university presses in the UK. We publish academic books and journals in our selected subject areas across the humanities and social sciences, combining cutting-edge scholarship with high editorial and production values to produce academic works of lasting importance. For more information visit our website: edinburghuniversitypress.com

© editorial matter and organisation Janay Nugent, Cathryn Spence and Mairi Cowan, 2024, 2026
© the chapters their several authors, 2024, 2026

Edinburgh University Press Ltd
13 Infirmary Street
Edinburgh EH1 1LT

First published in hardback by Edinburgh University Press 2024

Typeset in 10/13 Giovanni by
Cheshire Typesetting Ltd, Cuddington, Cheshire, and
printed and bound by CPI Group (UK) Ltd,
Croydon, CR0 4YY

A CIP record for this book is available from the British Library

ISBN 978 1 3995 1298 5 (hardback)
ISBN 978 1 3995 1299 2 (paperback)
ISBN 978 1 3995 1300 5 (webready PDF)
ISBN 978 1 3995 1301 2 (epub)

The right of Janay Nugent, Cathryn Spence and Mairi Cowan to be identified as editors of this work has been asserted in accordance with the Copyright, Designs and Patents Act 1988 and the Copyright and Related Rights Regulations 2003 (SI No. 2498).

Gender in Scotland, 1200–1800

For Professor Elizabeth Ewan

'Gender in Scotland'
by *Jamie Reid Baxter*

Doors are there to be opened,
Paths untrod to be taken,
Nonsense contradicted,
False certainties shaken.

Contents

List of Figures and Tables vii
Notes on the Contributors ix
List of Abbreviations xiv
Preface xvi

Introduction: Engendering Scottish History for the Medieval and Early
Modern Periods 1
Cathryn Spence, Janay Nugent and Mairi Cowan

PART ONE Place

1 Mary, Queen of Scots, Three Noblewomen and a Fife 'Murder
   Mystery' 13
   Jane E. A. Dawson

2 'Scottish Portias' Revisited: Women in the Courts in Early Modern
   Scottish Towns 31
   Rebecca Mason

3 Punching Back against Patriarchy: The Story of Jean Weir 48
   Michael F. Graham

4 Always at the Gate? Unlocking Medieval Women's Stories in
   Modern-day Edinburgh 62
   Rachel M. Delman

PART TWO Faith

5 'She displays by her speeches': Marion Walker, Catholic Speech and Local Resistance in Early Modern Glasgow 87
Daniel MacLeod

6 Memory and Materiality: John Knox and the Resilience of Relic-thinking in the Continuity and Gender of Cult in Late Medieval and Early Modern Perth 104
Mark A. Hall

7 'She-zealots' and 'Satanesses': Women, Patriarchy and the Covenanting Movement 123
Michelle D. Brock

8 Emotion, Authority and Griefwork in the Spiritual Poetry of Lilias Skene 141
Sarah Dunnigan

PART THREE Politics

9 Displaying Support for Women's Lineage: Late Medieval Seals and Family Identity 161
Rachel Meredith Davis

10 Another Damsel in Distress? Katherine Beaumont, a Disinherited Noblewoman in Fourteenth-century Scotland 179
Iain A. MacInnes and Morvern French

11 Negotiating Youth, Old Age and Manhood: A Comparative Approach to Late Medieval Scottish Kingship 193
Lucinda H. S. Dean

12 Sons and Daughters, Mothers and Mercenaries: Agency and Agenda in the Cross-North Channel Context, c. 1550–c. 1600 210
Alison Cathcart

Conclusion: New Vistas and the Future for Scottish Gender History 224
Cathryn Spence, Janay Nugent and Mairi Cowan

Bibliography 226
Index 257

Figures and Tables

Figures

1.1	Relationships between the four women	14
4.1	Façade of the Magdalen Chapel, Cowgate, Edinburgh	71
4.2	Trinity Apse and the Leonardo Royal Hotel, Chalmers Close, Edinburgh	71
4.3	Interior of the Magdalen Chapel, facing south-east	75
4.4	Plaque on the exterior of the Magdalen Chapel, Cowgate, Edinburgh	76
4.5	Site of the tomb of Jonet Rynd in the Magdalen Chapel	77
4.6	Interior of Trinity Apse, Edinburgh, in 2018	80
4.7	Information board on the main gate of Trinity Apse, Chalmers Close, Edinburgh	82
6.1	General view of Marian chandelier, St John's Kirk, Perth	107
6.2	Glover Incorporation portrait of St Bartholomew	107
6.3	Detail view of Marian chandelier to show contrasting multiplicity of match-marks	110
6.4	Detail of additional shoe added to enable re-fitting of bracket	111
6.5	The presumed John Knox candlestick	115
6.6	The John Knox walking stick	115
9.1	Seal cast of Alexander, Earl of Menteith	164
9.2	Seal cast of Walter Steward	164
9.3	Seal cast of Alan Stewart of Menteith	164
9.4	Seal cast of Alexander Abernethy	164
9.5	Seal of Katherine Beaumont, Countess of Atholl	168
9.6	Seal cast of Margaret Stewart, Countess of Angus and Mar	170
9.7	Seal cast of George Douglas, Earl of Angus	171
9.8	Seal cast of Walter Leslie, Lord of Ross (1371)	172
9.9	Seal cast of Euphemia Leslie, Countess of Ross	172

9.10	The arms and crest of Walter Leslie	173
9.11	Seal cast of Walter Leslie (1367)	173
9.12	Seal cast of Donald, Lord of the Isles	175
9.13	Seal cast of Alexander, Earl of Ross and Lord of the Isles	176
9.14	Seal cast of John, Earl of Ross and Lord of the Isles	176
9.15	Descendants of Sir Alexander Abernethy in the fourteenth and early fifteenth centuries	177

Tables

2.1	Women involved in debt and estate litigation in Glasgow's burgh court, June 1657 to June 1658	41
2.2	Marital status of female litigants in debt and estate litigation in Glasgow's burgh court, June 1657 to June 1658	43

Notes on the Contributors

Michelle D. Brock is Professor of History at Washington and Lee University in Virginia. She completed her PhD at the University of Texas at Austin. A scholar of religion and the supernatural in early modern Scotland, she is the author of *Satan and the Scots: The Devil in Post-Reformation Scotland* (2016). She is also co-editor of *Knowing Demons, Knowing Spirits in the Early Modern Period* (2018) and the forthcoming *Routledge History of the Devil in the Western Tradition*. Additionally, she is co-director of *Mapping the Scottish Reformation*, a digital prosopography of the Scottish clergy between 1560 and 1689. Her second monograph, *Plagues of the Heart: Crisis and Covenanting in a Seventeenth-Century Scottish Town*, is forthcoming with Manchester University Press.

Alison Cathcart is Professor of Early Modern Scottish and Archipelagic History at the University of Stirling though she would describe herself as a historian of the peripheries. Following publication of her second monograph, *Plantations by Land and Sea: North Channel Communities of the Atlantic Archipelago, c. 1550–1625* (2021), her current focus is on insular communities across the archipelago that exist at the interface of land and sea, and their interaction with central authorities, while drawing on maritime, legal, environmental and economic dimensions to such relationships. She is involved also in interdisciplinary research projects with a focus on fishing.

Mairi Cowan is Associate Professor in the Department of Historical Studies, University of Toronto Mississauga. She is the author of *Death, Life, and Religious Change in Scottish Towns, c. 1350–1560* (2013) and *The Possession of Barbe Hallay: Diabolical Arts and Daily Life in Early Canada* (2022). She has also written articles about tensions of international theology, national politics and local tradition in twelfth-century Glasgow; experiences of childhood in the Renaissance court of James IV, King of Scots; the periodisation of Scottish history; colonial efforts to 'Frenchify' Indigenous people in seventeenth-century Québec; and

Jesuit missionaries' beliefs about demons in Indigenous societies of North America.

Rachel Meredith Davis received her PhD from the University of Edinburgh in 2020, where she wrote a thesis on how elite women's identities were constructed through seals and charters in late medieval Scotland. She is a teaching assistant at the Centre for History at the University of the Highlands and Islands. Current research interests include agency, gender and material culture in fourteenth- and fifteenth-century Scotland.

Jane E. A. Dawson is the John Laing Professor Emerita of Reformation History at the University of Edinburgh. Her books include *John Knox* (2015), *Scotland Re-formed, 1488–1587* (Edinburgh University Press, 2007) and *The Politics of Religion in the Age of Mary, Queen of Scots* (2002). She was Director of the Wode Psalter Project and the various 'Singing the Reformation' offshoots (2008–16). Her latest research is examining the exercise of female power in sixteenth-century Scotland.

Lucinda H. S. Dean is Senior Lecturer at the Centre for History at the University of the Highlands and Islands, focusing primarily on late medieval and early modern Scotland with a keen interest in its connections and comparisons in Europe. Her research, publications and teaching centre on interconnected themes and methods of ritual, ceremony, kingship, power and authority, courtly display, material culture, gender (particularly masculinity), the life cycle and public history. Her first monograph, *Death and the Royal Succession in Scotland, c. 1214–1543: Ritual, Ceremony and Power*, is forthcoming in 2024 and she is co-investigator on the Perth Charterhouse Project. She co-edited *Medieval and Early Modern Representations of Authority in Scotland and the British Isles* (2016), *The Routledge History of Monarchy* (2019), and is currently co-editing a special issue of *Royal Studies Journal* on 'Material Culture and Built Heritage: Manifestations of Scotland's Royal Past, Present and Future' (2025) as well as contributing to a new Routledge textbook on *Exploring Monarchy in Medieval Europe*. Her contribution to this volume is part of a new project exploring manhood, masculinity and coming of age of the Stewart kings.

Rachel M. Delman is the Heritage Partnerships Coordinator in the Humanities Division at the University of Oxford, where she is responsible for building research partnerships between members of the university and regional, national and international heritage organisations. Rachel returned to Oxford – where she completed her AHRC-funded doctorate in 2017 – after research fellowships at the universities of Edinburgh and York, including a Leverhulme Early

Career Fellowship. As a historian of late medieval Britain, she has published widely on topics relating to women's and gender history, material culture and the built environment. Rachel's monograph on elite women's residences in late medieval England is forthcoming with Oxford University Press. She also frequently acts as a historical consultant to heritage organisations, including Historic Environment Scotland.

Sarah Dunnigan is Senior Lecturer in English Literature at the University of Edinburgh. Her publications in the field of early modern Scottish literature include *Eros and Poetry at the Courts of Mary Queen of Scots and James VI* (2002) and, with C. Marie Harker and Evelyn S. Newly, as co-editor of *Women and the Feminine in Medieval and Early Modern Scottish Writing* (2002). She is editor of the Scots sections of the forthcoming *Women's Poetry in Ireland, Scotland, and Wale*s (2025), with Sarah Prescott, Cathryn Charnell-White, Marie-Louise Coolahan and Wes Hamrick. She also writes about traditional Scottish ballads; fairy tales; and the history of Scottish children's writing, and has most recently co-edited, with Shu-Fang Lai, *The Land of Story-Books: Scottish Children's Literature in the Long Nineteenth Century* (2019).

Morvern French is the Properties Historian at Historic Environment Scotland. Her work, focusing on the medieval and early modern periods, includes buildings and collections research and the creation of interpretation including guidebooks, panels and reconstruction illustrations. Morvern completed a PhD in medieval history at the University of St Andrews and has published on women's history, the Wars of Independence, and medieval and early modern material culture.

Michael F. Graham is Professor of History at the University of Akron in Ohio. His most recent book, *The Blasphemies of Thomas Aikenhead* (Edinburgh University Press, 2008), tells the story of the last person executed for the crime of blasphemy in Britain. His first book, *The Uses of Reform* (1996), a study of efforts to impose new standards of behaviour and belief in the first fifty years of the Scottish Reformation, won the Sixteenth Century Studies Society's Roland H. Bainton Book Prize for the best work on early modern history or theology published that year. He has held the James Cameron Faculty Fellowship at the University of St Andrews (2003) and been a visiting fellow of the Institute for Advanced Studies in the Humanities at the University of Edinburgh (2011). In 2003 he was elected a fellow of the Royal Historical Society.

Mark A. Hall is an archaeologist and museum curator based at Perth Museum and Art Gallery, Scotland. He has just finished working on a project to deliver a new Perth Museum, including the Knox relics discussed here. Dr Hall is an active member on several professional bodies and policy initiatives (including human remains in museums, Scotland's Archaeology Strategy and the Scottish Archaeological Finds Allocation Panel). He is currently Honorary Senior Research Fellow at Stirling University. His long-standing research interests include medieval material culture (including board games and play, the cult of saints and supernatural interactions and Pictish sculpture), cultural biography and cinematic re-imaginings of the past, on which he has published internationally.

Iain A. MacInnes is Senior Lecturer in Scottish History at the University of the Highlands and Islands, where he has worked for over fourteen years. His research is centred on Anglo-Scottish conflict in the fourteenth century, with a particular focus on the post-Robert I period. His first monograph, *Scotland's Second War of Independence*, was the first full-length academic consideration of warfare during this conflict and he continues to write on themes relevant to a war that is somewhat understudied. He is also increasingly branching out from this and has developed a research interest in modern depictions of medieval warfare in popular culture (predominantly in comics) and in the wider theme of medievalism.

Daniel MacLeod is Associate Professor and Director of the Jesuit Centre for Catholic Studies at St Paul's College, University of Manitoba. He earned a PhD in History from the University of Guelph where he studied in the Centre for Scottish Studies. His research examines Christianity in early modern Scotland with a particular focus on Catholicism and the Society of Jesus. In 2014 he edited (with Stuart Macdonald) *Keeping the Kirk: Scottish Religion at Home and in the Diaspora*. He has published on Scottish conceptions of time in the Reformation era, Scottish Jesuit St John Ogilvie, and lay religious experiences in sixteenth- and seventeenth-century Glasgow. He lives in Winnipeg, Manitoba, with his family.

Rebecca Mason is a multi-disciplinary feminist researcher, with a PhD in History from the Centre for Gender History at the University of Glasgow. She specialises in gender and feminist legal history, with a focus on women's navigation of legal systems and property relationships in early modern Scotland. She has held postdoctoral positions at the University of Glasgow (Economic and Social Research Council) and the Institute of Historical Research (Eileen Power Economic History Society Fellowship). She currently works for The Young Women's Movement, a non-profit feminist organisation that exists to ensure young women's voices and experiences are meaningfully heard and incorporated in research and policy to lead collective action and enact transformational change throughout Scottish society, systems and structures.

She is a Steering Committee Member of Women's History Scotland and sits on the Council of the Stair Society, Scotland's leading legal history society.

Janay Nugent is Associate Dean in the Faculty of Arts and Science and Associate Professor in the Department of History at the University of Lethbridge in Alberta, Canada. Her research is on gender, family and young people during the Scottish Reformation. She is co-editor with Elizabeth Ewan of *Finding the Family in Medieval and Early Modern Scotland* (2008) and *Children and Youth in Premodern Scotland* (2015). She also co-authored with Laura Stewart, *Union and Revolution: Scotland and Beyond, 1625–1745* (Edinburgh University Press, 2021) which was shortlisted for the Saltire Society's 2021 National Book Award in History.

Jamie Reid Baxter is an Honorary Research Fellow in Scottish History at Glasgow University. He has been active in bringing about and participating in live performances of Renaissance Scottish drama, poetry and music since 1982, and since 1993, has been publishing on these subjects, most recently the life and work of Jacobean Franco-Scot Esther Inglis.

Cathryn Spence is Associate Professor in the Department of History, University of Guelph. She is the author of *Women, Credit, and Debt in Early Modern Scottish Towns* (2016) and co-editor (with Aaron Allen) of *The Housemaills Taxation Book, 1634–6* (2014). She has also written articles about women's use of wills and testaments, credit and debt relationships, and early modern family business, work and economic endeavours.

Abbreviations

AFM	*Annála Rioghachta Éireann: Annals of the kingdom of Ireland by the Four Masters from the earliest period to the year 1616*, edited and translated by John O'Donovan, 7 vols. Dublin: Hodges, Smith & Co., second edn, 1856
AUL	Aberdeen University Library
BL	British Library
Chron. Bower	Walter Bower, *Scotichronicon*, edited by D. E. R. Watt et al., 9 vols. Aberdeen and Edinburgh: University of Aberdeen Press, 1987–98
Chron. Fordun	John Fordun, *Chronicle of the Scottish Nation*, translated and edited by W. F. Skene. Edinburgh: Edmonston and Douglas, 1872
Chron. Lanercost	*The Chronicle of Lanercost, 1272–1346*, translated by Herbert Maxwell. Glasgow: J. Maclehose, 1913
Chron. Wyntoun	*The Original Chronicle of Andrew of Wyntoun*, edited by F. J. Amours, 6 vols. Edinburgh: William Blackwood and Sons for the Scottish Text Society, 1903–14
CSPSc	*Calendar of State Papers Relating to Scotland and Mary, Queen of Scots*, edited by Joseph Bain et al., 13 vols. Edinburgh: HM General Register House, 1898–1969
DIB	*Dictionary of Irish Biography*
DOST	*Dictionary of the Older Scottish Tongue*; https://dsl.ac.uk
HMC	Historical Manuscripts Commission
IR	*Innes Review*
IRSS	*International Review of Scottish Studies*
JSHS	*Journal of Scottish Historical Studies*
LASP	Literary and Antiquarian Society of Perth
NLS	National Library of Scotland

NRS	The National Records of Scotland, formerly the National Archives of Scotland, formerly the Scottish Record Office
ODNB	*Oxford Dictionary of National Biography*, edited by H. C. G. Matthew and B. Harrison, 60 vols. Oxford: Oxford University Press, 2004; www.oxforddnb.com
PMAG	Perth Museum and Art Gallery
PSAS	*Proceedings of the Society of Antiquaries of Scotland*
RMS	*The Register of the Great Seal of Scotland (Registrum Magni Sigilli Regum Scotorum)*, edited by J. M. Thomson et al., 11 vols. Edinburgh, 1882–1914
RPC	*The Register of the Privy Council of Scotland*, edited by J. H. Burton et al., 37 vols. Edinburgh, 1877–
RPS	*Records of the Parliaments of Scotland to 1707*, edited by Keith Brown et al. St Andrews, 2007; www.rps.ac.uk
SBRS	Scottish Burgh Record Society
SHR	*Scottish Historical Review*
SHS	Scottish Historical Society
SPO	State Papers Online; https://www.gale.com/primary-sources/state-papers-online
SRS	Scottish Record Society
STS	Scottish Text Society
TNA	The National Archives
WHR	*Women's History Review*

Preface

Anybody who knows Professor Elizabeth Ewan recognises that twinkle in her eye when she gets excited about your research. They also know to have pen and notebook ready: she will have all sorts of ideas about what to read and who you should meet to discuss your project. Unfailingly generous with her time, advice and expertise, Professor Ewan encourages and inspires those around her. It is this generosity, combined with a gift for establishing collegial networks, that has brought together a community of scholars, a kind of scholarly kinship that crosses several oceans. Professor Ewan's influence has been felt far and wide through her quiet, yet fiercely dedicated support of others. From her graduate students to colleagues, and then to her colleagues' graduate students, she is regularly pulled into the mentorship of new and emerging historians. The relationship changes, but we continue to learn from her. And unlike most children, we never leave home.

During her more than three decades of innovative teaching Professor Ewan trained students far and wide, and ensured that the University of Guelph remain an internationally renowned centre for the study of Scottish history. To celebrate these many years of service to her students and to the study of Scotland, we wanted to honour Professor Ewan by editing a collection that pushes forward the discipline that she has helped shape. We have been struck by the warmth of responses from both authors and reviewers. These contributors represent a wide range of scholars, all very accomplished as critical voices and leaders in their fields, and they have unanimously declared themselves honoured to participate in a celebration of Elizabeth Ewan's work. Among them are former students and mentees, colleagues and people she meets regularly for coffee at the National Library of Scotland on George IV Bridge in Edinburgh. As they know, Professor Ewan is selfless in giving advice and comprehensive in the range of assistance she can offer. Contributors to this volume report that she has drawn maps of Edinburgh so that new arrivals from overseas would not lose their way between accommodations, cafés and archives; helped to find flat-mates to make research trips financially feasible; and lain on the floor of Stirling Castle to be best positioned for discussing the artistic and historical merits of the Stirling Heads.

Elizabeth Ewan's tradition of extraordinary mentorship and distinguished scholarship began with her Honours Bachelor of Arts degree in History at Queen's University, Canada. Upon completion of this degree, she spent a year researching an oral history of Queen's University women. Her father, Professor George Ewan, worked at this same institution as a leader in the field of particle astrophysics and became co-founder of the Sudbury Neutrino Observatory, which undertook research recognised by the Nobel Prize in Physics in 2015. Exceptional mentorship is clearly a family legacy as is a passion for the support and advancement of women in academia. Elizabeth's mother, Maureen Ewan (née Howard), was an active member of the Ban Righ Centre, set up to support mature women students at Queen's University in the 1970s. A room named in Maureen's honour testifies to her commitment to women scholars. In 1985, Elizabeth Ewan completed her PhD in Scottish History at the University of Edinburgh. She returned to Canada to pursue her career at the University of Western Ontario, and then at the University of Victoria, before settling in to the Scottish Studies programme and the History Department at the University of Guelph in 1988. Here, she held a University Research Chair, and was appointed as Associate Graduate Faculty at the Centre for Medieval Studies, University of Toronto. Over the course of thirty-two years, Elizabeth formally supervised three postdoctoral students, twenty-three PhD students and an astonishing forty-seven MA students, in addition to serving on the supervisory committees of twenty-eight more.

Alongside her unwavering commitment to teaching, Elizabeth Ewan has also dedicated an impressive amount of energy to research. In 1990 she published *Townlife in Fourteenth-Century Scotland* with Edinburgh University Press.[1] As Elizabeth's work on urban Scotland evolved, historical women began to emerge from the shadows of their homes to take their place as townspeople who were integral to all aspects of late medieval and early modern urban society.[2] In 1999, Elizabeth published *Women in Scotland, c. 1100–c. 1750* with co-editor Maureen Meikle.[3] This collection of essays definitively established that studying women was not just possible, but invaluable for understanding the Scottish

---

[1] Elizabeth Ewan, *Townlife in Fourteenth-century Scotland* (Edinburgh: Edinburgh University Press, 1990; paperback, 1992).

[2] Elizabeth Ewan, 'Mons Meg and Merchant Meg: Women in Later Medieval Edinburgh', in *Freedom and Authority: Scotland, c. 1050–c. 1650*, eds Terry Brotherstone and David Ditchburn (East Linton: Tuckwell Press, 1999); Elizabeth Ewan, 'Schooling in the Towns, c. 1400–c. 1560', in *The Edinburgh History of Education in Scotland*, eds Robert Anderson, Mark Freeman and Lindsay Paterson (Edinburgh: Edinburgh University Press, 2015).

[3] Elizabeth Ewan and Maureen M. Meikle, eds, *Women in Scotland, c. 1100–c. 1750* (East Linton: Tuckwell Press, 1999; reprinted 2002).

past. Its success reaffirmed the need to identify and document historical women, and led to *The Biographical Dictionary of Scottish Women*, co-edited with Sue Innes, Siân Reynolds and Rose Pipes in 2006.[4] The *Dictionary* quickly became woven into the fabric of any research programme that examined women and gender in Scotland. Public engagement with this volume was so great that from virtually the first day of its release, the editors received suggestions on how to expand entries and include more women deemed essential for the next edition. An update was planned and executed with Jane Rendall joining the editorial team after the loss of cherished colleague Sue Innes, and *The New Biographical Dictionary of Scottish Women* was published in 2018.[5]

The rescuing of women from obscurity in histories of the medieval and early modern past has been a running theme of Professor Ewan's research projects, as seen through her engrossing work on Black Agnes of Dunbar, Alison Rough and numerous other women she wrote about in the *Biographical Dictionaries* and the *Oxford Dictionary of National Biography*.[6] In addition to her research on individual women, Professor Ewan has also sought to place women more generally at the centre of how we understand medieval and early modern urban, economic and social life. Her work on female brewers and servants makes a convincing case for the economic significance of premodern women,[7] while her

---

[4] Elizabeth Ewan, Sue Innes, Siân Reynolds and Rose Pipes, eds, *The Biographical Dictionary of Scottish Women* (Edinburgh: Edinburgh University Press, 2006; paperback, 2007).

[5] Elizabeth Ewan, Rose Pipes, Jane Rendall and Siân Reynolds, eds, *The New Biographical Dictionary of Scottish Women* (Edinburgh: Edinburgh University Press, 2018).

[6] For Black Agnes of Dunbar see: Elizabeth Ewan, 'The Dangers of Manly Women: Late Medieval Perceptions of Female Heroism in the Second War of Independence', in *Woman and the Feminine in Medieval and Early Modern Scottish Writing*, eds Sarah M. Dunnigan, C. Marie Harker and Evelyn S. Newlyn (Basingstoke: Palgrave Macmillan, 2004); for Alison Rough see: Elizabeth Ewan, 'Alison Rough: A Woman's Life and Death in Sixteenth-century Edinburgh', *Women's History Magazine* 45 (Autumn 2003): 4–13. See also entries in the *Biographical Dictionary* on Margaret Crichton (1483–c. 1546), Annie Dunlop (1897–1973), Marjory Fleming (1803–1811), Christian Fletcher (fl. 1650–1662), Isabella Graham (1742–1814), Leah Leneman (1944–1999), Jean Livingston (1579–1600), Christiana MacRuairi (fl. 1290–1318), Alison Rough (c. 1480–1535), Agnes Randolph of Dunbar (before 1324–c. 1369), Marjory de Schireham (fl. 1326–31), Anna Scott, Duchess of Buccleuch (1651–1732), and Isabel Williamson (c. 1430–93). Entries in the *New Biographical Dictionary* include Elizabeth Cairns (1685–1741), Jane Campbell, Lady Kenmure (c. 1607–75), Christian Fletcher (1619–91 revised), Anna MacKenzie, Countess of Balcarres (1621–1707), and Grisie Baillie (1692–1759). Entries in the ODNB, https://www.oxforddnb.com/ include: Alison Rough, John Mercer, Forrester family, John Crab and Isabel Williamson.

[7] Elizabeth Ewan, '"To the Longer Liver": Provisions for the Dissolution of the Marital Economy in Scotland, 1470–1550', in *The Marital Economy in Scandinavia and Britain, 1400–1900*, eds Maria Ågren and Amy Louise Erickson (Aldershot: Ashgate, 2005); Elizabeth Ewan, 'Mistresses of Themselves: Domestic Servants and By-employments in Sixteenth-century Scotland', in *Domestic Service and the Formation of European Identity: Understanding the Globalization of Domestic Work, 16th–21st Centuries*, ed. A. Fauve-Chamoux (Bern: Peter Lang, 2004); Ewan, 'Mons Meg and Merchant Meg'; Elizabeth Ewan, 'For Whatever Ales Ye: Women as Consumers and Producers in Scottish Medieval Towns', in *Women in Scotland*, eds Ewan and Meikle.

studies on gender, slander, female crime and interpersonal violence challenge traditional narratives of women as quiet and peripheral to premodern Scottish communities.[8] As a corrective to the presumption that women were insignificant outside of the family, her work with Janay Nugent on *Finding the Family in Medieval and Early Modern Scotland* and *Children and Youth in Premodern Scotland* demonstrates that family life was anything but insular to the broader community.[9] In 2017, Lynn Abrams and Elizabeth Ewan edited *Nine Centuries of Man: Manhood and Masculinities in Scottish History* to illustrate the importance of paying attention to constructions of masculinity when seeking to understand the past.[10]

The extent of collaboration in Professor Ewan's work – including the outputs of eight co-edited books and a special journal issue – is very rare among historians. The projects that she undertakes are interdisciplinary in nature, drawing on the written record but also on archaeology, literature, art, material culture and heritage research.[11] As an editor, she has been exceptionally thoughtful

---

[8] Elizabeth Ewan, 'Beyond Borders and Boundaries: The Use of Banishment in Sixteenth-century Scottish Towns', in *Crossing Borders: Boundaries and Margins in Late Medieval and Early Modern Britain*, eds Sara M. Butler and Krista J. Kesselring (Leiden: Brill, 2018); Elizabeth Ewan, 'Impatient Griseldas: Women and the Perpetration of Violence in Sixteenth-century Glasgow', *Florilegium* 28 (2013 for 2011): 149–68; Elizabeth Ewan, 'Disorderly Damsels? Women and Interpersonal Violence in Pre-Reformation Scotland', *SHR* 89, no. 228 (Oct 2010): 153–71; Elizabeth Ewan, '"Tongue, You Lied": The Role of the Tongue in Rituals of Public Penance in Medieval Scotland', in *Hands of the Tongue*, ed. Edwin Craun (Kalamazoo: Medieval Institute Publications, 2007); Elizabeth Ewan, 'Crime or Culture? Women and Daily Life in Late Medieval Scotland', in *Twisted Sisters: Women, Crime and Deviance in Scotland Since 1400*, eds Yvonne Brown and Rona Ferguson (East Linton: Tuckwell Press, 2002); Elizabeth Ewan, '"Many Injurious Words": Defamation and Gender in Late Medieval Scotland', in *History, Literature and Music in Scotland, 700–1560*, ed. R. Andrew McDonald (Toronto: University of Toronto Press, 2002); Elizabeth Ewan, 'Scottish Portias: Women in the Courts in Mediaeval Scottish Towns', *Journal of the Canadian Historical Association* 3, no. 1 (1992): 27–43.

[9] Janay Nugent and Elizabeth Ewan, eds, *Children and Youth in Premodern Scotland* (Woodbridge: Boydell and Brewer, 2015); Elizabeth Ewan and Janay Nugent, eds, *Finding the Family in Medieval and Early Modern Scotland* (Aldershot: Ashgate, 2008). See also: Elizabeth Ewan, 'The Early Modern Family', in *The Oxford Handbook of Modern Scottish History*, eds T. M. Devine and Jenny Wormald (Oxford: Oxford University Press, 2012); Ewan, '"To the Longer Liver"'.

[10] Lynn Abrams and Elizabeth Ewan, eds, *Nine Centuries of Man: Manhood and Masculinities in Scottish History* (Edinburgh: Edinburgh University Press, 2017).

[11] J. Campbell, Elizabeth Ewan and Heather Parker, eds, *Shaping Scottish Identities: Gender, Nation and the Worlds Beyond* (Guelph: Centre for Scottish Studies, 2011); Sarah Dunnigan and Elizabeth Ewan, guest eds, '"Transformative Disorder": Scotland, 1550–1650', *Renaissance and Reformation* 30, no. 4 (Fall 2006/7); Sierra Dye, Elizabeth Ewan and Heather Parker, eds, *Gender and Mobility in Scotland and Abroad* (Guelph: Centre for Scottish Studies, 2018); Elizabeth Ewan, 'The Age of Bon-Accord: Aberdeen in the Fourteenth Century', in *New Light on Medieval Aberdeen*, ed. John S. Smith (Aberdeen: Aberdeen University Press, 1985), 228–44; 'Family, Gender and Lifecycle in Late Medieval Scotland', in *A Companion to Late Medieval Scotland*, ed. Andy King (Leiden: Brill, forthcoming); 'The Female Character: Early Scots Literature as a Source for the History of Scottish Medieval Women', *ACTA* 16 (1993 for 1989): 29–38; 'The Community of the Burgh in the Fourteenth Century', in *The Scottish Medieval Town*, eds Michael Lynch et al. (Edinburgh: John Donald Press, 1988), 32–45; '"Hamperit in ane Honeycamb": Sights, Sounds and Smells

in bringing the research of emerging scholars alongside that of more senior historians, and her astute advice has helped people at all stages of their careers improve their work until it shines with its best possible light.

Professor Ewan's collaboration extends beyond the walls of the academy too, and the accessibility of Scottish history to a wide audience has been clear in her vision through much of her scholarship. Her work on the *Biographical Dictionary*, the Scottish Women's History network, the Women in Scottish History digital history project, Historic Scotland's project on historic plaques and illustrations, and her consultancy work with the Real Mary King's Close have had a far-reaching impact, ensuring that people are reminded of both the presence and the significance of women in the past.

Even though this edited collection cannot give back to Elizabeth Ewan everything she has provided to us, we hope that it will let her know how much her work and her guidance have meant to the editors, to the contributors, and to so many others.

---

in the Medieval Town', in *Everyday Life in Medieval Scotland*, eds E. J. Cowan and Lizanne Henderson (Edinburgh: Edinburgh University Press, 2011), 109–44; 'A Land Fit for Heroines? The Biographical Dictionary of Scottish Women', *JSHS* 26 (2006): 1–13; 'Late Medieval Scotland: A Study in Contrasts', in *A Companion to Medieval Scottish Poetry*, eds P. Bawcutt and J. Hadley-Williams (Woodbridge: Boydell, 2006), 19–33; 'A Realm of One's Own? The Place of Medieval and Early Modern Women in Scottish History', in *Gendering Scottish History: An International Approach*, eds Terry Brotherstone, Deborah Simonton and Oonagh Walsh (Glasgow: Cruithne Press, 1999), 19–36; 'Scottish Burghs', in *Atlas of Scottish History to 1707*, eds Peter G. B. McNeill and Hector L. MacQueen (Edinburgh: Scottish Medievalists and Department of Geography, University of Edinburgh, 1996), 231–7; 'Town and Hinterland in Medieval Scotland', in *The Pre-Industrial Cities and Technology Reader*, eds Colin Chant and David Goodman (London: Routledge, 1999), 125–8; 'Townlife and Trade', in *Scotland: The Making and Unmaking of the Kingdom, c. 1100–c. 1707*, eds Bob Harris and Alan R. MacDonald (Dundee: Dundee University Press, 2006), 1–38; 'An Urban Community: The Crafts in Thirteenth-century Aberdeen', in *Medieval Scotland: Crown, Lordship and Community*, eds Alexander Grant and Keith J. Stringer (Edinburgh: Edinburgh University Press, 1993), 156–73; 'Protocol Books and Towns in Medieval Scotland', in *La Diplomatique urbaine en Europe du moyen age*, eds W. Prevenier and T. de Hemptinne (Ghent: Garant, 2000), 143–56; 'Women and the Biographies of Nations: The Biographical Dictionary of Scottish Women', in *True Biographies of Nations? The Cultural Journeys of Dictionaries of Biography*, ed. Karen Fox (Canberra: Australian National University Press, 2019), 119–37; Elizabeth Ewan and Gordon DesBrisay, 'Life in the Two Towns, 1100–1800', in *Aberdeen Before 1800*, eds E. P. Dennison et al. (East Linton: Tuckwell Press, 2002), 44–70; Elizabeth Ewan and S. Rigby, 'Government, Power and Authority, 1300–1540', in vol. 3 of *Cambridge Urban History of Britain*, ed. D. M. Palliser (Cambridge: Cambridge University Press, 2000), 291–312.

Introduction
Engendering Scottish History for the Medieval and Early Modern Periods

Cathryn Spence, Janay Nugent and Mairi Cowan

In 1999, Elizabeth Ewan and Maureen Meikle began their collection *Women in Scotland, c. 1100–c. 1750* with the qualification, 'This book is not about Mary Queen of Scots'.[1] More than twenty years later, the field of women and gender history in Scotland has grown to such an extent that we need no longer worry about the same limited expectations. Not only do we begin this collection with a chapter discussing Mary and a shocking murder, but the cover of this book features a statue inspired by the Queen of Scots. *The Queen*, by Trevor Leat, plays with gender norms through a woman hawking. The graceful willow sculpture is boldly installed in the grounds of Falkland Palace, inviting modern-day visitors to consider the role that gender played centuries ago in that place, in people's faith and politics. While loosely inspired by a famous queen, this sculpture stands as a witness to the fuller importance of adding women and gender to our imaginings of historical spaces.

Gender has now become an established critical lens through which to understand Scotland's history. This collection is a testament to the importance of gender scholars, and the ability of their work to deepen our understanding of women's and men's experiences. It builds on recent developments in women's and gender history, demonstrating the power of such history not only to present familiar topics in new ways, but also to open up new vistas for our historical sight.

While the field of women's history as a distinct branch of history began in the 1930s, and gained significant ground in the 1960s and 1970s, few examinations of women in Scottish history existed prior to the mid-1980s. During that decade, historians such as Rosalind Marshall, Leah Leneman and Rosalind Mitchison laid the groundwork for how to find women in historical

---

[1] Elizabeth Ewan and Maureen M. Meikle, 'Introduction', in *Women in Scotland, c. 1100–c. 1750*, eds Elizabeth Ewan and Maureen M. Meikle (East Linton: Tuckwell Press, 1999), xix.

records and study their impact on the Scottish past.² Also key at this time was the development of the study of witchcraft.³ In the 1990s, the consideration of women's place in Scottish history continued to deepen, thanks in no small part to Elizabeth Ewan. In 1995, she published 'Women's History in Scotland: Towards an Agenda'.⁴ At the end of the decade, two collections discussing women and gender in Scottish history appeared: *Gendering Scottish History*, edited by Terry Brothersone, Deborah Simonton and Oonah Walsh, as well as *Women in Scotland, c. 1100–c. 1750*, co-edited by Elizabeth Ewan and Maureen Meikle.⁵ Examinations of women's roles within and outwith the family, in religion, in politics, in law and economics have burgeoned in the years since. Ewan's work, and the work of her mentees and colleagues, has been at the forefront of this research.

Once women's history had been firmly established as a viable field of study in Scotland, scholars began to integrate more complex theoretical analyses building on Joan Scott,⁶ Merry Wiesner-Hanks⁷ and Natalie Zemon Davis.⁸ As Lynn Abrams noted in 2006, 'gender as a category of analysis [is] the conceptual leap that underpins historical understandings of culture, society, identity and experience'.⁹ Elizabeth Ewan led the way in taking this conceptual leap for pre-modern Scotland. As discussed in the Preface, her own scholarship, along with that of her collaborators, students and mentees, has continued to expand the potential of gender to 'enact a fundamental paradigm shift in historical enquiry'.¹⁰ Recently, considerations of masculinity have diversified gender in Scottish history, illuminating how men's roles were affected by issues

---

[2] Rosalind K. Marshall, *Virgins and Viragos: A History of Women in Scotland from 1080–1980* (London: Collins, 1983); Leah Leneman, *Living in Atholl: A Social History of the Estates, 1685–1785* (Edinburgh: Edinburgh University Press, 1986); Rosalind Mitchison, *Life in Scotland* (London: Batsford, 1978).

[3] Christina Larner, *Enemies of God: The Witch-hunt in Scotland* (Baltimore: Johns Hopkins University Press, 1981).

[4] Elizabeth Ewan, 'Women's History in Scotland: Towards an Agenda,' *IR* 46, no. 2 (Autumn 1995): 155–64.

[5] Terry Brotherstone, Deborah Simonton and Oonagh Walsh, eds, *Gendering Scottish History: An International Approach* (Glasgow: Cruithne Press, 1999); Ewan and Meikle, *Women in Scotland*.

[6] Joan W. Scott, 'Gender: A Useful Category of Historical Analysis', *American Historical Review* 91, no. 5 (1986): 1053–75.

[7] Merry E. Wiesner-Hanks, *Women and Gender in Early Modern Europe* (Cambridge: Cambridge University Press, 1993).

[8] Natalie Zemon Davis, *Women on the Margins: Three Seventeenth-century Lives* (Cambridge, MA: Harvard University Press, 1995).

[9] Lynn Abrams, 'Gendering the Agenda', in *Gender in Scottish History Since 1700*, eds Lynn Abrams, Eleanor Gordon, Deborah Simonton and Eileen Janes Yeo (Edinburgh: Edinburgh University Press, 2006), 3.

[10] Katie Barclay, Tanya Cheadle and Eleanor Gordon, 'The State of Scottish History: Gender', *SHR* 92, Supplement (2013): 83.

of class, status and ethnicity.¹¹ Here again, research by Ewan and her mentees has shaped the field's new directions. Feminist and gender scholars continue to demonstrate how theoretical perspectives help us understand the lives of people in the past and why those lives matter today, propelling Scottish historical scholarship to embrace the intersectional theories of Kimberlé Crenshaw in a quest for understanding through intersections of age and class.¹²

The employment of gender as a category of analysis has become a key component of Scottish historical scholarship. Barclay et al. noted in 2013 that there is 'an emerging consciousness that gender history in Scotland is reaching maturity'.¹³ This book provides clear examples of that maturity having been achieved. Although its organisation into sections on place, faith and politics might seem to follow traditional markers of Scottish distinctiveness, its chapters show that the integration of gender can advance even the most conventional fields, contributing to 'a fundamental paradigm shift in historical enquiry'. The ordering of the sections inverts the usual scholarly hierarchy by placing politics – the typical domain of elite men – at the end of the collection while situating place – which naturally includes all medieval and early modern Scots – at the outset. This upending of traditional scholarship is also evident in the fact that scholars not primarily engaged with gender history are perceiving how their research can be advanced by an analysis of gender. Through a creative consideration of a wide range of evidence, contributors listen to silences, read sources against the grain and employ social theory to investigate gender and intersectional forms of power. Their inclusion is particularly exciting given that, just a decade ago, a greater interest in gender history beyond gender historians was identified as an important future direction by Katie Barclay, Tanya Cheadle and Eleanor Gordon in their state of the field *SHR* article,¹⁴ and in 2023, Katie Barclay and Rebecca Mason still found reason to question how

---

[11] Lynn Abrams and Elizabeth L. Ewan, 'Introduction: Interrogating Men and Masculinities in Scottish History', in *Nine Centuries of Man: Manhood and Masculinities in Scottish History*, eds Lynn Abrams and Elizabeth Ewan (Edinburgh: Edinburgh University Press, 2017); Janay Nugent and Elizabeth Ewan, 'Guide to Further Reading' in *Children and Youth in Premodern Scotland*, eds Janay Nugent and Elizabeth Ewan (Woodbridge: Boydell and Brewer, 2015); Barclay, Cheadle and Gordon, 'The State of Scottish History'; Elizabeth Ewan and Janay Nugent, 'Guide to Further Reading' in *Finding the Family in Medieval and Early Modern Scotland*, eds Elizabeth Ewan and Janay Nugent (Aldershot: Ashgate, 2008); Elizabeth Ewan, 'A New Trumpet? The History of Women in Scotland, 1300–1700,' *History Compass* 7, no. 2 (March 2009): 431–46; Ewan, 'Women's History in Scotland'; womeninscottishhistory.org.

[12] Kimberlé Crenshaw, 'Demarginalizing the Intersection of Race and Sex: A Black Feminist Critique of Antidiscrimination Doctrine, Feminist Theory and Antiracist Politics', *University of Chicago Legal Forum* 139 (1989): 139–67; Kimberlé Crenshaw, *On Intersectionality: Essential Writings* (New York: New Press, 2017).

[13] Barclay, Cheadle and Gordon, 'The State of Scottish History', 83. See also Katie Barclay and Rebecca Mason, 'Scottish Women's and Gender History and Women Historians in Scotland: Past, Present and Future Directions', *SHR* 102, 2, no. 259 (August 2023), 189.

[14] Barclay, Cheadle and Gordon, 'The State of Scottish History', 107.

far the authority of gender historians has been accepted by those beyond the discipline.[15]

Historiographical developments are clear across all three sections of this volume. The first, 'place', refers of course to physical space, but also to the presence and importance of women and gender in distinct settings. Research by Julian Goodare, Janay Nugent, Rob Falconer, Michelle D. Brock, Cathryn Spence, Alice Glaze and Sierra Dye has already demonstrated women's presence within places that have traditionally been seen as male dominated, and expanded how this positioning relates to women's involvement in broader aspects of society.[16] Contributors to this volume continue the work of analysing how women understood their places in the past, and how we should understand that placement today.

The section on place starts with an essay about a physical place, a road in Fife. This road leads to an examination of the political landscape, showing how a historian's close attention to the details of specific places offers a new way of understanding larger political developments. As Jane E. A. Dawson discusses in Chapter 1, 'Mary, Queen of Scots, Three Noblewomen and a Fife "Murder Mystery"', some places – such as the roads upon which many travelled – were very public, while others – the birthing chamber for instance – were intimately private. Using a biographical approach to the people in these places, Dawson shows how a historian can 'recover female experiences, relationships and political agency', even unravel a centuries-old murder mystery. Chapter 2, 'Scottish Portias Revisited: Women in the Courts in Early Modern Scottish Towns', by Rebecca Mason, investigates women's actions in burgh courts. Mason's chapter focuses on women representing themselves within a public – and primarily masculine – space, making specific choices about how they can best present themselves to win whatever suit they are pursuing. In Chapter 3, 'Punching Back Against Patriarchy: The Story of Jean Weir', by Michael F. Graham, the place in question is the scaffold. Graham shows that here, Jean Weir, tried for incest and witchcraft, took control of the narrative surrounding her character

---

[15] Barclay and Mason, 'Scottish Women's and Gender History and Women Historians in Scotland', 202.

[16] Julian Goodare, *The Scottish Witch-Hunt in Context* (Manchester: Manchester University Press, 2002); Janay Nugent, '"None must meddle betuenne man and wife": Assessing Family and the Fluidity of Public and Private in Early Modern Scotland', *Journal of Family History* 35 (2010): 219–31; J. R. D. Falconer, *Crime and Community in Reformation Scotland: Negotiating Power in a Burgh Society* (London: Pickering and Chatto, 2012); Michelle D. Brock, *Satan and the Scots: The Devil in Post-Reformation Scotland, c. 1560–1700* (Farnham: Ashgate, 2016); Cathryn Spence, *Women, Credit, and Debt in Early Modern Scotland* (Manchester: Manchester University Press, 2016) and '"By her own mouth speaking": Women's authoritative voices in early modern wills and testaments', *SHR* 102, no. 2 (2023): 273–89; Alice Glaze. 'Women and Kirk Discipline: Prosecution, Negotiation, and the Limits of Control', *JSHS* 36, no. 2 (2016): 125–42; Sierra Dye, 'To Converse with the Devil? Speech, Sexuality, and Witchcraft in Early Modern Scotland', *IRSS* 37 (2012): 9–40.

and her impending death. Having endured the wrenching of private matters into public discussion, she used her voice to make her final moments as memorable as possible. Chapter 4, 'Always at the Gate? Unlocking Medieval Women's Stories in Modern-day Edinburgh', by Rachel M. Delman, incorporates the concept of place at two levels: modern Edinburgh is the (physical) place under consideration, yet Delman also examines the (metaphysical) place of historical women in that city's presentation of its history. In particular, Delman considers the Magdalen Chapel and Trinity Apse as examples of historical sites that are also places associated with medieval Scottish women, and argues that women's historical presence should be brought to the fore of public consciousness by historians and heritage professionals.

A common feature across these chapters is that each considers 'place' by moving from the private to the public. Dawson describes ostensibly small events from women's private lives and then builds to the public implications for such a well-known political figure as Mary, Queen of Scots. Mason analyses women bringing private matters into public courts. Graham shows how Jean Weir's experience was moulded by her intensely private relationship with her brother, and how this relationship became public spectacle through her prosecution and execution. Delman's focus centres on memorialising private lives in public histories. By employing a gendered analysis in tracing movements from private to public, this section challenges our preconceptions about where the boundaries around private and public places lie, showing that a seemingly private matter has the potential to disrupt a political system, or reinforce norms already in place.

The second section, on 'faith', comprises papers that examine how religion and spirituality shaped expressions of gender, as well as how gender shaped people's experiences of spirituality and religion. Historians have shown that people's beliefs could reach very far into different aspects of society. Works by Audrey-Beth Fitch, Mairi Cowan, Daniel MacLeod and Chris Langley have broadened considerations of religious belief before, during and after the Reformation, while works by Sarah Dunnigan, Gordon DesBrisay, David Mullan and C. Marie Harker have examined the role of gender beyond overtly religious structures.[17] Other scholars have explored connections between faith

---

[17] Audrey-Beth Fitch, *The Search for Salvation: Lay Faith in Scotland, 1480–1560*, ed. Elizabeth Ewan (Edinburgh: John Donald, 2009); Mairi Cowan, *Death, Life, and Religious Change in Scottish Towns, c. 1350–1560* (Manchester: Manchester University Press, 2013); Daniel MacLeod, 'Servants to St. Mungo' (PhD diss., University of Guelph, 2014); Stuart Macdonald and Daniel MacLeod, eds, *Keeping the Kirk: Scottish Religion at Home and in the Diaspora* (Guelph: Guelph Centre for Scottish Studies, 2014); Chris R. Langley, Catherine E. McMillan and Russell Newton, eds, *The Clergy in Early Modern Scotland* (Woodbridge: Boydell and Brewer, 2021). For gender and spirituality, see Sarah M. Dunnigan, C. Marie Harker and Evelyn S. Newlyn, eds, *Woman and the Feminine in Medieval and Early Modern Scottish Writing* (Basingstoke: Palgrave Macmillan, 2004); Gordon DesBrisay, 'Catholics, Quakers and Religious Persecution in Restoration Aberdeen', *IR*

and politics in the Covenanting movement.[18] Contributors to this volume develop all these areas further, and also offer new considerations of the roles of religion, religious artefacts and material culture in Scottish history.

Marion Walker's opposition to the largely masculine Reformed movement leads the section on faith. In Chapter 5, '"She displays by her speeches": Marion Walker, Catholic Speech, and Local Resistance in Early Modern Glasgow', Daniel MacLeod analyses the case of a woman doubly marginalised by both gender and confession, yet whose voice can still be heard through a sensitive interpretation of the historical evidence. Chapter 6, 'Memory and Materiality: John Knox and the Resilience of Relic-thinking in the Continuity of Gender and Cult in Late Medieval and Early Modern Perth', by Mark A. Hall, considers the consistency of masculine heroic imagery across the Reformation. In Chapter 7, '"She-zealots" and "Satanesses": Women, Patriarchy and the Covenanting Movement', Michelle D. Brock shows how women seized an opportunity presented by the religious changes of the covenanting movement to gain more political power, then faced resistance as the pendulum of patriarchal equilibrium swung back and eroded their advances. Chapter 8, 'Emotion, Authority and Griefwork in the Spiritual Poetry of Lilias Skene', by Sarah Dunnigan, takes a closer look at a more personal and inward approach to spirituality, with attention to emotions in intersection with gender as a way of understanding the faith and spirituality of Quakerism.

Each chapter in this section demonstrates how religious belief or spirituality could be used to express personal and internal motivations, often to a public audience, thereby externalising inward experience. As these beliefs went on display, they became part of the gendered identity that individuals presented to the world. In some cases, these presentations showed resistance to societal norms, as well as the struggle between public expectations and a desire to remain true to one's inner spiritual self. Early modern Scots invoked the shared symbols and meanings of gender to advocate for their own religious belief systems.

The section on 'politics' might at first appear to be the most traditional of the three, yet it too showcases exciting advances. Scottish kingship, queenship

---

47 (1996): 136–68; David G. Mullan, *Narratives of the Religious Self in Early-Modern Scotland* (Aldershot: Ashgate, 2010); David G. Mullan, *Women's Life Writing in Early Modern Scotland: Writing the Evangelical Self, c. 1670–c. 1730* (Farnham: Ashgate, 2003).

[18] David Stevenson, *Union, Revolution, and Religion in 17th-Century Scotland* (Aldershot: Variorum, 1997); Allan I. MacInnnes, *Charles I and the Making of the Covenanting Movement, 1625–1641* (Edinburgh: John Donald, 1991); Laura A. M. Stewart, *Rethinking the Scottish Revolution: Covenanted Scotland, 1637–1651* (Oxford: Oxford University Press, 2016); Allan Kennedy, '"A Heavy Yock Uppon Their Necks": Covenanting Government in the Northern Highlands, 1638–1651', *JSHS* 30, no. 2 (2010): 93–112; Chris R. Langley, ed., *The National Covenant in Scotland, 1638–1689* (Woodbridge: Boydell and Brewer, 2020). In the main, the Covenanting movement has largely been explored with regard to its masculine context, paving the way for a more thorough gendered analysis.

and noble power have been well documented and discussed by such notable historians as Geoffrey Barrow, Amy Blakeway, Stephen Boardman, Keith Brown, Rachel M. Delman, Archie Duncan, Julian Goodare, Michael Lynch, Rosalind Marshall, Colm McNamee, Cynthia Neville, Michael Penman and Jenny Wormald.[19] Recently, studies by Jane E. A. Dawson, Rosalind Carr and Katie Barclay, and Katharine Glover have advanced the discussion of the role of women and gender in early modern politics.[20] The essays in this collection continue to illuminate the relationship between politics and gender. By considering the importance of female lineage, the expectations and manifestations of masculinity in kingship, and the ways power could be exerted through family connections across the channel between Scotland and Ireland, new and varied considerations of Scottish political history emerge.

The section on politics begins with an examination of a symbol of noble power. Chapter 9, 'Displaying Support for Women's Lineage: Late Medieval Seals and Family Identity', by Rachel Meredith Davis, looks at how seals were used to assess and assert the importance of women's lineage to family identity. Davis considers how specific images were chosen to convey family influence, especially influence transferred through the female line, and argues that families chose to highlight the power of female lineage when it was convenient to do so. A woman's defence of her family is at the centre of Chapter 10, 'Another Damsel in Distress? Katherine Beaumont, a Disinherited Noblewoman in

---

[19] G. W. S. Barrow, *Robert Bruce: And the Community of the Realm of Scotland* (Edinburgh: Edinburgh University Press, 2005); Amy Blakeway, *Regency in Sixteenth-Century Scotland* (Woodbridge: Boydell, 2015); Stephen Boardman, *The Campbells, 1250–1513* (Edinburgh: John Donald, 2006); Keith M. Brown, *Noble Society in Scotland: Wealth, Family and Culture from the Reformation to the Revolution* (Edinburgh: Edinburgh University Press, 2000); Rachel Delman, 'Mary of Guelders and the Architecture of Queenship in Fifteenth-Century Scotland', SHR 102, no. 2 (2023): 211–31; A. A. M. Duncan, *Scotland: The Making of the Kingdom* (Edinburgh: Mercat Press, 1975, 1992); Julian Goodare, *State and Society in Early Modern Scotland* (Oxford: Oxford University Press, 1999); Michael Lynch, *Edinburgh and the Reformation* (Edinburgh: John Donald, 1981); Rosalind K. Marshall, *Queen Mary's Women: Female Relatives, Servants, Friends and Enemies of Mary, Queen of Scots* (Edinburgh: John Donald, 2006); Colm McNamee, *The Wars of the Bruces: Scotland, England and Ireland, 1306–1328* (East Linton: Tuckwell Press, 1997); Cynthia J. Neville, *Land, Law and People in Medieval Scotland* (Edinburgh: Edinburgh University Press, 2010); Michael Penman, *The Scottish Civil War: The Bruces and the Balliols and the War for Control of Scotland, 1286–1356* (Charleston: Tempus Publishing, 2002); Jenny Wormald, *Court, Kirk and Community: Scotland, 1470–1625* (Toronto: University of Toronto Press, 1981); Jenny Wormald, *Mary Queen of Scots: A Study in Failure* (London: George Philip, 1988 [republished in Edinburgh by John Donald, 2017]). For a survey of Scottish scholarship on gender and politics in the last decade see Barclay and Mason, 'Scottish Women's and Gender History and Women Historians in Scotland', 202–4.

[20] Jane Dawson, *Scotland Re-Formed, 1488–1587* (Edinburgh: Edinburgh University Press, 2007); Rosalind Carr, *Gender and Enlightenment Culture in Eighteenth-Century Scotland* (Edinburgh: Edinburgh University Press, 2014); Katie Barclay and Rosalind Carr, 'Women, Love, and Power in Enlightenment Scotland', WHR 27, no. 2 (2018): 176–98; Katharine Glover, *Elite Women and Polite Society in Eighteenth-Century Scotland* (Woodbridge: Boydell and Brewer, 2011).

Fourteenth-century Scotland', by Iain A. MacInnes and Morvern French. In this chapter, MacInnes and French reveal the circumstances surrounding a noblewoman protecting her home. They note the carefully gendered explanations or justifications for her actions in contemporary accounts, and explore the political reasons for Beaumont's inclusion in some historical sources, and exclusion from others. The seemingly contradictory narratives of heroine protecting her children and the family's basis for political and economic power, in contrast to English depictions of the 'damsel in distress', highlight the visceral and vivid gender imagery employed during periods of political and military struggle. In Chapter 11, 'Negotiating Youth, Old Age and Manhood: A Comparative Approach to Late Medieval Scottish Kingship', Lucinda H. S. Dean examines how age affected gendered expectations of behaviour – in this case the masculinity of medieval kings. Arguing that youth and old age could destabilise even the most powerful of Scottish masculine hierarchies, Scottish kingship, her analysis highlights the importance of intersections among categories of age, gender and social status. The final chapter, Chapter 12, 'Sons and Daughters, Mothers and Mercenaries: Agency and Agenda in the Cross-North Channel Context, c. 1550–c. 1600', by Alison Cathcart, examines the intersection of familial and political power. Cathcart devotes attention to the important and sometimes unexpected roles that women played in elite family relationships, revealing how Agnes Campbell and her daughter Finola MacDonald advanced their agenda in Ulster and within a militarising cross-North Channel world.

Key in this 'politics' section are family relationships. Gender shaped such relationships, whether through images on seals, inheritance rules, the forming of kings, defence of a home during periods of war or efforts drawing upon family networks to recruit others to a cause. Contemporaries recognised women in power, but relied on gender to ensure subservience to the norms of patriarchal society.

Beyond the questions of gender tied most closely to ideas of place, faith and politics, broader themes also run throughout this collection. One theme is that of agency. The essays in this collection add nuance to what intersectional scholarship has contributed to the critique of power and the analysis of how those who lacked power could act and effect change. By acknowledging that power had limits and by understanding how these limitations were gendered, scholars in this collection assess extraordinary moments where women and men used the rules in sometimes unexpected ways to make their voices heard. Although a lifelong victim of familial abuse and a subject of ridicule within the witch-hunting environment of early modern society, Jean Weir, as Graham argues, was able to express her anguish in her final moments on the scaffold. Here the public was forced to consider her performance and perhaps determine for themselves whether she was an impenitent sinner, a poor woman who was victimised by her life circumstances, or somewhere in-between. Equally attuned to complexity in her treatment of women and the law, Mason examines the legal spaces where women were afforded the opportunity to be heard. The burgh court records, while clearly constructed for the benefit of men, do show women asserting control over their own affairs. MacLeod's work on Marion Walker presents the sites of kirk courts and Walker's own home as places where she was able to advocate for her faith. A Catholic woman who appeared to live as a common townsperson, Walker followed her religious conscience into dangerous spaces, as did Lilias Skene. Dunnigan shows how Skene's poetry used gender to legitimise a marginalised spiritual conscience and engage in political activism on behalf of imprisoned allies. Religious righteousness provided a venue for voicing beliefs. This awareness of religious conscience and activism was more broadly embraced by Brock's covenanting women. From the mythical heroine of Jenny Geddes to the 'worshipers, rioters, witches and wives', covenanting women understood the perils of the patriarchal space (both physical and intellectual) that they inhabited, but also recognised that through religious righteousness they could claim a right to be heard in this space. The importance of agency is vividly illustrated in MacInnes and French's analysis of Katherine Beaumont's defence of her family's castle during the Wars of Independence, as well as in Cathcart's discussion of women and power in the North Channel context. The physical and conceptual spaces where these women engaged in traditionally masculine political acts provided legitimacy to their actions and were crucial to their successes.

While agency is a fraught concept, the authors in this collection take seriously individuals' desires to shape their own lives within the very real constraints imposed upon them. Dean's kings were powerful men, but even for them age functioned as a determinant of power with young and old kings being vulnerable to critiques. In Davis's seals are representations of women as central to establishing family social status. Elite women can also be found relying on expected gender roles in political acts with Katherine Beaumont's defence of her castle and women forging relationships in Mary, Queen of Scots' birthing and lying-in rooms. Marion Walker, a woman of much humbler social status, evoked gendered expectations of functioning largely within the private space of her home to shelter Catholic priests. Hall's chapter draws upon material culture to consider a popular use of gendered expectations that might not otherwise be visible in the documentary record. The question of agency is messy. We see complexity and ambiguity in how explicitly or consciously gender was used to assert control, how gender could be invoked to protect oneself while engaging in dangerous activities, and the extent to which gendered experience propelled individuals into actions that those of their social station might not otherwise undertake. Delman's chapter reminds us that this question of agency is still unsettled in our own time, demonstrating a relevancy of the history of gender to the tangible and intangible heritage of Scotland today.

What ties these individual essays together is the careful interpretation of the historical record to understand the motivations behind historical people's actions. People presented themselves purposefully, in many different contexts, acting to construct and display specific identities. These identities were designed to respond to, and often take advantage of, particular situations, showing awareness of local conditions (place), religious conformity and nonconformity (faith) and political intrigues (politics). Crucially, all the people discussed as central figures in these chapters are identifiable individuals, rather than merely tiny points within aggregate studies of big data. This focus on individual persons – all of whom are complex, all of whom are worthy of historical investigation – adds the texture of lived human lives to historical understanding. The application of a gendered analysis allows studies that would not have been possible otherwise. Whether showing a new side to the most famous – the great and powerful who would populate any typical history book – or uncovering the experiences and expectations of the more humble and less well-documented, this approach humanises people and the historical experience. By paying attention to gendered identity, these studies move us closer to understanding how individuals experienced and shaped the events of their day, advancing the study of gender in the past and its relevance to the present.

Part One

Place

ONE

Mary, Queen of Scots, Three Noblewomen and a Fife 'Murder Mystery'

Jane E. A. Dawson

'Cherchez la femme'[1]

The maxim, *'cherchez la femme'* or 'look for the woman', was the starting-point for unravelling a Fife 'murder mystery'. The phrase also points to Elizabeth Ewan's outstanding contribution to women and gender studies in Scottish history.[2] Resting upon what she has achieved (and her friendship and support over many years), this essay adopts a biographical approach to recover female experiences, relationships and political agency. By placing the three Fife noblewomen and Mary, Queen of Scots, centre stage the story behind two violent deaths in 1570 can be told. On Saturday, 15 April of that year on the road near Kinnear in Fife, John Forbes, younger of Reres, with his family and friends 'chancit to foirgadder' with John Wood, Regent Moray's secretary, and his party. Wood and Forbes were killed and the others escaped in this confrontation between Fife neighbours. These details were recorded by the Fife chronicler Robert Lindsay of Pitscottie, but Wood's slaughter never came to trial and the incident was tacked onto the regent's assassination the previous January and subsequently slipped from sight.[3] Moray's death had a profound impact upon his powerbase of Fife, making people travel for safety in groups and 'na man that

---

[1] The phrase originated with Alexandre Dumas in his 1854–9 novel *Les Mohicans de Paris* and became a cliché of detective fiction.

[2] Elizabeth Ewan's ground-breaking volume edited with Maureen M. Meikle, *Women in Scotland c. 1100–c. 1750* (East Linton: Tuckwell Press. 1999), galvanised the study of women in Scottish history. The *Women in Scottish History* website – https://womeninscottishhistory.org/ – and Professor Ewan's publications on specific studies of women and gender followed (see Preface and Bibliography). Elizabeth, alongside her fellow editors, steered through the original edition (2006) and *The New Biographical Dictionary of Scottish Women* (Edinburgh: Edinburgh University Press, 2018).

[3] *The Historie and Cronicles of Scotland ... by Robert Lindesay of Pitscottie*, ed. A. J. G. Mackay, 3 vols, STS, 42–3, 60, II 227–8 (1899–1911).

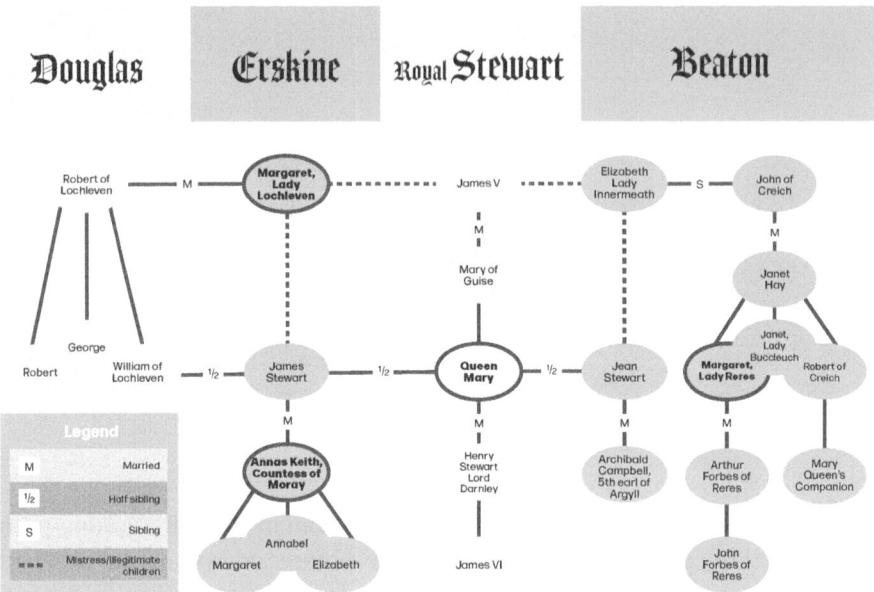

Figure 1.1 Relationships between the four women. Line drawing by Kennedy Robertson

met ane vthir be the way durst schaw him his mynd nor quhais man he was'.[4] The renewal of the Marian civil war produced a plethora of skirmishes between armed men undermining law and order throughout Scotland. Sufficient historical evidence has survived to look past the male violence at Kinnear and see in the background female networks, power and honour. Though none were present at the scene, the four women held the key to the actions of the men with blood on their hands. Revealing their relationship with each other has directly connected those particular Fife deaths to the dramatic events in national and international politics during Mary's reign.

The lives of early modern Scottish noblewomen centred upon family, kinship and service with every woman being required to uphold her own and her family's honour and legitimacy.[5] The core of that duty normally involved

---

[4] Pitscottie, II 289. Amy Blakeway, 'The Response to the Regent Moray's Assassination', *SHR* 88 (2009): 9–33.

[5] Barbara J. Harris, *English Aristocratic Women, 1450–1550* (Oxford: Oxford University Press, 2002), has provided an analysis of the lives of English noblewomen. Their Scottish counterparts form part of Keith M. Brown's study, *Noble Society in Scotland: Wealth, Family and Culture, from Reformation to Revolution* (Edinburgh: Edinburgh University Press, 2000). Individual women of this period appear in *Women in Scotland, c. 1100–c. 1750* or the *Biographical Dictionary of Scottish Women* or studies such as Margaret H. B. Sanderson, *Mary Stewart's People* (Edinburgh: Mercat Press,1987) covering Marion, Ogilvy; Jane Gordon; Janet Fockart; Mary Verschuur, *A Noble and Potent Lady: Katherine Campbell, Countess of Crawford*, Abertay History Society, no. 46 (Dundee:

marriage, child-bearing and rearing, running a household and maintaining her reputation, especially with regard to sexual conduct. Weddings and childbirth were among the central experiences that brought together women of different ages and forged their friendships.[6] For the four women highlighted in this essay, such occasions carried equal significance within 'mainstream' politics, an area traditionally viewed as a predominantly male sphere. Though rarely channelled through male-dominated 'public' institutions, female agency shaped the political life of sixteenth-century Scotland and the ways these women interacted.[7]

In order of age the women at the heart of this 'murder mystery' were Margaret Erskine, dowager Lady Lochleven; Margaret Beaton, Lady Reres; Annas Keith, Countess of Moray; and Mary, Queen of Scots. The first three were primarily based in Fife where the Queen was a frequent visitor. All were born into a high, or the highest, social rank and were at the heart of, or associated with, the royal court.[8] Enhancing the authority each woman received from her birth status, marriages, children and households, their strong personalities added to their power and effectiveness. During Mary's personal rule her gender ensured more women were placed at the Scottish court in positions of intimacy with, and possible influence over, the monarch. While offering elite women the opportunity to move closer to the centre of the political stage, greater prominence also brought greater vulnerability.[9]

2006). The broad issues concerning women and gender in Scottish early modern history were discussed by Elizabeth Ewan, 'A New Trumpet? The History of Women in Scotland, 1300–1700', *History Compass* 7, no. 2 (2009): 431–46; 'Gendering the Reformation', in *A Companion to the Reformation in Scotland, c. 1525–1638: Frameworks of Change and Development*, ed. William Ian P. Hazlett (Leiden: Brill, 2021), 511–41; Katie Barclay, Tanya Cheadle and Eleanor Gordon, 'The State of Scottish History: Gender', *SHR* 92, Supplement: no. 234 (2013): 83–107.

[6] Marriage, the family and childhood have been highlighted in two volumes edited by Elizabeth Ewan and Janay Nugent, *Finding the Family in Medieval and Early Modern Scotland* (Aldershot: Ashgate, 2008) and *Children and Youth in Premodern Scotland* (Woodbridge: Boydell Press, 2015). For a clear exposition of kinship and the law of marriage, David Sellar, 'The Family', in *A History of Everyday Life in Medieval Scotland*, eds Edward J. Cowan and Lizanne Henderson (Edinburgh: Edinburgh University Press, 2011), 89–108.

[7] For a recent discussion of women's agency, see Merry Wiesner-Hanks, ed., *Challenging Women's Agency and Activism in Early Modernity* (Amsterdam: Amsterdam University Press, 2021).

[8] 'Queenship and power' has received considerable scholarly attention including its own Routledge/Palgrave Macmillan series. A summary directly relating to Mary, Queen of Scots, can be found in Anna Groundwater's 'Afterword' in *Mary, Queen of Scots: A Study in Failure*, by Jenny Wormald (Edinburgh: John Donald, 2017), 211–20. For modern understandings of Mary through the lens of gender, Nia Clark, 'Re-imagining Mary, Queen of Scots in Contemporary Scottish Women's Writing', in *The Afterlife of Mary, Queen of Scots*, ed. Steven J. Reid (Edinburgh: Edinburgh University Press, 2024), Chapter 9.

[9] For Mary's reign, see Rosalind K. Marshall, *Queen Mary's Women: Female Relatives, Servants, Friends and Enemies of Mary, Queen of Scots* (Edinburgh: John Donald, 2006); for James V's reign, see Andrea Thomas, 'Dragonis baith and dowis ay in double forme": Women at the Court of James V, 1513–1542', in *Women in Scotland*, 83–94.

The older generation

By the time of Queen Mary's return to Scotland in 1561, Margaret Erskine and Margaret Beaton were mature married women who had survived multiple childbirths and were firmly established in Fife.[10] Margaret Erskine was born about 1515, the daughter of Margaret Campbell and John, fifth lord Erskine. As a married teenager she had become the mistress of King James V and bore him a son named James. Though an adulterous affair and illegitimate child usually brought a loss of honour, late medieval Scottish noble society condoned the taking of a mistress by a male monarch, particularly before he married. James V fathered nine illegitimate children, whom he openly acknowledged, all by different mothers.[11] The king held a special affection for Margaret Erskine and in 1536 enquiries were made in Rome about annulling her marriage to Robert Douglas of Lochleven. Nothing came of that approach, and mindful of his royal duty, James V sealed his French alliance by two marriages, first to Princess Madeleine and then to Mary of Guise. In 1538 Margaret's seven-year-old son went to St Andrews where his royal father had appointed him the Commendator Prior. The young James was raised in the priory and Margaret benefitted from priory grants that drew her further into the Fife noble and communications network.[12] Her base at Lochleven on the great north road from Queensferry to Perth also lay along routes into eastern and western Fife. Margaret knew the Fifer, Sir David Lyndsay of the Mount, Lyon King of Arms, who had been James V's mentor and friend. When Lyndsay alluded to Margaret as, 'the one who luffit you [the King] best', Fife noble society understood who was meant.[13] When her husband was killed at the Battle of Pinkie, Margaret

---

[10] The geography of Fife can be viewed in Blaeu's *Atlas*, nos 29–31, accessed 6 April 2022, https://maps.nls.uk/atlas/blaeu. Socially and politically, the shire was not dominated by a single aristocratic family because of the rivalry between the Leslies and the Lindsays (earls of Rothes and lords Lindsay). It possessed a group of interconnected greater lairdly families whose service to the crown gave them additional political clout. The Catholic Church, especially the Archbishop and Prior of St Andrews, held substantial estates and political and ecclesiastical authority, see Bess Rhodes, *Riches and Reform: Ecclesiastical Wealth in St Andrews, c. 1520–1580* (Leiden: Brill, 2019). For comparison, a fine study of the characteristics of another regional society, see Maureen M. Meikle, *A British Frontier?: Lairds and Gentlemen in the Eastern Borders, 1540–1603* (East Linton: Tuckwell Press, 2004); 'Victims, Viragos and Vamps: Women of the Sixteenth-Century Anglo-Scottish Frontier', in *Government, Religion and Society in Northern England, c. 1000–1700* (Gloucester: Alan Sutton, 1997), 172–84.

[11] Peter Anderson, 'James V, Mistresses and Children of', *ODNB*; Mairi Cowan and Laura E. Walkling, 'A "gret cradil of stait": Growing up with the Court of James IV', *Children and Youth in Premodern Scotland*, 15–31; Ishbel C. M. Barnes, *Janet Kennedy, Royal Mistress: Marriage and Divorce at the Courts of James IV and V* (Edinburgh: John Donald, 2007).

[12] Linda J. Dunbar, *Reforming the Scottish Church: John Winram (c. 1492–1582) and the Example of Fife* (Aldershot: Ashgate, 2002), 8–9; 12–13.

[13] Anderson, 'James V, Mistresses', *ODNB*; Rhiannon Purdie discussed Lyndsay's Fife audience in her edition of Squyre Meldrum, *Six Scottish Courtly and Chivalric Poems Including Squyer Meldrum*, eds Rhiannon Purdie and Emily Wingfield (Kalamazoo: Medieval Institute Publications, 2018),

was left a widow with six children. Until his succession in 1555, she managed the estates on behalf of William, her eldest Douglas son.[14] Five years earlier Margaret had organised a future for James outside the Church. In a manner usually associated with male family strategies, she used the wardship of her godchild, Christina, Countess of Buchan, to betroth the three-year-old girl to James, giving him access to the Buchan inheritance.[15]

Margaret Beaton understood Lady Lochleven's secure position in Fife society because her aunt, Elizabeth Beaton, Lady Innermeath, had been another of James V's mistresses and their daughter Jean Stewart, Countess of Argyll, was her friend and cousin. Margaret was born in the mid-1520s to Janet Hay and John Beaton of Creich, who held the hereditary keepership of the royal palace at Falkland, not far from Lochleven. Through their service at court the Beatons had acquired power, influence and appointments, most notably within the Church. Margaret's extended family included Cardinal David Beaton, Archbishop of St Andrews, and James Beaton II, Archbishop of Glasgow.[16] Among her cousins was James Hamilton, Duke of Châtelherault, and within Fife she was kin to the greater lairdly families of the Balfours and Melvilles who had also thrived in royal service. Margaret had married Arthur Forbes of Reres whose estates lay in the southern Fife parish of Kilconquhar and in the east at Leuchars. John, Margaret's eldest son, and his wife Barbara Sandilands lived at Westhous on the Eden estuary and controlled the hunting lodge at Pitlethie that entertained Stewart monarchs.[17] Combining the Forbes landed base with Beaton connections running along the northern Fife hills to Falkland, Margaret could command a sphere of information and influence across much of the shire. By 1561, secure in the authority generated by their families, households, estates and court connections, both Margarets were established and powerful Fife ladies.

172–5. It is possible that the character of 'Dame Sensualitie' in Lyndsay's play *The Satyre of the Three Estatis* was partly inspired by Margaret.

[14] 'Sir William Douglas, Laird of Lochleven, Earl of Morton, c. 1540–1606', Sanderson, *Mary Stewart's People*, 55–74. Examples of how Margaret managed the estates can be found in Margaret H. B. Sanderson, *A Kindly Place?: Living in Sixteenth-Century Scotland* (East Linton: Tuckwell Press, 2002), 114, 139, 141, 151.

[15] Dunbar, *Reforming the Scottish Church*, 163–4; Heather Parker, 'At thair perfect age': Elite Child Betrothal and Parental Control, 1430–1560', in *Children and Youth in Premodern Scotland*, 173–86.

[16] For the extended Beaton family, M. H. B. Sanderson, *Cardinal of Scotland: David Beaton, c. 1494–1546* (Edinburgh: John Donald, 2001), appendix 4. The archbishop remained Queen Mary's ambassador in France until her death.

[17] Owned by St Andrews Priory, Pitlethie was used by the Forbes, *Place Names of Fife*, https://fife-placenames.glasgow.ac.uk/placename/?id=3005.

The younger generation

By contrast, Queen Mary and Annas were beginning their adult lives. Like many women, they were drawn closer together by sharing their experiences of the pressure to make the best possible marriage and, once wed, facing the perils of childbearing.[18] Mary was born in 1542 shortly before her father died and never knew a time when she had not been queen. She spent much of her childhood at the French court seeing little of her mother, Mary of Guise, who remained in Scotland as regent from 1554 until her death in 1560. A year later, after the death of her first husband, King Francis II, Mary had to adjust to the disappearance of her shining future as Queen of France. Since a female could not inherit the French crown, Mary's upbringing had prepared her for the role of queen consort rather than direct rule. The nineteen-year-old widow returned to Scotland where she faced the multiple challenges of governing her kingdom in person. Although the only surviving legitimate child, Mary did have Stewart siblings. Her mother's care for James V's illegitimate children enabled Mary to draw a family group around her, including her only half-sister, Jean, Countess of Argyll. Having visited the queen in France to make his peace for leading the 1559–60 rebellion, James, her eldest and most prominent half-brother, became her chief political adviser.[19] The presence at court of her Stewart kin helped Mary replace the loss of daily contact with her French relatives but could not add the political weight of a noble kindred such as the House of Guise. 'Queen Mary's women' constituted a significant group and gave her court a strong sense of family and community.[20] Accompanying the queen from France were her Four Maries, including Mary Beaton. Margaret, Mary Beaton's aunt, became one of the ladies in waiting and Annas Keith quickly became one of the queen's favourites when she arrived at court in November 1561. Annas was born about 1540, the eldest daughter of Margaret Keith and William, third Earl Marischal and with her eleven siblings was well educated in their Protestant-leaning household. Within the noble marriage market, Annas was a major 'catch' and, as the richest earl in Scotland, her father provided the staggering sum of 10,000 merks for her tocher or dowry.[21] Rather than meekly following convention, Annas was clear about her marital future. Aided by their shared religious beliefs, she had developed a close relationship with James, Margaret

---

[18] For the attitudes about young wives, see Sarah Dunnigan, 'Sons and Daughters, "young wyfis" and "barnis": Lyric, Gender and the Imagining of Youth in the Maitland Manuscripts', in *Children and Youth in Premodern Scotland*, 187–201.
[19] Mark Loughlin, 'James Stewart, first earl of Moray', *ODNB*.
[20] Marshall, *Queen Mary's Women*, chs 7, 9, 10.
[21] *HMC 6th Report*, 647; Amy Blakeway, 'Keith Annas [Agnes], Countess of Moray and of Argyll (c. 1540–1588), *ODNB*.

Erskine's son. Though derailing Margaret's earlier provision, Annas had the queen's strong support for what contemporaries viewed as a love match.[22]

Making and patching marriages[23]

For every family, securing good marriages formed a central part of their strategy and was crucial to their success. Detailed negotiations were conducted between the two kin groups, with women playing a crucial, but seldom seen, part.[24] Since weddings provided one of the most important occasions for the display of status, power and wealth throughout her personal rule, Mary revelled in match-making and wedding organisation for relatives and friends and gave these events a high priority.[25] They would draw noblewomen as well as their menfolk into court life, cementing networks and friendships. In January 1562 the queen sponsored the wedding of her equerry, Arthur, Margaret Erskine's young brother, to Magdalen Livingstone, a maid of honour and sister of one of the Four Maries.[26] For Annas and Margaret this possibly felt like a dress rehearsal for the main event the following month.

From her experience at the Spectacles mounted by the French royal family, Mary understood the importance of displays of 'soft power' for domestic and international consumption and she chose a royal Stewart marriage to stage her own first royal Spectacle.[27] She employed the sumptuous wedding of Annas and James in February 1562 to display her political and dynastic power and her policies.[28] It emphasised Mary's Stewart family, represented by the groom and another half-brother Robert, Commendator of Holyrood Abbey, the venue

---

[22] James wrote to his mother he had 'falowed my hartis inclination in my mariage', 9 October 1562, *Registrum Honoris de Morton*, ed. T. Thomson (Edinburgh: Bannatyne Club, 1853), I 9–10; Randolph noted the couple's 'long love', *CSPSc*, eds J. Bain et al. (Edinburgh, 1898–1969), II 563.

[23] For the best study of Scottish marriage practices in this period, Heather Parker, '"In all gudly haste": The Formation of Marriage in Scotland, c. 1350–1600' (PhD diss., University of Guelph, 2012). For the later period including a discussion of intimacy and power, see Katie Barclay, *Love, Intimacy and Power: Marriage and Patriarchy in Scotland, 1650–1850* (Manchester: Manchester University Press, 2011).

[24] For example, Katherine Ruthven's role, Jane Dawson, ed., *Clan Campbell Letters, 1559–1583* (Edinburgh: SHS, 5th ser. 10, 1997), 28–34.

[25] Mary was criticised for attending a wedding immediately after Darnley's murder, see Wormald, *Mary*, 167–8.

[26] Marshall, *Queen Mary's Women*, 138, 160.

[27] Mary's mother was well aware of their importance, see Lucinda H. S. Dean, 'In the Absence of an Adult Monarch: Ceremonial Representations of Authority by Marie de Guise, 1543–1558', in *Medieval and Early Modern Representations of Authority in Scotland and the British Isles*, eds Katherine Buchanan, Lucinda H. S. Dean and Michael A. Penman (London: Routledge, 2016), 143–62.

[28] Sarah Carpenter, 'Performing Diplomacies: The 1560s Court Entertainments of Mary Queen of Scots', *SHR* 82 (2003): 194–225, at 201–2; Theo van Heijnsbergen, 'Advice to a Princess: The Literary Articulation of a Religious, Political and Cultural Programme for Mary, Queen of Scots',

for the celebrations. The level of magnificence at her court was signalled by the couple's stunning matching outfits in black with expensive jewellery and the commissioning of Hans Eworth's wedding portraits, then a relative novelty in Scotland.[29] The wedding service for this conspicuously Protestant pair was conducted by John Knox in the High Kirk, St Giles' Cathedral, Edinburgh. After the ceremony, 'with sik solemnitie as the lyk hes not bene sein befoir; the haill nobilitie of this realme being thair present, and convoyit thame doun to the Abbay of Halyrudhous, quhair the banket wes maid, and the Quenis Grace thairat'. A further three days of celebration followed, with masques, dancing, a fireball entertainment and further banqueting.[30]

Lavish hospitality, rich attire, courtly dances and masques were pursuits in which noblewomen were expected to excel. Mary, having developed these skills at the French court, fulfilled this royal role to perfection. At the final banquet she performed a diplomatic gesture confirming support for her brother's conduct of foreign policy. Mary toasted her cousin Queen Elizabeth and donated the heavy gold cup to the English ambassador, the couple's personal friend. This wedding united the four women as Annas and the queen took centre stage, supported by the groom's mother and Margaret Beaton, Mary's lady-in-waiting. It also brought honour and reflected glory to Fife, as Pitscottie was eager to note, with a number of Fife lairds being knighted when James was made an earl.[31]

For women, marriage altered their status and family allegiances to a greater degree than their male counterparts. In Annas's case she remained close to her Keith relatives while becoming part of the Erskine, Douglases of Lochleven and royal Stewart families. In common with other elite wives she was the lynch-pin of the marital alliance and her role was to maintain harmony among her kin. Annas's geographical location shifted when she moved her main residence to St Andrews.[32] With her husband, now earl of Moray, high in royal favour and frequently at court, Annas became acquainted with the priory's estates under the guidance of John Winram, the sub-prior.[33] That made her a significant figure within Fife society as well as a St Andrews neighbour to the Reres estate at Leuchars. She rapidly formed an affectionate bond with her mother-in-law,

---

in *Sixteenth-Century Scotland: Essays in Honour of Michael Lynch*, eds Julian Goodare and Alasdair A. Macdonald (Leiden: Brill, 2008), 99–122, at 120–1.

[29] Keith Brown labelled the portraits 'the power couple of the 1560s', *Noble Society in Scotland*, plates 19, 45. 'True black' dye was extremely expensive and the colour was frequently worn at court, without any association with mourning.

[30] *A Diurnal of Remarkable Occurrents …*', ed. T. Thomson (Edinburgh: Bannatyne Club, 1833), 70–1.

[31] He proudly recorded the remark by Mary's uncle that he had never seen such a bridal, not even for the French king, Pitscottie, II 17, n.7.

[32] Elizabeth Ewan, 'Living in the Late Medieval Town of St Andrews', in *Medieval St Andrews: Church, Cult, City*, eds Michael Brown and Katie Stevenson (Woodbridge: Boydell, 2017), 117–40.

[33] Annas had a long relationship with Winram; see Dunbar, *Reforming the Scottish Church*, 166–9.

being only a ride from Lochleven that passed Falkland Palace held by the Beatons. Annas and the two Margarets had no difficulty staying in touch and personal contact with the queen was maintained by Margaret Beaton and Annas's regular attendance at court.

When planning her royal progresses Mary could create opportunities to visit friends based outside her capital. She travelled frequently to Fife, especially to Falkland Palace and the royal residence at the New Inns, St Andrews.[34] All four women were brought together during the royal progress from February to May 1563. Annas hosted the queen in St Andrews and the obvious base for the hunt at Kinross was Margaret Erskine's 'Newhouse' on the shore at Loch Leven. While her brother Robert was keeper at Falkland, Margaret Beaton was probably in charge at the Pitlethie hunting lodge.[35] That spring the queen was concerned about the disintegration of her sister Jean's marriage to the earl of Argyll. Margaret Beaton was Jean's friend and through her Campbell mother Margaret Erskine was kin to the earl. Argyll was Moray's close personal friend leaving Annas in the awkward position of being friends with both parties. With this being a family concern for each of them as well as a public 'scandal', the women would have discussed the Argylls' marital troubles.[36] In the middle of April accompanied by Annas and Moray, Mary rode from St Andrews to Lochleven. Having specially summoned Knox for a consultation, this unlikely pair of marriage counsellors agreed Knox would tackle the earl while the queen had a stern talk with her sister. Mary's words to Jean were reinforced by a strategy, possibly suggested by her female friends. During the following year's royal progress, the queen visited Inveraray Castle thereby ensuring the earl and countess had to work together to host her and that reconciliation kept their marriage going until Mary's deposition.[37]

Succession

While the queen was busy arranging or patching up other people's marriages, she knew she needed to re-marry. A marital alliance was the most powerful diplomatic tool she possessed, and Mary wanted it to strengthen her position in the English royal succession. She also needed to fulfil the fundamental duty

---

[34] Edward Furgol, 'The Scottish Itinerary of Mary Queen of Scots, 1542–8 and 1561–8', *PSAS* 117 (1987): 219–31, fiche 1; C1–D6.

[35] Margaret Beaton also had to deal with her eldest son's marriage break-up after his wife's affair conducted at Pitlethie that resulted in the first Protestant divorce on grounds of adultery; Thomas M. Green, *The Spiritual Jurisdiction in Reformation Scotland: A Legal History* (Edinburgh: Edinburgh University Press, 2019), 167–70.

[36] Janay Nugent, '"None must meddle betuenne man and wife": Assessing Family and the Fluidity of Public and Private in Early Modern Scotland', *Journal of Family History* 35 (2010): 219–31.

[37] Jane Dawson, 'The Noble and the Bastard: The Earl of Argyll and the Law of Divorce in Reformation Scotland', in *Sixteenth-Century Scotland*, 147–68.

of every monarch (and noble) of securing the dynasty, though it brought the personal dangers of pregnancy. As a reigning queen, she faced the complications of how a wifely status affected her own authority and that of Scotland's position in Europe. For her subjects, the central issues of Mary's next marriage were who would be their king and which European alignment he would bring. The Franco-Scottish union created by her first marriage had been rejected by the successful Protestant rebellion of 1559–60 led by Moray who had steered her Anglophile policy since her return.

Four years after her return to Scotland, Queen Mary made that major political and personal decision. Her contentious choice in the spring of 1565 fell upon Henry Stewart, Lord Darnley, newly arrived from long-term exile in England. His elevation undermined Moray's political influence, overthrew Scotland's existing diplomatic alignment and appeared to threaten its religious settlement. When trying to win her brother's approval, the queen employed a significant line of argument. She did not speak about international relations nor dynastically about combining her own with Darnley's claim to the English throne. Instead Mary presented her choice as if it were solely a family marriage between Stewart relatives and appended a direct appeal to their father's memory. She wished Moray 'to be so much a Stewart as to consent with the keeping of the Crown in the family, and the surname, according to their father's will and desire, as was said of him a little before his death'.[38] Remaining opposed to the Darnley marriage, Moray was pushed into rebellion, followed by exile and his authority in Fife collapsed. With a rebellion and foreign policy crisis, there was no opportunity for the queen to turn her July wedding into a spectacular royal event. When Mary swept into Fife in September to assert her royal authority it was clear her marriage had split her Fife friends. She found support among many nobles who had previously looked to Moray, such as Lord Lindsay or Forbes of Reres, Margaret Beaton's husband.[39] Left in St Andrews managing the estates and awaiting the birth of another child, Annas was evicted from her home and went on the run in Fife as she attempted to join her exiled husband.[40] When the surrender of Lochleven Castle was demanded, Margaret Erskine drew upon her experience and friendship with Mary and made a successful appeal for clemency.[41]

---

[38] *John Knox's History of the Reformation in Scotland*, ed. W. C. Dickinson, 2 vols (Edinburgh: 1949), II 145.

[39] Gordon Donaldson, *All the Queen's Men: Power and Politics in Mary Stewart's Scotland* (London: Batsford, 1983), 73.

[40] For St Andrews events, see Dunbar, *Reforming the Scottish Church*, 140–2; the botched escape, Randolph to Leicester, 18 October 1565, *CSPSc*, II no. 284; Bedford to Privy Council, 12 November 1565, *Calendar of State Papers, Foreign Edward, Mary and Elizabeth*, eds J. Stevenson et al. (London: 1861–1950), VII no. 1668.

[41] William Douglas of Lochleven was seriously ill, *Registrum Honoris de Morton*, eds T. Thompson et al., 2 vols (Bannatyne Club, 94, Edinburgh, 1853), I:12–13.

The female domain of childbirth

Despite the upheavals of 1565, Annas's friendship with the queen was renewed in the following year. She formed part of a formidable trio (the countesses of Moray, Argyll and Mar) who kept Mary company as her pregnancy progressed.[42] Annabella Murray, Countess of Mar, was the sister-in-law of Lady Lochleven and was later placed in overall charge of Prince James's household. Annas and Mary had already shared the highs and lows of the birth and death of a child. During the 1564 Fife progress the queen returned to Falkland specifically to await the birth of Annas's child. During her labour, probably supervised at Lochleven by Margaret Erskine, Annas endured 'sore travail' and several weeks later her son died. By then in Edinburgh, Mary made an unscheduled journey to Lochleven where Annas was grieving and remained for nearly a week commiserating with her. Early modern society recognised that in such circumstances female support was natural and essential and no adverse comment was made over the queen's absence.[43] Preparing for her own first confinement in 1566 Mary made her will listing gifts of jewels to her ladies including Annas and her baby daughter, Elizabeth, and the other two countesses.[44] Childbirth was an almost exclusively female domain, with experienced women assisting alongside midwives. As the queen went into labour the rumour circulated that Margaret Fleming, Countess of Atholl, had cast a spell to transfer the queen's pains to Margaret Beaton.[45] This did not prevent a long labour for Mary before her son was born on 19 June. Mary Beaton rushed the news of the birth to the waiting James Melville of Halhill, her Fife neighbour who rode post haste to London with the tidings.[46] As Prince James's first governess, Margaret Beaton was given the official duty of showing the healthy baby to the English ambassador. The queen was determined to use James's baptism at Stirling to create an exceptional Spectacle for international and national audiences. Her female friends played important parts with her sister Jean given the prestigious post of deputising for Queen Elizabeth as James's godmother with Annas named

---

[42] This provoked Darnley's jealousy; see Marshall, *Queen Mary's Women*, 90.
[43] Lochleven accounts for 4–9 June 1564, Moray, MSS National Register of Archives of Scotland, 217 Box 2, no. 72. Randolph to Cecil, June 1564, *CSPSc*, eds J. Bain et al., 13 vols. (Edinburgh: 1898–1969), II 78.
[44] Michael Pearce, 'The Jewels Mary, Queen of Scots, Left Behind' (2016), accessed 6 April 2022, https://dundee.academia.edu/MichaelPearce. Elizabeth was Annas's first surviving child.
[45] The story was told by Andrew Lundie from Fife, *Memorials of Transactions in Scotland ... by Richard Bannatyne*, ed. Robert Pitcairn (Edinburgh: Bannatyne Club, 1836), 174. The later suggestion that Prince James was Margaret's son was refuted by R. K. Hannay, 'The Coffin in the Wall', *SHR* 15, vol. 58 (1918): 156–8. I am grateful to the anonymous reviewer for the Hannay reference.
[46] Marshall, *Queen Mary's Women*, 167; Melville later recorded Queen Elizabeth's reaction to the birth: 'the Quen of Scotlandis is leichter of a faire sonne, and that sche was bot a barren stok', *Memoirs of His Own Life. By Sir James Melville of Halhill*, ed. T. Thomson (Edinburgh: Bannatyne Club, 1827), 158–9.

as the second choice. Margaret Beaton received cloth for her baptismal attire and furnishings for the prince's nursery.[47] The triumphant celebrations at the christening emphasised the message that the Scottish queen had achieved her dynastic duty of providing a male heir and could look forward to a peaceful future resting upon the unity of the kingdom.[48]

Mary's healthy son brought dynastic security but held a potential threat to her own royal authority. In June 1567 Mary's deposition was only a viable option because the baby Prince James could be crowned. By that time the queen was in prison within the island castle of Lochleven. She was only permitted two domestic servants and none of her own ladies. The two Ladies Lochleven, Margaret and her daughter-in-law Agnes, were thrust into the dual roles of jailer and hostess. The pregnant Agnes slept in the same room as the queen who was herself carrying Bothwell's child. When Mary suffered a miscarriage of twins it was the female household who handled the situation. Officially no visitors were permitted, but Annas hurried to Lochleven and she and Mary cried together about the queen's predicament.[49] Modern commentators have noted discrepancies concerning the length of Mary's pregnancy.[50] The queen declared she was seven weeks pregnant, placing conception after she had married Bothwell on 15 May 1567. Since twins could be identified, it was probable they were conceived earlier when Bothwell raped Mary at Dunbar. No hint of that earlier conception date emerged when allegations about Mary's adulterous relationship with Bothwell were made later by George Buchanan or John Wood who were close to Annas and Margaret Erskine. The Lochleven women kept silent, protecting Mary's sexual honour and defending the female domain of childbirth from male interference and politicisation.

A later letter from Margaret Erskine to Annas revealed how the loss of a child was felt across generations. She had the painful duty of writing, 'that is has plesit God to tak your doichtor my bairne to himself, quhilk is the greittest greif that ever came to my hertt, for ony of hir yeiris owther of my awin beiring or of ony utheris'. While attempting to comfort Annas, Margaret expressed her own searing grief:

> I pray your ladyschip be of gud comfort, and treitt yourself weill that ye may lewe to bring wp the leif be honest folkis, for ne bodye hes gottin the greittest lois bott I. I dout nocht God sall send your Ladyschip barnis efter this to do you plesseur, for ye ar young

---

[47] 5 Sept 1566, D. Hay Fleming, *Mary Queen of Scots* (London: Hodder and Stoughton, 1898), 499–500.
[48] Michael Lynch, 'Queen Mary's Triumph: The Baptismal Celebrations at Stirling in December 1566', *SHR* 69 (1990): 1–21.
[49] Throckmorton to Queen Elizabeth, 26 July 1567, *CSPSc*, II 363.
[50] For example, Retha M. Warnicke, *Mary Queen of Scots* (Abingdon: Routledge, 2006), 163–4.

anewch, bot thair is neyn abill to do me sic plessour as sche did, bot I committ all thingis to the pleasour of God, quha conserue you eternalie.[51]

Blackening reputations

Shortly after the queen's miscarriage, Annas's husband returned to Scotland and visited Lochleven. Moray adopted the high moral tone of an elder brother and pressured Mary to agree he should become regent for her son James.[52] When Moray undertook the regency John Wood became his secretary and adviser. At the young king's first parliament in December 1567, rumours circulated that Moray was to be declared next heir to James.[53] An accusation that Moray was aiming to take the throne had previously appeared in 1559–60.[54] Seven years later the allegation had become explicitly linked to his mother. A propaganda rhyme supporting the queen's party written by 'Tom Truth' alleged Margaret Erskine had claimed, she 'precontract Was in most solemn wise Unto the King (James V), before that he Was married to the Gwyse'.[55] A similar accusation was expressed in 1581 by Nicol Burne who reported a discussion in London between Knox and Moray in April 1567 in which the preacher declared Margaret and King James to have been lawfully married. Moray would therefore be able to succeed to the crown because he was his father's 'reable' heir (i.e., capable of inheriting).[56] As Moray's surviving parent, Margaret found herself in the middle of the constitutional struggle about 'legitimacy' and the Scottish throne.

In 1568 the queen's escape from Lochleven was engineered by George, Margaret Erskine's third son, her page, 'little William' Douglas and Margaret Beaton's cousin, John.[57] Mary's freedom unleashed a vitriolic propaganda campaign starting with her proclamation before the Battle of Langside in which Moray and Wood were named in the blacklist of her enemies.[58] After Mary's defeat and flight to England, Wood was despatched by the regent to London and shuttled between the countries negotiating with William Cecil, Queen Elizabeth's chief adviser, concerning the proposed English 'commission' to

---

[51] Margaret Erskine to Annas, n.d. probably 17 March 1571, *HMC 6th*, 'Moray MSS' (London, 1877), 652.
[52] Melville later noted that interview had destroyed Mary's affection for Moray, see Melville, *Memoirs*, 194.
[53] *The History of Mary Stewart by Claude Nau*, ed. J. Stevenson (Edinburgh: William Paterson, 1883), 73–4.
[54] Knox, *History*, I:368; Melville, *Memoirs*, 81–2.
[55] *Satirical Poems of the Time of the Reformation*, ed. James Cranstoun, 2 vols (Edinburgh: STS old ser., 1891–3), no. IX 76, ll 205–12.
[56] Nicol Burne, *Disputation* in *Catholic Tractates of the Sixteenth Century*, ed. T. Law (STS, 1901), 164.
[57] John went to his brother, Mary's ambassador in Paris, 26 May 1568, *Calendar of State Papers, Venice*, eds R. Brown and G. Cavendish Bentinck (London, 1890), 7 1558–80, no. 425.
[58] Printed in Hay Fleming, *Mary*, 512–14.

pronounce on any stains to Mary's honour and reputation. In June, Wood's secret report to Moray was intercepted by the queen's party.[59] Copies of material to be included in the 'Casket Letters' case against Mary were also carried south by Wood. The suspicion within the queen's party that Cecil and Wood were conspiring to blacken Mary's name seemed confirmed by their behaviour at her 'first trial'.[60] Melville, his fellow Fifer, named Wood as the 'ringleader' of the radicals around Moray and described how at the trial Wood first refused to surrender the Casket Letters, then produced them from inside his doublet. The Bishop of Orkney whisked the packet from Wood's hand and laid them before the commissioners. Melville added, Wood and Cecil winked at each other and the other radicals laughed.[61] Wood was a traitor and a marked man to the queen's supporters.

As well as her staunch support for Mary, Margaret Beaton had a personal grievance against Wood whose family at Largo were close neighbours and distantly related to the Forbeses.[62] She had been included in the allegations presented to the English commissioners thereby impugning Margaret's personal reputation and the Forbes family's honour. Wood's colleague, George Buchanan, alleged Margaret was one of Bothwell's former lovers and was the 'principall instrument' connecting the earl to Mary.[63] Such a personalised attack from the leading propagandist for the king's party reflected how close Margaret had been to the queen. The suggestion that Mary had told Margaret Erskine and Moray that Lady Reres had betrayed her was intended to drive a wedge between them. In his *Dectectioun* Buchanan went as far as turning Margaret into the stock comic character of the middle-aged procuress:

> my ladie Rerese, a woman of maist vile vnchastitie ... wha now in her age had from the gayne of horedome betaken hir selfe to the craft of bawderie ... The Quene with Margaret Carwod ... dyd let her downe by a stryng ouer an auld wall into the next garden ... Behald, the strying sodenly brake, and downe with a great noyse fell Dame Rerese, a woman very heauy baith by vnweldy age and massy substance ... vp sche getteth, and winneth into Bothwels chamber; she gyt the dore open, and out of his bed,

---

[59] Drury to Cecil, 27 June 1568, *Calendar of State Papers, Foreign Series Edward, Mary, Elizabeth For* 8, 489. The packet's contents were described as 'nothing more hostile to Queen Mary herself, nothing more ruinous to her cause, could be either expressed or imagined' (Nau's, *History*, 188.)
[60] Gordon Donaldson, *The First Trial of Mary, Queen of Scots* (London: Batsford, 1969).
[61] Melville, *Memoirs*, 113.
[62] Wood's brother Andro, younger of Largo, stated he was related to John Forbes, *Register of the Ministers, Elders and Deacons of the Christian Congregation of St Andrews*, trans. and ed. David Hay Fleming (Edinburgh: SHS), I: 166–7.
[63] Case of Queen of Scots, c. 20 June 1568, *CSPSc*, II 709.

euen out of his wiues armes, halfe a slepe, halfe naked, sche forceably bringes the man to the Quene.⁶⁴

The assassinations of 1570

What had been said and done in 1568 added a lasting bitterness to the civil war between the king's and queen's parties that in 1570 entered a particularly violent and chaotic phase. In January of that year warnings reached Annas about the imminent danger her husband faced, so she dispatched John Wood to appeal to Moray not to enter Linlithgow.⁶⁵ He ignored her plea and was shot by Hamilton of Bothwellhaugh as he rode through the burgh. After the shock of the assassination, the pregnant Annas with Wood's help organised Moray's funeral and dealt with his creditors demanding repayment.⁶⁶ By then under house arrest in England, Mary wrote to Annas seeking restitution of royal jewels seized by the 'traitor' Moray. In a handwritten postscript the embittered queen showed little sign of their past friendship.

> As I mynd to pitie yow in your adversite yff yow doe your deuti, so be sur iff yow hold anithing pertins me from me, yow and your bernes and meinterners schal feel my displesour heuier nor wrangous geir profitable, and so I will be to yow, as yow schal deserue.⁶⁷

Within Fife the queen's party was in the ascendant making the region unsafe for Moray's household. Annas had initially explored the possibility of refuge in England, but travelled instead to the safety of her father's castle at Dunnottar, having politely declined the offer to give birth at Lochleven.⁶⁸ Meanwhile, her St Andrews house and possessions were overrun by creditors and those trying to gain control over the priory.⁶⁹ Knowing he was also a target, Wood told Annas on 4 April what to do in the event of his death:

---

⁶⁴ George Buchanan, *De Maria Scotorum Regina*, critical hypertext edition by Dana F. Sutton (2001), 1571, English translation, section 5, accessed 3 August 2022, https://philological.cal.bham.ac.uk/mqs/trans.html.

⁶⁵ Bannatyne, *Memorials*, 289–90.

⁶⁶ Wood to Annas, 24 Feb and 3 Mar 1570, *HMC 6th*, 650–1. Wood probably composed the Latin epitaph for Moray's tomb. Blakeway, 'Response', 25–6. For the broader context of Scottish women and debt, see Cathryn Spence, *Women, Credit and Debt in Early Modern Scotland* (Manchester: Manchester University Press, 2016).

⁶⁷ Queen Mary to Annas, 28 March 1570, *HMC 6th*, 638.

⁶⁸ 23 Feb 1570, *HMC 6th*, 649; *CSPSc*, III no. 140.

⁶⁹ Annas to William Douglas, 5 Feb and 26 Mar 1570, *Reg. Hon Mort.*, I 45–6, 51–2. The Priory disputes, Dunbar, *Reforming the Scottish Church*, 142–6.

Yff it pleis God to wisit me, my compt and your memorialis with all thingis in my handis salbe crawit of my brother James, for my rekenyngis and comptis ar in my tronk besyid your ladischippis self, and I sall leif with him the rest. Yff it sall pleis God to grant ws guid successe, and lyif be reseruit, I sall cum directly frome Glascow to your ladischip as my horse will beyr me.[70]

As John Wood was riding along the north Fife road to the Tay ferry on 15 April he knew he passed close to Creich, the Beatons' castle, and was overlooked by their allies, the Forrets of that ilk.[71] He would have readied himself for a confrontation once he recognised the Forbes's party. From his virulently anti-Hamilton viewpoint Buchanan's initial account of the fight, accused them, 'yat fetcheit men out of teviot daill to fyff to slay master Johnne Wod for na vyer cause bot for being ane gude seruand to ye croun and yat he had espyit out sum of yair practisis.'[72] Margaret Beaton was related to the Hamiltons and the Teviotdale men were probably linked to her sister, Janet, Lady Buccleuch. By killing Wood, the Forbes's group assumed they had avenged the slight upon their family's honour, removed a plotter against Queen Mary and demonstrated that her supporters dominated Fife and might be gaining control over the rest of the kingdom.

Aftermath

Despite the efforts of the male members of Margaret's family to restore her and their honour, over the centuries Buchanan's blackening of her reputation has survived. Whatever she thought about her honour, at Kinnear she had lost her eldest son. Her husband and second son, both named Arthur, were charged with Wood's slaughter, outlawed and forfeited. Three years later Margaret and Jean Stewart retreated to Edinburgh Castle with the last of the queen's supporters. When it fell to the English and king's party forces, Jean appealed to Queen Elizabeth for protection against her estranged husband Argyll, one of the besiegers. Probably with Margaret, Jean travelled to Fife where she was reported to be comfortable.[73] John Beaton, Mary's master of household, would have given his mistress news of the Kinnear killings. At this point Queen Mary's attention was concentrated upon events in England, though she might have felt a moment of satisfaction at Wood's death. His demise was not mentioned

---

[70] Wood to Annas, 4 Apr 1570, *HMC 6th*, 651–2.
[71] Henry Forret was named as one of Wood's killers, *Ancient Criminal Trials in Scotland from 1488 to 1624*, ed. R. Pitcairn (Edinburgh, 1833), I Pt II: 40.
[72] Text from the manuscript 'Exhortation Against the Hamiltons', *CSPSc*, II no. 123; George Buchanan, *Ane Admonitioun to the Trew Lordis*, in *Vernacular Writings*, ed. P. Hume Brown (STS 26, 1892), 33.
[73] Dawson, 'Noble and Bastard', 165.

in later Marian narratives where he was dismissed as 'a crafty and cunning fellow'.[74] After James VI succeeded to the English throne, he translated his mother's body from Peterborough Cathedral to Westminster Abbey, restoring her honour and building an elaborate final resting place that outshone the neighbouring tomb of Queen Elizabeth.[75] Over the centuries Mary's supporters have refuted Buchanan's version of her reign and created the potent image of the tragic queen.[76]

Around the time of Wood's death, Annas was giving birth to a daughter whom she named Margaret after her grandmother. Both women had hoped for a son to continue Moray's line, and Margaret's letter included a postscript referring to the Old Testament story of Ruth and Naomi, where the mother-in-law comforted her daughter-in-law. Margaret implied Annas should re-marry with the hope God would send more children. She reassured Annas any future bairns, 'salbe alss welcum to me yai beand gottyn wp lauchtfullye sua yai beand nocht my sonnis inneme'.[77] Though she wished to continue her close relationship with Annas, in that final caveat Margaret showed her priority lay with her surviving sons. 'Old' Lady Lochleven was able to weather the assassinations of Moray and Wood by utilising her previous experiences of loss. She could rest within the last and honourable stage of her maternal career with her sons settled, the Douglas lineage and estates secured and her daughters married into the leading Fife families of Lord Lindsay, Colville of Wemyss and Durie of that ilk.[78] Despite her eldest son's fragile health, William outlived his mother to succeed his kinsman, the earl of Morton, and Robert, her second son, held the earldom of Buchan by right of Christina, his wife. Even George, her youngest, whose support for Mary had sent him into exile in France, returned to Fife, was knighted and served on the St Andrews Kirk Session.[79]

For Annas the slaughter of Wood, her right-hand man, added one more blow to the loss of her beloved husband, her position as the first lady of the realm and her St Andrews' home and possessions. The security of her daughters became her chief concern, leading to a protracted battle over the royal jewels that formed their inheritance.[80] She had followed the advice to remarry and was assisted in the negotiations by Margaret's brother, John, Regent Mar. In January

---

[74] For example, Nau, *History*, 175, 186.
[75] Susan Doran, ed., *Elizabeth and Mary: Royal Cousins, Rival Queens* (British Library, 2021), 274–5.
[76] Steven Reid, ed., *The Afterlife of Mary, Queen of Scots* (Edinburgh: Edinburgh University Press, 2024).
[77] 16 Apr 1570, Dunbar, *Reforming the Scottish Church*, 168 n. 22 from NRAS 217, Box 15, no. 352.
[78] For a broader view of how married women settled their property and testaments, see Cordelia Beattie with Cathryn Spence, 'Married Women, Testaments and Property in Sixteenth-Century Scotland', *SHR* CII, no. 258 (2023): 1–33.
[79] *Register of the Ministers, Elders and Deacons of the Christian Congregation of St Andrews*, II civ and index under 'Sir George Douglas of Elenhill'.
[80] Pearce, *Jewels*.

1572 she wed Sir Colin Campbell of Boquhan, the earl of Argyll's brother. The following year the couple unexpectedly became the sixth earl and countess of Argyll and Annas's second family secured that senior Campbell lineage.

Enough biographical details have survived to unravel the mystery of the 1570 murder and recover the experiences of these three Fife noblewomen in the reign of Mary, Queen of Scots. Each of them faced and survived the losses of that year and contemporaries would have judged them to have succeeded in their 'duties' as wives and mothers. Adopting a gendered perspective has underlined how important it is not to take at face value the ideological formulations of the patriarchal society of early modern Scotland. At first glance the Kinnear killings appeared to belong exclusively to the male-dominated world of politics and warfare. Finding the women changed the narrative of that incident and uncovered female networks running between regional society and the royal court and government. This has given a fresh view of the complex politics surrounding Mary, Queen of Scots and the agency of the noblewomen of her kingdom. The last word belongs to Margaret Erskine, as was probably the case for most of her life. For families, kindred and the good of the kingdom, she understood it was misguided to concentrate so much upon male roles and primogeniture.[81] It was equally important that girls should be taught to recognise what they could do in their lives. When she was consoling Annas that Moray's posthumous child was not a male heir, Margaret wrote, 'bot ye lassis may be sua handlyt yair may alss mekyll gud cum of yaim as of laddis'.[82]

---

[81] For an introduction to masculinities, see L. Abrams and E. Ewan, eds, *Nine Centuries of Man: Manhood and Masculinities in Scottish History* (Edinburgh: Edinburgh University Press, 2017).
[82] Dunbar, *Reforming the Scottish Church*, 168 n. 22.

TWO

'Scottish Portias' Revisited: Women in the Courts in Early Modern Scottish Towns

Rebecca Mason

In early modern Scotland, women's legal status was largely dependent on their capacity to own, buy, sell and inherit property. It was within marriage that the law most rigorously regulated women's property rights and entrenched the subordination of women to men. Once married, Scottish women – like many of their European sisters – could not contract or sue in court without their husbands' consent. At the heart of Scots law lay a desire to uphold patriarchal values within marriage, placing the husband firmly at the head of the household and the wife in a subservient position. Yet, while the husband may have been superior, he was not to be a tyrant, with a married woman expected to keep her husband's marital powers in check. An overly submissive wife unable to challenge a wastrel husband was a dangerous match, with the law recognising the necessity for a careful balance of property rights and marital obligations. This essay explores how married women negotiated their legal status and property rights before the burgh (town) courts in early modern Scotland, uncovering the specific ways ordinary women wielded legal authority within marriage when property was involved. While husbands were expected to steer firmly at the helm of a ship, married women could influence its route and destination, with communities and the courts recognising women's capacity to pay bills and rent, oversee family businesses, sell goods and even invest land, on behalf of – and, on certain occasions, independent of – their husbands.

I am grateful to Mairi Cowan, Janay Nugent, Cathryn Spence, Michelle D. Brock and the anonymous peer reviewers for their insightful comments and suggestions on earlier drafts of this essay. All errors remain my own. I am also grateful to Elizabeth Ewan for ultimately inspiring my love of Scottish women's legal history. This article was researched and written with the financial support of an Arts and Humanities Research Council PhD Studentship 2015–19 [AH/L013568/1]; an Economic History Society Eileen Power Fellowship 2019–20 at the Institute of Historical Research; an Economic and Social Research Council Postdoctoral Fellowship 2020-1 [ES/V011847/]; and the Women's History Network Research Fellowship 2021–2.

Scottish women's legal history has made significant advances in recent years, largely thanks to the efforts of Elizabeth Ewan. In 1992, Ewan published 'Scottish Portias: Women in the Courts in Medieval Scottish Towns' in the *Journal of the Canadian Historical Association*.[1] Based on an analysis of fifteenth- and sixteenth-century legal records of several Scottish towns, her essay was among the first to explore the various roles of women in the burgh courts in pre-Reformation Scotland. Despite Scottish legal rules stipulating women's limited capacity for independent legal action, especially on marriage, Ewan discovered women pleading their own cases, buying and selling property, and even acting as procurators (lawyers) for others. According to Ewan, ordinary townswomen displayed a surprising level of legal prowess, showing great initiative in representing and defending their own property rights and those of their husbands and families. In her conclusion, Ewan urged historians to 'look beyond the formal codes to the actual functioning of the law' when uncovering women's roles in the legal world of medieval and early modern Scotland.[2] While the field has since considerably progressed, much work remains to be done to rejuvenate the study of Scottish women's legal history in history and law departments alike.[3]

In 'Scottish Portias', Ewan challenged the idea that married women were legally incapacitated before the medieval Scottish burgh courts, noting that the law did not state that men *must* represent their wives, but only that they *may* represent them.[4] This observation then prompted her to ask the following important question: does this perhaps suggest a somewhat more flexible

---

[1] Elizabeth Ewan, 'Scottish Portias: Women in the Courts in Mediaeval Scottish Towns', *Journal of the Canadian Historical Association* 3, no. 1 (1992): 27–43.

[2] Ewan, 'Scottish Portias', 42; For recent research on women's roles in early modern Scotland see Cathryn Spence, *Women, Credit and Debt in Early Modern Scotland* (Manchester: Manchester University Press, 2016); Katie Barclay, *Caritas: Neighbourly Love and the Early Modern Self* (Oxford: Oxford University Press, 2021); Chris Langley, 'Clergy Widows in Early Modern Scotland', *Scottish Church History* 50, no. 2 (2022): 111–32; J. R. D. Falconer, *Crime and Community in Reformation Scotland: Negotiating Power in a Burgh Society* (London: Pickering and Chatto, 2012); Michelle D. Brock, '"The Man Will Shame Me": Women, Sex and Kirk Discipline during the Cromwellian Occupation', *Scottish Church History* 51, no. 2 (2022): 133–56.

[3] John Finlay, 'Women and Legal Representation in Early Sixteenth-Century Scotland', in *Women in Scotland, c. 1100– c. 1750*, eds Elizabeth Ewan and Maureen M. Meikle (East Linton: Tuckwell Press, 1999), 165–75; Winifred Coutts, *The Business of the College of Justice in 1600: How it Reflects the Economic and Social Life of Scots Men and Women* (Edinburgh: Stair Society, 2003), 140–44; Thomas Green, *Consistorial Decisions of the Commissaries of Edinburgh 1564 to 1576/7* (Edinburgh: Edinburgh University Press, 2014). Feminist legal academics are leading the charge in recovering Scottish women's struggle for justice and fair legal opportunities. See Alison Lindsay, '"This Fair Lady, in her Laces": Margaret Howie Strang Hall, the First Woman in Scotland to Try to Become a Lawyer', *WHR* 29, no. 4 (2019): 555–62; Sharon Cowan, Chloë Kennedy and Vanessa E Munro, eds, *Scottish Feminist Judgments: (Re)creating Law From the Outside In* (Oxford: Oxford University Press, 2019); Seonaid Stevenson and Maria Fletcher, 'A Century of Women in the Scottish Legal Profession', in *Law and Justice: A Collection of Essays in Memory of Professor Ian Willock*, eds E. P. H. Keane and P. Robson (Vancouver: Fairleigh Dickinson University Press, 2023).

[4] Ewan, 'Scottish Portias', 30.

attitude on the participation of Scottish women in court than in some other contemporary societies? This essay is an attempt to build on such reflections raised in 'Scottish Portias' by returning to the position and treatment of Scottish women in legal sources to better understand women's varied interaction with the courts in daily life. It re-examines the view of women held by Scottish men of law, with particular focus on the legal status of the married woman, and considers their treatment by and participation in the Scottish legal system at a local and central level. It then goes on to explore the role of married women in the Scottish burgh courts, paying close attention to their actions as pursuers and defenders in suits concerning their property rights, roles and relationships.

Surveying a wide range of points of contact between Scottish women and the law – from their appearance in legal writings and treatises, to their presence or treatment as litigants or named parties in courts – this essay calls for closer consideration of women's rights within the standard narratives of classical Scottish legal history and mainstream Scottish history, and for re-examination of some previous conclusions on the relationship between married women and the law. In doing so, it argues that Scottish men of law – from university-educated judges and advocates in the central court in Edinburgh to town baillies and notaries in burgh courts in towns – did not always think of women's legal actions in relation to definitive or authoritative statements of fixed legal rules, and that married women's access to justice in early modern Scotland was considerably more fluid and multi-layered than has been previously recognised.

Women and the law

During the medieval and early modern periods, the legal position of Scottish women was primarily discussed in legal handbooks (popularly known as 'Practicks'), as well as in parliamentary statutes, court records and legal papers written by procurators, advocates, clerks and notaries – all of whom were men. Prominent Scottish legal writers – including Sir John Skene, Sir James Balfour, Sir Thomas Hope, Sir Thomas Craig, Sir George Mackenzie and Sir James Dalrymple (Lord Stair), among many others – primarily discussed women's rights when commenting on property-holding and legal capacity, with the legal position of married women and heiresses taking centre stage in their writings.[5]

---

[5] For medieval legal opinions of women see Alice Taylor, ed., *The Laws of Medieval Scotland: Legal Compilations from the Thirteenth and Fourteenth Centuries* (Edinburgh: Edinburgh University Press, 2019), esp. 269, 469; John Reuben Davies with Alice Taylor, *Regiam Maiestatem: The Earliest Known Version* (Edinburgh: Stair Society, 2022), 429; For early modern legal opinions of women see P. G. B. McNeill, ed., *The Practicks of Sir James Balfour of Pittendreich*, 2 vols (Edinburgh, 1962–3), 93–8; *The Jus Feudale by Sir Thomas Craig of Riccarton*, trans. Lord Clyde (Edinburgh, 1933), II:17, 1; J. A. Clyde, ed., *Hope's Major Practicks, 1608–1633* (Edinburgh, 1937–8), 2:17; J. Dalrymple, *Viscount Stair, Institutions of the Lawes of Scotland* (1st edn 1681; 6th edn by D. M. Walker, 1981), I, IV, IX, 27–28.

In Scots law, girls and young women under the age of twenty-one were unable to pursue or defend suits as independent persons. As 'minors', girls and underage women were represented in court by their fathers; if their fathers were deceased, they were represented by relatives from their mothers' and fathers' kingroup, usually consisting of two relatives from each family, or their mother if she remained unmarried.[6] Importantly, this rule also applied to boys and young men under the age of twenty-one.[7] Scottish women who had reached the age of twenty-one and were not yet engaged to be married could finally plead and respond in suits without requiring male legal representation.[8] This would, of course, change upon marriage. The legal status and capabilities of unmarried women varied across Europe: in Sweden, unmarried women were always represented in court by male legal guardians until marriage, while in Brittany, a region of France from 1532, custom dictated that unmarried women had full legal capacity.[9]

Married women, on the other hand, were unable to purchase or sell property as independent persons in Scots law, and always required their husbands' consent before initiating and defending suits.[10] Similar rules existed elsewhere in Europe: in German-speaking territories, the legal system did not regard a married woman as a legal adult, instead placing her under the guardianship of an adult male (often her husband) called a *Kriegsvogt* (meaning 'war governor' or 'war overseer').[11] In England, the common law doctrine of coverture similarly vested power and authority in the husband alone – as well as losing her family

---

[6] Balfour, *Practicks*, 114, 121–2.

[7] Balfour, *Practicks*, 335.

[8] Much work remains to be done on the legal status of single women in early modern Scotland. For an English comparison see Cordelia Beattie, '"Living as a Single Person": Marital Status, Performance and the Law in Late Medieval England', *WHR* 17, no. 3 (2008): 327–40.

[9] Mia Korpiola, 'A Litigating Widow and Wife in Early Modern Sweden: Lady Elin Johansdotter [Månesköld] and her Family Circle', in *Litigating Women: Gender and Justice in Europe, c. 1300–c. 1800*, eds Teresa Phipps and Deborah Youngs (London: Routledge, 2022), 173–92, at 173, 176–7; Nicole Durfournaud, 'Between Parental Power and Marital Authority: How Merchant Women Stood the Test of Customary Laws in Brittany in the Sixteenth to Seventeenth Centuries', in *Gender, Law and Economic Well-Being in Europe from the Fifteenth to the Nineteenth Century: North Versus South?*, eds Anna Bellavitis and Beatrice Zucca Micheletto (London: Routledge, 2018), 47–61, at 47.

[10] For a discussion of the legal status of married women, see Balfour, *Practicks*, 93; Rebecca Mason, 'Women, Marital Status and Law: The Marital Spectrum in Seventeenth-Century Glasgow', *Journal of British Studies* 58, no. 4 (2019): 787–804; Paton, 'Husband and Wife,' 100–1; Forte, 'Some Aspects', 110; Coutts, *Business of the College of Justice*, 140; Spence, *Women, Credit and Debt*, 13.

[11] Sheilagh Ogilvie, 'Married Women, Work and the Law: Evidence from Early Modern Germany', in *Married Women and the Law in Premodern Northwestern Europe*, eds Cordelia Beattie and Matthew Frank Stevens (Woodbridge: Boydell and Brewer, 2013), 213–39, at 215 and 224; Margareth Lanzinger and Janine Maegraith, 'Women Negotiating Wealth: Gender, Law and Arbitration in Early Modern Southern Tyrol', in *Litigating Women: Gender and Justice in Europe, 1100–1750*, eds Teresa Phipps and Deborah Youngs (Routledge: London, 2022), 152–72, at 154.

surname on marriage, an English wife was unable to sue or be sued without her husband.[12] That a married woman required her husband's consent when appearing before the courts served as a powerful reminder of the superior status of husbands in terms of patriarchal authority and household management. Yet, while many of these legal rules may appear harsh, the legal restrictions a married woman suffered resulted not from a denial that she was a person, but from the assumption of legal authorities that a married couple's legal interests were firmly merged, thus making the wife's independent legal action almost impossible.[13] On widowhood, a Scottish woman once again regained her independent legal status, entitling her to sue or be sued without male assistance.[14]

The limitations ascribed to Scottish wives in legal theory clearly did not fully encapsulate the complexities of their roles in daily life. If the law was as rigid as one might assume, a husband would be expected to accompany his wife to the marketplace every time she wished to purchase meat from a flesher (butcher), follow her to court every time she wished to raise a minor complaint against a craftsman for selling faulty goods, or escort her to the notary's office when she wanted to draw up a discharge (receipt) detailing the sale of foodstuffs to a neighbour's domestic servant. The legal requirement for the husband's consent in authorising his wife's everyday activities was not practical, nor was it always possible. To recognise this, customary rules entitled Scottish wives to operate as agents of their husbands (as *praeposituras*) when purchasing and selling household 'necessaries', such as food, drink and merchandise – ultimately recognising their role as co-managers of their husbands' business contacts and marital economies.[15] Similar rules existed alongside other legal regimes in Europe: a communal decree from Frankfurt in 1674 recorded 'matter-of-factly' that Jewish women and wives would naturally be involved in procuring buyers for the wares sold by their families, despite their limited legal position under the law.[16] In England, the 'law of agency' or 'law of necessaries' also entitled married women to independently contract small-scale debts on behalf of their husbands, effectively undermining legalistic attempts to prevent women from

---

[12] Amy Louise Erickson, *Women and Property in Early Modern England* (London: Routledge, 1993), 47–8, 99–101, 153–5; Tim Stretton, *Women Waging Law in Elizabethan England* (Cambridge: Cambridge University Press, 1998), 101–28; Amy Erickson, 'Mistresses and Marriage: Or, a short history of the Mrs', *History Workshop Journal* 78 (2014): 39–57.

[13] Tim Stretton, 'The Legal Identity of Married Women in England and Europe, 1500–1700,' in *Europa und seine Regionen: 2000 Jahre Rechtsgeschichte*, eds Andreas Bauer and Karl H. L. Welker (Cologne: Bohlau, 2007), 309–22.

[14] Balfour, *Practicks*, 93.

[15] Coutts, *Business of the College of Justice*, 139; Katie Barclay, *Love, Intimacy and Power: Marriage and Patriarchy in Scotland, 1650–1850* (Manchester: Manchester University Press, 2011), 49–52; Spence, *Women, Credit and Debt*, 12–13.

[16] Debra Kaplan, 'Women and Worth: Female Access to Property in Early Modern Urban Jewish Communities', *Leo Baeck Institute Year Book* 55, no. 1 (2010): 93–113, at 98.

making financial or legal decisions without their husbands' consent.[17] Because of such diverse legal rules and customs surrounding married women's capacity for legal agency, historians and legal scholars have thus described the early modern legal system as 'Janus-faced' – serving both as an instrument of women's repression and also as a tool for change.[18]

A surface reading of Scots law would suggest that married women had limited opportunity to represent their legal interests separately from their husbands, with only a glimmer of autonomy relating to their position as mere helpmeets and 'hussies' (Scots for 'housewives').[19] In daily life, however, the operation of strict legal rules was not automatic, nor practicable. From the Court of Session to the burgh courts, Scottish men of law did not always agree on the extent to which married women should be allowed to represent their own interests without their husbands' consent. Moreover, men of law only ever addressed and debated the question of the competence of married women as legal persons when the issue was brought to their attention – theoretical rules alone did not necessarily deter married women from attempting to bring suit in court.

Clarifying consent

If a married woman always relied on her husband's consent to plead or defend a suit, what happened if her husband refused his consent? In a 1623 case heard before the Court of Session in Edinburgh, the Lords of Session sustained an action at the instance of a married woman as it involved the implementing of a contract conceived in her own favour. In this case, the defender alleged that because the husband 'concurred not' (did not consent) to his wife's legal action, she was not authorised to stand before the court as a sole pursuer. Commenting on this particular legal argument, the Scottish advocate Thomas Haddington (1563–1637) stated:

> I proponed to the Lords, that the husband was naturally obliged to give his consent, and authorise his wife in her lawful pursuits, not hurtful to him, and in effect was *loco curatoris*, who refusing to authorise his minor in lawful causes might be removed, or another

---

[17] Joanne Bailey, 'Favoured or Oppressed? Married Women, Property and "Coverture" in England, 1660–1800', *Continuity and Change* 17, no. 3 (2002): 351–72; Margot Finn, 'Women, Consumption and Coverture in England, c. 1760–1860', *Historical Journal* 39, no. 3 (1996): 703–22.

[18] Lindsay Moore, *Women Before the Court: Law and Patriarchy in the Anglo-American World, 1600–1800* (Manchester: Manchester University Press, 2019), 9; Sara L. Kimble and Marion Röwekamp, 'Introduction: Legal Cultures and Communities of Female Protest in Modern European History, 1860–1960s', in *New Perspectives on European Women's Legal History*, eds Sara L. Kimble and Marion Röwekamp (London: Routledge, 2016), 1–24.

[19] 'Hussy', DOST, https://dsl.ac.uk/entry/dost/hussy.

might be offered by the Judge, to assist the minor judicially in his lawful and profitable pursuit, and the like reason was militant betwixt the husband and wife, chiefly since the delay of her action might make her condition worse in case her debtor died.

In other words, Haddington argued that it was proper for a husband to support his wife in her legal endeavours (so long as they were not harmful to him) and he could not, without reason, deny his consent. On this occasion, the Lords authorised the married woman to stand in judgment without her husband's consent as the property was promised to her in her marriage contract, finding that there was 'a legal authorising of the pursuit to *her* behoof'.[20]

The issue of a husband's lack of consent was again raised before the central court less than a year later. In 1624, a married woman alleged that her husband had promised to 'infeft' (to invest with legal possession of heritable property) her in land and that he had since refused to fulfil his promise. In reply, the husband argued that his wife was not entitled to stand in judgment without his consent. It was then noted that:

> The Lo[rds] reasoning among themselves thought it ane hard matter that the woman should be frustrat[ed] found the charge valiabell she obteaining the concurse (consent) of her father or some of [her] nearest friends.[21]

> The Lords discussing it among themselves thought it a difficult matter that the woman should be frustrated found the command valid, if she obtained the consent of her father or some of her nearest friends (kin).

This particular observation was scribbled in a lawyer's handbook currently housed in the Signet Library in Edinburgh, alongside a list of other cases relating to women's legal status that both puzzled and divided judges and advocates in the central court.[22] In the end, the Lords of Session allowed the married woman to plead without her husband's consent, on the condition that she appointed her father or another relative to stand on her behalf. As commented on by Katie Barclay and Emily Ireland, an English wife could sue by a 'next friend' (a representative in court who was theoretically liable for the plaintiff's costs) when seeking separate maintenance upon the irrevocable breakdown of marriage, suggesting a degree of flexibility in other patriarchal legal regimes.[23]

---

[20] William M. Morison, *Decisions of the Court of Session, from Its Institution until the Separation of the Court into Two Divisions in the Year 1808, Digested under Proper Heads, in the Form of a Dictionary*, 42 vols (Edinburgh: Printed for Archibald Constable, 1811), XV–XVI, Marshall against Marshall and Yule, January 1623, 6036–7. My emphasis.

[21] Signet Library, MS 20, Lawyer's handbook, c. 1643.

[22] Signet Library, MS 20, Lawyer's handbook, c. 1643.

[23] Katie Barclay and Emily Ireland, 'The Household as a Space of the Law', *Law and History* 7, no. 2 (2021): 98–126.

While the strict letter of the law required a husband to consent to his wife's legal action, there were clear exceptions to the rule in practice.

Scottish men of law continued to debate the thorny issue of the requirement of the husband's consent throughout the seventeenth century. In a case in the Court of Session in 1674, a married woman pursued a reduction of a disposition (a formal deed transferring ownership of heritable property) of lands made by her father while he was on his deathbed, insisting that the transfer had no legal standing. The defender alleged that the pursuer, as a married woman, was not authorised to seek the reduction without her husband's consent. In response, however, the married woman's legal counsel alleged that the summons was raised at the instance of the husband 'for his interest' and that the Lords ought 'in justice to authorise the wife to insist, this being a heritable right, wherein the husband could have no more interest but by his right of *jus mariti* (ownership of moveable goods)'. The stock phrase 'for his interest', while referring to the husband's 'interest' in his wife's legal matters, also alludes to his claim to the possession or use of her inherited property during marriage, without necessarily owning the property outright. In the end, the Lords sided with the married woman, agreeing that the husband had no interest 'further than his right of *jus mariti* and the courtesy (liferent on his wife's death)', and that the married woman was lawfully entitled to litigate on the basis of her heritable rights, which remained her own separate property during marriage.[24] The doctrine of *jus mariti* – a legal principle that ultimately symbolised the practice of patriarchy within marriage – was not resolute, and did not extend to matters that concerned a wife's separate or inherited estate.

That a wife could informally contract household debts and purchase 'necessaries' on behalf of her husband as a *praepositura* was widely accepted by Scottish men of law in the central court. Nonetheless, the assumption that a married woman was always acting at the behest of her husband when purchasing and selling goods as a *praepositura* held the potential to create problems that could be exacerbated before the courts. What if a married woman purchased goods beyond her husband's status and rank? What if she damaged his credit rating? And what if he disputed her purchase or sale of items that she deemed 'necessary'? As noted by a Lord of Session in 1698, 'a man may be silent at the management and actings of an imperious wife, and yet must be construed to oppose of the same, else she might bring him into inconveniences enough'.[25]

While agreeing that a married woman could informally contract debts on behalf of her husband, Scottish men of law debated how far the office of *praepositura* extended. In a case in the Court of Session in 1609, a merchant pursued

---

[24] Morison, *Decisions of the Court of Session*, XV–XVI, Hacket against Gordon, July 1673, 6039.
[25] Morison, *Decisions of the Court of Session*, XV–XVI, Arnot against Stevenson, November 1698, 6017–8.

a husband for debts allegedly incurred by his wife as a *praepositura*. In the suit, the merchant alleged that he had sold and delivered barrels of wine worth £800 Scots (approximately £8,500 by today's standards) to the defender's wife, and that he was still awaiting payment in full.[26] In response, the husband alleged that his wife did not purchase the property at his command, and that she had no right to contract any such debt without his consent. In response, the pursuer insisted that the wife held an 'open wine tavern, and commonly sold wine by her husband's knowledge', and she was therefore known as a '*praeposita tabernae*' – alluding to a blend of her role as a married woman and her occupation as a tavern keeper.[27] In the end, the Lords agreed that the merchant had 'good action to pursue the husband for payment of the prices thereof' as the wife had at the very least purchased the wine with her husband's knowledge, if not his consent.[28] A year later, however, the Lords were informed that the tavern wife had since deserted her husband, and that she now 'dwelt apart from him very slanderously and dishonestly', presumably with another man. Only then did the Lords decide to sustain the action solely against the wife, not her husband. In doing so, they ruled that 'the decree should have no action against the husband in his person, land or goods', effectively releasing the husband from settling his wife's debts, both then and in future.[29] Deserted husbands could legally disallow their wives' debts by registering a letter of inhibition with the court or displaying a notice at the town's mercat cross – a formal method to warn bypassers not to deal with their runaway wives.[30]

For many Scottish men of law, the crux of the matter was whether the married woman's legal action threatened to 'prejudice her husband', with the Lords of Session noting on numerous occasions that the husband might be ignorant of the alleged debt or arrangement, and therefore at risk of financial destitution at the behest of a spendthrift or unruly wife.[31] When a married woman's legal action did not directly threaten or undermine her husband's status or rights,

---

[26] By 1600, £12 Scots was worth £1 sterling; £1 Scots was worth 1s. 6d. sterling. 1 Scottish merk was worth 1s. 1d. sterling. See A. J. S. Gibson and T. C. Smout, *Prices, Food and Wages in Scotland, 1550–1780* (Cambridge, Cambridge University Press, 1995); TNA Currency Converter: 1270–2017: https://www.nationalarchives.gov.uk/currency/ Accessed 27 October 2022.

[27] '*Praeposita tabernae*' is perhaps comparable to those working wives who acted as *femme soles* in towns in early modern England. See Marjorie K. MacIntosh, 'The Benefits and Drawbacks of Femme Sole Status in England,' *Journal of British Studies* 44 (2005), 410–38, at 413.

[28] Morison, *Decisions of the Court of Session*, XVXVI, Muirhead against Douglas, November 1609, 6020.

[29] Morison, *Decisions of the Court of Session*, XV–XVI, A against B, January 1610, 6020.

[30] Deborah Simonton, 'Community of Goods, Coverture and Capability in Britain: Scotland versus England', in *Gender, Law and Economic Well-Being in Europe from the Fifteenth to the Nineteenth Century*, 31–46, at 39.

[31] Morison, *Decisions of the Court of Session*, XV–XVI, John Allan against The Earl and Countess of Southesk, July 1677, 6005–7; Muirhead against Douglas, November 1609, 6020–21; Lady Boot and Her Husband against the Sheriff of Boot, January 1666, 520.

and instead concerned her own rights and arrangements, Scottish men of law tended to agree that a married woman could represent herself in court or, at the very least, appoint another male representative to plead or answer on her behalf. The husband's consent in permitting his wife's legal action was significant but perhaps not entirely crucial, especially when certain legal scenarios required immediate attention.[32]

Women in the towns

Women in the central court often brought suits relating to significant amounts of property, which required detailed legal examination by trained and educated men of law. Women in the burgh courts, on the other hand, typically brought suits relating to small-scale debts and economic transactions in and around the town, alongside a range of other legal business, and often with limited legal representation.[33] As commented on by Cathryn Spence, participation in the Scottish burgh courts was an activity 'open to nearly all members of society', from servants to merchants, indwellers to burgesses, men and women, both the married and the unmarried.[34] A snapshot of a year (June 1657 to June 1658) in the burgh court of Glasgow highlights ordinary women's active role in property litigation in early modern Scottish towns. Table 2.1 shows the participation of female litigants in Glasgow's burgh court over the course of a year in the mid-seventeenth century, broken down by the number of suits involving female pursuers and defenders as primary litigants.[35] In total, approximately 700 suits relating to debts and estates were heard and decided on before the burgh court of Glasgow, with women appearing as primary pursuers in 20 per cent of cases and primary defenders in 27 per cent of cases. These figures are largely consistent with other work on Scottish women's litigation in burgh courts. Spence, for instance, found that women accounted for more than a third of creditors and debtors named in Edinburgh's burgh court between 1560 and 1640, and around 20 per cent of

---

[32] For the English perspective on this argument, see Emily Ireland, 'Re-examining the Presumption: Coverture and "Legal Impossibilities" in Early Modern English Criminal Law', *Journal of Legal History* 43, no. 2 (2022): 187–209.

[33] David Walker, *A Legal History of Scotland: The Seventeenth Century* (Edinburgh: T. & T. Clark, 1996), 323–4.

[34] Cathryn Spence, 'Negotiating the Economy: Gender, Status, and Debt Litigation in the Burgh Courts of Early Modern Scotland', in *Crossing Borders: Boundaries and Margins in Medieval and Early Modern Britain: Essays in Honour of Cynthia J. Neville*, eds Sara Butler and Krista J. Kesselring (Leiden: Brill, 2018), 174–92, at 174.

[35] For instance, if a married woman initiated a suit, with her husband named 'for his interest', she was recorded as a primary female litigant. Table 2.2 provides a breakdown of female litigants in relation to their marital status.

Table 2.1 Women involved in debt and estate litigation in Glasgow's burgh court, June 1657 to June 1658[i]

Sex of litigants	Pursuers	Defenders	Total
Male	562 (80%)	508 (73%)	1070
Female	138 (20%)	192 (27%)	330
Total no. of litigants	700	700	1400

[i] A total of 700 civil suits relating to debt and estate litigation were heard and settled before Glasgow's burgh court over the course of the year. The above table does not include all named parties, but rather covers the sex of primary pursuers and defenders. Married women suing or defending with their husbands' consent were therefore categorised as 'female'. 'Male' covers cases that did not involve or mention a woman.

Source: Glasgow City Archives, Glasgow burgh court, court book 1657–59, B1/1/5/fols 1rv–134rv.

creditors and debtors in the burgh courts of Haddington and Dundee during the same period.[36]

As pursuers, women typically appeared when seeking the repayment of debt from a business contact or relative, like the widow Geillis Young who sued her sister Jonet Young, the wife of Alexander Quhyt, for the repayment of 5 merks 6s. 8d. Scots she had loaned a year previous.[37] As defenders, women were typically charged with failing to settle outstanding debts in a timely manner, like the widow Catherine Findlay who was ordered to pay the carpenter John Merburn £4 Scots for a deed's chest she had purchased from him three months previous.[38] Interestingly, women were more likely to be called to the burgh court to defend a suit than initiate a complaint, with the town baillies denouncing those who failed (or rather refused) to appear under oath to answer for their actions. This suggests that not only were ordinary women economically and legally active in Scottish towns, but that they were held responsible for their actions and debts, regardless of their gender and marital status.

When not pleading or responding, women were named in litigation as 'cautioners' for relatives and friends in economic arrangements, suggesting a level of trustworthiness and esteem within their families and communities. In Scotland, a 'cautioner' was a person (usually a man) who vouched for another, often in legal agreements involving debt. In Glasgow's burgh court in 1657, two women appeared as cautioners for family members: the widow Jonet Weir for her son Patrick Turbour, and the wife Bessie Hamilton for her sister Margaret Hamilton, also a married woman. Both arrangements related to small-scale debts: Jonet Weir promised to pay William Henderson 38s. 8d. Scots for merchandise purchased by her son a year previous, while Bessie Hamilton agreed to pay 8 merks to the merchant Robert Semple for 'lintseed' recently purchased

[36] Spence, *Women, Credit and Debt*, 38–40.
[37] GCA, Glasgow's burgh court, court book, 25 December 1657, B1/1/5/71v.
[38] GCA, Glasgow's burgh court, court book, 1 December 1657, B1/1/5/55v.

by her married sister Margaret.[39] The ability to assume liability to act on behalf of another had both a practical and symbolic significance: it increased women's chances of acting as guardians, creditors and property owners, and confirmed their important legal responsibilities as participants in burgh life. It also acknowledges women's competencies in areas where they traditionally or officially were deemed to have no power or rights.

More information can be gleaned by breaking down the marital status of female litigants in the burgh court of Glasgow, as seen in Table 2.2. Distinguishing married women from unmarried women is relatively straightforward in Scottish burgh court records, mainly because women were most often identified by their name and as the daughter, wife or widow of a man. On the whole, married women appeared in greater numbers than unmarried or widowed women in Glasgow's burgh court, accounting for 57 per cent of female litigants. Over a third of female litigants were identified as widows, while women without a marital designator were named as litigants in around 8 per cent of cases. Single women are quite difficult to definitively locate in Scottish court records as clerks rarely recorded their unmarried status, though a small number can be identified by their occupation, like the domestic servant Jonet Walker who sued her mistress Janet Hamilton and her husband David Sat 'for his interest' for unpaid wages of £6 Scots.[40]

The legal actions of married women can be divided into three separate but related categories: wives as primary litigants, with a husband named 'for his interest'; wives as co-parties, named after a husband; and wives as remarried widows.[41] Married women suing or defending with a husband named 'for his interest' formed the majority of married female litigants in Glasgow's burgh court – accounting for 77 and 84 per cent of those pleading and responding. While the majority of cases related to married women's responsibilities as agents of their husbands, many suits also alluded to their separate property arrangements, like the wife Grissell Maxwell who sued another wife for failing to return clothes she had pledged in exchange for credit.[42] Others were standing in lieu of an absent husband, like the wife Jonet Martein who, as a defender, was held legally responsible for the payment of £6 Scots while her husband was abroad on business.[43]

---

[39] GCA, Glasgow burgh court, court book, 13 August 1657, B1/1/5/29v. That Bessie stood as a 'cautioner' for her married sister is quite unusual as a husband was legally responsible for his wife's debts.
[40] GCA, Glasgow's burgh court, court book, 15 June 1658, B1/1/5/119v.
[41] Rebecca Mason, 'Property Over Patriarchy?: Remarried women as litigants in the courts of seventeenth-century Glasgow', in *Litigating Women: Gender and justice in Europe, 1100–1750*, eds Teresa Phipps and Deborah Young (London: Routledge, 2022), 133–51, at 143.
[42] GCA, Glasgow's burgh court, court book, 3 November 1657, B1/1/5/34r.
[43] GCA, Glasgow's burgh court, court book, 31 July 1657, B1/1/5/20r.

Table 2.2 Marital status of female litigants in debt and estate litigation in Glasgow's burgh court, June 1657 to June 1658

Marital status	Pursuer	Defender	No. of cases with a female pursuer or defender
Widows	44	73	117 (35%)
Married women	74	113	187 (57%)
husband 'for his interest'	57	95	
co-party with husband	12	14	
remarried widow	5	4	
Daughter	3	1	4 (1%)
Unknown	17	5	22 (7%)
Total	138 (42%)	192 (58%)	330 (100%)

Source: GCA, Glasgow burgh court, court book 1657–59, B1/1/5/fols 1rv–134rv.

Why, then, did married women appear in such great numbers before the courts in early modern Scotland? While difficult to answer, Scottish historians have discussed various reasons as to why married women are so visible in Scottish court records. Firstly, Scottish wives (unlike their English counterparts) kept their family surnames on marriage, which meant that women were nearly always referred to as 'wife of' or 'spouse of' a man when documented in court records.[44] Without this information, it would be nearly impossible for historians to distinguish Scottish wives from single women or widows. Moreover, as urban marriages were understood as partnerships, married women routinely entered into demands of business and investment alongside their husbands, with their names included in deeds, documents and lawsuits.[45] When a husband was named 'for his interest', the clerk was carefully recording that while the wife might have purchased or sold the goods in question, her husband was ultimately responsible for (or at the very least aware of) her business dealings. The frequent mobilisation of Scottish men for war and for activities at sea or abroad might also partially explain why so many married women appeared as primary litigants in burgh courts, with many appearing on behalf of their absent husbands.[46]

Yet another important explanation, and one that is often overlooked, relates to the operation of Scots law at a local and central level. Scots law was based on more or less easily comprehensible principles, and did not require the same knowledge of cases and the minutiae of procedure as did, say, English common

---

[44] Mason, 'Women, Marital Status and Law'.

[45] Aaron Allen, *Building Early Modern Edinburgh: A Social History of Craftwork and Incorporation* (Edinburgh: Edinburgh University Press, 2018), 69–76.

[46] Gordon DesBrisay, 'Aberdeen and the Dutch Atlantic: Women and Woolens in the Seventeenth Century,' in *Women in Port: Gendering Communities, Economies, and Social Networks in Atlantic Port Cities, 1500–1800*, eds Douglas Catterall and Jodi Campbell (Leiden: Brill, 2012), 69–102.

law, even by the seventeenth century.[47] In early modern England, the common law doctrine of coverture eclipsed a woman's legal status on marriage, preventing her from pleading or responding before the English borough (town) courts, and other common law jurisdictions, as independent persons. As a result, an English wife had to approach a favourable jurisdiction and court, such as equity in the Court of Chancery, when seeking justice. In Scotland, however, a married woman could appear before any jurisdiction and court as equity was not a distinct branch of Scots law and, unlike England, there was no institutional separation of courts dealing with law and equity.[48]

As coverture was a defining feature in women's legal experiences in England, married women rarely featured in English borough courts as litigants, and when they did appear they always appeared alongside their husbands.[49] In England, the borough courts were ruled by common law overseen by the king's central courts, and typically heard civil suits relating to debt and trespass. Because of the restrictions common law placed on English wives, their participation in borough courts was thus limited. For instance, Craig Muldrew found that women only appeared as plaintiffs in 11 per cent of cases heard before the Great Yarmouth borough court in 1677 and 1678, while only appearing as defendants in 5 per cent of cases during the same year.[50] Lindsay Moore, on the other hand, located women as litigants in the London Mayor's Court in around 10–11 per cent of cases in the seventeenth century, with married women only accounting for 14 per cent of female litigants.[51]

At a local and central level, the Scottish legal system arguably treated married women more equitably than common law courts in England because of the system's emphasis on lay pleading and more simplified court procedures.[52] As noted by Rab Houston, early modern Scotland was 'under-lawyered' when compared with England.[53] It has been estimated that England and Wales in 1640 had around 2,500–3,000 legal practitioners (barristers and attorneys or

[47] John Finlay, 'The Lower Branch of the Legal Profession in Early Modern Scotland', *Edinburgh Law Review* 11, no. 1 (2007): 31–61.

[48] D. J. Carr, 'Are Equity and Law in Scotland Fused, Separate or Intertwined?', in *Equity and Law: Fusion and fission*, eds J. C. P. Goldberg, H. E. Smith and P. G. Turner (New York: Cambridge University Press, 2019), 179–200.

[49] Lindsay Moore, 'Women, Property, and the Law in the Anglo-American World, 1630–1700', *Early American Studies: An Interdisciplinary Journal* 14, no. 3 (Summer 2016): 537–67, at 547–8.

[50] Craig Muldrew, '"A Mutual Assent of Her Mind"? Women, debt, litigation and contract in early modern England', *History Workshop Journal* 55 (2003): 47–71, at 54–5, also discussed and cited in Moore, 'Women, Property, and the Law', 546.

[51] Moore, 'Women, Property, and the Law', 546.

[52] Mark Godfrey, 'Royal Councils, Law Courts and Governance: The role of litigation in early modern Scotland', in *Rechtsgeschichte heute: Religion und Politik in der Geschichte des Rechts – Schlaglichter einer Ringvorlesung*, eds N. Jansen and P. Oestmann (Tübingen: Mohr Siebeck, 2014), 77–94.

[53] Rab Houston, 'The Composition and Distribution of the Legal Profession, and the Use of Law in Britain and Ireland, c. 1500–c. 1850', *Legal History Review* 86 (2018): 123–56, at 127.

solicitors) in a population of around 5 million: roughly one for every 1600 inhabitants. By contrast, Scotland in 1640 had many fewer practitioners: about seventy working writers to the signet (like attorneys and solicitors) and 100 advocates (like English barristers, usually found pleading in the central courts) in a population of about 1 million.[54] Even by the early seventeenth century, formally trained lawyers did not monopolise the provision of legal advice or representation in Scotland's burgh courts – any person, man or woman, could do so. As a result, Scottish women did not require a professional lawyer to plead or answer on their behalf – they only needed a notary to confirm the authenticity of a property agreement before initiating or defending a suit.

The informal, small-scale nature of much civil legal business in burgh courts meant that ordinary women could simply appear in court and rebuke a pursuer's charge under oath, without the assistance of a lawyer. In 1657 the married woman Elizabeth Hall was cited before Glasgow's burgh court as a defender in a suit concerning the purchase of malt. Hendrie Paterson, the pursuer, alleged that he had sold Elizabeth (with her husband named 'for his interest') malt worth £7 12s. Scots a year previous, and that she had since refused to pay. The clerk noted that Elizabeth appeared 'personallie in judgement' before the town baillies, alleging that she would only pay Hendrie £3 12s. as 'the malt was not sufficient'. After extensive questioning from the town baillies, Hendrie 'succumbed' to Elizabeth's defence; the court agreed that Elizabeth should only have to pay £3 12s. in total.[55]

This is, of course, not to say that married women were suing or defending suits en masse without their husbands' knowledge or consent. The burgh courts were careful to uphold the patriarchal authority of husbands, only permitting wives' independent legal action when they were adhering to highly gendered roles as household mistresses and obeying wives. In fact, the large number of married women in burgh courts can arguably be viewed as a result of the patriarchal construction of household gender relations: wives were expected to provision the household as subservient but dependable mistresses, and husbands were expected to support their wives' economic and legal activities as patriarchal heads of households. When married women sought legal intervention on matters considered beyond their scope or control, Scottish men of law tended to uphold the husbands' superior status and rights. For instance, in his protocol book in 1562, the notary Gilbert Grote deleted the consent of John Rowan, the husband of Katherin Brussoun, noting in the margins that 'he wes nocht present nor consentit nocht heirto' to the alienation of her land;

---

[54] For the English figures, see Christopher Brooks, *Lawyers, Litigation and English Society since 1450* (London: Hambledon Continuum, 1998), esp. 21, 130, 182–5; for Scottish figures and discussion see Houston, 'The Composition and Distribution of the Legal Profession', 125–8.
[55] GCA, Glasgow burgh court, court book, B1/1/5/64rv.

presumably removed at John's request at a later date.[56] Likewise, in Inverness burgh court in 1560, the clerk noted that Thomas Paterson, the husband of Jannet Duff, protested that:

> quhat ewyr hys wyf confesis be nocht prejudiciall to hyme, be resson scho is his maret wyf and onder his dominion and aucht nocht to ansuer by his adwyse.[57]

> Whatever his wife confesses is not prejudicial to him, by reason that she is his married wife and under his dominion and ought not to answer without his advice.

Men undoubtedly had the final say: if the wife's legal action 'prejudiced' her husband's patriarchal power, she was forbidden from pursuing or defending a complaint, especially when the sale or dispute concerned land or other forms of immoveable property. However, that some husbands felt the need to reiterate their patriarchal status before the courts, and for clerks and notaries to formally record such statements in court books, does suggest that it was not unusual for married women to plead or respond without always providing evidence of their husbands' consent. As commented on by Gordon DesBrisay and Karen Sander Thomson, the presumption that a married woman operated in concert with her husband was 'so ingrained' in early modern Scotland that an aggrieved husband would have to go to considerable lengths to *stop* people (and, one might add, the courts) dealing with his wife on his account.[58]

Conclusion

This essay has challenged the pervasive idea that married women were legally incapacitated as property owners and litigants in early modern Scotland. While women were, of course, legally at a significant disadvantage in comparison to men, this did not mean that they were invisible in legal spaces or excluded from participating in legal conversations. The requirement of the husband's consent in authorising his wife's legal actions was clearly negotiable and not easily applicable to a multitude of scenarios. While the legal process was undoubtedly riddled with biases, highly ideological interpretations, and efforts to maintain the interests of married men in particular, Scottish men of law recognised that women's marital status should not automatically prevent them from pleading or responding in litigation, especially when their husbands simply refused consent. Moreover, it seems that married women's legal status was only ever

---

[56] William Angus, ed., *Protocol Book of Mr Gilbert Grote, 1552–1573* (Edinburgh, 1914), 46.
[57] William Mackay and Herbert Cameron Boyd, eds, *Records of Inverness Burgh Court Books: 1556–86*, I (Aberdeen, 1911), 49.
[58] Gordon DesBrisay and Karen Sander Thomson, 'Crediting Wives: Married Women and Debt Litigation in the Seventeenth Century', in *Finding the Family in Medieval and Early Modern Scotland*, eds Elizabeth Ewan and Janay Nugent (Aldershot: Ashgate, 2008), 85–98, at 86–7.

debated in the courts in certain circumstances: when queried by another litigant, when a husband was abroad or noticeably absent, or when the marital relationship was in some way unconventional or turbulent. Obstreperous husbands were reprimanded by judges and lawyers when refusing consent without reason, while deserting wives were denied access to the benefits that marriage entailed.

Women's interaction with the burgh courts was commonplace throughout the early modern period, and married women's appearance in particular was usual, rather than exceptional. The flexible procedures of burgh courts, and their far-reaching jurisdiction in matters concerning women's status and rights, meant that women – young, middle-aged or old; single, married or widowed; poor, middling or wealthy – routinely appeared as litigants in suits concerning their property rights, roles and responsibilities. Economic necessities clearly warranted married women's inclusion within the legal sphere and business of the burgh courts, especially when acting on behalf of their husbands and administering their marital economies as household mistresses. Women were clearly trusted by their husbands (and their husbands' business contacts) to manage or co-manage the family business, with that underlying trust revealing itself in the records of the burgh courts. Early modern legal records – from the central court in Edinburgh to burgh courts in towns across Scotland – contain thousands of references to married women engaged in the legal process to bolster and defend their status and rights. Not only did these women act on their own, but they empowered others to act on their behalf, and acted on behalf of others. Perhaps now, thirty years on from Ewan's plea, is the time to include these 'Scottish Portias' in the male-dominated history of Scots law.

THREE

Punching Back against Patriarchy: The Story of Jean Weir

Michael F. Graham

Victimised by what appears to have been long-term sexual abuse by her elder brother, and then further by a legal system that saw her as a co-perpetrator (rather than a victim) of incest, Jean Weir (d. 1670) deserves to be better remembered. To the extent that she is remembered at all it is as part of her abuser's story. Some of the people writing that story (either as a cautionary tale or an ideological weapon) could not even get her name right. One called her 'Jane', and others the even-less-homophonic 'Grizel'.[1] Her brother received his own entry in the *Oxford Dictionary of National Biography* but she does not even get that recognition, although she does have one in the *Biographical Dictionary of Scottish Women*.[2] While she lived to be more than sixty-five years old (no mean feat in seventeenth-century Scotland), she only really entered the historical record in the last week or so of her life, and had the label 'witch' added to her reputation as a parting insult on the way out.

Jean Weir is best known as half of one of the most notorious couples in Scotland's history. Her brother, Major Thomas Weir, a leading figure in Edinburgh's Covenanting circles, was executed on 11 April 1670 for sexual crimes including bestiality and incest. Jean, convicted as his partner in incest, was hanged the following day. Not surprisingly, as the differences between the Weirs' public and private lives came into the open, they were cast as hypocrites,

---

[1] For her as 'Jane' see [George Hickes], *Ravillac redivivus: being a narrative of the late tryal of Mr. James Mitchel a conventicle-preacher, who was executed the 18th of January last, for an attempt which he made on the sacred person of the Archbishop of St. Andrews. To which is annexed, an account of the tryal of that most wicked Pharisee Major Thomas Weir, who was executed for adultery, incest and bestiality* (London: Henry Hills, 1678), 64–7. For her as 'Grizel' see, among others, NLS ms Adv. 32.4.7 – Πρόνοια. *Providentia. Divina Providentia in Rebus Humanis. Divine Providence in humane affaires. A Collection of Providential Passages Antient and Modern Foreign and Domestick by Master James Fraser Minister At Kirkhill. Written Anno 1678'*, 156v.

[2] David Stevenson, 'Weir, Thomas', *ODNB*; Scott Moir, 'Weir, Jean (aka Grizel)', in *The Biographical Dictionary of Scottish Women*, eds Elizabeth Ewan, Rose Pipes, Jane Rendall and Siân Reynolds (Edinburgh: Edinburgh University Press, 2006), 439.

and the Devil was invoked as a useful explanation for why they had strayed so far off the righteous path. The bulk of the negative attention focused on Thomas, both because he had been the more public figure, and also because his admitted sexual crimes were more manifold. Jean slipped into the background. But, at its centre, the story of the Weirs was a dysfunctional family drama, one first brought to the attention of officials in part through the efforts of Margaret Weir, a third sibling.

While contemporaries (and particularly the legal system) showed no mercy toward Jean, a modern, dispassionate examination of what happened to the Weirs could see her as the long-suffering victim of an abusive elder brother in a family which tried to sweep that abuse under the rug. If we try to shift our focus to her part in the story, what emerges is indeed a narrative of victimisation in a harshly patriarchal environment. Yet while many chapters in that story are obscure, another theme clearly emerges toward the end. Yes, Jean was a victim. But on her final day of life she sought to turn the tables on those who came to witness her humiliation, punching the hangman and calling out the crowd assembled in Edinburgh's Grassmarket for its own hypocrisy. Unlike her brother, who appeared nearly insensible at his execution, she fought back until the noose strangled her. Victimised for much of her life, she refused the role of penitent sinner at the end, seeking to shift the focus from her own offenses to what she saw as Scotland's collective offense: the abandonment of the mid-century Covenants which had defined its particular Calvinist identity.

The last scholarly treatment of the Weirs, a 1972 article by David Stevenson (reprinted without notes in 1996), sought to cast them as early Scottish Antinomians, even 'Justified Sinners.'[3] While Stevenson's effort constituted an interesting speculative excursion into Calvinist psychology, its primary focus was on Thomas, and Stevenson did not really question the extent to which Jean was a willing partner in their notorious crimes. He merely seemed to assume that she was, suggesting that the Weirs were so confident in their election to salvation that

> [t]heir crimes would then not be crimes, for they could do no wrong. Their godliness and devotion to the covenants would not be hypocrisy if they were convinced that they had received divine grace and were justified in all they did. The fact that they kept their crimes secret and outwardly obeyed moral law would be merely a matter of expediency to guard themselves against the reprobate who did not understand the divine will so well as they did.[4]

---

[3] David Stevenson, 'Major Weir: A Justified Sinner?', *Scottish Studies* 16 (1972): 161–73. See also his *King or Covenant? Voices from Civil War* (East Linton: Tuckwell Press, 1996), 65–77.
[4] Stevenson, 'Major Weir', 169.

But what if, rather than being full of such confidence, Jean was terrified by her brother, and justifiably lived in fear of what might happen to her if his abuse of her came to light?

As with so many Scots of the early modern period, particularly Scotswomen who were not queens or noblewomen or poets, we cannot piece together anything like a complete life of Jean Weir. The vast majority of the sources that mention her are trial records or reports of that trial and its aftermath. They were written and compiled in such a way as to condemn her, so, to give her her due, we must read between the lines and against the grain of these sources. But even then we can only sketch the broadest of outlines until we get to her final days. She was born about 1604, the daughter of Thomas Weir of Kirkton, an estate near Carluke in Lanarkshire. Her brother Thomas had already entered the world, and younger sister Margaret would be born a few years later. Given that Jean's mother was also named Jean, she was likely the eldest daughter. The voices of Jean and Margaret come to us (admittedly, in mediated fashion) only through the justiciary court records, including the relevant folios of the High Court minute book and book of adjournal, and a small bundle of process papers, all held in the National Records of Scotland, although others later claimed to have gotten additional information from Jean.[5]

The whole legal process appears to have begun on Monday, 4 April 1670 when Thomas Weir began speaking to others, in his home, about his crimes. One of those present was Anna Ker, the wife of a local bookbinder, who had been specifically asked by Margaret Weir to visit Thomas's house because she (Ker) was 'a friend to the major'.[6] In retrospect it appears that Margaret, who would give evidence against her brother – some of which would also be used against her sister, although it is not clear that was her intent – sensed that Thomas was ready to confess and wanted him to do so in front of a sympathetic figure who might also be particularly shocked by the revelations. Soon the bailies were summoned and he repeated the confessions. As a result, he was taken to Edinburgh's tolbooth and, while the trial records do not explicitly say so, it appears that Jean was also placed in the tolbooth that same day.[7]

---

[5] The minute book and book of adjournal are only available as image sets in a 'virtual volume'; the originals are no longer produced for readers due to their fragile condition. So all citations below will be by frame number and will indicate right or left in the frame. The process papers are still available in traditional form. NRS, JC2/13 (book of adjournal), images 9–13; JC6/8 (minute book), images 97–101; JC26/37 (process papers for 1670). James Fraser, minister at Kirkhill, later reported information he had allegedly received from an Edinburgh minister who had spoken with Jean between her brother's execution and her own. For that, see below.

[6] For Ker's testimony about this, see NRS, JC2/13, image 12 left.

[7] An account published in England in 1678 by George Hickes, which was extremely hostile to presbyterians and covenanters in general, claimed that presbyterian ministers in Edinburgh had been aware of Thomas Weir's crimes 'for several months' until one of them told the (episcopalian) provost of Edinburgh. This may be true, but it is not a version of events reflected in the trial records. See Hickes, *Ravillac Redivivus*, 62.

On Wednesday, 6 April the magistrates of Edinburgh successfully petitioned the Scottish Privy Council to have the lord advocate (Sir John Nisbet of Dirleton) prosecute various prisoners in the tolbooth, 'and especially one major Weir and his sister for most abominable & odious crymes'.[8] That day, in preparation of the case, the lord advocate took statements from Thomas and Jean Weir, and both statements survive. He probably also took a statement from Margaret, although it has not survived. Its contents, however, can be inferred from her recorded testimony in the court records.[9] She, then fifty-six, attested that when she was seventeen and living in her parents' house in the west of Scotland (thus circa 1631), she had caught her older brother (naked) and sister in bed together 'and that she heard the bed move and shaike and heard scandalous languadge and discoursse betuixt them and … she heard her sister offer he had gottin his will of her'. At that time, Thomas would have been more than thirty, and Jean in her mid-twenties. Margaret had told her mother about this and, shortly thereafter, Jean had been sent away to Edinburgh.[10]

The first recorded account of any of this from Jean's perspective was also gathered on that Wednesday, in a statement which covered many details of the incest. She said her brother first attempted to have sex with her when she was ten, although he did not succeed in doing so until six years later. She corroborated her sister's account of the latter having discovered them in bed, and said her brother had continued to have 'carnall deal' with her for forty years – first in their parents' home and lands, and then in Edinburgh after they both moved there. It is worth noting that while Jean is recorded as having confessed to the charges against her (essentially all those listed in this Wednesday statement) at her trial on Saturday, she, who was literate enough to have kept a school (see below), did not sign the Wednesday statement. Possibly she initially regarded it as evidence against her brother rather than a confession. Thomas Weir did sign his Wednesday statement, which was much shorter than Jean's, but it only covered an incident of his bestiality from the early 1650s. From that point on, Thomas made no further revelations, so his conviction at the Saturday trial was mostly based on the testimonies of others.[11] From all of this it appears that Jean was a victim of sexual abuse within her family starting at age ten and her parents (or at least her mother) had chosen to cover this up and send her

---

[8] NRS, JC26/37 – High Court Process Papers 1670, first item in bundle labelled 'Major Weir and his sister process'.

[9] The fact that the first draft of the indictments ('dittays') against Thomas and Jean are dated Thursday, 7 April, and include information provided by all three siblings, suggests that Margaret's statement was taken on Wednesday, along with Thomas and Jean's statements.

[10] The official record of Margaret Weir's testimony is NRS, JC2/13, image 11 right.

[11] The statements from Thomas and Jean Weir, both given on Wednesday, 6 April, are on the same folded sheet which is in the bundle of process papers, and followed by a blank space prefaced to suggest that it was intended for a further statement from Thomas Weir on 7 April. See NRS, JC26/37, bundle marked 'Major Weir and his sister process 1670'.

away (although, it would turn out, not permanently), rather than endanger the family's upright reputation. We can only speculate at the sort of psychological damage this could have caused. While we should be wary of applying modern diagnostic categories in an early modern environment (given how culturally constructed many diagnoses are), it certainly would not strain credulity to suggest that Jean's upbringing would have left her permanently damaged and, as a result, tending to behave in ways that might not always make sense to us.[12]

The various references – literary, scholarly and popular – to the Weirs in the centuries since the case took place have shrouded it in a cloak of diabolism, a tendency which developed early on, possibly as a means of explaining something which otherwise seemed so inexplicable: how an upright pillar of the covenanted community such as Thomas Weir (and, by extension, Jean) could have turned out to be such a fraud. Even someone as well-versed in the Scottish witch-hunt as Julian Goodare has referred to Thomas Weir as 'Scotland's best-known male witch'.[13] While he certainly came to be viewed as a witch (or warlock or even wizard) in popular culture in the years following the Weirs' executions, he was not charged with witchcraft or any sort of demonic pact at his trial. But Jean was – perhaps demonstrating through a tiny sample of two the ways in which women were much more vulnerable than men to witchcraft accusations, or interpretations of behaviour that involved witchcraft.

In the (unsigned) statement which she gave on Wednesday, 6 April, after attesting to the incest with her brother, Jean recounted an additional, seemingly unrelated story which, along with the information on the incest, was then included in the dittay (that is, indictment) presented against her at her trial on Saturday, 9 April. She said that some years previously (the specific year is left blank in her original statement as well as in its incorporations into the dittay), when she was keeping a school in Dalkeith at which she taught children, she was visited by a woman who offered 'to speik wi[th] ye queen of feirie and to streik and batell on [Jean's] behalf nightlie ye gudman, meaning undoubtedlie ye divill'. The next day, she was visited by a different woman (described as 'litel' in Jean's original statement, although that was left out of the dittay) who gave her 'a peec of trie or ye root of some herb or trie and did tell [Jean] that als long as you hade ye saimen ye should be able to do whatsoever you should desyre'. The particular power that this gave her was the ability to spin wool at what seemed a superhuman speed. This, coupled with the other instructions from

---

[12] Valerie J. Edwards, George W. Holden, Vincent J. Felitti and Robert F. Anda, 'Relationship Between Multiple Forms of Childhood Maltreatment and Adult Mental Health in Community Respondents: Results from the Adverse Childhood Experiences Study,' *American Journal of Psychiatry* 160 (2003): 1453–60, found a strong correlation between childhood sexual abuse and adverse adult mental health outcomes.

[13] Julian Goodare, 'Women and the Witch-Hunt in Scotland', *Social History* 23, no. 3 (1998): 288–308, at 305. Jean Weir did claim in her recorded testimony that her brother had the Devil's mark on his shoulder. See NRS, JC2/13, image 12 right.

the second visitor which Jean said she followed (that she place her foot on a cloth the woman had put in her doorway and her hand on the crown of her head and repeat three times 'all my crose and trubles go to ye doors') was taken by the lord advocate as evidence of a pact with the Devil and a renunciation of baptism. Jean said nothing explicit about offering her soul to anyone; in fact she reported giving the second visitor payment in silver and meal.[14] Ultimately, on the day of the Weirs' trial, the lord advocate told the justices and the members of the assize that he was insisting 'upon ye uthir action of sorcerie [against Jean] only as ane aggravatione', meaning that he did not regard it as central to the case against her, so she was condemned to death for the incest alone.[15] Perhaps the idea of Jean dabbling in diabolism would not have withstood the test of legal probation but was included because it made her overall story more plausible: someone who had an unnatural relationship with her brother would no doubt be open to the enticements of the Devil as well. But detailed witchcraft narratives contain the voices of the suspect as well as the interrogator, and we must consider the possibility that Jean's was the primary voice here. Who was this 'divel' against whom she needed 'to streik and batell ... nightlie'? Might it have been her own brother? Writing in an early modern German context, Lyndal Roper has written that while 'witchcraft confessions have been understood as the projections of a male-dominated society', we must not read them exclusively in that way. To do so 'is to ignore the creative work which the witch herself carried out, translating her own life experiences into the language of the diabolic, performing her own diabolic theatre'.[16]

It does not appear that Jean told this story as a result of torture. While many Scottish witchcraft suspects were in fact tortured, the employment of torture officially required a special warrant from the Privy Council.[17] There is no evidence of one being issued in Jean's case and given that this trial was taking place at the highest level – Edinburgh's Justiciary Court, which would soon be transformed into the High Court of Justiciary – it seems unlikely that undocumented torture would have been employed. So this story probably reflected in part Jean's own recollection of two incidents which occurred in rapid succession in her life, with a diabolical interpretation put on them, either by the authorities, or by Jean in conjunction with the authorities. Given that suspects were often asked leading questions during interrogation it might be a something of a joint production, with Jean's voice the primary, but certainly

[14] Quotations drawn from NRS, JC6/8, images 99 right to 100 left, checked against NRS, JC2/13, image 10 right.
[15] NRS, JC 6/8, image 100 left, JC2/13, image 11 left. Interestingly, though, the marginal reference that marks the beginning of her case in the book of adjournal claims she was convicted of 'witchcraft [and] sorcerie' with no mention of incest. See NRS, JC2/13, image 10 left.
[16] Lyndal Roper, *Oedipus and the Devil: Witchcraft, Sexuality and Religion in Early Modern Europe* (London: Routledge, 1994), 20.
[17] Brian Levack, *Witch-hunting in Scotland: Law, Politics and Religion* (New York: Routledge, 2008), 22.

not the only, contributor. It certainly contains some classic Scottish folkloric tropes, such as the Queen of Fairy, and also puts Jean in the position of a person beaten down by her life and therefore tempted by an offer of magical assistance.[18] It is also plausible that an increased capacity for wool-spinning (to augment her school-teaching) could have enhanced her economic and personal independence (literally as a spinster). She had certainly experienced crosses and troubles she might have wanted to cast away. But as with so many putative demonic pacts, she got the worst of the bargain. She was not able to maintain her independence, and moved back to Edinburgh to live with her brother after his wife's demise, probably in the 1650s.[19] What sort of desperation and/or psychic damage might have spurred her in that direction?

In fact, moving from Dalkeith back to Edinburgh to live with her brother again was not Jean's first return to her abusive situation. Though Margaret Weir reported that her sister had been sent away from the family home to Edinburgh after Margaret told their mother that she had found Thomas and Jean having sex, Jean, according to her dittay, 'did most obstinatelie and wickedlie return y[er]unto and did continew and walow in ye s[ai]d abominable wickedness with [her] brother without any sens of remorse'.[20] The assumption of a lack of remorse of course held Jean as fully responsible for her own behaviour. The same dittay charged that Margaret, when she first discovered them, was 'frighted and troubled with the terror of so great an abominatioune', and argued that, even as a ten-year-old whose brother had tried to sexually assault her, Jean's knowledge of 'his forsaid wicket inclinatiouns & practyces should have made you more circumspect and watchefull and should have obleidged you to have avoided his cumpanie & tentatioune yet you did not …'.[21] Was it a temptation or an unavoidable situation? It should be noted that by their very nature indictments did not offer any sympathy to those accused of crimes. A dittay was designed to encourage the assize jury to convict the defendant by presenting the case against them in the strongest terms possible. But an early twenty-first-century reading of this dittay might question what other choices Jean really had. How, as an adolescent, could she avoid the company of her older brother when living under the same roof? As the eldest daughter of a lairdly family, she probably would have received some sort of basic education and been raised in the expectation that she would eventually marry and run a household of children and servants. Being sent away to Edinburgh in her mid-twenties could not have enhanced those prospects. Margaret's deposition reported that Jean

---

[18] Lizanne Henderson has noted that 'a significant number of Scottish witch trials contain elements of fairy beliefs'. See her *Witchcraft and Folk Belief in the Age of Enlightenment: Scotland, 1670–1740* (Basingstoke: Palgrave Macmillan, 2016), 120, n.85.
[19] Stevenson, 'Major Weir: A Justified Sinner?', 165.
[20] NRS, JC6/8, image 99 right.
[21] NRS, JC6/8, image 99 left.

was sent away, but made no mention of the situation she was sent into. Was it for schooling (although she would have been old for that)? Was it to work as a servant in the household of a relative or someone else connected with her family? This is one of many lacunae in this fragmentary biography. But it, along with Jean's future occupation as a schoolmistress, suggests that her marriage prospects were diminishing.

The fortunes of her birth family were also diminishing. In December 1636, when Jean would have been thirty-two, her parents sold the family estate to George Barber, a resident of Edinburgh. The entry in the Registry of the Great Seal stipulated that this was done with the consent of Thomas Weir, listed as the elder Thomas Weir of Kirkton's 'son and heir-apparent'.[22] If he had not already done so, Thomas would soon move to Edinburgh where, early in 1642, he married Isobel Mein, widow of a merchant, served briefly in the army fighting the Irish rebellion and, according to his 1670 dittay, eventually took to sexually abusing his stepdaughter, marrying her off to an Englishman when she became pregnant.[23] His marriage had given him burgess status, and in 1648 he was elected captain of the town guard, so he had managed to secure a good landing spot in Edinburgh even though circumstances had forced his family to sell their estate.[24] Sometime during this period, Jean, with rather less status, would have been running the school in Dalkeith. While one otherwise well-informed 1670 account of the Weirs' trial and executions claimed that Jean had been married at some point, no other contemporary source included that detail and, if it were true, she probably would have been identified as a spouse or 'relict' (widow) in the trial records.[25] In any case, after the death of Thomas's wife (and perhaps the marriage of his stepdaughter), Jean moved to Edinburgh to live with him once again.

This last return is a problematic detail in a narrative where Jean is understood primarily as victim. Before returning to Edinburgh to live with her brother again, she surely had a modicum of independence. But it can make sense if we consider the possibilities of economic necessity coupled with the likelihood that she lived in fear of her brother (and had done so from an early age).

---

[22] *RMS*, 9:170–1. For a later sale which refers to the earlier sale, see *RMS* 11:122–3.

[23] Henry Paton, ed., *Register of Marriages for the Parish of Edinburgh, 1595–1700* (Edinburgh: SRS, 1905), 729; NRS, JC6/8 frame 98 left.

[24] Charles B. Boog Watson, ed., *Roll of Edinburgh Burgesses and Guild-Brethren, 1406–1700* (Edinburgh: SRS, 1929), 519; Marguerite Wood, ed., *Extracts from the Records of the Burgh of Edinburgh, 1642–1655* (Edinburgh: Oliver and Boyd, 1938), 179.

[25] *Diary of Mr John Lamont of Newton, 1649–1671* (Edinburgh: Maitland Club, 1830), 218, states that Jean 'was maried to another' during at least one of the periods in which they committed incest. While her sister Margaret may be the Margaret Weir who married Alexander Weir, a resident of Carluke (given his geographic origins close to the old family seat) in Edinburgh in 1647, none of the six Jean Weirs recorded as marrying in Edinburgh between 1631 and 1652 can be even tentatively identified with the subject of this chapter. See *Register of Marriages for the Parish of Edinburgh, 1595–1700*, 728.

The upheavals of the Wars of the Three Kingdoms hit Scotland particularly hard. While they provided opportunities for advancement via military service (and strong alignment with the hardline presbyterian party) for some men like Thomas Weir, they (and the Cromwellian occupation after 1651) also caused widespread death and economic upheaval.[26] One source reported that Jean 'lived upon alms' at the time she was visited by the mysterious strangers in Dalkeith.[27] Jean's apparent livelihoods (school-teaching and wool-spinning) could well have collapsed. She may no longer have been able to support herself. At that point, the opportunity to move back to Edinburgh to live with her well-established brother, while a poisoned chalice, might have been one she felt she had to take. There is also evidence that she was terrified of him and the possibility that he might expose their incest. People in such straits do not always behave rationally.

The most detailed source we have on Jean Weir which was not produced by the Justiciary Court is an interesting and idiosyncratic account by James Fraser, minister at the northern parish of Kirkhill, who included the story of the Weirs in his 1678 'Collection of Providential Passages Antient and Modern Foreign and Domestick'.[28] The well-travelled Fraser claimed to have met Thomas Weir in 1660 and, while he referred to Jean as 'Grisel', in other respects he offered a strikingly sympathetic picture of Jean. As an episcopalian, Fraser might have had a bias against both of the strongly presbyterian Weirs.[29] But it also meant that he had good sources among the episcopal clergy, including those in Edinburgh, who staffed the Restoration Scottish Kirk. He was certainly a believer in the reality of witchcraft and the possibility of magic, but had been appalled at some excesses in witch-hunting around his home parish.[30] His account of the Weirs highlighted (one could say even promoted) the alleged supernatural elements in the story. One of these was a walking stick that Thomas Weir was said to always carry. There was no mention of this item in the original trial records.[31] In Fraser's telling, this stick had magical qualities. Several sources attested to

---

[26] See, among others, Keith M. Brown, *Kingdom or Province? Scotland and the Regal Union, 1603–1715* (London: Macmillan, 1992), 123–39.

[27] NLS, Adv. 32.4.7, 158r.

[28] NLS, Adv. 32.4.7. This manuscript also appears to have been one of the major sources (sometimes copied verbatim) in the account of the Weirs that George Sinclair appended as a postscript to his *Satan's Invisible World Discovered* (Edinburgh: John Reid, 1685).

[29] David Worthington, 'Fraser, James', *ODNB*.

[30] David Worthington, *Rev. James Fraser, 1634–1709: A New Perspective on the Scottish Highlands before Culloden* (Edinburgh: Edinburgh University Press, 2023), chapter 5. I am grateful to Professor Worthington for sharing this chapter with me prior to its publication.

[31] There is a reference to it in the version of the Weirs' trial given in W. G. Scott-Moncrieff, ed., *The Records of the Proceedings of the Justiciary Court Edinburgh, 1661–1678*, 2 vols. (Edinburgh: SHS, 1905), 2:15, but that is in the commentary provided by the unknown compiler of the manuscript used as the source for that publication, who had drawn on the Justiciary records but added additional material as well.

Thomas Weir's remarkable skills in leading extemporaneous prayers, but Fraser claimed 'it was observed yt he could not officiat in any holy duty without the black staff or rod in his hand and leaning upon it', and reported that the staff had been given to Weir by the Devil.[32] In his account of the Weirs' arrests, Fraser wrote that the bailies asked if there was any money in the house. Thomas said there was none, but Jean directed them to money hidden in various places 'to the value of 5 Dollars in parcells'. Then '[h]is sister advised the Magistrates to secure his staffe of specially, which they did'.[33] Jean appears to have been offering cooperation, but her concern about the staff in particular seems significant; she had allegedly been concerned about it on previous occasions as well.

Fraser wrote that one of Edinburgh's episcopalian ministers, who had not visited Thomas Weir during his imprisonment, did visit Jean in the tolbooth in the afternoon after Thomas Weir's execution, doing so because, unlike her brother, she 'had some remorse'. (By all accounts Thomas Weir refused the prayers of all ministers in his final days.) This minister told Jean that her brother had been hanged and burned, and at first she would not believe it. But after he repeatedly assured her that this was true, she asked what had happened to his staff, 'for she knew that his strength & life lay therein'.[34] When her visitor told Jean that the staff had been burned with her brother she, despite her advanced age,

> nimbly & in a furious rage fell on her knees, uttering words horrible to be remembered & in riseing up, as she was desired, her rageing agony closed w[i]t[h] these words. O Sir I know he is w[i]t[h] the Divils for w[i]t[h] them he lived.

Fraser wrote that she then shared with the minister details of her life that the latter vowed 'must die with him', although he did report some of them. For example, she said that her brother stopped having sex with her when she was fifty-six because he 'then loathed her for her age'. Asked whether she had ever become pregnant as a result of sex with her brother, she replied that 'he hindered that by means abominable, which she beginning to relate, the preacher stopt her'. She also said she thought her mother had been a witch (this being the mother who had covered up Jean's victimisation) and she revealed what she thought might be the 'devil's mark' in the shape of a horseshoe on her own forehead, a physical trait which she said her mother also possessed. Thinking that she had found a sympathetic clergyman (and surprisingly, given her strongly presbyterian background, one from the established Episcopal Church), Jean asked him if he would attend her on the scaffold the next day.[35] What comes out of this account is a sense that Thomas Weir's death liberated

---

[32] NLS, Adv. 32.4.7, 156v.
[33] NLS, Adv. 32.4.7, 157r.
[34] NLS, Adv. 32.4.7, 157v.
[35] NLS, Adv. 32.4.7, 158r–v.

his sister, despite her knowledge that she herself would be executed the next day. She also seems to have firmly believed that the staff was critical to his power (and perhaps his sway over her). Fraser reported that she told his ministerial source that on earlier occasions she had tried to hide the staff from her brother, 'becaus without it he could do nothing, [but] he would threaten & vow to discover yer incest feareing wh[ich] she would deliver it again'.[36] This was abusive blackmail, but now the spell that it had cast was broken.

Fraser suggested that the minister agreed to attend Jean on the scaffold only because 'She intreated [him] to visit her & attend her to her death, w[hil]k at her violent importunity he yeldid unto, though it was not his course to wait upon condemned persones.'[37] Perhaps he was trying to prevent his informant from being implicated in her final performance, which certainly did not follow the traditional script. Numerous historians, under the influence of Michel Foucault's *Discipline and Punish*, have seen public executions as teaching moments with the power of the state and its justice system on display.[38] Members of the assembled crowd would be warned against emulating the crimes of the convicted, but would also be reassured that the condemned person was truly repentant and reconciled to their fate. Those about to be executed might ask for the crowd's forgiveness and reassure the hangman that they bore him no ill will. Through the sacrifice of one, the social body was theoretically healed from the stain of transgression. Challenging that model in an English context, Thomas Laqueur has argued that this theatre of execution did not always deliver such clear messages. Many hangings (even those at London's Tyburn) took place at considerable distance from monuments of state power and 'through laughter, outrageous clothes, misplaced sentimentality and silence some prisoners subverted the roles assigned to them'.[39] On the one hand, the location of Jean's execution (Edinburgh's Grassmarket, just below the West Bow neighbourhood in which she and her brother had lived and a short walk from where she had been imprisoned and tried) was certainly close to the symbols of state power. But, on the other hand, she subverted the role which she had been assigned.

The most detailed accounts of Jean's behaviour on the scaffold come from Fraser and the Fife diarist John Lamont. Fraser's source may well have been the episcopal minister who accompanied her to the scaffold, although there would

---

[36] NLS, Adv. 32.4.7, 158r.
[37] NLS, Adv. 32.4.7, 158r.
[38] Michel Foucault, *Discipline and Punish: The Birth of the Prison*, trans. Alan Sheridan (New York: Random House, 1979), 48.
[39] Thomas W. Laqueur, 'Crowds, Carnival and the State in English Executions, 1604–1868', in *The First Modern Society: Essays in English History in Honour of Lawrence Stone*, eds A. L. Beier, David Cannadine and James M. Rosenheim (Cambridge: Cambridge University Press, 1989), 305–55, at 312–3, 319.

have been plenty of other witnesses to the scene.[40] Lamont probably was not an eyewitness, as the bulk of his 'journal' (including an account of a horse race in Cupar on the day Jean was hanged) concerned events in Fife.[41] But Jean's final act was so remarkable that the news probably spread widely. Lamont's account supports that of Fraser but adds additional information. Among other likely eyewitnesses was the future Lord of Session John Lauder of Fountainhall. Contrasting Jean's scaffold performance with her brother's near silence, he wrote that Jean was 'but a very lamentable object, for she ran on the other extreem and praesumed exceidingly on the mercy of God, wheiras their ware no great evidences in hir of soull contrition'.[42] There was, however, plentiful evidence of her anger and her refusal to die quietly. While Lauder of Fountainhall's laconic account hints at something broader (and more dramatic), Fraser's supplies the details: Fraser reported that on the morning of her execution day, Jean

> told the Minister she resolved to die w[i]t[h] all the shame she could to expiat under mercy her shamefull life; this he understood to be an ingenuous confession of her sins, in opposition to her brothers despare & desperat silence, to which he did incurage her.

Then, 'at her parting w[i]t[h] him, she gave him hearty thanks for his pains & shakeing & kissing his hands she repeated the same words q[uhi]lk he bade her perform'.[43] But Jean apparently had different words in mind.

> [A]scending up the ladder she spake someq[uha]t confusedly of her sins, of her brother & his inchanting staff & w[i]t[h] a ghastly conntenance, behalding a multitud of spectators, all wondering & some weeping, she spake aloud, There are many here this day wondering and greeting for me but alas few mourns for a broken --------------, at which words many seemed angry.[44]

Some printings of George Sinclair's *Satan's Invisible World Discovered* supplied the missing word, which the episcopalian Fraser may have been wary of including – 'covenant'.[45] In a city and kingdom in which covenanted

---

[40] Fraser's version is echoed (sometimes verbatim) in Sinclair, *Satan's Invisible World Discovered* and Hickes, *Ravillac redivivus*.

[41] While the published version of Lamont's diary styles him 'of Newton', he probably was not the laird of that estate. He appears to have been the son and grandson of ministers of Scoonie. See *Diary of Mr John Lamont of Newton, 1649–1671* (Edinburgh: Maitland Club, 1830), v–viii, corrected by Alexander du Toit, 'John Lamont', *ODNB*.

[42] Donald Crawford, ed., *Journals of Sir John Lauder, Lord Fountainhall, with his observations on public affairs and other memoranda, 1665–1676* (Edinburgh: SHS, 1900), 232.

[43] NLS, Adv. 32.4.7, 158v.

[44] NLS, Adv. 32.4.7, 158v.

[45] George Sinclair, *Satan's Invisible World Discovered* (Edinburgh: John Reid, 1685), 239 (but unpaginated). 'Covenant' appears in the National Library of Scotland and British Library copies, but not in the copy included in Early English Books Online.

presbyterianism had been officially supplanted a decade before by an episcopalian Church, Jean was casting shame on her co-religionists for abandoning the cause of the godly to which she (and, for that matter, her brother) had publicly adhered. Those in the crowd might have thought about James Sharp, once active in the presbyterian cause but now Archbishop of St Andrews. By invoking the covenant, Jean could claim a different role for herself: not a penitent sinner (or victim) but a champion of the national godly cause from which so many had turned away.

Laura Stewart has recently commented on the active roles played by women in the covenanting movement from its inception and carrying on through the seventeenth century:

> The most positive and long-lasting political legacy of the 1640s was communal swearing of the Covenant by people of all social ranks. This event may have been a particularly potent experience for women, who were ordinarily denied participation in governance, and may partially explain their continued prominence in Presbyterian crowds later in the century.[46]

In reminding the assembled crowd of the covenant, Jean might have been trying to remind herself of something more inspirational in her own life than the viciously repeating pattern which had brought her to that place.

But Jean was not done. As some of those near her 'called to her to mind higher concerns' and her ministerial companion struggled to keep his composure, Jean began ripping off her clothing as she 'prepared to die stark naked'.[47] Lamont reported that the bailie supervising the execution tried to stop her from removing any more clothing and entreated the hangman to hurry up and secure the rope around her neck. But he had not yet tied her hands behind her back, so 'she smote the execwtioner on the cheike'. Probably shocked by this development, the hangman quickly kicked the ladder away, but not quickly enough, because Jean was able to grab at it as she dropped and then 'labored to recover hir selfe, and put in hir head betwixt two of the steps', a posture she was able to maintain 'till she was put from itt', presumably by having the ladder forcibly ripped away. Fraser averred that the hurried scuffle meant that the hangman 'was forced to throw her over openfaced, which afterward he covered, after the usual manner with a cloath'. Thus, attendees could have watched Jean's face as she suffocated. Lamont concluded that the whole performance showed that Jean, like her brother, died impenitent.[48] That may have been true in a technical sense, but I suspect Jean's intended message was more complex.

---

[46] Laura A. M. Stewart, *Rethinking the Scottish Revolution: Covenanted Scotland, 1637–1651* (Oxford: Oxford University Press, 2016), 331.
[47] NLS, Adv. 32.4.7, 158v.
[48] *Diary of Mr John Lamont*, 218.

Victimised for much of her life by her brother, an apparent paragon of the covenanted community, she was not about to reward a crowd she saw as rife with hypocrisy with a show of public contrition. In that respect, her execution bears at least some resemblance to that of the covenanters Isabel Alison and Marion Harvie, executed (like Jean Weir, at the Grassmarket) for treason in 1681. Laura Doak has recently examined their performance, both before the Privy Council where Harvie invoked the covenants and on the scaffold where the pair protested in word and song and Harvie allegedly shouted 'I leave my blood on all ungodly and profane wretches'.[49]

While Alison and Harvie were known Cameronian activists, Jean Weir, three times their ages, came to the scaffold through a very different life history, one marked by abuse at the hands of a covenanting stalwart. She knew hypocrisy in ways that they did not. As a result, she tried to shift her narrative while roaring out the cumulative pain of her life. Possibly she failed in that effort. An anonymous lawyer who made a copy of the Weirs' trial records and inserted bits of commentary claimed that Thomas 'died in despair declaring that he had no hopes of mercy, and the woman died folishly [sic]'.[50] The known commentators (all of them male, of course) seemed to see primarily impenitence in Jean's end, despite Fraser's implied recognition that she was a victim of her brother. Mostly they passed over her story, dwelling at much greater length on her brother, his double life and his supposedly magic walking stick. But who can say how the crowd (full of women and men, all informed by their own particular experiences of religion, family life and sexual politics) might have read Jean's final performance?[51] If 'many seemed angry' at her invocation of a broken covenant, was their anger directed at her, or elsewhere? More than three centuries later, it's hard to know. But reading against the grain of the few sources which tell us of Jean Weir's life we might direct most of our anger elsewhere, and more of our sympathy to her.

---

[49] Laura Doak, 'Militant Women and "National" Community: The Execution of Isabel Alison and Marion Harvie, 1681', *Journal of the Northern Renaissance* 12 (2021): 18, 23–4.
[50] Scott-Moncrieff, ed., *The Records of the Proceedings of the Justiciary Court*, 2:14.
[51] Laqueur, 'Crowds, Carnival and the State in English Executions, 1604–1868', 346–9 notes the wide range of emotions and behaviours execution audiences might display.

FOUR

Always at the Gate? Unlocking Medieval Women's Stories in Modern-day Edinburgh

Rachel M. Delman

Elizabeth Ewan has been a trailblazer in establishing the field of medieval women's and gender history in Scotland. Equally noteworthy yet less discussed, however, are Ewan's pioneering efforts in bringing medieval women's stories to non-specialist audiences beyond the academy. In 2003, Ewan collaborated with the developers of one of Edinburgh's star visitor attractions, The Real Mary King's Close on the Royal Mile, a network of historic streets buried underground during the building of the Royal Exchange in the eighteenth century, to illuminate the story of Alison Rough (c. 1480–1535), a woman of middling status whose life is unusually well-documented.[1] Following the collaboration, Rough was presented to public audiences through processions, on merchandise in the form of tea towels and mugs and even projected onto Edinburgh City Chambers as part of an advent calendar. Rough's story became one of the many told to visitors by the costumed guides at the site. Ewan said of the experience, '[f]or me, Alison Rough is my own Black Agnes, brought back from historical oblivion, creating a stir, and always at the gate'.[2] In using Black Agnes's well-known defence of Dunbar Castle as a metaphor for medieval women's and gender history in Scotland more generally, Ewan reminds us that women are present in the historical record, waiting for their stories to be told; they just require historians and heritage professionals – gatekeepers with specialist training and access – to unlock the gate and enable them to enter the public consciousness.

This chapter focuses on the representation of medieval women's stories in the heritage interpretation of Edinburgh's Old Town. It argues that despite piecemeal efforts to tell women's stories in Edinburgh over the years, the Old Town of Scotland's capital city, one of the UK's top tourist destinations and a

---

[1] For Rough's story see Elizabeth Ewan, 'Alison Rough: A Woman's Life and Death in Sixteenth-century Edinburgh,' *Women's History Magazine* 45 (Autumn, 2003): 4–13.
[2] 'Undergraduate Scholarship to Honour Professor Elizabeth Ewan', The Scottish Studies Foundation, https://p10.secure.hostingprod.com/@scottishstudies.com/ssl/elizabeth-ewan.htm.

UNESCO World Heritage Site, has not fully utilised its built and archival medieval heritage to tell the stories of other historical women like Alison Rough, and thus capitalise on the associated potential of such stories for creating more inclusive and representative heritage experiences. Taking two centrally located, extant medieval buildings that were commissioned by late medieval women, namely Magdalen Chapel on Cowgate and Trinity Apse on Chalmers Close, as case studies, this chapter elucidates how centring women's lives at the two sites could help counter the male biases of the city's current public narrative and transform the existing visitor experience. It advocates for the curation of medieval women's stories as a means of creating a more inclusive and dynamic visitor experience with the potential for significant cultural, social and economic impact. In doing so, the chapter seeks to illuminate some of the ways in which public historians and heritage professionals might go about opening the gate, not only for the medieval women who are ever ready to enter, but also for the modern-day visitors whose histories have traditionally been absent(ed) or marginalised in heritage interpretation.

Gendered interpretations in urban heritage

Gender is by no means synonymous with women's issues, but the absence of women in heritage interpretation, and the lack of diversity in the stories told about them, are salient issues in critical heritage discourse.[3] Laurajane Smith observes that

> where gender issues are identified in the heritage literature, two issues tend to stand out. The first concerns the degree to which sites and places of significance to women's history and experience are neglected in registers of conserved or preserved heritage and, secondly, the degree to which the stories told at heritage places and museums tend to convey and legitimize gender stereotypes of men and women.[4]

As Karen Dempsey and others have also noted of castle sites, there is still an issue of 'women equating to care and the domestic while men equat[e] to public life and power', with little variation or nuance.[5]

---

[3] For a recent reflection on gender and heritage discourse see Elena Settimini, 'Women's Representation and Participation in UNESCO Heritage Discourse', *International Journal of Heritage Studies* 27, no. 1 (2021): 1–15.
[4] Laurajane Smith, 'Heritage, Gender and Identity', in *The Ashgate Research Companion to Heritage and Identity*, eds Brian Graham and Peter Howard (Abingdon: Routledge, 2008), 159–78, at 162.
[5] Karen Dempsey, Roberta Gilchrist, Jeremey Ashbee, Stefan Sagrott and Samantha Stones, 'Beyond the Martial Façade: Gender, Heritage and Medieval Castles', *International Journal of Heritage Studies* 26, no. 4 (2019): 352–69.

The inherent masculinity of built heritage in towns and cities is also widely recognised.[6] Indeed, Dolores Hayden argues that urban heritage is synonymous with the few architectural monuments that become associated with male elites as city fathers, rather than representing the lives of working men and women.[7] In 2017–18, a popular media campaign recognised that in the City of Edinburgh there are fewer statues of named women than of animals.[8]

In recent years, stakeholders in urban centres have sought to redress the gender bias and tell women's stories through both the tangible and intangible heritage of UK towns and cities. Efforts have taken various forms, from exhibitions and walking tours on women's history, to the commissioning of new statues and plaques celebrating the lives of women and other marginalised groups. The past five years, in particular, have seen a considerable drive towards the implementation of permanent monuments to women. The uncovering of a statue of the pioneering nineteenth-century fossil hunter and palaeontologist Mary Anning in Lyme Regis in Dorset, the creation of a monument to the thirteenth-century Jewish businesswoman Licoricia of Winchester in the city of Winchester, and the naming of a college building at the University of York after the Yorkshire landowner and 'first modern lesbian', Anne Lister, all in 2022, are prime examples of the ways in which a feminist reclaiming of urban space has translated into the creation of permanent legacies.[9]

Critical reflections on methodological approaches to telling women's histories at heritage sites and spaces have shown that it is not sufficient to simply insert women's lives into places and stories that have hitherto been considered 'masculine', but to rather create a broader cultural shift whereby visitors come to embrace, and indeed expect, diverse narratives.[10] Challenging default assumptions is one way that this shift in culture can be achieved. Responding to the seemingly inherent masculinity of Scotland's heritage, Sara Sheridan's 2019 publication, *Where are the Women? A Guide to an Imagined Scotland*, published in association with Historic Environment Scotland, provides an 'imagined atlas' of fictional streets, buildings, statues and monuments, which are dedicated to real women.[11] The reimagining of iconic Edinburgh landmarks and streets, such

---

[6] Smith, 'Heritage, Gender and Identity', 161–7.
[7] Dolores Hayden, 'Making Women's History Visible in the Urban Landscape', *City and Society* 10, no. 1 (1998): 9–20, at 9.
[8] 'Where are the Statues of Scots Women?', *The Scotsman*, 23 January 2016.
[9] In the case of Licoricia of Winchester, the implementation of the statue has been accompanied by a series of events, publications and activities, thus linking tangible and intangible heritage. See, for example, History of the Project and the Time: Licoricia of Winchester. Licoricia of Winchester | Fundraising for a statue of Licoricia of Winchester in Jewry Street, Winchester, https://licoricia.org/licoricia-of-winchester/.
[10] Nicole Deufel, 'Telling her Story of War: Challenging Gender Bias at Culloden Battlefield Visitor Centre', *Historical Reflections/Réflexions Historiques* 37, no. 2 (2011): 72–89.
[11] Sara Sheridan, *Where are the Women? A Guide to an Imagined Scotland* (Edinburgh: Historic Environment Scotland, 2019).

as Arthur's Seat in Edinburgh as St Triduana's Seat, is a powerful reminder of how many of the place names that we use unthinkingly in everyday discourse are gendered male. Sheridan also illuminates the role that imagination can play in bringing awareness to, and indeed challenging, our default male perspective. Sheridan's work represents a reclaiming of space, by which women are shown in locations where they have always been, yet have not been memorialised through place names or monuments due to the continued androcentrism of our towns and cities. The accessibility and affordability of Sheridan's book, which is sold in Historic Environment Scotland gift shops and via the organisation's website, also gives it a wider reach than academic publications which use technical language and are often hidden behind paywalls.[12]

Many of the efforts to curate women's stories through urban heritage interpretation to date have thus involved the creation of new monuments or a re-imagining of urban space. Less common have been attempts to re-centre women's lives through permanent or long-term interpretation at existing buildings and sites with which they were historically associated. The dominance of the former approaches is in part due to a perceived lack of surviving evidence for women's histories, which is also one reason why the stories of medieval and early modern women, in particular, are told in fewer numbers than those of their more recent counterparts. Where they do survive, buildings commissioned, owned and used by women and other underrepresented groups from the more distant past remain under-utilised despite their considerable potential for creating a more inclusive heritage narrative, as this chapter will elucidate.

While scholarship on the implementation of women's stories in urban contexts remains in its infancy, critical studies of museum settings have shown that telling women's stories as an integrated part of a gendered methodology applied to objects, and artefacts can be especially productive for enhancing visitor engagement and for transforming visitors' understanding of both their past and their present. The cultivation of more inclusive and representative visitor experiences, rooted in tangible remains from the past, creates a greater sense of belonging and ownership in groups who have otherwise been marginalised or excluded from the stories told through the heritage surrounding them.[13]

This chapter advocates for the potential of urban buildings to similarly provide a tangible link to 'hidden' or underrepresented stories, which might likewise counter misconceptions about historical gender dynamics to foster a more inclusive present. The purpose of the discussion is not to determine the 'best'

---

[12] For a reflection on Open Access and feminism, see Carys J. Craig, Joseph F, Turcotte and Rosemary J. Coombe, 'What's Feminist about Open Access? A Relational Approach to Copyright in the Academy', feminists@law 1, no. 1 (2011): 1–35, https://journals.kent.ac.uk/index.php/feministsatlaw/article/view/7/54.

[13] James Daybell, Kit Heyam, Svante Norrhem and Emma Severinsson, 'Gendering Objects at the V&A and Vasa Museums', *Museum International* 72, no. 102 (2020): 106–17.

forms that revisionist interpretation might take – which, it is argued, would be more productively achieved through multi-stakeholder collaboration – but instead to elucidate the unique potential of the two buildings for offering an alternative, gendered lens through which to view the medieval heritage of Edinburgh's Old Town.

Edinburgh's Old Town as a tourist destination

Edinburgh, Scotland's capital city since the fifteenth century, is one of the world's most popular tourist destinations.[14] Together, the medieval Old Town and the Georgian New Town form a UNESCO World Heritage Site, which attracts millions of visitors from around the globe each year. Of the two parts of the World Heritage Site, the Old Town represents 'the most significant area of tourism activity in terms of attractions and speciality retailing' in Edinburgh.[15] Medieval history features prominently in the Old Town's heritage landscape: among its most visited sites are Edinburgh Castle and Holyrood Palace, which bookend the Old Town's main artery, the Royal Mile.[16] Half way up the Mile stands the High Kirk of St Giles, with its iconic crown spire. Despite considerable alterations in subsequent centuries, the Castle, Holyrood Palace and St Giles' are medieval in origin. All three sites rank highly on the list of the city's top heritage attractions with Edinburgh Castle, which is cared for by Historic Environment Scotland, consistently awarded first place across a wide range of heritage and tourism sites.[17]

The footfall of the Old Town's tourism falls predominantly on the Royal Mile, where the medieval and early modern stories told through heritage tourism largely centre on the lives of men and masculine themes of war and conflict. At Edinburgh Castle, statues of William Wallace and Robert the Bruce flank the entrance, while inside, 'Fight for the Castle', a permanent, immersive exhibition installed in 2018, which focuses on the Wars of Independence, reinforces the widely popularised notion of the middle ages as a period defined by conflict.[18] The military soundscape of clanging metal and dimmed lighting conveys a

[14] In 2022, *Time Out* voted Edinburgh the best city in the world to visit.
[15] Graham Parlett, John Fletcher and Chris Cooper, 'The Impact of Tourism on the Old Town of Edinburgh', *Tourism Management* 16, no. 5 (1995): 355–60.
[16] Though largely a seventeenth-century creation, Holyrood palace incorporates the ruins of the medieval abbey.
[17] In 2019, the number of the visitors to the castle peaked at 2.2 million, making it the most visited of Historic Environment Scotland's sites prior to the Covid-19 pandemic. 'Another Record-Breaking Year for Scottish Heritage Sites', Historic Environment Scotland, accessed 18 February 2023, https://www.historicenvironment.scot/about-us/news/another-record-breaking-year-for-scottish-heritage-sites/.
[18] 'New Exhibition Officially Opens at Edinburgh Castle', Historic Environment Scotland, last modified 15 November 2018, https://www.historicenvironment.scot/about-us/news/new-exhibition-officially-opens-at-edinburgh-castle/.

middle ages filled with darkness and drudgery. While a label accompanying an exhibition case containing a spindle whorl and other ordinary domestic items acknowledges that 'despite the turmoil, life went on for the women and men who lived and worked [in the castle]', no information is given on what those lives may have looked like. Thus, the overarching narrative of the exhibition, and indeed the castle more broadly, remains focused on the military endeavours of elite men. The literature that visitors take away with them also reinforces a male-dominated narrative. A survey of Edinburgh Castle guidebook, which was published as recently as 2014, revealed that in comparison to ninety-two named men, only thirteen named women appear in the text.[19] Men are also often refered to in places where there is no obvious need for them to be, whereas women, conversely, are absent in places where they warrant mention.[20]

The one early modern woman who does appear repeatedly in the Old Town's heritage narrative is Mary, Queen of Scots. Even her story, however, is often sensationalised and told in relation to the men around her. While Edinburgh Castle focuses on Mary's role as mother to James VI, elsewhere she is defined by her male contemporaries, particularly John Knox, whose statue stands outside St Giles' Cathedral, as well as her husband, Lord Darnley, and secretary, David Rizzio, whose infamous stabbing dominates the interpretation of the queen's private rooms at Holyrood Palace.

One of the most popular and commercially successful attractions on the Mile, the abovementioned Real Mary King's Close, makes some attempt to counter the Old Town's elite, male biases by telling the stories of ordinary men and women.[21] The attraction prides itself on telling 'authentic truths' about Edinburgh's hidden social history, as indicated by the use of 'real' in the title. The visitor experience blends a historical tour with costumed interpretation given by character guides, some of whom take on the personas of historical women, among them the attraction's namesake and seventeenth-century burgess and merchant, Mary King, Alison Rough and one of Mary King's daughters, who has been renamed 'Ash' for modern audiences.

A search of the near 19,000 reviews for the Real Mary King's Close on the popular reviewing website TripAdvisor using the terms 'woman/women' (seventy-seven results), 'female' (twenty-three results), 'Mary King'

---

[19] Dempsey et al., 'Beyond the Martial Façade', 357; Méline Potoczny, 'Report on the Representation of Women in Historic Environment Scotland's Guidebooks and Statements of Significance' (Unpublished report, Historic Environment Scotland, 2022). I am grateful to Dr Morvern French at Historic Environment Scotland for sharing this report with me.

[20] Potoczny, 'Report on the Representation of Women'.

[21] In February 2023, the Real Mary King's Close was ranked seventh out of 520 attractions in Edinburgh on TripAdvisor, with 18,915 reviews. 'The Real Mary King's Close, Edinburgh', TripAdvisor, accessed 13 February 2023, THE REAL MARY KING'S CLOSE (Edinburgh) – All You Need to Know BEFORE You Go (tripadvisor.co.uk).

(1,000 results), 'Alison (seven results)' and 'Alison Rough (0 results)' returned a number of reviews which commented specifically on the inclusion of women's history, mostly in a positive way.[22] While TripAdvisor reviews are by no means a comprehensive record of the visitor experience, the website is widely recognised as a valuable resource for visitor engagement with heritage tourism, particularly as it enables reviewers to co-construct their heritage experience through user-generated content. In turn, the easily searchable, open access reviews left by visitors then inform future visitors' expectations of those same places.[23]

The TripAdvisor reviews that comment on the inclusion of women's histories at the site in a positive light tend to characterise Mary King's achievements as remarkable and unexpected for a person of her gender and status. One visitor to The Real Mary King's Close from China in 2019 wrote: 'What interests me the most is how Mary King was so influential during her time that a Close was named after her. As a woman, this would have been an incredibly huge [sic] achievement during that time!'[24] Another visitor from the US commented that the tour guide 'did not spare any details and given the current heightened awareness around gender equality it was quite impressive to hear the story of how Mary King's Close was named and the remarkable women of the 17th Century'.[25] A UK visitor commented that 'it was nice to hear about the history of an ordinary woman rather than a royal or a well to do man'.[26]

The reviews were not unanimously positive, however. One reviewer complained that 'there is one story about a woman [Alison Rough] who could not marry her daughter, so she offered a fake dowry and then killed her husband when he asked for it. This has nothing to do with Mary King's close, so not sure why this is even presented.'[27] In actual fact, the murder took place on Craig's Close, which is one of the streets forming part of the attraction. The review also belies larger issues; namely that there is potential for misunderstanding and misinformation when interpretation relating to women's histories is only

---

[22] Search carried out on 13 February 2023, The Real Mary King's Close (Edinburgh) – All You Need to Know BEFORE You Go (tripadvisor.com).

[23] Laura Hodson, '"I expected … something": Imagination, Legend, and History in TripAdvisor Reviews of Tintagel Castle', *Journal of Heritage Tourism* 15, no. 4 (2020): 410–23, at 411–12.

[24] 'Mrshhs', Hong Kong, China, Tripadvisor, reviews: The Real Mary King's Close, review left 9 November 2018, https://www.tripadvisor.co.uk/Attraction_Review-g186525-d191321-Reviews-or10-The_Real_Mary_King_s_Close-Edinburgh_Scotland.html. Accessed 11 December 2022.

[25] 'Mdinonno', Marina del Rey, CA, Tripadvisor, Reviews: The Real Mary King's Close, Review left 7 July 2018, https://www.tripadvisor.co.uk/Attraction_Review-g186525-d191321-Reviews-or10-The_Real_Mary_King_s_Close-Edinburgh_Scotland.html.

[26] 'Samantha D', Chester, UK, Tripadvisor, Reviews: The Real Mary King's Close, Review left 19 August 2018, https://www.tripadvisor.co.uk/Attraction_Review-g186525-d191321-Reviews-or10-The_Real_Mary_King_s_Close-Edinburgh_Scotland.html.

[27] 'Tricia B' [no location given], Tripadvisor, Reviews: The Real Mary King's Close, Review left 15 August 2017, https://www.tripadvisor.co.uk/Attraction_Review-g186525-d191321-Reviews-or10-The_Real_Mary_King_s_Close-Edinburgh_Scotland.html.

communicated through temporary or ephemeral forms of interpretation, and also that women's stories are often challenged or deemed irrelevant in ways that are rarely the case for those of men. At Mary King's Close, Alison Rough's permanent legacy has also been erased, as in recent years, a display on Rough has been replaced by one on the better-known Mary, Queen of Scots.

Reflecting on the erasure and displacement of women's stories during her keynote at the 'Women and Materiality in Medieval and Early Modern Scotland' symposium, held in Edinburgh in 2018, Elizabeth Ewan argued that scholars and heritage professionals are constantly forced to reinvent the wheel when women's stories are only temporarily highlighted. For Ewan, school education is one important way in which women's stories might begin to become more fully integrated into permanent heritage interpretation: if children expect to see such stories from a young age, then they will be mindful of incorporating or asking for them when they work in or visit heritage sites as adults.[28] Having a central physical and/or digital space where such efforts are recorded, bookmarked and archived is another way in which the duplication of efforts might be prevented in future: indeed, Glasgow Women's Library is a prime example of a repository which preserves the stories of historical and contemporary women for future generations.[29] These wider, ongoing challenges thus provide important context for how the female narratives attached to Magdalen Chapel and Trinity Apse might be preserved and communicated going forward.

Magdalen Chapel and Trinity Apse

The case studies chosen for this study have been selected on the grounds that they are significant examples of medieval built heritage in Edinburgh's Old Town and World Heritage Site that were commissioned by women, yet they are currently neglected as part of Edinburgh's heritage offer. Both the sixteenth-century Magdalen Chapel on Cowgate and the fifteenth-century Trinity Apse on Chalmers Close have been designated as Category A listed buildings, meaning that they are of 'special architectural or historic interest' and 'outstanding examples of a particular period, style or building type'.[30] Both buildings are located within walking distance of the Royal Mile, making them two of only twenty-two pre-seventeenth century buildings in Edinburgh's Old

---

[28] For the day's discussions see Rachel M. Delman, 'Women and Materiality in Medieval and Early Modern Scotland Symposium Report', Women's History Network, https://womenshistorynetwork.org/women-and-materiality-in-medieval-and-early-modern-scotland-symposium-report/.

[29] Glasgow Women's Library, https://womenslibrary.org.uk/.

[30] 'What is a Listing? Categories of Listing', Historic Environment Scotland, https://www.historicenvironment.scot/advice-and-support/listing-scheduling-and-designations/listed-buildings/what-is-listing/#categories-of-listing_tab.

Town Conservation area.[31] As urban buildings with well-documented narratives centring on the lives of women, they hold unrivalled potential for telling the stories of late medieval women to locals and the millions of tourists who visit Edinburgh each year on their own terms, and for adding nuance to existing public perceptions concerning the lives and experiences of medieval women.

Magdalen Chapel stands at number 41 Cowgate, the street which connects Holyrood Road with the Grassmarket and runs parallel to the Royal Mile (Figure 4.1). Today, Cowgate is populated by nightclubs and is, along with the neighbouring Grassmarket, at the epicentre of Edinburgh's drink tourism industry. In the daytime areas of Cowgate can seem run-down and dark, in part because of a lack of daylight activity, and because the street is quite literally overshadowed by the nineteenth-century George IV Bridge above. In the evenings, it is an area of the city associated with anti-social behaviour and vandalism. Trinity Apse is likewise centrally yet awkwardly located. In its current incarnation, the Apse stands on Chalmers Close, which is one of the narrow alleyways linking the Royal Mile to the New Town, its fifteenth-century Gothic stonework juxtaposed against the backdrop of the Leonardo Royal Hotel, formerly Jury's Inn, which was built in the 1990s (Figure 4.2). Few tourists venture down Chalmers Close, which is one of the less picturesque alleyways of the Old Town.

A lack of visitor engagement with the two sites is evidenced in the low number of reviews left on TripAdvisor. For Trinity College Kirk (listed as Trinity College Church) there is only one review, while for Magdalen Chapel there are twenty-two.[32] Despite the paucity of reviews, those that do exist are valuable in that they are the only publicly available form of written evidence for visitor engagement with the two sites. The language used in them is also revealing: the single reviewer for Trinity describes the church as a 'hidden gem', which is 'tucked away'.[33] Four of the twenty-two reviews for Magdalen Chapel also use the phrase 'hidden gem' to describe the chapel. These reviewers thus show appreciation for the uniqueness and historical value of the two sites, but also recognise that the buildings (and their associated histories) are not readily signposted or displayed.

---

[31] 'Pre-1750 Buildings in Edinburgh Old Town Conservation Area', Edinburgh City Council, City Development Department, Pre 1750 Buildings In Edinburgh Old Town Conservation Area: Free Download, Borrow, and Streaming: Internet Archive, https://www.edinburgh.gov.uk/downloads/file/24351/pre-1750-buildings-in-edinburgh-old-town-conservation-area#:~:text=Surviving%2017th%20century%20ecclesiastical%20buildings,Surgeons'%20Hall%2C%20Drummond%20Street.

[32] Figures correct as of 17 February 2023. TripAdvisor, 'Trinity College Church', Accessed 17 February 2023, TRINITY COLLEGE CHURCH (Edinburgh) – All You Need to Know BEFORE You Go (tripadvisor.co.uk); TripAdvisor, 'Magdalen Chapel', Accessed February 17, 2023 Magdalen Chapel, Edinburgh (tripadvisor.co.uk).

[33] 'malc1005', Kettering, UK, Tripadvisor Reviews: Trinity College Church, Edinburgh, Review left 27 May 2021, TRINITY COLLEGE CHURCH (Edinburgh) – All You Need to Know BEFORE You Go (tripadvisor.co.uk).

Figure 4.1 Façade of the Magdalen Chapel, Cowgate, Edinburgh. © Rachel Delman

Figure 4.2 Trinity Apse (centre) and the Leonardo Royal Hotel, formerly Jury's Inn (left), Chalmers Close, Edinburgh. © Rachel Delman

Accessibility is a further barrier to visitor engagement with the two buildings. Following the lockdowns associated with the Covid-19 pandemic, Magdalen Chapel, which is now the headquarters of the Scottish Reformation Society, has been open on selected weekdays by appointment only. Prior to the pandemic, the building was open on three weekdays between 10 a.m. and 2 p.m., and otherwise by arrangement. A visitor from Texas in September 2022 expressed their disappointment at finding the chapel locked on the day they visited, while other TripAdvisor reviewers commented that they had found the chapel open by chance.[34] At present, Trinity Apse is closed to the public, and the future of the building remains uncertain. In the 1980s, the Apse housed the Edinburgh Brass Rubbing Centre, while, more recently, it has been used by Edinburgh City Council's Culture Service as an occasional venue for public events and festival activities. In October 2020, the Finance and Resources Committee approved a twenty-five-year lease to a prospective tenant seeking to create a whisky heritage centre experience for tourists, yet the tenant withdrew their interest due to uncertainty around the state of international travel resulting from the Covid-19 pandemic. In 2021, 'The Crafting Cartel Ltd', who applied for a ten-year lease with the intention of running the building as an open-plan multi-use destination incorporating a houseplant and homewares store, a coffee bar, crafting workshop and outdoor street food terrace, were the Council's preferred bidder, yet, at the time of writing approximately two years later, the building remains empty.[35]

Jonet Rynd and Magdalen Chapel

The sixteenth-century Magdalen chapel, which stands among more modern bars, nightclubs and student hostels, is the only tangible marker of Cowgate's past as a thriving hub of mercantile activity. By the sixteenth century many of Edinburgh's markets had relocated to Cowgate from the High Street, which was encompassed within the Flodden Wall from 1513.[36] Cattle and other livestock were stabled outside the West Port at the street's western end, while butter, cheese and wool were traded at the east end.[37]

---

[34] 'frankhoustonTexas', Tripadvisor, Reviews: Magdalen Chapel, Review left 14 October 2022, https://www.tripadvisor.co.uk/Attraction_Review-g186525-d213562-Reviews-Magdalen_Chapel-Edinburgh_Scotland.html.

[35] Finance and Resources Committee, 'Trinity Apse, Edinburgh – Proposed New Lease: Meeting Thursday 12th August 2021', https://democracy.edinburgh.gov.uk/documents/s35960/Item%208.9%20-%20Trinity%20Apse%20Edinburgh%20Proposed%20New%20Lease.pdf.

[36] Cathryn Spence, *Women, Credit and Debt in Early Modern Scotland* (Manchester: Manchester University Press, 2016), 16.

[37] Julie Franklin et al., 'The Development of Candlemaker Row, Edinburgh, from the 11th to the 20th Centuries: Excavations at Greyfriars Kirkhouse', *Scottish Archaeological Internet Reports* 71 (2017): 1–35, at 31.

The vibrancy and busyness of Cowgate in the sixteenth century made it the ideal location for a building project intended to celebrate the wealth, piety and status of an illustrious mercantile couple, who were key figures in Edinburgh's bustling urban community. In the 1530s, Edinburgh burgess and merchant Michael McQueen made plans to establish a chapel.[38] McQueen's poor health and death soon after, however, meant that he never set the plans for his project in motion. Instead, his widow Jonet Rynd (variously Janet Rhind), a successful businesswoman in her own right with her own trading booth in Edinburgh, brought the project to fruition.[39] Jonet did not passively carry out her husband's wishes, but made the project her own, adding a further £2000 Scots to the £700 Scots that Michael had invested in the foundation. She also added a hospital for the sustenance of a chaplain and seven poor men or bedesmen. The chapel was dedicated to Jesus, the Virgin Mary and St Mary Magdalen and was to serve both as a religious chapel and a guildhall for the Incorporation of Hammermen, an Edinburgh craft guild encompassing all those who worked metal with hammer. Jonet and Michael's connections to the Hammermen's guild are not readily apparent, although it is probable that Jonet, who herself was from a prominent Edinburgh family, among them a goldsmith, counted members of the guild among her relatives. At the very least, the couple's prominent standing within Edinburgh would have made them aware of the guild's activities and religious patronage. Jonet's support of the guild also appears to have been in part due to her desire to occupy a house on the nearby Niddry's Wynd, which she received (after protracted negotiations) in exchange for the guild's patronage of Magdalen Chapel during her widowhood.

Piety, fear of the afterlife and the desire for salvation were undoubtedly key factors influencing Michael's, and subsequently Jonet's, decision to establish Magdalen Chapel and hospital. In a deeply religious age, the creation of pious and charitable foundations such as chapels, almshouses and hospitals created living communities whose prayers for the dead were believed to help shorten the deceased's time in purgatory and thus quicken their route to heaven.[40] For Jonet, who was around fifty years old at the time of Michael's death, the foundation would have also helped cultivate an image of pious widowhood. The chaplain and bedesmen of the foundation were to dedicate their lives to praying to God for the salvation of the souls of Mary, Queen of Scots; Michael and Jonet; their fathers and mothers; all who had assisted them in the work; the patrons; the guild of Hammermen; and the souls of anyone from whom Jonet had received anything which she had not returned. The foundation charter, which dates to 1547 and comprises almost five thousand words, stipulates that

---

[38] Thomas Ross and G. Baldwin Brown, 'The Magdalen Chapel, Cowgate, Edinburgh', *The Book of the Old Edinburgh Club* 8 (1916): 1–78.
[39] For Jonet Rynd see, Mairi Cowan, *Death, Life, and Religious Change in Scottish Towns, c. 1350–1560* (Manchester: Manchester University Press, 2013), 139–44.
[40] Cowan, *Death, Life, and Religious Change*, 21.

the bedesmen were to be over sixty years old and were to exhibit punctuality when attending the chapel's twice-daily services. In the event that the members of the foundation failed to uphold its statutes, Jonet's natal family – notably not her marital family – were to be her beneficiaries.

Jonet's later years were dominated by the dispute with the Hammermen over the house in Niddry's Wynd, which stood only a short distance from her foundation. She eventually moved in during the final years of her life. Jonet died in 1553, and was buried in the chapel of her foundation, in a prominent position directly to the south of the main altar. Her gravestone, which is still in situ despite the much-altered fabric of the Magdalen Chapel, reads: 'Heir lyes ane honorabil woman Janet Rynd spous of umquhile Micel Maquhen burgess of Edin and founder of this place and decessit ye III day of Decr. An Dom M. VcLIII.'

Jonet's is the only marked tomb in the chapel, making it a rare survival and a fitting testament to her role as an energetic and determined patron. For medieval widows such as Jonet, whose lives were otherwise hidden behind or determined by those of their husbands, the location and design of funerary monuments provided an important means through which they expressed choice over how and where they wanted to be commemorated.[41] As the only marked tomb in the chapel, in the highest status position to the south of the altar, Jonet's tomb is a powerful statement of her own role in bringing the project to fruition, and of how she wished to be commemorated within her local community.

The continued use of the Magdalen Chapel as a meeting place into the present day makes for a busy aesthetic with multiple layers of post sixteenth-century history (Figure 4.3). The steeple was completed in the seventeenth century, along with much of the surviving fabric. Two walls are covered in panels recording gifts made by the Hammermen to the chapel up until the nineteenth century. Extant evidence of the chapel's earlier history takes the form of stained-glass roundels – the only examples of pre-Reformation glass surviving in situ in Scotland – featuring the arms of Mary of Guise, McQueen and McQueen impaling Rynd, and carved stone bosses representing the bedesmen of Jonet and Michael's original foundation.

Jonet's story is not absent from the current interpretation of the chapel, but details of her life are minimal, and her remarkable achievement is significantly downplayed. When the chapel is closed, a plaque on the wall directly to the left of the main entrance offers a summary of the building's history. Jonet's involvement in the project is briefly acknowledged, with the plaque describing how Michael planned the chapel, while Jonet built it (Figure 4.4).

Inside the chapel, Jonet's tomb is also difficult to locate as it is now covered by a raised slab, which is carpeted in the same colour as the main carpet,

---

[41] Barbara Harris, *Aristocratic Women and the Fabric of Piety, 1450–1550* (Amsterdam: Amsterdam University Press, 2018).

Figure 4.3 Interior of the Magdalen Chapel, facing south-east. © Rachel Delman

making it incongruous with the surroundings (Figure 4.5). A tiny paper sign located close to the ground reads:

> Beneath this carpet and raised stone is the burial place of Janet Rynd, wife of Michael MacQuhane who devised the plan of the chapel. He died before it was built, and Janet Rynd continued the project from 1537 to 1541.

In this instance, Jonet's role in devising the plan of the chapel is notably acknowledged, yet the phrase 'continued the project' reinforces the notion that she was merely fulfilling her husband's wishes, despite the fact that she personally made a significant financial investment in the project and added a hospital. At the very least, the interpretation of Jonet as the person responsible for devising the chapel is incongruous with the underwhelming curation of the site of her tomb, which could be easily missed by visitors. One local reviewer wrote on TripAdvisor that one of several ways in which the visitor experience could be improved would be by 'uncovering the tomb of Janet Rynd by removing the carpet and making that a bit more of a spectacle'.[42]

[42] 'Weekak', May 2021, https://www.tripadvisor.co.uk/Attraction_Review-g186525-d213562-Reviews-Magdalen_Chapel-Edinburgh_Scotland.html.

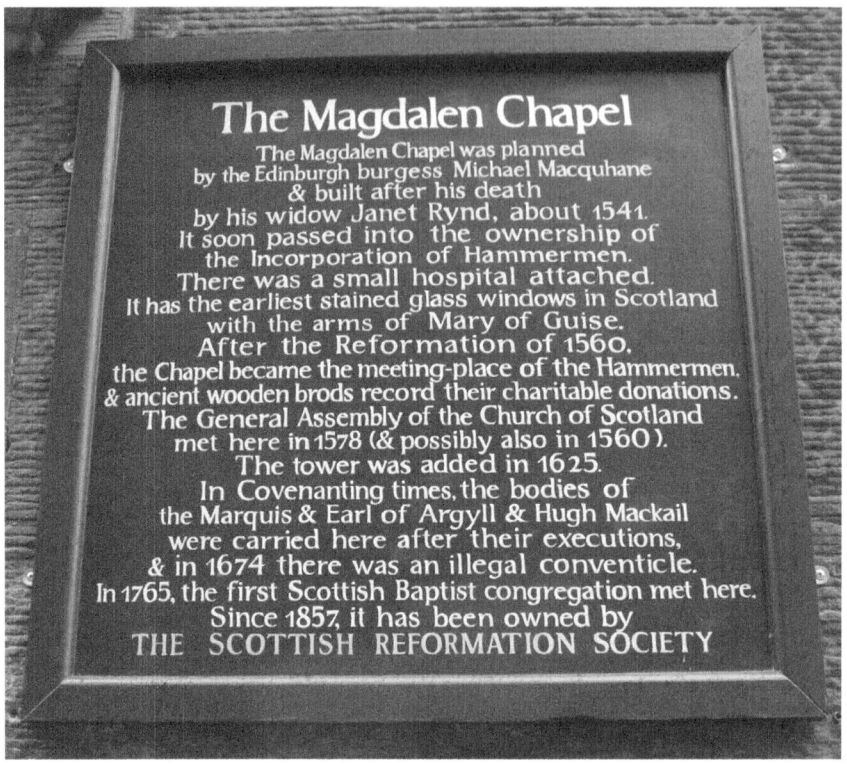

Figure 4.4 Plaque on the exterior of the Magdalen Chapel, Cowgate, Edinburgh.
© Rachel Delman

The remains of the tomb itself are by no means remarkable in stylistic terms, yet the fact that there is an identifiable, fixed location within the building that is associated with a named medieval woman patron offers considerable scope for telling the story of Jonet, and the historic neighbourhood in which she lived and operated. While the historic fabric of the building may not lend itself to the addition of fittings and fixtures, Jonet's tomb provides rare surviving in situ evidence of how and where a late medieval woman wished to be commemorated and therefore offers a tangible starting point for the implementation of interpretation, both static and ephemeral, exploring her life and context. More broadly, Jonet's tomb could provoke wider consideration of how belonging and exclusion have been expressed in the city of Edinburgh through a gendered lens, both historically and today. One way in which this might productively be achieved is through co-curated outputs involving multiple stakeholders, whereby the Scottish Reformation Society collaborates with medieval historians, heritage professionals, local residents, school groups, creatives, policy makers and other relevant parties to enhance knowledge of, and pride in, place.

Figure 4.5 Site of the tomb of Jonet Rynd in the Magdalen Chapel, with the small paper sign above. © Rachel Delman

Mary of Guelders and Trinity Apse

The building on Chalmers Close, now referred to as Trinity Apse, originally formed part of a larger collegiate church and hospital, which stood, until the nineteenth century, on the site now occupied by Waverley train station. When Waverley was built, the chapel was dismantled and the stones were numbered and placed on Regent Road, close to Calton Hill. Only the section of the chapel now known as Trinity Apse was rebuilt in the new location of Chalmers Close, however, where it stands juxtaposed against the Leonardo Royal Hotel.

Trinity Collegiate Church was founded in 1460 by Queen Mary of Guelders (d. 1463, variously Gueldres), who after the death of her husband, James II, commissioned the collegiate foundation and accompanying hospital as a familial and personal mausoleum on the outskirts of Edinburgh, in what was then St Ninian's suburb.[43] Like Michael McQueen and Jonet Rynd, Mary of Guelders's motivations for founding a chapel and hospital undoubtedly included the outward display of piety and concern for the afterlife. Mary's foundation was dedicated to 'the praise and honour of the Holy Trinity … the Virgin Mary, St Ninian the confessor (to whom Mary appears to have had an especial dedication and in whose suburb the foundation stood) and all saints'.[44] The buildings were to include a perpetual college, or collegiate church, for one provost, eight chaplains or prebendaries and two choristers. The hospital was larger than that attached to the Magdalen Chapel, being devised to house thirteen poor bedesmen who were dependent on Mary's charity. The chapel was also to be the queen's final resting place.

As well as being a tangible display of Mary's piety and concern for the afterlife, the foundation was a grand statement of the queen's role as the curator and custodian of familial and personal memory at a point when her husband's death was fresh in the Scottish political consciousness. As with Magdalen Chapel, the purpose of the perpetual chantry was to secure masses for the souls of the royal family, including Mary's deceased husband, James, his ancestors, Mary's natal ancestors from the ducal house of Guelders and for Mary herself. By making provisions for such prayers, Mary blended her natal and marital heritage to define her identity, much like Jonet, as a devoted daughter and widow. In Mary's case, her presentation of herself as a grieving, pious widow, as expressed through her foundation, also served an important political purpose, signalling her intention to remain unmarried and thus crystallising her identity as queen dowager in the process.

---

[43] See Rachel M. Delman, 'Mary of Guelders and the Architecture of Queenship in Fifteenth-Century Scotland', *SHR* 102, no. 2 (2023): 211–31.

[44] J. D. Marwick, ed. *Charters and Documents Relating to the Collegiate Church and Hospital of the Holy Trinity and the Trinity Hospital, Edinburgh*, AD *1460–1661* (SBRS, 1871).

Mary took a close personal interest in her foundation, reserving the right to make any amendments or additions to its rules and statutes whenever she pleased.[45] Jill Harrison argues that Mary's 'care for all aspects of its construction and provision make it a personal as well as a spiritual project and a visible sign of her queenship'.[46] Contemporary documents are authenticated with the queen's personal seal, and the prebendaries and bedesmen were expected to exhibit exemplary behaviour and to perform masses around the queen's tomb.[47]

Mary's choice to be buried within a foundation of her own making demonstrated that she had sufficient wealth and status to afford an impressive burial site. It also demonstrated personal choice and agency over where and how she and her family were to be remembered. Although only the apse, choir and transepts of Trinity collegiate church were completed during Mary's lifetime, the foundation was regarded as one of the finest examples of medieval Gothic architecture in Scotland.[48] The queen invested over £1000 in the project, and the tierceron vault, bosses and elaborate foliate carving which are still present today in the rebuilt section of the chapel on Chalmers' Close are indicative of a grand and impressive mausoleum. Within, the chapel was sumptuously furnished, containing images of the Trinity, the Virgin Mary, and saints Margaret and Catherine. Many of the vessels and vestments displayed the queen's arms.[49]

Today, the interior of Trinity Apse, unlike Magdalen Chapel, is sparsely decorated (Figure 4.6). Devoid of its original paintwork, the inside of the chapel comprises a single open space with tall, narrow windows and a high, tierceron-vaulted ceiling. Architectural features of note include an elaborately carved piscina (a stone basin used in Catholic churches for draining water during the Mass), which is set into the wall, as well as several gargoyles, a carved fifteenth-century fireplace believed to have been salvaged from a neighbouring property and the vaulted ceiling. At its upper end, the space is crudely divided by a modern, temporary screen, behind which is a storage space, modest kitchen facilities and a toilet. A large, cardboard replica of the Trinity Altarpiece, the original of which was commissioned for the chapel approximately a decade

---

[45] *Charters and Documents*.
[46] Jill Harrison, 'Fresh Perspectives on Hugo van der Goes' Portrait of Margaret of Denmark and the Trinity Altarpiece', *The Court Historian* 24, no. 2 (2019): 120–37, at 122.
[47] *Charters and Documents*. See also Helen Sarah Brown, 'Lay Piety in Later Medieval Lothian, c. 1306–c. 1513' (PhD diss., University of Edinburgh, 2007), 88.
[48] T. Rickman, *Essay on Ecclesiastical Architecture*, cited in Daniel Wilson, 'St Ninian's Suburb, and the Collegiate Church of the Holy Trinity, Founded at Edinburgh by Queen Mary of Gueldres, the Widow of James II, in 1462', *PSAS* 18 (1884): 128–70, at 138. The tower was never finished, giving the building a rather squat appearance, which can be seen in surviving nineteenth-century drawings and photographs.
[49] Brown, 'Lay Piety in Later Medieval Lothian', 89.

Figure 4.6 Interior of Trinity Apse, Edinburgh, in 2018, showing the temporary partition dividing the main space from the storage, toilet and kitchen facilities. © Rachel Delman

after Mary's death and is now housed in the National Gallery, stands propped against the wall. Outside, a small, overgrown courtyard garden contains several pieces of carved masonry that were once set into the fabric of the chapel. The outer walls of the Apse still bear the numbers that were etched into them when the chapel was dismantled during the nineteenth century.

As with Jonet Rynd's legacy at Magdalen Chapel, very little information is provided in the current interpretation about Mary's patronage of the chapel. An interpretation board attached to the (often locked) gates outside the Apse provides information on the history of the church, describing it as 'a medieval jigsaw puzzle', which was 'founded in 1460 by Mary of Gueldres in memory of her husband King James II' (Figure 4.7). Here again, although Mary is named as the founder of the chapel, the building works are said to have been carried out purely in her husband's memory, with no reference to her other motivations, or of the ways in which the foundation celebrated her own life and identity.

In response to a lack scholarly and local knowledge surrounding the existence and history of Trinity Apse and the associated story of Mary of Gueldres, in 2020, an interdisciplinary group of academics founded the 'Reviving the Trinity' network, with the aim of producing new content, events and information relating to the building and its associated history.[50] Since its inception, the network has hosted an online symposium, as well as a Heritage Open Day in May 2021, which was held at the Apse and attracted over sixty attendees. The event included a guided tour, as well as expert talks on Mary of Gueldres, the history of the Apse and related aspects of medieval history. Written and anecdotal feedback from attendees was overwhelmingly positive, with visitors requesting further events on the Apse and its history. Future plans include an edited volume based on the symposium proceedings, an Open Access article and a self-guided trail of stones that once belonged to other parts of the church but have since ended up in various museums, gardens, yards and other locations around Edinburgh. The developments mark important strides towards showcasing the foundation's history at a pivotal moment in the building's future, and the network has actively embedded itself within the local community to heighten awareness and produce outputs that are responsive to the interests and needs of those beyond academic institutions. The potential for revisionist, in-situ interpretation remains subject to the attitudes of the incoming leaseholders, and their level of interest in cooperating with members of the network to tell the Apse's story, yet the network's ongoing activities are key to creating an awareness of the building's significance beyond its mere architectural value, with the story of Mary of Gueldres central to those efforts.

---

[50] 'Reviving the Trinity' Network, https://blogs.ed.ac.uk/trinitynetwork/the-trinity-network-who-are-we/.

Figure 4.7 Information board on the main gate of Trinity Apse, Chalmers Close, Edinburgh. © Rachel Delman

Conclusions

This chapter has shown that Magdalen Chapel and Trinity Apse are unique examples of Edinburgh Old Town's built medieval heritage with considerable potential, not only for educating locals and visitors about the Old Town's medieval past but also for countering an otherwise androcentric urban narrative to create a more inclusive heritage offer. As rare surviving examples of built heritage commissioned by medieval women, the buildings offer a prime opportunity for telling the histories of women's contributions to the built environment of Edinburgh on their own terms. The revival and celebration of the stories of Jonet Rynd and Mary of Guelders at the two sites could make a substantive contribution to a feminist reclaiming of urban space, enabling a greater percentage of the population to see themselves represented in the built environment, and, by association, take greater pride in the heritage around them.

Through an exploration of the two case studies and the interpretation pertaining to medieval women's histories as presented at both Magdalen Chapel and Trinity Kirk, this chapter has advocated for a critical review of the current visitor interpretation, both in terms of the level of information provided on the two women and with respect to the nature of the content about them. More detailed information about the lives and patronage of Jonet and Mary, it has been argued, would prove particularly beneficial for illuminating the histories of the two sites, as would revisionist attention to how their stories are told. A reframing of the passive language in the current interpretation boards, which suggests that the women merely continued their husbands' projects solely in memory of them, would help elucidate the women's roles as active, innovative patrons who defined their own legacies through their patronage.

The discussion has raised suggestions but has purposefully not been prescriptive about preferred forms that outputs based on the two women's stories might take, which would be counterproductive when advocating for the need for co-produced heritage interpretation based on the findings of historical research. The involvement of multiple stakeholders, such as universities, heritage groups, schools, members of the local community and policy makers, would be beneficial for the preservation of both tangible and intangible heritage and meaning-making in relation to the two sites and their place within the urban landscape. A recent study of Gladstone's Land, another of the Royal Mile's key heritage attractions dating to the sixteenth century, for example, has shown that the involvement of local stakeholders in co-creating the heritage experience enabled the demand for an engaging visitor experience to be met, while also providing a soundboard for local identity.[51] In a similar vein, the Trinity Network has already made important strides in raising awareness around Mary of Guelders's foundation and its history through the engagement of academic researchers with members of the local community, connections which continue to grow and diversify.

In order for the stories of Jonet Rynd and Mary of Guelders to enter the public consciousness, the interpretation at the two sites also needs to be accessible

---

[51] Christina Louise Mijnheer and Jordan Robert Gamble, 'Value Co-creation at Heritage Visitor Attractions: A Case Study of Gladstone's Land', *Tourism Management Perspectives* (2019): 1–12.

both on and off site, particularly if the two buildings are to remain physically inaccessible most of the time. Digital methods and tools could be a useful way of providing remote access, as well as a means of stripping back the layers of modernity to suggest how the buildings might have appeared in the late medieval period. Encouraging increased visitor engagement through the implementation of revisionist interpretation at the Magdalen Chapel and Trinity Kirk, both of which stand in less visited yet centrally located parts of the Old Town, could additionally serve the practical function of spreading the tourist footfall beyond the Royal Mile, and in making the two sites destinations.

The cultivation of interdisciplinary, co-created research, which brings together the multiple stakeholders invested in the City of Edinburgh and invites them to play an active role in meaning-making, could therefore be transformative for the existing visitor experience at the two sites, and generate the income necessary to fund the resulting outputs. In order for the Magdalen Chapel and Trinity Kirk to be recognised as core heritage attractions, they also need to be better integrated into the Old Town's existing heritage offer. This could be achieved by contextualising the stories of Jonet Rynd and Mary of Guelders against those of better-known contemporary women, such as Mary, Queen of Scots, and by linking the sites to the other, more frequently visited medieval attractions in the Old Town. Until such steps are taken, however, Mary and Jonet, like many other medieval women, will wait patiently at the gate, ever ready to enter.

Part Two

Faith

FIVE

'She displays by her speeches': Marion Walker, Catholic Speech and Local Resistance in Early Modern Glasgow

Daniel MacLeod

Introduction

Recent generations of research on the Scottish Reformation have focused and re-focused our attention on the people at the heart of the religious change in the late sixteenth and early seventeenth centuries. While Michael Graham and Margo Todd's work revealed a greater attention to discipline and 'religion in the pew', other research has reassessed our interpretations of reformed leaders like John Knox, as well as his collaborators, the newly Reformed Scottish clergy.[1] This work has revealed numerous themes and entanglements that shaped the Reformation world profoundly. Like our lives, the lives of the Scottish people living in the period of the Reformation were shaped by a series of loyalties, devotions, ideas and habits that were influenced by their religious beliefs and coincided to form the direction of the Scottish Reformation. Among other phenomena, gender, town-life and speech, essential themes in the sparkling career of scholarship of Elizabeth Ewan, have come to be seen as critical considerations for achieving a fulsome analysis of the period. This chapter aims to further this analysis through examination of the case of Marion Walker, a Glasgow widow whose life demonstrates the nexus of gender, speech, Catholicism and resistance in the later decades of the sixteenth century and the first decades of the seventeenth.

After a brief discussion of the Catholic community in post-Reformation Glasgow and Walker's familial connections across the Reformation divide, the

---

[1] Michael Graham, *The Uses of Reform: 'Godly Discipline' and Popular Behavior in Scotland and Beyond, 1560–1610* (Leiden: Brill, 1996); Margo Todd, *The Culture of Protestantism in Early Modern Scotland* (New Haven: Yale University Press, 2002); Jane Dawson, *John Knox* (New Haven: Yale University Press, 2015); Chris R. Langley, Catherine E. McMillan and Russell Newton, eds, *The Clergy in Early Modern Scotland* (Woodbridge: Boydell and Brewer, 2021). See also Michelle Brock and Chris Langley's 'Mapping the Scottish Reformation: A Database of the Scottish Clergy, 1560–1689', http://mappingthescottishreformation.org.

chapter interrogates Walker's presence in the disciplinary records of the Scottish Kirk. Here, Walker's resistance to the ministry and the larger structures of the reformed kirk demonstrates the roles speech played in refining resistance in early modern Glasgow. More specifically, Walker's case exemplifies the utility of adding Catholic speech to the analytical tools historians can apply to early modern Scotland. Her speech helps historians approach recusancy, anticlericalism and the material culture of Catholic survival with more precision by nuancing our understanding of these phenomena and adding complexity to the lives of Catholics in Protestant Scotland. In doing so, Marion Walker's life is simultaneously evidence of the nature of Catholic resistance in Glasgow and a challenge to understand it more fully by listening more carefully to its voices in the records and how these voices mingle with other aspects of Catholic survival. Following Ewan's lead, this chapter hopes to demonstrate the continued value of seeking out women's voices to improve our understanding of the Scottish past. Walker's life shows how these under-studied cases provide historians with new paths of inquiry that converge and diverge with many fields of history and approaches to the past. In this way, research on Marion Walker's life reveals Catholic women's voices to be essential in telling the Reformation story in Scotland.

Those familiar with the trial of the Scottish Jesuit John Ogilvie, who was executed in Glasgow in 1615, may already know something of Marion Walker.[2] In the documents from Ogilvie's trial, Walker features prominently as an enabler of his mission.[3] She is the only woman mentioned within the so-called 'Depositions of the Papists' collected during his trial, where she is recorded as having hosted masses and religious debates at her home in the period before Ogilvie's arrest.[4] Each deposition notes that a mass occurred 'in Marion

---

[2] Basic biographical details on Walker can be found in Daniel MacLeod, 'Marion Walker' in *The New Biographical Dictionary of Scottish Women*, ed. Elizabeth Ewan et al. (Edinburgh: Edinburgh University Press, 2018), 443.

[3] A copy of the 1615 Douai printing of Ogilvie's prison writing (*Relatio*) and testimony from his fellow prisoners (*Continuatio*) is held at the National Library of Scotland (BCL.S165). It is printed in William James Duncan, ed., *Miscellaneous Papers Principally Illustrative of Events in the Reigns of Queen Mary and King James VI* (Glasgow: Edward Khul, 1834), 79–108. The crown's perspective can be found in John Spottiswoode, 'A True Relation of the Proceedings Against John Ogilvie, A Jesuit', in Robert Pitcairn ed. *Ancient Criminal Trials of Scotland*, vol. 3, part 1 (Edinburgh: Bannatyne Club, 1833), 350–4. The trial documents are compiled in William E. Brown, *John Ogilvie: An Account of His Life and Death with a Translation of the Documents Relating Thereto* (London: Burns Oates and Washbourne, 1925), 171–201, as well as in William Forbes-Leith, ed., *Narratives of Scottish Catholics under Mary Stuart and James VI* (Edinburgh: Paterson, 1889), 297–316.

[4] Much more work is needed on those who collaborated with the Jesuit mission to Scotland, especially the role of women. On the Jesuits, see Michael Yellowlees, *'So Strange a Monster as a Jesuite': The Society of Jesus in Sixteenth-century Scotland* (Argyle: House of Lochar, 2003), 191. For Jesuits and women, see Gemma Simmonds, 'Women Jesuits?', in *Cambridge Companion to the Jesuits*, ed. Thomas Worcester (Cambridge: Cambridge University Press, 2008), 120–35; Lisa

Walker's house' or 'in the house of Marion Walker' and her home was clearly a muster-point for Ogilvie's mission. In subsequent analyses she is nearly always mentioned among Ogilvie's associates in Glasgow.[5]

Indeed it is difficult to hear the story of John Ogilvie without hearing the name Marion Walker. But it is correspondingly difficult to hear much of substance about Walker herself. In some descriptions she reaches near martyr status due to her death shortly after Ogilvie's while under house arrest in Glasgow for her associations with him.[6] In others, she is included among the collection of obstinate Catholics associated with Ogilvie. Overall, the dearth of analysis of Marion Walker leaves the impression that we might associate her with what one historian describes as the 'quiet, domestic, and reflective' faith among women in Catholic-minority communities.[7]

These perspectives would misrepresent Marion Walker, however, as Walker was not a meek, reserved woman tidying up for John Ogilvie. She was an active and consistent resistor of the newly established religion in Glasgow. In fact, her presence elsewhere in the records helps re-contextualise Walker's role in Ogilvie's case and re-presents her as a woman who ties together many of the themes of Catholic resistance that we find in other analyses.

Glasgow's Catholic community

Paul Goatman and John Durkan have helped unpacked kinship relationships among Catholics in early modern Glasgow.[8] Scott Spurlock has documented similar patterns elsewhere in Scotland, as these networks facilitated continued Catholicism in specific, if limited, circumstances.[9] This work shows that tolerance for Catholicism was subject to a changing political climate or interest from the crown and that it sometimes served to consolidate the power of

---

McClain, 'On a Mission: Priests, Jesuits, "Jesuitresses," and Catholic Missionary Efforts in Tudor-Stuart England', *Catholic Historical Review* 101, no. 3 (2015): 437–62; Olwen Hufton, 'Altruism and Reciprocity: The Early Jesuits and their Female Patrons', *Renaissance Studies* 15, no. 3 (2001): 328–53.

[5] John Durkan, 'John Ogilvie's Glasgow Associate', *IR* 21, no. 2 (Autumn 1970): 153–70.

[6] Thomas Collins, *Martyr in Scotland: The Life and Times of John Ogilvie* (New York: Macmillan, 1955), 227. The 'Scottish Martyr's Committee' investigated a potential cause for sainthood for Walker. It is referenced in a 1923 'Circular Letter' from the Scottish Catholic hierarchy, a copy of which can be found in the NLS (APS.2.78.23) among materials related to Ogilvie's cause.

[7] Michael Mullett, *The Catholic Reformation* (New York: Routledge, 1999), 175–6.

[8] Durkan, 'John Ogilvie's Glasgow Associates'; Paul Goatman, 'Exemplary Deterrent or Theatre of Martyrdom?: John Ogilvie's Execution and the Community of Glasgow', *Journal of Jesuit Studies* 7, no. 1 (2020): 47–66.

[9] R. Scott Spurlock, 'The Laity and the Structure of the Catholic Church in Early Modern Scotland', in *Insular Christianity: Alternative Models of the Church in Britain and Ireland c. 1570–c. 1700*, eds Robert Armstrong and Tadhg O'Hannrachain (Manchester: Manchester University Press, 2013), 231–51, and Spurlock, '"I do disdain both Ecclesiasticke": Lay Catholic Identity in Early Modern Scotland', *Records of the Scottish Church History Society* 38 (2008): 5–22.

local Catholic magnates.¹⁰ It has nuanced traditional interpretations suggesting that Scottish Catholics depended on networks facilitated by the Scots colleges or continental Catholicism, and instead stresses Catholic survival as a more domestic phenomenon influenced by the political risk/reward relationships affecting Catholic allegiances after 1560.¹¹ Goatman makes this point particularly for Glasgow, noting that continued Catholic presence among the town's power brokers was connected to broader national interests.¹² Still, religious survival in this climate as a member of a minority religion was complicated, and maintenance of key elements of Catholic life such as the sacraments was severely threatened by the absence of the clergy and hierarchy.

Other research shows a high degree of integration within the local Catholic web in Glasgow.¹³ This community included Marion Walker's late husband John Mure and her son Archibald Mure who went on to marry another prominent Catholic in the town with connections to Ogilvie's trial. Walker's associations with Glasgow's Catholic community were not, however, limited to the early decades of the seventeenth century. Her kin relationships took her directly to the Catholic hierarchy at the time of the Reformation parliament, enabling her to transcend traditional gender roles at the local level. Her father, William Walker, was the chamberlain for James Beaton II, Archbishop of Glasgow at the time of the change, and William was responsible for managing Beaton's affairs after the archbishop departed for France in 1560.¹⁴ In William Walker's correspondence with Beaton we see a devoted servant trying to manage changing and difficult circumstances in the town. The correspondence reveals the beginnings of a post-Reformation Catholic Church's interaction with the lay community tasked with operating and leading a clerical church without the clergy. One letter to Beaton is telling in its account of the context around Marion Walker's Catholic network. In the 1569 letter William Walker tells his boss that the bishop's lands were being redistributed among the townspeople by the provost and baillies of Glasgow. Walker writes that he had argued with the authorities on the bishop's behalf, and he had insisted they had no legal right to the lands. Ultimately, he argued without success, but there is little doubt as to Walker's devotion to Beaton. Disappointed in his ability to effect change on behalf of the bishop and no doubt suffering some workplace-related stress, Walker wrote to Beaton that his anxieties were now 'known outwardly

---

¹⁰ Paul Goatman, 'Religious Tolerance and Intolerance in Jacobean Scotland: The Case of Archibald Hegate Revisited', *IR* 67, no. 2 (2016): 159–81.
¹¹ On the Scots Colleges, see Tom McInally, *The Sixth Scottish University: The Scots Colleges Abroad, 1575 to 1799* (Leiden: Brill, 2012).
¹² Goatman, 'Exemplary Deterrent or Theatre of Martyrdom?', 51–8.
¹³ Goatman, 'Exemplary Deterrent or Theatre of Martyrdom?' See also, Daniel MacLeod, 'Servants to St Mungo' (PhD diss., University of Guelph, 2014).
¹⁴ Collins, *Martyr in Scotland*, 78.

by the changing of the colors of my hair, which was black and now is white'.[15] So it is in this context that Marion Walker was raised and in which Glasgow's recusant Catholic community was formed – with a hierarchy exiled to the continent, a layman tasked with the business of the dismantling of the Catholic infrastructure of the town, and the remaining Catholic community charged with carving out space for itself amidst a newly hostile framework.

Marion Walker and John Cooper

Yet, just as we are wise to avoid focusing merely on Marion Walker's association with John Ogilvie, so too is it instructive to move beyond her familial links to fully demonstrate her place in post-Reformation Catholic Glasgow. Walker's emergence as a public nuisance in her own right coincides with the minister John Cooper's time as the second minister in the town, which began in 1587.[16] By the later 1590s he and Walker were in regular conflict, which was not uncommon for Cooper.[17] His acrimonious leadership was characterised by his thin skin, which resulted in his calling detractors before the session and presbytery for insulting him in person or in writing. In 1594, Cooper brought Walter and William Bowie before the presbytery for blaming him for their wife and mother's death.[18] In 1599, two men were brought before the burgh court for posting a piece of writing on the minister's gate containing 'blasphemous, vile and menacing words'. They were fined and made to promise not to repeat their crime.[19] Another case saw parishioners upset that Cooper denied them the sacraments, particularly baptism, because they refused to receive them in the Blackfriars church, preferring the cathedral. The dispute culminated in a man raising a sword to Cooper and snatching an infant out his hands at a baptismal ceremony because the minister refused to baptise children from outside the parish.[20] These cases and others testify to relatively consistent complaints in Glasgow against both Cooper and the larger ministry, whom in the year before Cooper's arrival one Glasgow man called 'wreckers and demolishers of the kirk.'[21]

---

[15] 'Letter from William Walker to the Archbishop of Glasgow', in Duncan, ed., *Miscellaneous Papers*, 23.

[16] NRS, Glasgow Kirk Session Records, CH2/550/1/175.

[17] More work is needed on Cooper's time in Glasgow, but biographical material can be found in Duncan Shaw 'Cowper, John (d. 1603), Church of Scotland minister', *ODNB*.

[18] NRS, Glasgow Presbytery Records, CH2/171/31, 212-19, 229.

[19] J. D. Marwick, ed., *Extracts from the Records of the Burgh of Glasgow, 1573-1642*, 2 vols (Glasgow: SBRS, 1914), I:200-1.

[20] See Daniel MacLeod, 'Their Own Parish Kirk: Sacramental Spaces and Jurisdictional Jealousy in Early Modern Glasgow', in *Where Mortal and Immortal Meet: Essays in Celebration of the 85th Anniversary of the Society of Friends of Glasgow Cathedral*, ed. Andrew G. Ralston (Eugene: Wipf and Stock, 2021), 182-97.

[21] NRS, Glasgow Kirk Session Records, CH2/550/1/101.

It is in conflict with Cooper that we see Marion Walker's most consistent appearance in the records. The initial strife surrounded the trial and execution of Margaret Aiken, the 'Great Witch of Balwearie'. Aiken was arrested for witchcraft in Fife in 1597 and in order to avoid her execution convinced some ministers, most notably Cooper, that she could detect witches by looking into their eyes.[22] Excited by this, Cooper engaged in a three-month commission seeking out witches 'especially at Glasgow' and several were condemned and burnt.[23] Over time, however, Aiken's methods were exposed as fraudulent. As Spottiswoode put it: 'In [the] end she was found to be a mere deceiver (for the same persons on the one day she had declared guilty, the next day in another habit she cleansed).' Aiken admitted her deception and was executed, and Spottiswoode notes that 'the credulity of the minister (Cooper)' was thought to have contributed to the 'great forwardness' in the execution of witches.[24] In all, Cooper's handling of the Aiken case contributed to what Julian Goodare has called the 'Scottish witchcraft panic of 1597' and further tarnished Cooper's reputation in the town.[25]

Marion Walker's involvement with the case began in October of 1597 when she and several others were brought before the presbytery as part of an effort to discover the original version of Aiken's confession, copies of which had been circulating in Glasgow.[26] As ever, Cooper was upset because the confession 'tended to (his) reproach'. Although the confession itself has not survived, its circulation was enough to motivate an 'Act Against Slanderers of the Ministry of Glasgow' from the Glasgow Presbytery in November of 1597 that threatened the branks and other punishments for any who claimed 'the ministry of the said city as the author of putting to death the persons lately executed for witchcraft.'[27] Here we see the kirk's preoccupation with controlling speech. This preoccupation was held in common with civil courts and which Ewan, Todd and others have shown was both tied to preservation of an individual's reputation within the town, and also associated with gender and witchcraft in that even unproven and disproven accusations of witchcraft had lasting effects on the accused.[28]

---

[22] A narrative of Aiken's story can be found in John Spottiswoode, *History of the Church of Scotland*, ed. M. Russell, 3 vols (Edinburgh: Spottiswoode Society, 1847–51), III:66–7.

[23] Spottiswoode, *History of the Church of Scotland*, 67.

[24] Spottiswoode, *History of the Church of Scotland*, 67.

[25] Julian Goodare, 'The Scottish Witchcraft Panic of 1597', in *The Scottish Witch-Hunt in Context*, ed. Julian Goodare (Manchester: Manchester University Press, 2002), 51–72.

[26] NRS, Glasgow Presbytery Records, CH2/171/32B, 178.

[27] NRS, Glasgow Presbytery Records, CH2/171/33, 122–3.

[28] Elizabeth Ewan, '"Many Injurious Words": Defamation and Gender in Late Medieval Scotland', in *History, Literature and Music in Scotland, 700–1560*, ed. R. A. McDonald (Toronto: University of Toronto Press, 2002), 163–86; Todd, *Culture of Protestantism*, 244–9. See also John Harrison, 'Women and the Branks in Stirling, c. 1600 to c. 1730', *Scottish Economic and Social History* 18,

Walker refused to give testimony in the case that attempted to uncover the original source of Aiken's confession, of which she had a copy. Ultimately, the presbytery threatened her with excommunication, a threat commonly made against men charged with the same violation. As the time of her excommunication neared she again refused to acknowledge her slander or provide further information on the writings that were 'blasphemously used to the slander of Mr. John'.[29] Walker's boldness in this case is notable. Her refusal to capitulate, in combination with her familial connections, her possession of the confession, and the frequency with which she criticised the clergy, indicate the status held by Marion Walker, at least locally in Glasgow. In this way, she expands our understanding of the roles played in Scotland by Catholic women who would be doubly marginalised in the years after the Reformation.[30] Although Alasdair Roberts was correct in noting the key place of noblewomen in Catholic survival, Walker's role in the Aiken case, even though it did not explicitly involve preservation of Catholicism, provides a different face for Catholicism in early modern Scotland.[31] Here, a Catholic woman directly confronts local church authorities and stares them down when threatened with a significant punishment. It may be easy to sideline Walker's Catholicity in the Aiken case, but it is essential to understanding her attitudes toward the clergy, the new kirk, and her perceptions of this kirk's authority to punish her speech. In this sense, all of Marion Walker's speech is Catholic speech and the criticisms she directs toward the clergy can be understood as part of a broader effort of Catholic survival in the town as well as the mettle Margaret Sanderson associated with Scottish recusant women.[32]

Walker and anticlericalism

Walker's criticisms of Cooper display aspects of 'soft anticlericalism' described by Robert Swanson in his assessment of anticlericalism in the medieval world.[33] For Swanson, criticisms of the clergy were often targeted at a particular member or group of clergymen and did not always produce a larger movement that coheres into an identifiable pattern. Walker conformed to this more restricted

---

no. 2 (1998): 114–31; Sierra Dye, 'To Converse with the Devil? Speech, Sexuality, and Witchcraft in Early Modern Scotland', *IRSS* 37 (2012): 9–40.

[29] NRS, Glasgow Presbytery Records CH2/171/32B, 211–12.

[30] Additional insight into Scottish Catholic laywomen can be found in Ryan Burns, 'Gender, Resistance and Conformity in Early Modern Scotland, 1560–1650', *IRSS* 44 (2020): 57–84.

[31] Alasdair Roberts, 'The Role of Women in Scottish Catholic Survival', *SHR* 70, no. 190, part 2 (October 1991): 129–50.

[32] Margaret H. B. Sanderson, 'Catholic Recusancy in Scotland in the Sixteenth Century', *IR* 21 (Autumn, 1970): 87–107, at 100.

[33] Robert Swanson, 'Medieval Anticlericalism: Terms and conditions', *History of Religions* 61, no. 1 (2021): 6–29, at 13–15.

pattern and confirmed her 'soft anticlericalism' in noting that the explicit target of her angst was Cooper rather than the ministry more generally. In 1599 she was accused of missing the communion in Glasgow and of being a 'railer against the ministry'.[34] Walker insisted she had attended the communion and denied the charges against her. She told the presbytery that she had only 'spoken against them that had done wrong to her', clearly indicating to both Cooper and the larger ministry the focus of her criticisms.[35] In a likely recognition of Cooper's failings and combative nature, the presbytery offered Walker a chance to air her grievances. The other two ministers in the town, David Wemyss and John Bell, offered to meet with Walker after Sunday service to discuss 'any grief she has conceived in her mind against any of the ministry.' The results of that meeting surely legitimised her claims against Cooper as the presbytery's discipline for Walker was a basic warning not to rail against the ministry in the future.[36]

The particular focus of Walker's criticisms of Cooper provides insight into the role of anticlericalism in the Scottish Reformation, a reality that requires much more attention in the historiography. In research on the phenomenon in the eighteenth and nineteenth centuries, Callum Brown notes that the nature of Scottish presbyterianism meant that 'anticlericalism did not, perhaps could not, enter the country's heart'.[37] This may be so, but even if it failed to enter the country's heart, it certainly entered the hearts of some of its people in the Reformation era. The session records are littered with people spending time on the stool of repentance for insulting the clergy. Part of the problem for historians, of course, is the myriad ways in which anticlericalism has been used by historians and non-historians alike. In 1994, Heiko Oberman's broad definition of the term provided us with numerous points of entry for the concept and significant loci for inquiry, but little in terms of a clear and direct path toward finding anticlericalism in the records.[38] Swanson recently built on this work noting the difficulty of gaining purchase on the concept at all, stating that anticlerical behaviours do not always 'congeal into an "ism"', thereby necessitating constant clarification of the 'terms of use', which might ultimately reduce the term's usefulness.[39] Yet these precautions do not and cannot erase the term's place amidst the terminology of the study of the Reformation, so its continued use must entail refinement and contextualisation.

---

[34] NRS, Glasgow Presbytery Records, CH2/171/33, 122.
[35] NRS, Glasgow Presbytery Records, CH2/171/33, 122–3.
[36] NRS, Glasgow Presbytery Records, CH2/171/33, 123.
[37] Callum G. Brown, 'Rotavating the Kailyard: Re-imagining the Scottish "Meenister" in Discourse and the Parish State Since 1707', in *Anticlericalism in Britain, c. 1500–1914*, eds Nigel Aston and Matthew Cragoe (Stroud: Sutton, 2001), 138–58, at 155.
[38] Heiko Oberman, 'Anticlericalism as an Agent of Change', in *Anticlericalism in Late Medieval and Early Modern Europe*, eds Peter A. Dykema and Heiko Oberman (Leiden: Brill, 1994), ix–xi.
[39] Swanson, 'Medieval Anticlericalism', 28.

For Scotland, a recent essay by Chris Langley is the first to tackle the subject of anticlericalism in the early modern period.[40] His study of parish visitation records demonstrates that the deep integration of the ministry in their parishes meant that the reformed clergy were rarely criticised in the same fashion as were their medieval counterparts for absenteeism or failure to integrate into parish communities. Complaints made against ministers ultimately mimicked the mechanisms of the visitation, demonstrating the empowerment of the laity to control and assess the behaviour of the clergy. Although complaints were still made against the ministry, which was natural enough considering the ministers' disciplinary responsibilities, Langley shows that the angriest vitriol was reserved for those who intruded into local affairs from the level of the presbytery or synod. He concludes, in line with Margo Todd, that 'there was no general anticlericalist movement in early modern Scotland'.[41]

Though a national campaign of anticlericalism may have been absent, complaints from the likes of Marion Walker and others show evidence of dissatisfaction with the clergy. These complaints are worthy of historians' attention, and their failure to coalesce into the same patterns of complaint we see targeted at the medieval Catholic clergy are more likely evidence of the changing nature of anticlerical language and behaviour than the absence of anticlericalism altogether. Irrespective of what we call them, studying these complaints can provide fruitful paths of inquiry, as Langley's work has shown. They can tell us a great deal about what people expected from the clergy as well as the specialised function of the clergy in a new religious context. Among Marion Walker and her Catholic community in Glasgow, the Catholic clergy would play a much different role than its Protestant counterpart. As Swanson has noted, 'the absolute centrality of priesthood to the salvational system' of Catholicism was important for anticlerical behaviours.[42] This is, of course, why Marion Walker was harboring John Ogilvie and hosting secret masses in her home and why she and her community were sneaking him around town. The reformed communion was relatively easily accessible in Glasgow, but these Catholics desired a different kind of communion that could only be provided by a Catholic priest. This is not to say that the reformed kirk did not value the sacraments. The fracas at the baptism discussed above shows the centrality of the new sacramental system.[43] But complaining parishioners complained differently, and about different phenomena, as beliefs changed. Walker's complaints help us identify these changes and sharpen our lens in the process.

---

[40] Chris Langley, 'Anticlericalism in Early Modern Scotland?', in *The Clergy in Early Modern Scotland*, 89–107.
[41] Langley, 'Anticlericalism', 106; Todd, *Culture of Protestantism*, 375.
[42] Swanson, 'Medieval Anticlericalism', 21.
[43] Further discussion of the changing nature of sacraments can be found in MacLeod, 'Their Own Parish Kirk', 189–94.

Catholic speech

A final case documenting Marion Walker's conflicts with kirk authorities further supports the value of considering Catholic aspects of anticlericalism. Although not as lengthy or prominent as her other encounters with kirk authorities, Walker's March 1604 appearance before the presbytery provides a brief but remarkable insight into Catholic life in the period and Walker's role in maintaining it in Glasgow through a marriage of word, object and deed. This explicit joining of the three occurred when Walker appeared before the presbytery because a crucifix was found in her home. Walker admitted that the object was hers, told the presbytery where she had bought the crucifix and stated that she would have purchased more of them if she 'had the silver'.[44] The case ends with the presbytery removing the crucifix from her home and destroying it because, the entry notes, 'it is an idol to the said Marion, which she displays by her speeches'.[45] The presbytery's comment is striking for the degree to which it explicitly notes Walker's speech as an aggravating factor for her transgression. Her words had a profound influence on the problem she faced, as possessing a crucifix was simply a different problem than possessing an idol.

The relationship between the speech and the object as stated in this case is fascinating for several reasons. First, it draws us to the close eye the sessions and the presbytery kept on the circulation of Catholic materials in the early decades of reformed Scotland. Townspeople in Glasgow routinely found themselves called before the presbytery for possession of Catholic objects or iconography. One man was ordered to stop painting pictures of God and the crucifix in people's homes.[46] Another was made to endure an examination of his doctrine because he was found in possession of 'an old papist book', Archbishop Hamilton's catechism.[47] Another found himself disciplined by the presbytery for selling 'erroneous books', among them *The Golden Legend* and a catechism written by Nicol Burne.[48] Other Catholic materials were found in the home of Margaret Mure, who was called before Glasgow's kirk session in February of 1592.[49] Mure not only had Catholic books in her loft, but also chrism oil, two stolls, images of the Virgin Mary and infant Jesus, mass cloths, mass books and a priest's hat. Mure said she had received the items from her dead husband, George Herbertson, but the session was suspicious and questioned her as to

---

[44] NRS, Glasgow Presbytery Records, CH2/171/1/3/267.
[45] NRS, Glasgow Presbytery Records, CH2/171/1/3/267.
[46] NRS, Glasgow Presbytery Records, CH2/171/32B, 167.
[47] NRS, Glasgow Presbytery Records, 198; Alastair Mann has noted the increased presence of Catholic books in Scotland as counter-Reformation activities increased on the continent in the seventeenth century. Mann, *The Scottish Book Trade: Print Commerce and Print Control in Early Modern Scotland* (East Lothian: Tuckwell Press, 2000), 169.
[48] NRS, Glasgow Presbytery Records, CH2/171/33, 119.
[49] NRS, Glasgow Kirk Session Records, CH2/550/1, 377–8.

whether she 'passed secretly to her loft to pray', a charge she denied.[50] The session instructed her to burn the material publicly at Glasgow Cross. In this case, as in Walker's, the criticism of the object was intimately tied to the intentions of the user and not merely to the object itself.

Speech's capacity to clarify the context of the material objects of the Reformation is also important for assessing the nature and degree of religious change in Glasgow and nearly everywhere in Reformation Europe. Here, the broader historiography of Reformations is helpful in situating the Scottish case. The material culture of churches carried obvious practical and theological implications. Alexandra Walsham's work on material survivals in England demonstrates what she calls 'recycling the sacred' amidst the changing religious landscape of the period.[51] Here desacralisations or re-use of church furnishings and objects help us locate ideas that underpinned religious change, whether these were related to iconoclasm, sacrilege or the larger theological ideas of the Reformation.[52] As ever, regional differences complicated the relationships between Christians and the materials their churches created. Luther's notions about *adiaphora* or the spiritual indifference of the objects themselves met with other Reformation ideas about 'superstition' and 'idolatry' to create a variety of complex settlements where some objects and churches were worthy of saving or re-purposing and others were deemed a bridge too far.[53] Even Lutheran commitment to indifference was subject to change as Lutherans attempted to distinguish themselves from reformed Christians who took a harder line against surviving Catholic material culture.[54] Amidst the variations of local Reformations, it remained the interactions among religious people and material culture, however, that determined their larger significance. As Walsham notes, 'human and object histories are inextricably intertwined'.[55] These interactions also feature prominently in the groundbreaking work on sacred spaces by Andrew Spicer, which has focused largely and church buildings in Scotland

---

[50] NRS, Glasgow Kirk Session, 378.
[51] Alexandra Walsham, 'Recycling the Sacred: Material Culture and Cultural Memory after the English Reformation', *Church History* 86, no. 4 (2017): 1121–54; Alexandra Walsham, 'Domesticating the Reformation: Material Culture, Memory, and Confessional Identity in Early Modern England', *Renaissance Quarterly* 69, no. 2 (2016): 566–616.
[52] On iconoclasm in Scotland, see David McRoberts, 'Material Destruction Caused by the Scottish Reformation', in *Essays on the Scottish Reformation, 1513–1625*, ed. David McRoberts (Glasgow: Burns, 1962), 415–62.
[53] On adiaphora, see Andrew Spicer, 'Adiaphora, Luther and the Material Culture of Worship', *Studies in Church History* 56 (2020): 246–72; Caroline Walker Bynum, '"Are Things Indifferent"? How Objects Change our Understanding of Religious History', *German History* 34, no. 1 (2016): 88–112.
[54] Spicer, 'Adiaphora, Luther and the Material Culture of Worship', 266–72.
[55] Walsham, 'Recycling the Sacred', 1124.

and in a comparative context.[56] Some of Spicer's recent work on adaptation has demonstrated how the preservation of churches and their material reorganisation were part of an effort toward rendering services and buildings as accessible as possible, responding to both increased attendance requirements and the preoccupation with preaching in reformed Scotland.[57] According to Spicer, re-casting of both church buildings and the larger parish structures remained unevenly executed, however, and subject to interactions with townspeople, with some communities relying on their medieval places of worship and others engaging in building campaigns that responded to the moment.[58]

The dynamics between people and objects in the study of sacred space are instructive for unpacking how Marion Walker's words clarified her use of the idol and asserted her Catholicity. Late sixteenth- and early seventeenth-century Scotland was awash in reminders of its Catholic past, which had been legally transformed from spaces of transcendence to places of potential transgression by the Reformation. In Glasgow, the cathedral, which held the remains of the town's patron, stood as just the most obvious case of those things that Carolyn Bynum has shown 'carry with them past devotion'.[59] Holy wells and pilgrimage sites continued to attract pilgrims to locations long after the Reformation.[60] Their importance to pre-Reformation Christians explains why they were monitored so closely by kirk authorities.[61] And as townspeople sometimes continued to follow Catholic patterns for daily life, so too did authorities seek to prevent

---

[56] Sarah Hamilton and Andrew Spicer, eds, *Defining the Holy: Sacred Space in Medieval and Early Modern Europe* (Aldershot: Ashgate, 2005); Spicer, '"Accommodating of Thame Selfis to Heir the Worde": Preaching, Pews and Reformed Worship in Scotland, 1560–1638', *History* 88, no. 291 (2003): 405–22; Andrew Spicer, '"God Hath Put Such Secretes in Nature": Conventicles, Consecrations and the Concept of the Sacred in Post-Reformation Scotland', in *Sacred Space in Early Modern Europe*, eds Will Coster and Andrew Spicer (Cambridge: Cambridge University Press, 2005), 81–103.

[57] Andrew Spicer, 'The Scottish Reformation and Church Architecture, 1560–ca.1638', in *A Companion to the Reformation in Scotland, ca.1525–1638*, ed. Ian Hazlett (Leiden: Brill, 2022), 313–42; Andrew Spicer, 'Iconoclasm and Adaptation: The Reformation of the Churches in Scotland and the Netherlands', in *The Archaeology of the Reformation, 1480–1580*, eds David R. M. Gaimster and Roberta Gilchrist (Leeds: Maney Publishing, 2003), 29–43.

[58] Spicer, 'The Scottish Reformation and Church Architecture', 335.

[59] Bynum, '"Are Things Indifferent"?', 111. In *Where Mortal and Immortal Meet*, Ralston, has compiled a number of important articles and chapters on Glasgow cathedral.

[60] For important discussion of intercession, relics and the saints in late-medieval Scotland, see Mairi Cowan, *Death, Life, and Religious Change in Scottish Towns, c. 1350–1560* (Manchester: Manchester University Press, 2013), 52–81, and Priscilla Bawcutt, '"Holy Words for Healing": Some Early Scottish Charms and their Ancient Religious Roots', in *Literature and Religion in Late Medieval and Early Modern Scotland*, ed. Luuk Houwen (Leuven, Belgium: Peeters, 2012), 127–44.

[61] Ryan Burns, 'Enforcing Uniformity: Kirk Sessions and Catholics in Early Modern Scotland, 1560–1650', *IR* 69, no. 2 (2018): 111–30, at 120–1; Todd, *Culture of Protestantism*, 182–226.

them from doing so.⁶² The ubiquity of Catholic things necessitated that their uses might require clarification. As Walsham writes:

> The meanings they carried must also have shifted as they travelled down the generations from parents to children and as they were bought, borrowed, pawned and sold ... individual artifacts acquired fresh inflections depending upon the people into whose hands they fell and the locations in which they were shown.⁶³

Thus a Catholic object had its 'significance reconfigured' amidst the religious changes in the town.⁶⁴ Objects now required Catholics to define them anew, a task accomplished most directly through speech.

The case of Walker's crucifix demonstrates the value in incorporating Catholic speech more fully into the matrix of understanding how speech influenced town life in post-Reformation Scotland. The session records are incredibly helpful for doing so, as they supply not only the complaints made against townspeople but also sometimes the responses, excuses or reactions to these complaints that further demonstrate meaning and intent. Ewan's pioneering work carefully layers our understanding of cases like these by demonstrating relationships among speech, gender, violence, ritual, family and civic life.⁶⁵ Social status intersects with gender, law and speech to create boundaries that were both 'porous' and 'visible'.⁶⁶ Further nuancing speech by more explicitly identifying its religious implications adds another needed lens for understanding how gender, ritual or power intersected with a changing Christianity. Speech's capacity to clarify is important in this sense. Nearly all of Walker's presence in the records offers precise indications of her meaning. She was annoyed by this minister, not that one; she wanted the sacrament in this way, not that way; she attached this meaning to a sacred object, not that meaning. Most of these clarifications confirmed her open Catholicity, which was always accompanied by her gender and the implications it would carry for the expression of her beliefs.

It is difficult to assess with precision where and how gender influenced Walker's treatment by the authorities, but Paul Goatman's recent research on

---

[62] MacLeod, 'Making Time Protestant in Early-Modern Glasgow', *Reformation and Renaissance Review* 20, no. 2 (2018): 168–84, at 179–81.
[63] Walsham, 'Domesticating the Reformation', 581.
[64] Walsham, 'Domesticating the Reformation', 605.
[65] Elizabeth Ewan, 'Crossing Borders and Boundaries: The Use of Banishment in Sixteenth-Century Scottish Towns', in *Crossing Borders: Boundaries and Margins in Medieval and Early Modern Britain*, eds Sara M. Butler and Krista J. Kesselring (Leiden: Brill, 2018), 237–57; Elizabeth Ewan, 'Impatient Griseldas: Women and the Perpetration of Violence in Sixteenth-Century Glasgow', *Florilegium* 29 (2011): 149–68; Elizabeth Ewan, '"Tongue You Lied": The role of the tongue in rituals of public penance in late medieval Scotland', in *The Hands of the Tongue: Essays on Deviant Speech*, ed. Edwin D. Craun (Kalamazoo: Medieval Institute Publications, 2007), 115–36.
[66] Ewan, 'Crossing Borders and Boundaries', 255.

Archibald Hegate provides a helpful comparator. Like Walker's, Hegate's case was an opportunity to examine an example of 'the "middling sort" in Scottish society' who also happened to be a known Catholic.[67] Hegate, a notary public and clerk in the town, was no longer in Glasgow at the time of Ogivlie's trial, but his children, Robert and James, were among those implicated with Walker. Goatman suggests that Archibald Hegate's decision to quit Glasgow for the continent was possibly inspired by an increased intolerance that emerged as Archbishop Spottiswoode attempted to assert episcopacy in the town.[68] Unlike Walker, Hegate would have been able to tap into these continental facilitators of upward mobility and ultimately rise to the point of receiving a pension from Urban VIII.[69] Goatman concludes that the sons' treatment by the authorities for their associations with Ogilvie (Robert was banished from the kingdom while James, who eventually became a Benedictine monk, was fined) was influenced by this hardening of the bishop's line on religious conformity combined with the possibility that Archibald aided in organising Ogilvie's mission.[70] This treatment exemplified the ebbs and flows of religious tolerance in the town as discussed above, which were heavily influenced by the king's changing positions on the matter.[71] Walker's case would be similar. There was space for her complaints to be heard, but this space was constantly subject to change, and she clearly had to be careful to avoid more severe punishments. The unique aspect of her case lies in the interplay between the availability and tolerance for protest and her willingness to resist the authorities. Speech thus existed at a unique nexus between opportunity and ability, which Walker seized upon to assert her point of view.

With this in mind, as new research emerges demonstrating Catholicism's intersection with gender or social status in recusant cases across Scotland, unpacking the varieties of speech can be fruitful. New studies of hidden Catholicism, which are likely to be derived from lay Catholic experiences in session and presbytery records, reveal dynamics related to marriage, sacraments or the regional persistence of Catholicism, and are ripe for including Catholic speech as a further dimension of analysis.[72] They also provide points of comparison and contrast among the laity themselves like those seen with Hegate

---

[67] Goatman, 'Religious Tolerance and Intolerance', 180.
[68] On Spottiswoode's relationship with the king, see Julian Goodare, 'How Archbishop Spottiswoode Became an Episcopalian', *Renaissance and Reformation* 30, no. 4 (2006): 83–103.
[69] Goatman, 'Religious Tolerance and Intolerance', 164.
[70] Goatman, 'Religious Tolerance and Intolerance', 178–9.
[71] Goatman, 'Religious Tolerance and Intolerance', 176.
[72] Some recent examples include Catherine McMillan, '"Scho Refuseit Altogidder to Heir His Voce": Women and Catholic Recusancy in North East Scotland, 1560-1610', *Scottish Church History* 45, no. 1 (2016): 36–48; Burns, 'Enforcing Uniformity'.

and Walker, or with the lay magnate power discussed by Spurlock presenting a different dynamic than that found in the towns.[73]

Examinations of Catholic speech are also helpful in developing a kind of infrastructure of behaviour, expression and complaint among Scottish Catholics that allow us to better assess the scope and character of Catholic activity in the decades after the Reformation. Amidst new studies that remove the 'historiographical varnish' from early modern Scotland over the past few decades, Catholicism, in both its pre- and post-Reformation varieties, has emerged from the records as more vibrant than previously acknowledged.[74] In these studies, the reformed kirk is no longer a monolith led merely by Knox and others, but instead a church trying to find its way, operating in varied 'theological contexts' that were subject to negotiation and local realities, and often heavily influenced by Catholics.[75] Incorporating a broader sense of Catholic complaint, agitation and viability into this historiography is valuable. For example, research on repentance rituals that endured beyond the Reformation have been presented as characteristic of an effort – even a strategy – on the part of the reformed ministry to facilitate a more complete religious change by serving it 'with a sauce of practical tradition'.[76] This approach seems to downplay the presence of negotiation by assigning too much emphasis to the strategic guile of the ministry while removing complaint or local Catholic power from explanations for why some rituals endured while others did not. Surely the continued presence of Catholic people and ideas influenced, however mildly, the character of the rituals that endured. Few in the reformed ministry would endorse a strategy of maintaining Catholic ritual in a Protestant milieu. As Jane Dawson has noted, Scottish Protestantism was 'defined as much by Catholic beliefs not held as by the basic tenets of Reformed doctrine that were'.[77] The difficult humiliations witnessed in recusancy cases bear out this interpretation.[78] Identifying Catholic agency thus situates religious change amidst the protracted and negotiated settlement acknowledged in the recent historiography.

Susan Karant-Nunn has shown us the fruits of centralising negotiation in our understanding of religious change in this period. For Karant-Nunn, ritual was negotiated among Catholic, Protestant, state and folk traditions in early

---

[73] Spurlock, 'The Laity and the Structure of the Catholic Church in Early Modern Scotland' and 'I Do Disdain both Ecclesiasticke and Politick Popery'.
[74] Langley, McMillan and Newton, 'Introduction', in *The Clergy in Early Modern Scotland*, 1–12, at 6.
[75] Langley, McMillan and Newton, 'Introduction', 4; Goatman, 'Religious Tolerance and Intolerance'.
[76] Todd, *Culture of Protestantism*, 232; Langley, McMillan and Newton, 'Introduction', 7.
[77] Jane Dawson, *Scotland Re-Formed, 1488–1587* (Edinburgh: Edinburgh University Press, 2007), 232.
[78] Burns, 'Enforcing Uniformity', 112–13.

modern Germany.[79] Here, attempts to change marriage rituals resulted in 'popular resistance to the imposition of ritual from above' as townspeople refused to attend all parts of the newly instituted marriage rituals that emphasised 'bureaucratic pronouncements' to which they were unaccustomed.[80] Instead, they attended later in the ceremony, waiting to 'witness the supernatural function of the clergyman' when he pronounced the change in the couple's supernatural status during the rite.[81] The degree of agency demonstrated by Karant-Nunn encourages historians to avoid merely counting recusancy cases when we search for evidence of religious conservatism or change and instead cast a wider net. In Scotland, Michael Graham has shown that the endurance of Catholic rituals necessitated that 'traditional religious practices associated with the old religion' became more of a focus for the St Andrews kirk session than obvious cases of recusancy.[82] Catholic behaviours were as much a problem as Catholic people. As we have seen with Marion Walker, Catholic complaints or recusant activity could lead to a fine, a punishment, an excommunication or a public dressing-down from the ministry. It is interesting to consider the influence these Catholic complaints may have had in Glasgow. Subtle and overt inclusions of Catholicity in the dynamics of an emerging religious settlement in Glasgow might alter how we consider Walker's influence, John Ogilvie's trial or the continued presence of a viable Catholic minority in the town.[83] In doing so, they might also influence how we assess broader developments in the early modern period and its myriad negotiations.

Conclusion

Marion Walker's presence in the church records for Glasgow provides an excellent apparatus for understanding post-Reformation Scottish Catholicism. As Elizabeth Ewan has shown us, seeking out the often-neglected voices of Scottish women leads historians in new directions, while also weaving together so many of the themes of other research. Several of the elements that characterised Catholic survival in the nation and elsewhere in the early modern Catholic world are present in Walker's interactions with the kirk. By way of her familial connections to the pre-Reformation church and her participation in the local Catholic network in the town, she demonstrates the key role that

---

[79] Susan Karant-Nunn, *The Reformation of Ritual: An Interpretation of Early Modern Germany* (New York: Routledge, 1997), 35–8.
[80] Karant-Nunn, *Reformation of Ritual*, 38.
[81] Karant-Nunn, *Reformation of Ritual*, 37.
[82] Graham, *Uses of Reform*, 92.
[83] Goatman, 'Exemplary Deterrent or Theatre of Martyrdom?'; MacLeod, 'Declining His Majesty's Authority: Treason Revisited in the Case of John Ogilvie', in John McCallum, ed., *Scotland's Long Reformation: New Perspectives on Scottish Religion, c. 1500–c. 1660*, St Andrews Studies in Reformation History, 1 (Leiden: Brill, 2016), 179–201.

mutual support played in the maintenance of Catholic life. Her housing of John Ogilvie provides insight into differences among the Catholic and Protestant clergy, the Jesuit mission in Scotland, and the lengths Catholics went to in difficult conditions to smuggle priests and celebrate the Catholic mass. Most importantly, however, Walker's presence in the records reveals a unique voice. Walker's clarity in articulating her displeasure with the ministry or her feelings about Catholic objects calls us to take more seriously aspects of religious life that might remain hidden in relatively plain sight in the records. Walker's cases call us to look elsewhere for people like her who contributed to the protracted negotiations that produced reformed Scotland. In reminding historians to tease voices like hers out of the records, Marion Walker is still heard loud and clear more than four centuries later.

SIX

Memory and Materiality: John Knox and the Resilience of Relic-thinking in the Continuity and Gender of Cult in Late Medieval and Early Modern Perth

Mark A. Hall

Introduction: cult practice in later medieval Perth

In a perceptive series of publications, Professor Elizabeth Ewan has pushed forward the exploration of social and individual identities of women, men and children in medieval and early modern Scotland. These include her co-edited volume *Nine Centuries of Men* (2017) and her monograph *Townlife in Fourteenth Century Scotland* (1990), the interdisciplinarity of which struck me, as a museum curator and archaeologist new to Scotland and getting to grips with the medieval excavation assemblages from the city of Perth. The latter became one of a small group of pivotal accounts that facilitated my own explorations of everyday life and practices in medieval Perth and in a European context. Superstition is not the term used here to describe these practices, but it is a term that has been invoked in the debate from ancient times, whether to describe unorthodox religious practice in pagan and pantheistic China, Greece and Rome[1] or in Christian medieval Europe, or to describe irrational belief and practice ignorant of science since at least the Enlightenment.[2] An ongoing strand of that exploration is my seeking to understand the what, why and how of Perth's typically European experience of supernatural engagements and Christian heterodoxy. Fundamental to this exploration is the collection of pilgrimage souvenirs and related material culture from Perth and its immediate

---

[1] Hugh Bowden, 'Before Superstition and After: Theophrastus and Plutarch on *Desidaimonia*', *Past and Present* 199, Supplement 3 (2008): 56–71; Richard Gordon, '*Superstitio*, Superstition and Religious Repression in the Late Roman Republic and Principate (100 BCE –300 CE)', *Past and Present* 199, Supplement 3 (2008): 72–94; T. H. Barrett, 'Superstition and its Others in Han China', *Past and Present* 199, Supplement 3 (2008): 95–114.

[2] Michael D. Bailey, 'Concern over Superstition in Late Medieval Europe', *Past and Present* 199, Supplement 3 (2008): 118.

hinterland, which offers rich insights into pilgrimage as a movement across and embedded in the landscape and as a source of devotional, magical practices in home life.[3] My previous discussions have also sought to set the ritual devotional practices alongside other cultural and ritual practices.[4] As a human social construction, religion and belief practices have always been gendered. Medieval religion was dominated by men who represented a particular form of masculine spirituality,[5] but there was no simple gender binary of masculine and feminine in operation, rather something more graded, varied and complex.[6] Through the examination of a selection of material culture connected to religious leaders of Perth, this paper argues for an unexpected continuity of the role that male heroic imagery played in the devotional religious practices of the masses from the medieval church through the Reformation.

To set the scene for the following discussion on the Reformation transition, I recap three elements from my prior Perth discussions, here re-nuanced to further bring out their gender dimension. A previous assessment of Marian devotion in medieval Perth situated it in the wider European cult (whose adherents could subvert Church dogma and both delight in and satirise the blessed intercession of the Virgin) and through a range of material culture revealed its local context and practice, encompassing men and women and probably all social classes.[7] We know little about the individual lives of the majority of women who lived in medieval Perth. What we do know largely

---

[3] Mark A. Hall, 'Burgh Mentalities: A Town-in-the Country Case Study of Perth, Scotland', in *Town and Country in the Middle Ages: Contrasts, Contacts and Interconnections, 1100–1500*, eds Katherine Giles and Christopher Dyer, Society for Medieval Archaeology Monograph 22 (Leeds: Society for Medieval Archaeology, 2005), 211–28; Mark A. Hall, 'Of Holy Men and Heroes: The Cult of Saints in Medieval Perthshire', *IR* 56, no. 1 (Spring 2005): 60–87; Mark. A. Hall, 'Crossing the Pilgrimage Landscape: Some Thoughts on a Holy Rood Reliquary from the River Tay at Carpow, Perth and Kinross, Scotland', in *Beyond Pilgrim Souvenirs and Secular Badges: Essays in Honour of Brian Spencer*, ed. Sarah Blick (Oxford: Oxbow, 2007), 75–91; Mark A. Hall, 'Wo/men Only? Marian Devotion in Medieval Perth', in *The Cult of Saints and the Virgin Mary in Medieval Scotland*, eds Stephen Boardman and Eila Williamson (Woodbridge: Boydell, 2010), 105–24; Mark A. Hall, 'The Cult of Saints in Medieval Perth: Everyday Ritual and the Materiality of Belief', *Journal of Material Culture* 16, no. 1 (March 2011): 80–104.

[4] Mark A. Hall and D. D. R. Owen, 'A Tristram and Iseult Mirror-Case from Perth: Reflections on the Production and Consumption of Romance Culture', *Tayside and Fife Archaeological Journal* 4 (1998): 150–65; Hall, 'Burgh Mentalities'.

[5] Felice Lifschitz, 'Priestly Women, Virginal Men', in *Gender and Christianity in Medieval Europe*, eds Lisa M. Bitel and Felice Lifshitz (Philadelphia: University of Pennsylvania Press, 2008), 87–102.

[6] Jacqueline Murray, 'One Flesh, Two Sexes, Three Genders?', in *Gender and Christianity in Medieval Europe*, eds Lisa M. Bitel and Felice Lifschitz, 34–51 (Philadelphia: University of Pennsylvania Press, 2008); Ruth Mazo Karras, 'Thomas Aquinas's Chastity Belt: Clerical masculinity in medieval Europe', in *Gender and Christianity*, eds Lisa M. Bitel and Felice Lifshitz; Leslie Brubaker and Julia M. H. Smith, eds, *Gender in the Early Medieval World: East and West, 300–900* (Cambridge: Cambridge University Press, 2004); Dawn M. Hadley, ed., *Masculinity in Medieval Europe* (London: Routledge, 1999).

[7] Hall, 'Wo/men Only?'

reflects their legal identities, extensions to those of their fathers and husbands. Endowments of Marian altars were not exclusively male or female: they could be endowed by both, singly or in partnership, and they could be endowed by men for women. Salvation was not contingent upon gender, but on earth the gate-keepers were the male priesthood. While Mary was perceived as capable in aiding the salvation of all, it was arguably the male church leaders who largely defined the pattern and behaviour of female Marian devotion.[8] One of the objects highlighted in this analysis was a late medieval Flemish/Low Countries gilt brass chandelier (Figure 6.1), of which many examples were imported into Britain in the medieval period.[9] The central figure of the chandelier is the Virgin and Child. She holds a sceptre and stands within a sunburst, indicating her role as *Beata Maria in Sole* ('Our Lady of the Sun'), as described in the book of Revelation. This hollow-cast figure sits atop a central stem from which branch twelve candle-supporting brackets, symbolising the Apostles. The base of the stem terminates in a lion's head biting an open ring – presumably to help raise and lower the whole on a pulley so as to replace and trim candles. The chandelier has aways been understood as having survived the Reformation intact. It came to antiquarian notice in the late eighteenth century (passing into the collections of the Literary and Antiquarian Society of Perth shortly afterwards) when it was linked to the altar of the Shoemaker Incorporation in St John's kirk. Helping to define and direct devotion at an altar was also the purpose of the wood-panel portrait of St Bartholomew, probably painted as the reredos of the Glover Incorporation altar in St Johns parish kirk, Perth[10] (Figure 6.2). The Apostle St Bartholomew was an extensively culted saint in the medieval period – his bodily relics (including his skin) were venerated in several cathedrals notably in Italy, Germany and the eastern Mediterranean. Popular legends had him active in Armenia, Ethiopia and India in the mid-first century CE. He was martyred around 70 CE and the most popular tradition has him being flayed alive and then beheaded. The most prominent of flayed Christian martyrs, he was widely depicted in art, sometimes shown being skinned alive, sometimes holding the skinning knife and sometimes holding his removed skin 'body-suit' (most famously in Michelangelo's Last Judgement, in the Sistine Chapel). He was principally patron of various skin-working crafts, including shoemakers, leatherworkers, skinners, tanners, book binders, curriers and related trades including butchers and salt merchants.[11]

[8] Marina Warner, *Alone of All Her Sex: The Myth and Cult of the Virgin Mary* (London: Weidenfeld & Nicolson, 1976).
[9] M. Q. Smith, 'Medieval Chandeliers in Britain and their Symbolism', *The Connoisseur* 190 (1975): 266–71; R. Fawcett, *St John's Kirk of Perth* (Perth: Friends of St John's Kirk, 1987), 25.
[10] David McRoberts, 'A Sixteenth-Century Picture of St Bartholomew from Perth', *IR* 10, no. 2 (1959): 281–6; Hall, 'Burgh Mentalities', 220.
[11] For his background see, for example, Jacobus de Voragine, *The Golden Legend: Readings on the Saints*, translated by William Granger Ryan (Princeton: Princeton University Press, 1993),

Figure 6.1 General view of Marian chandelier, St John's Kirk, Perth (Perth Museum registration number: 2011.178). © and courtesy PMAG

Figure 6.2 Glover Incorporation portrait of St Bartholomew (Perth Museum registration number: 17/1967). © and courtesy PMAG

In Perth, the Shoemaker and Glover Incorporations were the notable umbrella for leatherworking crafts (though the town's bookbinders were part of the Hammermen Incorporation) and, like all the town's incorporations, the preserve of male craftsmen and merchants (of necessity women could be admitted but only as an extension of their fathers and husbands). Collective male decisions determined particular saints' dedications for altars and the acquisition of relics for those altars in the communal parish kirk. The Perth St Bartholomew portrait has him holding a fleshing knife, the instrument of his martyrdom – thus bringing together the male heroism of his death and the male craft of leather-working, the former blessing the latter in what anthropologists may call a reflex of sympathetic magic (which dictated that because Bartholomew was skinned alive he would be very effective as the patron for workers whose trade was to skin animals).

The chandelier and the portrait were axiomatic in the practice and continuity of male Christian devotional practice, with that continuity seen as a strong signal of resistance to the Reformation. Relic theory, as described below, aids in this analysis. The struggle for Reformation was undeniably violent[12] in both directions but this was only one thread of a complex, ambiguous and nuanced contestation. To take just these two objects, it is clear that both can be understood in ambiguous and nuanced ways and in doing so they help to underpin the broader discussion we now turn to about evolving ritual and cultural practices[13] within the often-paradoxical mix of continuity and change in Catholic and Protestant church practices.[14] Late medieval and early modern religious practice, particularly the determining and laying-down of orthodoxy, has been increasingly recognised as having a gender dimension including significant work in Scotland.[15] This essay contributes to that discussion by suggesting where this becomes particularly visible and deserving of further analysis.

495–501; Rosa Giorgi, *Saints in Art* (Los Angeles: J. Paul Getty Museum, 2003), 51–2; Frances Spilman, *The Twelve: Lives and Legends of the Apostles* (New York: Lulu.com, 2017), 62–89.

[12] Eamon Duffy, *The Stripping of the Altars: Traditional Religion in England, 1400–1580*, 2nd edition (New Haven: Yale University Press, 2005).

[13] Cf. Margo Todd, *The Culture of Protestantism in Early Modern Scotland* (New Haven: Yale University Press, 2002); David R. M. Gaimster and Roberta Gilchrist, eds, *The Archaeology of Reformation, 1480–1580* (Leeds: Maney Publishing, 2003).

[14] For example, Todd, *Culture of Protestantism*, 183–226, with a range of Perth practices considered at 197–226.

[15] Key examples include Bitel and Lifschitz, *Gender and Christianity*; Scott Hendrix and Susan Karant-Nunn, eds, *Masculinity in the Reformation Era* (Kirksville, MO: Truman State University Press, 2008); Amy E. Leonard and Karen L. Nelson, eds, *Masculinities, Violence, Childhood: Attending to Early Modern Women – and Men* (Newark: University of Delaware Press, 2000); Stuart Macdonald and Daniel MacLeod, eds, *Keeping the Kirk: Scottish Religion at Home and in the Diaspora* (Guelph: Guelph Centre for Scottish Studies, 2014); Steven Ozment, *When Fathers Ruled: Family Life in Reformation Europe* (Cambridge, MA: Harvard University Press, 1983); Lyndal Roper, *The Holy Household: Women and Morals in Reformation Augsburg* (Oxford: Clarendon Press, 1989). For the Scottish example see Janay Nugent, "The Mistresse of the Family Hath a Special Hand": Family,

Reformation and beyond: new cults and old

Let us return then to both the St John's chandelier and the St Bartholomew portrait, before extending the discussion to the culting of two sacred and heroic men, King James I and John Knox, 'the Great Reformer', both on either side of a religious divide but sharing the male authority that helped to heroise them within religious practice.

Illuminating relics: St John's Chandelier and St Bartholomew's portrait

The St John's kirk chandelier has been in the Perth collections since 1812, when it was purchased by the LASP. It still hangs in the kirk, where it has been on loan since the completion of Lorimer's restoration in the 1920s. A return to Perth Museum in 2010, for display purposes, facilitated a closer analysis of the chandelier than had been possible for many years.

There were many kinds of bronze, brass and ceramic lamps used to light medieval churches, but by the sixteenth century perhaps the most common was the multi-branched chandelier of this type, mostly made in workshops in the Low Countries and Germany. However, very few have survived, not least because the metal was a valuable commodity and their un-reformed iconography further encouraged melting them down for reuse. The altars of St John's kirk are likely to have been lit by several of these chandeliers, but this is the only one to survive. Or is it? Actually, this example appears to be a chandelier made up of the parts from several chandeliers – the parts probably escaping total destruction during the Reformation, and then brought back into use possibly in the seventeenth and eighteenth centuries when the surviving elements were put back together to make one chandelier. Such chandeliers produced for export were generally sold in pieces, each marked for easy assembly on arrival at their destination.[16] With such chandeliers we should expect a set of marks that enabled the detached branches to be matched to the attachment points on the body or baluster of the chandelier. In this case, there are multiple sets of differing marks indicating that the branches, candle holders and dripping pans were drawn from several chandeliers and re-set with new marks for guidance (Figure 6.3). Dots, triangles, oblique slashes and notches can clearly be distinguished. In most instances the 'final' sets of marks used match, but there are

---

Women, Mothers and the Establishment of a "Godly Community of Scots"', in *Keeping the Kirk*, eds Macdonald and MacLeod, 2014; Janay Nugent, 'Reformed Masculinity: Ministers, fathers and male heads of households, 1560–1660', in *Nine Centuries of Man: Manhood and Masculinities in Scottish History*, eds Lynn Abrams and Elizabeth Ewan (Edinburgh: Edinburgh University Press, 2017), 39–54.

[16] Alexander Fleming and Roger A. Mason, eds, *Scotland and the Flemish People* (Edinburgh: Birlinn, 2019), 94–5.

Figure 6.3 Detail view of Marian chandelier to show contrasting multiplicity of match-marks.
© and courtesy PMAG

instances where they do not. For example, branch 3 of the lower tier has three notches on the body attachment point, mis-matched against six notches on the branch. This suggests that most of the pieces had been numbered several times and that in the final, present assembly, the best fit had to be made with what pieces had survived from multiple chandeliers. Several of the branches and dripping pans also exhibit traces of damage and repair (including new brass inserted into breaks, cracks in branch stems, soldered repairs to the pans and new feet added to make for secure attachments between branch and body – see Figure 6.4), and the use of some post-medieval securing screws, further testament to their troubled biography-accumulating trajectories.

The Perth Glover Incorporation's portrait of their patron saint, Bartholomew, was commissioned during the Reformation. It carries the date 1557, indicating completion just two years before the incendiary speech made by Knox in St Johns kirk. It was saved from destruction and continued in use for Glover ceremonies, only being fully replaced in 1829, when a new, fashionable portrait was commissioned. It was brought out of retirement about 1865 and hung alongside the new portrait. During that long period of use the painting was reworked several times to maintain its social currency. McRoberts suggested that the head of St Bartholomew is the only surviving original feature, testament to a competent, probably local, artist.[17] By 1580, the Reformation was firmly

[17] McRoberts, 'A Sixteenth-Century Picture', 284–6.

Figure 6.4 Detail of additional shoe added to enable re-fitting of bracket to body of Marian chandelier.
© and courtesy PMAG

established, and the first change to the portrait made: its 'popish', presumed inscription asking for prayers for the dead for its donor had to be removed. It was painted over in green paint and the date of 1557 reapplied. Various accoutrements of the Glovers' craft were added to show the picture was not an idol but a symbol of the incorporation. In 1629 the Glovers acquired their first formal hall, in Curfew Row, and the picture hung there from that time. When a new hall was built in 1787, in George Street, the ageing picture was restored, including the addition of a vignette of the Old Hall, in the bottom right-hand corner. Further restoration followed around 1900, refreshing the colours, adding two bunches of nutshells and painting out the Old Hall vignette. The picture has now been made more complex by the discovery, in June 2022, of new information pertaining to the Glovers' use of Bartholomew imagery. The Glovers' papers include two charters, both dated 11 August 1490 and both recording donations of annual rents to the chaplain of the St Bartholomew altar in St Johns kirk.[18] The sasines for both took place as a symbolic handing over of a penny 'ymagini Sancti Bartholomei', that is, at the image of St Bartholomew. Although the location of the image is not stated, it is inferable that it was at the St Bartholomew or Glovers' altar, in St Johns kirk. The likelihood is that this reference is to a previously unknown image of the patron saint created

[18] A. K. Bell Library, Perth, MS67/2/17/Bundle 37.

somewhat before 1490 for use at the Glovers' altar. It appears not to survive and was presumably replaced by the first iteration of the surviving picture (which may have looked back to it). That said, it remains possible that this lost image was perhaps an earlier iteration of the painting seemingly made in 1557. A long arc of devotional adherence by the Glovers to their patron's 'icon' spanning the fifteenth and sixteenth centuries and beyond would make sense in the context of cult practices and continuities considered here. Each iteration perpetuated a muscular, male self-perception of their crafting role – which encompassed the bloody skinning of animals as a male craft – and its endorsement by God and the church.

King and reformer: culting James I and John Knox

King James I was intimately associated with two of Perth's monastic houses, the Dominican or Blackfriars and the Carthusian or Charterhouse. Blackfriars had been the main royal lodging in Perth for some 200 years by the time James was assassinated there in 1437. The Charterhouse, the only house of the Order founded in Scotland, was endowed by James in 1424, on his return from captivity in England. He saw the Carthusians as a good model to inspire ecclesiastical reform in Scotland. James always seems to have conceived of the Perth Charterhouse as his mausoleum. His burial in the presbytery would have been accompanied by an elaborate tomb, no doubt topped by an effigy. He was joined there by his queen, Joan Beaufort, following her death in 1445. Other family members followed. James's memory was promoted, and his cult flourished for well over a century, no doubt helped by Joan persuading the Papal Nuncio to kiss the wounds of the washed body of the king, an effective act of sanctification. For several years in the 1430s and 1440s payments were made, recorded in the Exchequer Rolls, for the upkeep of the tomb and shrine, including the addition of railings in 1438 – for which £30 was paid for Spanish iron, delivered to the prior, John of Bute. In 1440 a payment of £48 12s. 5d. was made by Cristini de Dunyn, a Perth Custumar, at the king's anniversary, for expenses relating to the fabric of the tomb, including smith-work and paintings around the enclosure. Initially, James's heart was not buried in Perth, but removed and taken on pilgrimage to the Holy Land, as had been done for the hearts of Robert I and Edward I, a shared attribute understandable as a privileged, male desire to posthumously embark on the masculine military pilgrimage tradition of crusading. James's heart did not reach Jerusalem as Ottoman power in the eastern Mediterranean made reaching Jerusalem safely impossible. A Hospitaller knight of St John returned the heart to Perth about 1443. He received payments of almost £100 through Custumars in both Edinburgh and Perth for his expenses in returning the heart. Various records also record several grants of land-rents, money and goods to the Carthusians by Joan and her son, James II, for the care of James's tomb.[19] The culting of James I is further confirmed by the Charterhouse's possession of the doublet worn by James when he was assassinated, no doubt kept or shown beside the tomb as a relic of the king. Seemingly this relic doublet was not destroyed at the Reformation but was salvaged and kept for some time privately in the town, for display to the faithful who were wedded to the belief in the supernatural agency of kings, males of sacral, heroic worth. The seventeenth-century verse history of Perth, *The Muses Threnodie*, records a witness – George Ruthven – to this cult practice:

> And in this place, where he doth buried lye,
> Was kept the relict wherein he did dye
> His doublet, as a monument referv'd
> And when this place was raz'd, it was preferv'd,
> Which afterwards I did fee for my part,
> With hols through which he stab'd was to the heart.[20]

The 'place' referred to is the priory, levelled during decades of the Reformation, but there is no record of the tombs or bodies of James and Joan being saved from destruction. Holy relics passing into private possession was not unusual – a wooden statue, probably of St Flannan, was preserved around Kirkintilloch because of its long association with bringing luck when housed in St Flannan's chapel.[21]

The tombs of James and Joan may have been swept away by the Reformation tide of destruction; their bodily remains may yet lie in their place of internment in the now vanished Charterhouse. As we leave James it is worth noting – a point we will return to shortly in discussing Protestant relic culture, particularly with respect to Knox and Luther – that the continuity of practice represented by James's cult echoes that already discussed above with respect to St Bartholomew's portrait and the Marian chandelier. It also has about it the hint of a very specific Scottish relic tradition, that of Dewars, community-based custodians of holy relics linked to named saints and whose role often continued

---

[19] RSRS v = G. Burnee, ed., *Rotuli scaccarii regum Scotorum / Exchequer Rolls of Scotland, volume 5* (Edinburgh: H.M. Register House, 1882) and discussions in John Parker Lawson, *The Book of Perth* (Edinburgh: Thomas G. Stevenson, 1847), 34–5; Robert Scott Fittis, *Ecclesiastical Annals of Perth to the Period of the Reformation* (Perth and Edinburgh: Gemmel and Cowan, 1885), 224–7; Samuel Cowan, *The Ancient Capital of Scotland: The Story of Perth from the Invasion of Agricola to the Passing of the Reform Bill*, 2 vols (London: Simpkin, Marshall, hamilton and Kent, 1904), 304–5.

[20] Henry Adamson, *The Muses Threnodie, or Mirthful Mournings on the Death of Mr Gall ...* (Perth: James Cant, 1638; 1774 edition), 37–8.

[21] John Higgitt, *'Imageis Maid with Mennis Hand': Saints, Images, Belief and Identity in Later Medieval Scotland* (Whithorn: Friends of the Whithorn Trust, 2003), 18 n.83.

through the Reformation and beyond.[22] The office of Dewar was very much a Gaelic tradition, a return to which may have appealed to reformers who redefined early, 'Celtic' Christianity as an aesthetically purer, non-popish, prefiguring strand of Protestantism. We may have a further glimpse of its continuation in practice, if not in name, in the popular culting of John Knox, icon of the Scottish Reformation.

Critical to the commencement of Reformation destruction in Perth was the speech John Knox made there in 1559.[23] The mob's destructive zeal would likely have included the likes of the chandeliers discussed above. Knox's physical presence in Perth and the changes wrought by the Reformation enshrined his place in the history of the burgh. At a time when history was often perceived through the footprints of mighty men, John Knox was a key figure of interest for the historical enquiries of LASP, founded in 1784. In 1832, two different objects were brought to the attention of the Society, which it was excited to acquire. The first was a sixteenth-century brass candlestick said to have belonged to John Knox and the very one that deflected an assassin's bullet fired through the window of his Edinburgh house (Figure 6.5). The second was a walking-staff or stick said to have been used by Knox in his old age and passed down through his family (Figure 6.6). The Society made their initial record in their Minute and Letter Books. They were consecutively accessioned as 'The Authentic Walking Stick of the Great Reformer John Knox – handed down and attested by a document in the Society's reports of the year 1832' and 'The Candlestick which belonged to the same celebrated reformer John Knox and was standing before him when he was Shot at. See on it the mark of the bullet.'[24] The verifying details of the candlestick were repeated in a 1930s re-registering of the collection:

> John Knox candlestick. Info supplied by donor. This candlestick belonged to the celebrated John Knox & was standing before him when he was shot at and the ball went through the bottom of it. How it came into the possession of my gt.Grandfather the Rev Williamson who was minister of St Cuthbert's in King Charles II's time I do not know but since then it has been in the family of the Williamsons till it was left to me by my uncle J. Williamson Esq., when he died 7 April 1826. Signed Alex Murray. Presented by Alex Murray of Ayton 1832.[25]

---

[22] Mark A. Hall, 'An Ivory Knife Handle from the High Street Perth, Scotland: Consuming Ritual in a Medieval Burgh', *Medieval Archaeology* 45 (2001): 176–9; Gilbert Markus, 'Dewars and Relics in Scotland: Some Clarifications and Questions', *IR* 60, no. 2 (2009): 95–144.

[23] Jane Dawson, *John Knox* (New Haven: Yale University Press, 2015), 177–81; Todd, *The Culture of Protestantism*, 197.

[24] PMAG Archives of the LASP 39, 38 and 43 respectively.

[25] Perth Museum accession register ('pencil' register).

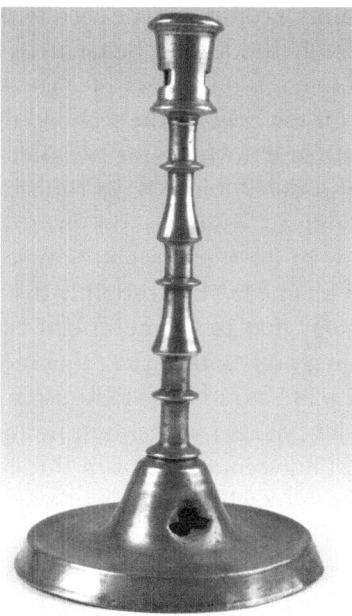

Figure 6.5 The presumed John Knox candlestick with presumed bullet hole deflection (Perth Museum registration number: 83). © and courtesy PMAG

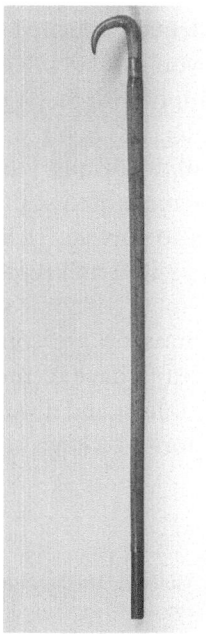

Figure 6.6 The John Knox walking stick with (a) detail of handle and (b) detail of tip (Perth Museum registration number: 154). © and courtesy PMAG

The candlestick is certainly a common type used in the sixteenth century and the damage is consistent with the idea of it being hit by a musket ball. However, there is no such known attempt on Knox's life. The swirling mists of Knox's cult made equally solid for the believer the real and the imagined episodes of his life. After Knox's death and down to the twentieth century, several myths accumulated around the so-called John Knox's House, Netherbow, Edinburgh. These included the attempted assassination in 1571, with a musket-ball fired through the window of his study, a tradition so appealing that Guthrie argued that it should be retained.[26] It is certainly historically true that during 1571 there was great anxiety that an attempt might be made on Knox's life by members of the Hamilton group, to the extent that members of the Edinburgh congregation mounted a guard around Knox's house at night.[27] So, in one sense the candlestick with bullet hole is not real but, in another sense, it verifies a powerful legend of masculine-centred heroism through its tangible, material reality, a typical mechanism by which relics worked, in this instance marking out the male Knox as deserving of divine protection (and from a God understood in male terms). I return to this point below.

The walking stick encouraged the expending of somewhat more ink in recording the circumstances of the donation. The walking cane had been in the possession of the Davidson family, descended from Knox's daughter. On the death of Mrs Davidson of Barnhills Cottage, Perth, the cane passed to a relative in London, named Laing, along with the cottage. Seemingly when the donor visited the cottage, he accidentally touched 'the Stick', and the executor, Mr Murdock, remarked 'Mr Laing, you'll not deprive us of that relic?' Laing made enquiry and agreed at once to comply with Mr Murdock's request to present it to the LASP. Twenty-two years later, the nephew of the now deceased Laing contacted the Society to confirm all the details. On 13 September 1954 Laing's nephew sent the Society an endorsement of the cane written by his uncle before his death, but this does not seem to survive.[28] The Society practised copying all letters into their Letter Book, as well as keeping the original correspondence but did not copy the endorsement for some reason. Visually the wooden cane with its bone handle and brass tip are consistent with sixteenth- and seventeenth-century types[29] but clearly have elements that could be renewed. In later life Knox was increasingly infirm and a walking aid would have added dignity as well as symbolising authority – a key attribute of many walking staffs

---

[26] Robert Miller, 'Where did John Knox Live in Edinburgh? And the Legend of "John Knox's House"', *PSAS* 33 (1899): 10; Charles J. Guthrie, 'The Traditional Belief in John Knox's House at the Netherbow Vindicated', *PSAS* 33 (1899): 267.
[27] Dawson, *John Knox*, 298.
[28] PMAG Archive 38 (LASP *Letter Book*).
[29] Catherine Dike, *Walking Sticks* (Aylesbury: Shire Publications, 1990).

and canes.³⁰ As a relic it had the potential to combine an appropriate, austere aesthetic with a symbolism of male authority, matching canes and staffs in the Catholic church (such as the well-known staff/cane of St Peter in the treasury of Cologne Cathedral, Germany). Such objects signify the male authority of their users and so indicate a shared attribute of gender that crossed pre- and post-Reformation cult practices.

The custodianship of the candlestick and walking stick are not described in detail but certainly involve heirloom-like descent through the families concerned; there are hints here that suggest their custodianship is reminiscent of the families being hereditary Dewars, the Gaelic relic-keeping office discussed above (the same may have been the case for James's doublet). The office of Dewar was not exclusively male. As late as 1726, the wooden image of St Fumac, at Botriphnie, Banffshire, was kept by an old woman whose duties included washing the image every year on the saint's feast day (3 May) in the waters of his eponymous holy well.³¹ Both this case and that of Knox's relics, with indications of women's roles in their keeping, also recall a wider medieval tradition of women as keepers of heirlooms and so family memories, traditions and history.³² This female role might seem at odds with the male gate-keeper role identified above in terms of access to sanctity, but it may be that this is a late, gender-nuanced expression of Dewar as a familial, motherly intercessor. Where Knox was concerned, the LASP effectively became his relics' more secular dewars when they acquired them. They were brought into the fold of an entirely male society that did not admit women and admired Knox as a key historical figure (whilst also lamenting the loss of fine medieval architecture prompted by his words); in 1835 they also acquired the anonymously painted seventeenth-century painting *The Scottish Reformers*, with Knox at its centre.

In *The Perth Hand-book* of 1848, the Knox relics were described as a highlight of the LASP displays.³³ Subsequently, they seem to have faded into obscurity in

---

³⁰ Joseph A. Amato, *On Foot: A History of Walking* (New York and London: New York University, 2004); Joseph A. Amato, *Everyday Life: How the Ordinary Became Extraordinary* (London: Reaktion Books, 2016).

³¹ Higgitt, 'Imageis Maid with Mennis Hand', 18, n.82.

³² Roberta Gilchrist, 'The Materiality of Medieval Heirlooms: From Biographical to Sacred Objects', in *Mobility, Meaning and the Transformation of Things*, eds Hans Peter Hahn and Hadas Weiss (Oxford: Oxbow Books, 2013), 170–82; Mark A. Hall, 'Status, Magic and Belief: Exploring Identity through Dress Accessories and other Amulets in Medieval Scotland: A Perthshire Case Study', *SHR* 100.3, no. 254 (December 2021), 469–92; Elisabeth M. C. van Houts, *Memory and Gender in Medieval Europe, 900–1200* (London: Macmillan, 1999); Matthew Innes, 'Keeping it in the Family: Women and Aristocratic Memory, 700–1200', in *Medieval Memories*, ed. Elizabeth van Houts (Harlow: Longman, 2000), 17–35; Rose Walker, 'Images of Royal and Aristocratic Burial in Northern Spain, c. 950–c. 1250', in *Medieval Memories*, ed. Elizabeth Van Houts (Harlow: Longman, 2000), 150–72.

³³ Anon., *The Tourist's Hand-Book to Perth and Neighbourhood with Historical Notanda, Civil and Ecclesiastical* (Perth: James Dewar and Son, 1848), 7.

terms of public attention. That said, there was clearly a wider culting of Knox at work by the mid-nineteenth century, if not before. At Glen Vale, on the edge of the Lomonds, Fife, looking down on Loch Leven was 'John Knox's Pulpit'. This was a precipitate rock formation that resembled a pulpit (blown-up as unsafe in 2004) and formerly known as the 'Preaching Rock' in reference to seventeenth-century covenanting meetings and which in the mid-nineteenth century became more widely known as John Knox's Pulpit, though there is no known direct historical association with Knox[34]. In 1849, the so-called John Knox House in Edinburgh (a late fifteenth-century timber framed house on the Royal Mile) was saved from demolition in the 1840s because of the presumed and traditional Knox association. Knox had stayed there but briefly before his death in 1572; it is now a museum commemorating Knox's life.[35] Both Pulpit and House display the 'stickiness' of popular belief that is essential for a personal cult to persist. The authenticity of the two relics as items which Knox physically handled could be questioned, but that is not the point of interest here – cults do not work through scientific authenticity but through perceptions of belief and the desire for an active presence of deceased figures that hold heroic and sacral authority that can act as conduits to the supernatural and define identities of belief and practice. Undoubtedly between Knox's lifetime and these items becoming relics, there was an evolutionary, biographical trajectory from initial post-Knoxian function as memorabilia and heirlooms to relics. The boundaries between all three – memorabilia, heirloom and relic – are ambiguous and psychologically, warmly fuzzy, with all three categories invested with notions of male heroism, rooted in long held aspirational spirituality and social structuring. They underpinned the Reformation's emphasis of male authority especially in mediating the divine.

To more fully understand the probable apprehension of these Knox memorabilia as relics, we need to briefly take account of some intersecting circles of behaviour that give us a sharpened context of understanding of relics within European, Protestant cultures. The groundwork for this broader context has been set by introducing above the template of medieval ritual practices, specifically the cult of saints, and charting adherence to it through the Reformation. Critically, we have to understand this as a more complex development than the binary of Catholic resistance and Protestant change: the practice was embraced and reconfigured by Protestants, chiefly because the appeal of relics is much deeper than its Christian veneer. Briefly, then, let us consider the wider cult of relics and the Protestant expression of it. In two papers published in 2014 Stephen Hooper sought to remind us of this deeper stratum of human ritual

---

[34] Simon Taylor and Gilbert Markus, *The Place-Names of Fife*, vol. 4: *North Fife between Eden and Tay* (Donnington: Shaun Tyas, 2010), 691–2; and online at the Glasgow University Fife Place-name database: https://fife-placenames.glasgow.ac.uk/placename/?id=3201.

[35] Miller, 'Where did John Knox Live?'; Guthrie, 'The Traditional Belief in John Knox's House'.

behaviour with a cross-cultural theorisation connecting equivalent patterns of human behaviour,[36] formulating a tripartite schema of relic behaviour: Relics of substance (i.e., corporeal or body relics); Relics of association (i.e., contact/touch relics); and Relics of equivalence (i.e. image or other substitute forms equivalent to the body of a special personage).[37] As Hooper observed of widespread, cross-cultural, human behaviour, the special personage is a particular cult context in which relics are attributed with significant powers, qualities and high status. The context need not be explicitly religious but the behaviour pattern towards the special person will have a religious character including veneration, adulation, respect and special journey, leading to altered material, psychological and emotional states. For some this would always be seen as superstitious behaviour (an abiding theme in religious/supernatural discourse[38]) and it is a striking paradox that Knox, a great admoniser of what he regarded as 'superstition', should be so culted. The Knox relics deliberated here would fall under Hooper's second category, relics of association, linked to Knox through a supposed touch of his original/core body: 'by the putative operation of contagious or sympathetic magic, or of "holy contagion", items that have been touched, used or created by the special personage, or that have touched their remains, have transferred to them the specialness of the core body'.[39] We might see it as inevitable that 'heroic' ministers of the Reformation might eventually become culted, albeit with an emphasis on memory and demonstrations of ideal behaviour.[40] The more bodies and objects were revealed in their bodiliness and materiality, the more they and their containers were encrusted with jewels and gold, underlining their permanence and closeness to – perhaps even their residence in – the heavenly Jerusalem. The more they were fragmented, displayed and circulated as parts, the more prestige was attached not only to their accumulation but also to exhibiting them in forms, such as reliquary altars or even the purely secularised wonder collections kept by aristocrats that make the multiplicity of the relic fragments clear. In the early sixteenth century, for example, the Elector of Saxony, Frederick the Wise, who became the protector of Martin Luther, had a collection of some 19,000 pieces

---

[36] Hall, 'Of Holy Men and Heroes', 62.
[37] Stephen Hooper, 'Bodies, Artefacts and Images: A Cross-Cultural Theory of Relics', in *Matter of Faith: An Interdisciplinary Study of Relics and Relic Veneration in the Medieval Period*, eds James Robinson, Lloyd de Beer and Anna Harnden (London: British Museum, 2014; Research Publication 195), 196; Stephen Hooper, 'A Cross-Cultural Theory of Relics: On Understanding Religion, Bodies, Artefacts, Images and Art', *World Art* 4, no. 2 (2014): 194.
[38] For example, see Bailey, 'Concern over Superstition'; Barrett, 'Superstition and its Others'; Bowden, 'Before Superstition and After'; Gordon, '*Superstitio*, Superstition and Religious Repression'; A. Rowlands, '"Superstition", Magic and Clerical Polemic in Seventeenth-Century Germany', *Past and Present*, Supplement 3 (2008): 157–77.
[39] Hooper, 'A Cross-Cultural Theory of Relics', 197.
[40] Cf. Nugent, 'Reformed Masculinity'.

that included the supposed body of one of the holy innocents slain by Herod.[41] What then of Luther?

The susceptibility of Luther to be remembered and sacralised through the cult of relics has long been recognised and suggested to be more than commemorative representations.[42] This recognition has been put on a new and expanded footing through the collective scholarship that marked the five hundredth anniversary of the publication of Luther's *Ninety-Five Theses*,[43] a scholarship indebted to the archaeological analysis of Luther's home.[44] Many objects owned by Luther, genuine and fake, excited veneration and an expectation of intervention, including his beer mug, ink blots allegedly made from his inkwell, ragged pieces of buildings he had lived in and splinters of wood from furniture and room paneling. Toothpicks made from Luther's deathbed were believed to cure toothache. The practice of taking splinters endures to our own time.[45] The evidence for Luther in this respect is strong but it is clear that he was not alone and that there was a wider sense of Protestant relic making. This was often text based (including books and sermon texts), reflecting the evolution of the Reformation which marked a transition from visual to literate culture, including text as image, but did not dispense with ritual.[46] From early on in the reformed Scottish church, ministers were seen as effective bridges to the supernatural, including through prophecy and charismatic sermonising, with the latter often leading to congregants recording the sermons in note form, which were then preserved as relics. Todd has suggested that sermon notebooks are worthy of re-evaluation as Protestant relics. She cites the example of William Cowper (sometime Minister of Perth), who died in 1618. So beloved was he that 'it was thought for grief that the wives of Edinburgh came to him and showed to him his own books'.[47] Here we see a distinctly Protestant display of relics, an inflection of an already existing grammar for approaching the supernatural, that also saw ministers revered as prophets and miracle workers.

---

[41] Caroline Walker Bynum, *Christian Materiality: An Essay on Religion in Late Medieval Europe* (New York: Zane Books, 2011), 132.

[42] R. W. Scribner, 'Incombustible Luther: The Image of the Reformer in Early Modern Germany', *Past and Present* 110 (February 1986), 38–68; Roper, *The Holy Household*; Ulinka Rublack, 'Grapho-Relics: Lutheranism and the Materialization of the Word', *Past and Present*, Supplement 5 (2010): 144–66.

[43] Anne-Simone Rous, ed., *Martin Luther and the Reformation* (Halle: Landesamt für Denkmalpflege und Archäologie Sachsen-Anhalt & Sandstein Verlag, 2016), especially contributions by Dietmann, Nebelsick and Kimmig-Völkner.

[44] Harald Meller, ed., *Fundsache Luther: Archäologen auf den Spuren des Reformators* (Stuttgart: Theiss Verlag, 2008).

[45] Katrin Herbst, ed., *Martin Luther: Treasures of the Reformation* (Halle: Landesamt für Denkmalpflege und Archäologie Sachsen-Anhalt & Sandstein Verlag, 2016), 374–85.

[46] Todd, *The Culture of Protestantism*, 392–3; Higgitt, 'Imageis Maid with Mennis Hand'; Edward Muir, *Ritual in Early Modern Europe*, 2nd ed. (Cambridge: Cambridge University Press), 2005.

[47] Todd, *The Culture of Protestantism*, 393.

Conclusion

Using cross-cultural theory allows us to step outside the immediate religious debate in which the Protestant church as defined by Knox, adhering to Calvin's teaching, sought to eradicate relic cults. Within that debate the notion that Knox would provoke a relic-based cult would be seen as an almost nonsensical paradox. Outside that framework, we can recognise that Knox's significance would still influence adherents to reflect his importance, through the typical human ritual behaviour of relicisation. Relics and relic-related behaviours are a fundamental element of religious practice and supernatural engagements by which those humans derive or perceive benefit from those practices.

The evidence for Knox relics is admittedly slender but it does follow wider patterns evident before, during and beyond the Reformation. They also make sense in the context of Perth as a crucible of Reformation in which Knox had a masculine, heroic role to play. His male authority and divine approval are explicit in the two surviving relics, one testifying to his invulnerability and the other to his elder status. It can seem a little paradoxical that Perth, a place that played a leading role in Reformation restructuring,[48] also desired to maintain material traditions of supernatural engagement as witnessed by the St Bartholomew portrait, the Skinner's chandelier and the doublet of James I.[49] In a town with strong craft traditions the male craftsmen were both at the forefront of change but also attached to their social investments in things like altars and their material demonstration of their different craft patrons. It would also have seemed natural to those steeped in traditions of supernatural engagement that regardless of a change in personnel, still hierarchies, authority and God should remain ritually approachable, especially through his agents on earth. The Reformation did not upend male authority or control; if anything the opposite occurred. We should perhaps not be surprised that access to the supernatural was still sought and that Knox and other ministers were the frontline of that access, replacing saints as a focus. Male domination of reformed, Protestant religion inevitably shaped the perception of its founders as its heroic male counterparts to the Catholic saints. The debates about masculinity in the middle ages frequently invoke a third gender, rooted in ecclesiastical chastity (for both men and women);[50] the Reformation dismantled the more fluid possibilities by disavowing clerical chastity. This further limited control of church and family to men as the gendered options decreased. Across Europe

---

[48] Dawson, *John Knox*; Todd, *The Culture of Protestantism*.
[49] Todd, *The Culture of Protestantism*, 119–25; Hall, 'Burgh Mentalities', 220–4.
[50] Felice Lifschitz, 'Gender Trouble in Paradise: The Case of the Liturgical Virgo', in *Images of Medieval Sanctity: Essays in Honour of Gary Dickson*, ed. Debra Higgs Strickland (Leiden: Brill, 2007), 25–39; Lifschitz, 'Priestly Women, Virginal Men', 2008; Murray, 'One Flesh, Two Sexes, Three Genders?'; Karras, 'Thomas Aquinas's Chastity Belt'.

people were not theologically expert but they were very adept in terms of ritual behaviour[51] and so were able to redefine the new orthodoxy as they had the old. To echo Bynum, the Reformation was a touchstone for many arguments about how the divine intersected with the material.[52] This paper and Todd's already mentioned analysis of sermon notebooks as relics (along with hints of other material reverences including the uniform-like coats worn by ministers) show that there was a heroic male-dominated relic-cult practice around the reformers that needs further investigation.

Acknowledgments

I am grateful to TAFAC, the EAA and the Wallace Collection for the opportunities to present variant versions of some of this content at their conferences and seminars, to David Perry for sharing his recent archive discovery pertaining to St Bartholomew's portrait, and two anonymous referees (one in particular) and the editorial team (especially Janay Nugent) for steering me in the right direction to hone the paper's gender thread.

---

[51] Muir, *Ritual in Early Modern Europe*.
[52] Bynum, *Christian Materiality*, 165.

SEVEN

'She-zealots' and 'Satanesses': Women, Patriarchy and the Covenanting Movement

Michelle D. Brock

The best known episode in the early covenanting revolution is, in part, a fiction. As the story goes, when James Hannay, Dean of St Giles' Cathedral in Edinburgh, attempted to read from the recently introduced – or imposed, depending on who one asked – Book of Common Prayer on 23 July 1637, a great tumult arose in the pews. Deeply offended by the intrusion of episcopacy into the presbyterian services held in Charles I's northern kingdom, a woman called Jenny Geddes purportedly lifted her stool high above her head and hurled it in anger at the unfortunate reader. Within minutes, a full-blown riot ensued and spilled into the High Street of the town.

No documentary evidence proving the existence of Geddes has been found, and her legend probably owes more to presbyterian nostalgia and the blending of local stories than to reality.[1] Historians have also debated the extent to which the stool-tossing turmoil was orchestrated by men and even commandeered by men dressed as women.[2] Regardless, a wide range of female protestors, including 'the meaner sort', clearly had prominence of place in the riots that took place at St Giles' and elsewhere in Scotland throughout that summer.[3] The following year, within months of the initial subscriptions of the National Covenant, Scottish women asserted their presbyterian commitments by rejecting, at times violently, the actions and authority of anti-covenanters in the kirk. So visible was female involvement in the early covenanting revolution that some feared tales of disorderly women would be used as a cudgel to discredit

---

[1] Laura A. M. Stewart, 'Geddes, Jenny', in *The New Biographical Dictionary of Scottish Women*, eds Elizabeth Ewan, Rose Pipes, Jane Rendall and Siân Reynolds (Edinburgh: Edinburgh University Press, 2018, 2nd ed.), 158.
[2] Jamie Murdoch McDougall, 'Covenants and Covenanters in Scotland, 1638– 1679' (PhD diss., University of Glasgow, 2017), 56–7.
[3] Walter Balcanquhall, *A Large Declaration Concerning the Late Tumults in Scotland* (London, 1639), 23.

the movement.[4] As Elizabeth Ewan writes of these women, they, like so many others during the long saga of the Scottish Reformation, 'have remained nameless but were an essential part of the history of these years'.[5]

The women of the early covenanting movement had been invited into activist roles that at once bucked and buttressed the traditional patriarchal order. The swearing of the National Covenant in 1638 called on Scottish women to participate in a moral, ecclesiastical and political revolution. Soon after, the whole of the British Isles descended into civil war. Five years later, Scottish covenanters joined the English parliamentarians against the king, both sides adopting another covenant in defence of the reformed faith against 'popery' and 'prelacy'. Like its predecessor, the Solemn League and Covenant was distributed to parishes for communal subscription. These acts of corporate, ritualistic solidarity often explicitly included women, though they infrequently signed either covenant. In Ayr, for example, all 'men women and all bouth younge and old' were told to stand in sacred space, arms upheld, and pledge their fidelity to God and the 'true religion'.[6] In 1643, the Perth kirk session ordained that 'the new covenant be read, sworne, and subscryvit' by every man and that 'the women also wer mowit to stande and sueir'.[7] So marked the beginnings of an important moment in the development of female religious and political activism in Scotland, which invited both praise and derision; so too marked the early years of a campaign of moral reform that at times placed women in the crosshairs of the machinery of kirk discipline.

In 2013, after surveying the state of gender in Scottish history, Katie Barclay asked 'where are our modern histories of Covenanting women?'[8] Happily, in recent years historians have paid increasing attention to the role of women in the covenanting revolution and its long legacy. As this work has shown, seventeenth-century women acted not only as swearers of the covenants in towns across Scotland, but also as rioters, petitioners, influential wives and widows of ministers, prophetesses and more.[9] This literature has emphasised

---

[4] Laura A. M. Stewart, *Rethinking the Scottish Revolution* (Oxford: Oxford University Press, 2016), 56–8.

[5] Elizabeth Ewan, 'Gendering the Reformation', in *A Companion to the Reformation in Scotland, c. 1525–1638*, ed. William Ian P. Hazlett (Leiden: Brill, 2021), 511.

[6] NRS, Ayr Kirk Session Records, CH2/751/2, 293r.

[7] *Chronicle of Perth: A Register of Remarkable Occurences, Chiefly Connected with that City, from the Year 1210 to 1688*, ed. John Maitland (Edinburgh: Maitland Club, 1831), 38.

[8] Katie Barclay, Tanya Cheadle, and Eleanor Gordon, 'The State of Scottish History: Gender', *SHR* 90, Supplement: no. 234 (2013): 83–107, at 106. The only published book fully devoted to covenanting women is James Anderson, *The Ladies of the Covenant* (Glasgow: Blackie and Son, 1851).

[9] Alasdair Raffe, 'Female Authority and Lay Activism in Scottish Presbyterianism, 1660–1740', in *Religion and Women in Britain, c. 1660–1760*, eds Sarah Petrei and Hannah Smith (Farnham: Ashgate, 2014), 59–74; Alan James McSeveney, 'Non-Conforming Presbyterian Women in Restoration Scotland: 1660–1679' (PhD diss., University of Strathclyde, 2005); Stewart,

the ways in which the covenanting movement, perhaps unwittingly, created space for women to take on more participatory and even leadership roles in a developing culture of public dissent.[10] As Jamie McDougall has demonstrated, while Scottish women had long been important figures in religious movements, the early years of the covenanting movement witnessed 'the beginnings of a more assertive and radical female activism' inspired by participation in the covenants.[11] This activism stalled during the apex of the covenanters' power – 1638 to 1652 – but after the return of episcopacy to Scotland in 1662, women became central, visible figures of nonconformity, petitioning the privy council, attending and hosting conventicles and composing accounts of their own religious experiences in the face of persecution.[12]

Despite this growing historiography on women and the covenants, there is still much to explore. First, we need to know more about the gendered impact of the covenanters' disciplinary regime; indeed, most Scottish women experienced the covenanting revolution through its leadership's vigorous attempts to prevent and punish sin. Second, the shifting roles of women over the course of the movement have not been fully accounted for. Scholars have yet to unpack whether the gendered meanings of covenanting fundamentally changed in these years and the extent to which covenanting politicised women in new ways.[13] These interrelated issues in mind, this chapter explores contemporary reactions to female activism to demonstrate the gendered paradox at the heart of covenanting. Despite containing the seeds of transformative potential for Scots of all sorts, the movement was fundamentally constructed and performed as a masculine, patriarchal project. From the outset, there was pronounced anxiety about the political involvement of covenanting women, even as they

Rethinking the Scottish Revolution, esp. 112–5; McDougall, 'Covenants and Covenanters in Scotland'; Louise Yeoman, 'A Godly Possession? Margaret Mitchelson and the Performance of Covenanted Identity', in *The National Covenant in Scotland, 1638–1689*, ed. Chris R. Langley (Woodbridge: Boydell, 2020), 105–25; Louise Yeoman, 'Away with the Fairies', in *Fantastical Imaginations: The Supernatural in Scottish History and Culture*, ed. Lizanne Henderson (Edinburgh: Birlinn, 2009), 29–46; David G. Mullan, 'Women in Scottish Divinity, c. 1590–1640' in *Women in Scotland, c. 1100–c. 1750*, eds Elizabeth Ewan and Maureen M. Meikle (East Linton: Tuckwell Press, 1999), 29–41; Laura Doak, 'Militant Women and "National" Community: The Execution of Isabel Alison and Marion Harvie, 1681', *Journal of the Northern Renaissance*, 12 (2021).

[10] Stewart, *Rethinking the Scottish Revolution*, 38–43. On the role of women in the development of public opinion, see Karin Bowie, *Public Opinion in Early Modern Scotland, 1560–1707* (Cambridge: Cambridge University Press, 2020).

[11] McDougall, 'Covenants and Covenanters in Scotland, 1638–1679', 56.

[12] On the roles of post-Restoration presbyterian women, see Raffe, 'Female Authority and Lay Activism', and McSeveney, 'Non-Conforming Presbyterian Women'.

[13] A recent exception to this is Laura A. M. Stewart, 'Contesting Reformation: Truth-telling, the female voice, and the gendering of political polemic in early modern Scotland', *Huntington Library Quarterly* 84, no. 4 (Winter 2021): 717–43. On these issues during the English Revolution, see Ann Hughes, '"Gender Trouble": Women's Agency and Gender Relations in the English Revolution', in *Oxford Handbook of the English Revolution*, ed. Michael J. Braddick (Oxford: Oxford University Press, 2015), 347–62.

were key to some critical early episodes. Moreover, the disciplinary project of the covenanters centred on eradication of sin and involved increased anxiety about women as purveyors of moral misdeeds. Only after the Restoration, when disciplinary fervour cooled as radical presbyterians struggled to maintain a political and ecclesiastical foothold, did women's activism return to the forefront as what remained of the covenanting movement became more about protest and personal relationships than clerical and state power.

Guiding my thinking in this chapter is Judith Bennett's concept of patriarchal equilibrium: the idea that at various moments when women could potentially have gained some advantage in their lives, such transformations were effectively countered by responses from patriarchal institutions; women's status in relation to men remained comparatively static.[14] This idea reminds us that, as Alice Glaze, Katie Barclay and others have pointed out, women too can act as agents of patriarchy and that men are also impacted by patriarchal norms.[15] This is a particularly essential point to bear in mind when thinking about the disciplinary program of the covenanters. To note that the kirk, during the covenanting period or otherwise, was a patriarchal institution is not to insinuate that that was all it was, or that maintenance of patriarchy was its primary intent, or that women did not have critical agency within and beyond its structure. As Bennett explains, 'almost all patriarchal institutions served other purposes that were not patriarchal in intention or effect, but one of their effects was to assist in the maintenance of a patriarchal equilibrium'.[16] Such framing does not suggest that covenanting women defended their cause and took up space self-consciously as female activists. Instead, they usually participated in protest in explicit support of some men – most often their ministers and husbands – while in overt defiance of others. Throughout, their motivations were rooted in genuine religious conviction that we must take seriously. Nor does it deny the extent to which the politics of the covenants created space for greater female activism inspired by the fundamental 'heart-work' of the movement.[17] But historicising patriarchy helps us to understand the covenanting revolution and why, ultimately, it did little to transform the role of women within kirk or state.

---

[14] Judith Bennett, *History Matters: Patriarchy and the challenge of feminism* (Philadelphia: University of Pennsylvania Press, 2010), ch. 4. Thank you to Cathryn Spence for suggesting this as a potential frame in tracing the evolution of women in the covenanting movement.
[15] Bennett, *History Matters*, 59. See Alice Glaze, 'Women and Kirk Discipline: Prosecution, negotiation, and the limits of control', *JSHS* 36, no. 2 (2016): 125–42; and Katie Barclay, *Love, Intimacy and Power: Marriage and Patriarchy in Scotland, 1650–1850* (Manchester: Manchester University Press, 2011).
[16] Bennett, *History Matters*, 178.
[17] Louise Yeoman, 'Heart-work: Emotion, Empowerment and Authority in Covenanting Times' (PhD diss., University of St Andrews, 1991).

'Disorderly Damsels' of the covenants[18]

The women at the centre of the prayerbook riots in late July 1637, as well as those who participated in similar rebellions later that summer, ranged in status from 'matrons of the mercantile community' to servants.[19] The responses elicited by their actions were equally varied. Reflecting on what had transpired at St Giles', presbyterian minister William Row praised the 'holy and religious women' whom the Lord had made 'instrumental in many good affairs for the promoting of the blessed Reformation'.[20] On the other side, royalist Walter Balcanquhall lambasted those who had 'raised such a barbarous hubbub in that sacred place'.[21] Sir James Balfour, in a letter to an unspecified woman written around the time of the riots, offers insight into what Laura Stewart has described as the 'general anxiety felt by men at the prominent role "religious" women afforded themselves'.[22] Balfour, a staunch presbyterian and equally staunch royalist, reminded the letter's recipient that women had been divinely created as a 'helper' to man and that 'in nature it is monstrous to see the hands leges and other members dominion over the head'. He accordingly encouraged her to cease any 'unwomanlike' behaviour and strive to 'learne humility' so that she could achieve a 'contented spirit'.[23] In other words, he was giving his female friend the unsolicited advice to calm down.

The letters of Robert Baillie offer a less polemical but still revealing chronicle of female activism in the early covenanting movement. He relayed how in August 1637, William Annand, at the time the much-maligned minister of Ayr, preached in defence of the new prayer book at a meeting of the Glasgow synod, resulting in his being assaulted by 'some hundredths of inraged women, of all qualities'.[24] So brutal was their assault that 'poor Mr. William', in danger of losing his life, had to be escorted to his horse the next morning so he could leave town, for, as Baillie put it ominously, 'more women were waiting'.[25] The following summer was also full of feminine disorder and violent turmoil, much of which involved familiar modes of women's dissent.[26] In Kinghorn parish a group of women attacked a man suspected of being an episcopal agent and an

---

[18] This subtitle is inspired by Elizabeth Ewan, 'Disorderly Damsels? Women and interpersonal violence in pre-reformation Scotland', *SHR* 89, no. 228 (2010): 153–71.
[19] Allan I. Macinnnes, *Charles I and the Making of the Covenanting Movement, 1625–1641* (Edinburgh: John Donald, 1991), 160.
[20] William Row, *The Life of Mr Robert Blair*, ed. Thomas M'Crie (Edinburgh, 1848), 154.
[21] Balcanquhall, *A Large Declaration*, 23.
[22] Stewart, *Rethinking the Scottish Revolution*, 56.
[23] NLS, Sir James Balfour's Letters, 1630–43, Adv.Ms.33.7.26, 15r.
[24] Robert Baillie, *The Letters and Journals of Robert Baillie*, ed. David Laing, 3 vols (Edinburgh: Bannatyne Club, 1841–2), I:20–1.
[25] Baillie, I:20–1.
[26] For a discussion of medieval modes of female violence against authorities, see Ewan, 'Disorderly Damsels?'.

enemy to the covenants. He escaped, but not without 'wounds and blood' from their stoning. When a minister in Colinton who had made his parishioners kneel before communion – an action deemed 'popish' and unacceptable to many in the presbyterian kirk – tried to leave the church, he was met by a group of waiting women who did 'shoare [threaten] him with stroaks'.[27] It is noteworthy that many of these incidents in 1637–8 ended with reports of other men spiriting the beleaguered victims to safety, out of the clutches of womanly wrath. Intentional or not, male solidarity against the excesses of female enthusiasm appears repeatedly in the accounts of critics and co-religionists alike.

Of course, most of the ways that women demonstrated their support for presbyterianism or the covenants left little trace in the archives. There are accounts of 'honest women' who generously provided needed food and supplies for the covenanter army, wives who supported clerical husbands or managed the home fronts while their men were away and, above all, those who swore the covenants alongside their fellow parishioners.[28] But the episodes that attracted the most national attention involved elements of performative drama, amplified by Scotland's growing print culture. In autumn of 1638, Edinburgh's Margaret Mitchelson began to deliver ecstatic speeches and prophecies to audiences of prominent covenanters, most notably Archibald Johnston of Wariston. In them, she praised the true kingship of Jesus (in explicit contrast to Charles I) and condemned the so-called King's Covenant – Charles I's rejoinder to the National Covenant – as an 'invention of the Sathan'.[29] Her audience interpreted these revelations as a clear sign of God's favour for the covenanting movement, which relied upon a potent combination of affective piety and polemic to demonstrate its legitimacy.[30] As Louise Yeoman has persuasively demonstrated, Wariston's own emotional, at times ecstatic religiosity had quite a lot in common with that of Mitchelson, but the key difference was that elite male figures like Wariston 'did not need to make a public spectacle to get a hearing'.[31] Their covenanter identity could be embodied in their positionality, no dramatic performance necessary.

---

[27] Baillie, I:76.
[28] Baillie, I:225. On clerical wives, see Chris R. Langley, 'Clergy Widows in Early Modern Scotland', *Scottish Church History* 51, no. 2 (2022): 111–32.
[29] Balcanquhall, *A Large Declaration*, 227.
[30] On establishing the legitimacy of the Covenanting movement, see Stewart, 'Authority, Agency and the Reception of the Scottish National Covenant of 1638', in *Insular Christianity: Alternative Models of the Church in Britain and Ireland, c. 1570–1700*, eds Robert Armstrong and Tadhg Ó hAnnracháin (Manchester: Manchester University Press, 2013). On the effective piety essential to covenanting, see Yeoman, 'Heart-work', and Nathan C. J. Hood, 'Corporate Conversion Ceremonies: The Presentation and Reception of the National Covenant', in *The National Covenant in Scotland*, ed. Langley, 21–38.
[31] Yeoman, 'A Godly Possession?', 118.

Some critics painted women like Mitchelson as unwitting tools of covenanting men. Balcanquhall deemed her 'raving fits' as having been motivated by the 'blind zeale' for the covenants instilled in her by ministers who set her up as 'a very fit instrument to abuse the people'.[32] Irish Bishop Henry Leslie wrote that the presbyterians 'advanced their faction … by insinuating into the weaker *sexe* in whom there is least ability of Iudgment'. He went on to explain that

> it is naturall unto the daughters of *Eve* to desire knowledge, and those men puff them up with an opinion of science, inabling them to prattle of matters of divinity … for these teachers allow them to be at least quarter-masters with their husbands, insomuch that I have not observed that faction to praevaile but where husbands have learned to obey their wives, and where will and affection weare the breeches.[33]

As Leslie's criticism makes clear, the activism of some covenanting women transgressed both biblical and social norms of appropriate female behaviour, in ways that not only offended God but emasculated men.

Those advocating for the National Covenant at times also expressed concern that their cause might be marred by association with troublesome female protesters. In 1639, a petition presented to the Lord Chancellor of Scotland in 'name of all the men, women, children, and servants of Edinburgh' against the new service book asked that his lordship consider that 'this businesse is a matter of so great weight and consequence as should not appeare to bee a needlesse noyse of simple women'.[34] Even Robert Blair's laudatory description of the women who caused a 'great tumult' at St Giles' was followed by a qualifier as to their characters: they were 'zealous and holy mostly'.[35] So grieved by the actions of those women at Kinghorn was Baillie that he feared their 'unhappie and ungodly violences hurt our good cause: they are lamented by us'.[36] In other words, this female disorder was unsanctioned by kirk leadership. Never mind that women had been purposely enlisted as rabble-rousers in other protests; the disapproval in Baillie's words was both evident and, to some extent, emblematic. Even as many covenanting leaders greatly respected the support, piety, and council of godly women – half of Samuel Rutherford's extant letters are addressed to his female confidantes, for example – their place in the wider movement remained circumscribed and easy to transgress.[37]

---

[32] Balcanquhall, *A Large Declaration*, 227–8.
[33] Henry Leslie, *A Treatise of the Authority of the Church* (London, 1639), preface.
[34] As described by Balcanquhall, *A Large Declaration*, 41.
[35] Row, *Life of Blair*, 150.
[36] Baillie, I:94.
[37] John Coffey, *Politics, Religion and the British Revolutions: The Mind of Samuel Rutherford* (Cambridge: Cambridge University Press, 1997), 97.

This was the gendered paradox at the heart of the covenanting movement: women performed a critical role in publicising the National Covenant and in shaping its varied meanings for a range of audiences, from the elite men who composed the document to ordinary Scots who observed the spectacle of women assailing anti-covenanter ministers or prophesying about national affairs. For covenanting leaders, women's words and actions, even unbidden, could be useful expressions of enthusiasm for the growing revolution. Yet left unbridled, female activism could also be dangerous and damaging to the reputation of the movement, which itself was born of and existed in a patriarchal social and religious order.

Realising the revolution

As the covenanters gained the sacred and secular power to enact their revolution, they needed to restore, as Stewart has put it, 'the structures that reinforced the ideals of a patriarchal, hierarchal society', which 'now existed in tension with the enhanced spiritual authority conferred on lay men and women by the events of 1637 and 1638'.[38] By the close of the decade, the spaces for Scottish women to protest, petition and prophesy were now occupied by an established covenanted kirk. Between 1638 and 1651, more than 230 ministers were ousted from their parishes by the new regime, and in the second half of the 1640s the movement was rife with rancorous debates over the extent to which it should cooperate with Charles I and, later, his son Charles II.[39] During these years, women continued to play important roles in vetting (and at times testing) local clergy for reasons personal and political. There was, for example, a great scuffle in the kirk of Lamington in the summer of 1644, when the presbytery of Biggar tried to install Andrew McGrie as minster of the parish. Led by Dame Grissell Hamilton, a group of prominent women stood guard over the pulpit and refused to let McGrie enter to preach. Their issue was not necessarily with the new minister himself but the insistence on proper procedure: the central patron of the kirk, Sir William Ballie, could not be present for McGrie's trial.[40] Despite this ongoing culture of dissent and the uptick in female activism in the early 1650s with the notorious Dunning Riot, there are, however, far fewer prominent examples of activist women responding directly to the ecclesiastical debates that preoccupied the covenanting movement at its height.[41]

---

[38] Stewart, 'Authority, Agency and the Reception of the Scottish National Covenant', 97.
[39] David Stevenson, 'Deposition of Ministers in the Church of Scotland under the Covenanters, 1638–1651', *Church History* 44, no. 3 (September 1975): 321–35.
[40] *RPC*, 2nd series, vol. 8, 31–4.
[41] On the Dunning Riot, see R. Scott Spurlock, *Cromwell and Scotland: Conquest and Religion, 1650–1660* (Edinburgh: John Donald, 2007), 103. More research is needed into female activism and dissent in the 1650s to determine its extent.

The shifting role of women is illustrated by the fact that the attention paid to Margaret Mitchelson dissipated just before the Glasgow Assembly in late October 1638. Yeoman suggests this may have been due to fault lines in how covenanting leaders felt about expressions of religious enthusiasm, but it also exemplifies a trend of highly visible, activist covenanting women being central to the movement only as it sought traction.[42] Once in power, the leadership encouraged mostly passive participation from Scottish women; their prescribed role was now to conform rather than perform. It is worth considering the extent to which the 'negative press' about the prominence of women in the movement's early years may have dampened the willingness of covenanting leaders to encourage certain types of female activism. On a more logistical level, women after 1638 were also likely preoccupied with the practical concerns of war and occupation. Ann Hughes has noted that women's involvement during the English Revolution ought to be understood within the context of the conflict, which brought with it loss of life, greater financial and physical precarity, and a range of other gendered burdens; much the same can be said for the Scottish experience.[43] If we want to understand Scottish women both *as* covenanters and as impacted *by* covenanters, we ought to situate them within in the experience of wartime hardship.

As important, we should interrogate the effects of the covenanted regime's dogged pursuit of a religious revolution that both upheld initiatives in place since the Reformation and introduced new strategies for reform.[44] Locally, ministers and elders worked in tandem with civil magistrates to implement heightened standards of morality among their parishioners. At the national level, the covenanters pushed for legislation that they hoped would establish a 'morally pure covenanting kingdom'.[45] Such efforts reached their apex when, in the first months of 1649, parliament passed a dozen acts tackling sins ranging from adultery to profanity to witchcraft, representing the height of dogmatic presbyterian power.[46] This agenda had a discernible effect on the lives of all Scots but affected women in specific and complex ways. On the one hand,

---

[42] Yeoman, 'A Godly Possession?', 122.

[43] Hughes, *Gender and the English Revolution*, 4–5. For examples of the wartime experiences of Scottish women, see Baillie, II:255, 334; III:286, 299.

[44] For disciplinary initiatives following the Reformation, see Margo Todd, *The Culture of Protestantism in Early Modern Scotland* (New Haven: Yale University Press, 2002) and Michael F. Graham, *The Uses of Reform: 'Godly Discipline' and Popular Behaviour in Scotland and Beyond, 1560–1610* (Leiden: Brill, 1996). On the disciplinary initiatives of the covenanted kirk, see Claire McNulty, 'The Experience of Discipline in Parish Communities in Edinburgh, Scotland, 1638–1651' (PhD diss., Queen's University Belfast, 2021).

[45] John Young, 'The Covenanters and the Scottish Parliament, 1639–1651: The Rule of the Godly and the Second Scottish Reformation', in *Enforcing Reformation in Ireland and Scotland*, eds Elizabethanne Boran and Crawford Gribben (London: Routledge, 2006), 132.

[46] Paula Hughes, 'Witch-Hunting in Scotland, 1649–1650', in *Scottish Witches and Witch-Hunters*, ed. Julian Goodare (London: Palgrave, 2013), 87.

it offered Scottish women additional means of resolving the domestic and neighbourly disputes that greatly shaped their lived experiences.[47] Through swearing the covenants, they had also been given an explicit stake not only in the 'remaking of the political order' but in the enforcement of discipline at the local level.[48] On the other, however, they could generally only collaborate with the arbitrators of institutional power within a system that was fundamentally patriarchal. Moreover, they could be targeted by the revitalised disciplinary program of the covenanters in ways determined not only by their gender but also other forms of social hierarchy.[49]

In enacting their vision of reform, one of the sins the covenanters took particular aim at was – unsurprisingly, given longstanding preoccupations of the kirk – illicit sexual behaviour.[50] Such was the concern for unlawful sex on the eve of the Cromwellian occupation that the General Assembly encouraged parliament to extend the death penalty for adultery to unmarried persons who had engaged in the crime with their married lovers.[51] While the courts usually held men and women to similar moral standards, when it came to sexual crimes 'the burden of proof fell on women rather than men'.[52] This burden was augmented by the Wars of the Three Kingdoms and Cromwellian occupation, which brought a steady stream of troops into local communities. This influx of soldiers meant increased opportunities – invited and not – for sexual involvement with single (at least situationally) men. Towns with a steady military presence grappled with an onslaught of cases of sexual impropriety, and women were punished accordingly by kirk sessions anxious to maintain during a period of heightened turmoil the standards of godliness prescribed by the covenants.[53] Adding to the gendered burdens created by policing sexual behaviour, new legislation in 1649 greatly increased fines for offenders. While Claire McNulty has shown that not all kirk sessions abided by these standard fines in considering individual cases, any increase in fees fell disproportionately on women, who were often in more precarious financial positions than their male co-offenders.[54] Thus even though the kirk may have punished the

---

[47] McNulty, 'The Experience of Discipline', 119.
[48] Stewart, *Rethinking the Scottish Revolution*, 3.
[49] Harriet J. Cornell has emphasised that social control in Scotland operated not only along a gender binary, but also according to social status. See Cornell, 'Gender, Sex and Social Control: East Lothian, 1610–1640' (PhD diss., University of Edinburgh, 2012), 2.
[50] Young, 'The Covenanters and the Scottish Parliament', 152.
[51] *Records of the Commissions of the General Assemblies of the Church of Scotland, 1650*, eds Mitchell and Christie, vol. II (Edinburgh, 1892), 411–15. This statute was rarely enforced.
[52] Cornell, 'Gender, Sex and Social Control', 262.
[53] See also Brock, 'Keeping the Covenant in Cromwellian Scotland', *SHR* 99 (2020): 392–411; Brock, 'The Man Will Shame Me': Women, Sex and Kirk Discipline During the Cromwellian Occupation', *Scottish Church History* 51, no. 2 (2022): 133–56.
[54] On the disproportionate nature of disciplinary fines, see Gordon DesBrisay, 'Twisted by Definition: Women under Godly Discipline in Seventeenth-Century Scottish Towns', in *Twisted*

transgressions of men and women in nominally equal fashion, the practice of discipline was fundamentally gendered by the nature of the crimes pursued, the function of reputation and the social and material impacts of punishments.[55]

The prosecution of purported witches – 85 per cent of the accused witches in Scotland were female – was one of the most dramatic, if comparatively limited, ways that the covenanting apparatus disproportionately impacted the lives of Scottish women.[56] As early as 1640, the General Assembly commenced regular lobbying of parliament for increased action against witchcraft. Such efforts were not in vain, for the number of known accusations for witchcraft reached subsequent peaks during the hunts of 1649–50 and 1661–2. 1649 saw not only new legislation but, according to Christina Larner, perhaps 'the greatest number of executions in the whole history of Scottish witch-hunting'.[57] As John Young and Paula Hughes have shown, this enthusiasm for witch-hunting ought to be understood as part of the broader program of moral reform implemented by a hardline regime seeking to create a godly state.[58] Little wonder, for the act of becoming a witch was 'the ultimate betrayal of the Scottish people's covenants with God'.[59] One of the most notable aspects of the witchcraft trials during the covenanting era was the explicit rhetoric of witches entering into a covenant – as opposed to a pact – with the devil. In 1644, for example, Margaret Watson was convicted of 'enterit in covenant with Sathan'.[60] Isobel Gowdie, in arguably Scotland's most sensational trial, confessed in 1662 to having met the devil at the kirk of Auldearn and 'ther covenanted, in a maner, with him'.[61] More than mere semantics, this shift in the typical language of the demonic pact reveals both a reconceptualising of all sins as threats to the covenants as well as heightened, even apocalyptic, anxiety about the actions of the devil seeking to impede the aims of the covenanted kirk and state.[62] Given the intense concerns about dangerous, even demonic, misbehaviour and sexuality at the height of the covenanting movement, the protests of unruly women may have been more

---

Sisters: Women, Crime and Deviance in Scotland Since 1400, eds Yvonne Galloway Brown and Rhona Ferguson (East Linton: Tuckwell Press, 2002), 141–2.

[55] For a recent summary of historiographical debates about gender and kirk discipline, see Ewan, 'Gendering the Reformation', 519–21.

[56] For a summary of an ongoing debate about gender and witchcraft, see Julian Goodare, 'Women and the Witch-Hunt in Scotland', *Social History* 23, no. 3 (October 1998): 288–308.

[57] Julian Goodare, Lauren Martin, Joyce Miller and Louise Yeoman, 'The Survey of Scottish Witchcraft', http://www.shca.ed.ac.uk/witches/ (archived January 2003, accessed 23 September 2022); Christina Larner, *Enemies of God: The Witch-Hunt in Scotland* (Baltimore: Johns Hopkins University Press, 1981), 78.

[58] John R. Young, 'The Scottish Parliament and Witch-Hunting in Scotland under the Covenanters', *Parliaments, Estates and Representation* 26, no. 1 (2006): 53–65, and Hughes, 'Witch-Hunting in Scotland'.

[59] Hughes, 'Witch-Hunting in Scotland', 87.

[60] *RPC*, 2nd series, vol. 8, 149.

[61] Robert Pitcairn, ed., *Criminal Trials in Scotland*, vol. 3 (Edinburgh, 1833), 603.

[62] Hughes, 'Witch-Hunting in Scotland', 87.

discomfiting and untenable than ever. As such, the relative lull in women's activism deserves further interrogation – or at least greater situation – within the context of the regime's attempts to combat sin at the local and national level.[63]

Post-Restoration female activism

The Restoration of 1660 brought dramatic change to Scotland's ecclesiastical and political establishment. Within a few years, bishops were back, three of the most prominent covenanting leaders were publicly executed, an Oath of Allegiance to the monarch replaced the covenants as a requirement for public office, the new government rescinded nearly all of the acts passed by covenanter-led parliament in the 1640s, and one-third of the ministry was deposed.[64] Most Scottish men and women conformed to these changes, accommodating their varied views on the covenants to the Erastian settlement.[65] For others, however, the reintroduction of episcopacy could not be countenanced; it was a threat to their deeply held faith and identity. As historians have noted, women played a prominent, highly visible role in the resistance to the post-Restoration ecclesiastical settlement, one that both reprised and deviated from their involvement in the early covenanting movement.[66]

Scottish women strove to defend their interpretation of the covenants – and, by extension, the liberties of the nonconforming ministers in their lives – through a wide range of means. As early as December 1661, Archbishop James Sharp lamented to Patrick Drummond that he had heard that some of the material from two sermons he had given on 'matters relating to the Church' had been 'carped at & misrepresented by some women, & capricious persons'.[67] James Kirkton relayed an account of how the earl of Middleton, commissioner of Scotland and one of the architects of the episcopal settlement, met 'a poor countrey woman' near the Tweed on his way back to England after an unwelcome tour of the western shires in 1662. The woman reportedly told Middleton that 'since he hade been so bussie to destroy their ministers', he would soon lose his position of power in Scotland. As Kirkton put it, 'from what spirit she spake I know not but then as she said so it came to pass', articulating

---

[63] Sierra Dye, 'To Converse with the Devil? Speech, Sexuality, and Witchcraft in Early Modern Scotland', *IRSS* 37 (2012): 9–40.
[64] For an overview of the Restoration period, see Tim Harris, *Restoration: Charles II and his Kingdoms, 1660–1685* (London: Penguin, 2005).
[65] On conformity and partial conformity during the Restoration period, see McDougall, 'Covenants and Covenanters in Scotland', ch. 4, and Alasdair Raffe, *The Culture of Controversy: Religious Arguments in Scotland, 1660–1714* (Woodbridge: Boydell, 2012), ch. 7.
[66] The two best works on post-Restoration female activism are Raffe, 'Female Authority and Lay Activism', and McSeveney, 'Non-Conforming Presbyterian Women in Restoration Scotland'.
[67] *The Lauderdale Papers*, ed. Osmund Airy, 3 vols (London, 1884), 1:61.

the ongoing belief in the ability of women to prophesy.[68] Still other women continued the long tradition of female religious protest, especially in areas with a history of presbyterian radicalism. William Row described how, in 1663, 'the Prelates [were] now busied to fill the places of outed ministers' with 'a number of the most profane insufficient creatures', which prompted spirited opposition from women in places like Kirkcudbright or Irongray in the south-west.[69]

By the 1670s, networks of female activism had grown increasingly organised and were crucial to 'presbyterianism's endurance in the face of government suppression'.[70] In 1674, a group of women in the parish of Liberton made 'tumult and invasion' against ministers from Edinburgh who had come to install episcopalian cleric Ninian Paterson. Four of the women stole the keys to the kirk from a church official, and for this they spent an hour in the pillory.[71] This must have left a lasting impression on Paterson, who published a poem nearly a decade later that called female nonconformists 'she-Fanaticks' who, worse than even 'Papists', worshiped presbyterian ministers as idols.[72] That same year, a group led by the wives and widows of deposed ministers gathered in Edinburgh, 'because the men durst not', to petition the Privy Council so that 'a gospel ministry might be provided for the starving congregations of Scotland'.[73] The document, which described how the removal of presbyterian ministers had caused 'the greif of the harts of many thousand in this land', became known as the 'Women's Petition'.[74] Most prominently, throughout the post-Restoration period nonconforming women from across the social spectrum – 'not only men but women, married and unmarried, yea servants' – were key figures in attending and even hosting conventicles.[75] In 1679, for example, Margaret Stewart, wife of a prominent Glasgow magistrate, ran afoul of the Privy Council for holding conventicles in her home.[76] Other women dissented more subtly, only partially conforming to the dictates of the new regime. They may not have been throwing stools, but they expressed their disapproval through actions like avoiding communion and generally refusing to acknowledge the authority of clerics who denounced the covenants. Moreover, the line between conformity and fealty to the covenants was very blurred; for many women, attending a

[68] James Kirkton, *A History of the Church of Scotland, 1660–1679*, ed. Ralph Stewart (Lewiston: Edwin Mellen, 1992), 90.
[69] Row, *Life of Blair*, 437; on the incidents at Kirkcudbright and Irongray, see McSeveney, 'Non-Conforming Presbyterian Women in Restoration Scotland', chs 4 and 5.
[70] Raffe, 'Female Authority and Lay Activism', 63.
[71] *RPC*, 3rd series, vol. 4, 147–8.
[72] Ninian Paterson, *The Fanatick Indulgence Granted Anno 1679* (Edinburgh, 1683), 9.
[73] Kirkton, *A History of the Church of Scotland*, 203.
[74] NLS, 'Petition of the Honest Women of Edinburgh', Wodrow MSS, 32, 231r.
[75] Row, *Life of Blair*, 536. For a list of women cited by the Privy Council between 1669 and 1679 for hosting or attending conventicles in Edinburgh, see McSeveney, 'Non-Conforming Presbyterian Women in Restoration Scotland', 218–21.
[76] *RPC*, 3rd series, vol. 6, 139–40.

service from an indulged minister one week and a conventicle the next posed little contradiction.[77]

In the latter decades of the seventeenth century, elite presbyterian women also wrote at length about their personal piety and commitment to the covenants. The narratives of two sisters, Katharine and Jean Collace, exemplify this genre of women's self-writing.[78] These women were often very close to nonconforming ministers, who lauded their piety and recognised the importance of their moral and material support. James Hog, who penned the forward to Katharine's *Memoirs*, wrote that he 'respected and honoured her', for 'she was a person of most equal spirit'.[79] Katharine's narrative describes how she had 'entered into an everlasting covenant' with God at the age of fourteen, though she continued to be tested by Satan and her own sin. As she grew more radical in the late 1660s and became a great supporter of men like Thomas Hog and James Welwood, she was deeply troubled by her prior willingness to listen to the words of clerics who had taken the Oath of Supremacy. As she put it, she had 'sworn to the extirpation of prelacy' and accordingly 'abhorred [herself] for countenancing them as ministers'.[80] Similarly, Jean detailed her grief for having committed 'that woefull and sad sin of hearing the curates', which equated to 'breaking covenant with God'.[81] She described Hog – for both sisters, the ideal of a godly minister – as 'the instrument made use of by God for my direction and establishment'.[82] The Collace sisters' writings reflect that, much like the hardliners of the 1640s, they believed 'the land's delivery from the bondage of prelacy' depended on observing a steadfast, strict commitment to the covenants, which took on an almost biblical immutability in their minds.[83] Yet for both, the crucial means to guard against episcopacy was not rooted in 'force', which Katharine explicitly rejected after the assassination of Sharp in 1679, or even in the power of the state, but in having the liberty to hear godly preaching in the company of like-minded friends.[84]

Many post-Restoration critics of nonconforming ministers portrayed their female followers as 'captive silly Women' led astray by enthusiastic preaching

---

[77] On the blurred lines between conformity and nonconformity, see McDougall, 'Covenants and Covenanters in Scotland', 188–9.

[78] Katharine Collace, 'Memoirs or Spiritual Exercises of Mistress Ross', and Jean Collace, 'Some Short Remembrances of the Lord's Kindness to me and his Work on my Soul, for my Own Use', in *Women's Life Writing in Early Modern Scotland: Writing the Evangelical Self, c. 1670–1730*, ed. David G. Mullan (Aldershot: Ashgate, 2003), 39–94; 95–135.

[79] Collace, 'Memoirs or Spiritual Exercises of Mistress Ross', 40.

[80] Collace, 'Memoirs or Spiritual Exercises of Mistress Ross', 52.

[81] Collace, 'Some Short Remembrances of the Lord's Kindness to me and his Work on my Soul, for my Own Use', 97.

[82] Collace, 'Some Short Remembrances of the Lord's Kindness to me and his Work on my Soul, for my Own Use', 99.

[83] Collace, 'Memoirs or Spiritual Exercises of Mistress Ross', 59.

[84] Collace, 'Memoirs or Spiritual Exercises of Mistress Ross', 89.

and fanatical ideas.[85] The earl of Rothes, a central figure in Charles II's administration of Scotland, complained in 1665 to the earl of Lauderdale that 'thes roges sitrs up the wimin so as they are wors than deivils'.[86] Yet the reality is that Scottish women led presbyterian dissent according to their own ideas, interpretations and initiatives. So dominant were female nonconformists in populating these illegal worship meetings that Rothes wrote that if women could be kept away from illicit worship, the country would 'have litill trubell with conventickils'.[87] Authorities struggled with how to deal with women who they viewed, paradoxically, as at once unyielding trouble-makers overstepping their appropriate roles and subservient pawns of radical men. After a group of Edinburgh women presented the so-called Women's Petition in 1674 – quickly condemned by Charles II as 'that seditious petition of many women' – the Privy Council interrogated them as to whether a man had in fact authored the petition.[88] What McSeveney calls the 'persistent attempt to prove that a male Presbyterian was behind the action of his female Presbyterian counterpart' should be understood as a form of backlash against female activism rooted in the evident discomfort with women's circumvention and at times outright rejection of gendered norms of political participation.[89] The most pointed reactions came from committed episcopalians like Sharp, who in 1669 railed against nonconforming women, calling them 'she-zealots' and 'Satanesses'.[90] Like their southern neighbours during the English Revolution, Scottish women who sought participation in the political process through activities like petitioning transgressed the boundaries of proper feminine behaviour and could face condescension, condemnation and even violence from their ideological opponents.[91]

Though the female activism after 1660 has been fruitfully explored, the sharp rise in the verve and visibility of nonconforming women invites further exploration. A range of possibilities have been proposed. V. G. Keirnan has pointed out that in the wake of the civil wars, many Scottish women had been left without husbands – due to death, imprisonment or abandonment – and thus relied especially heavily on their bonds with covenanting ministers and their godly circles.[92] Scott Spurlock has suggested that the 'alternative religious

---

[85] Alexander Rose, *A Sermon Preached Before the Right Honourable the Lords Commissioners of His Majesties Most Honourable Privy Council* (Glasgow, 1684), 29.
[86] *Lauderdale Papers*, I:234.
[87] *Lauderdale Papers*, I;234.
[88] *RPC*, 3rd series, vol. 4, 211.
[89] McSeveney, 'Non-Conforming Presbyterian Women in Restoration Scotland', 206.
[90] Row, *Life of Blair*, 523.
[91] Hughes, *Gender and the English Revolution*, 55.
[92] V. G. Kiernan, 'A Banner with a Strange Device: The Later Covenanters', in *Covenant, Charter, and Party: Traditions of Revolt and Protest in Modern Scottish History*, ed. Terry Brotherstone (Aberdeen: Aberdeen University Press, 1989), 35–6.

communities' introduced to Scotland by the Cromwellian forces provided greater space for women to participate more assertively in religious debates.[93] Jamie McDougall has noted that because the swearing of the covenants entailed investment in their ongoing success, once the venture was imperilled, women 'were ready to fulfil their Covenanted obligations to oppose toleration, Episcopacy, and Erastianism'[94] The thread that unites these interpretations is the grounding of post-Restoration female activism in two overlapping contexts: the hardships women had faced over the previous two decades of war and occupation – events themselves rooted in the spiritual politics of covenanting – and the augmented stake they had explicitly been given in the trajectory of Scotland's religious future by participation in the swearing of the covenants. Critical too to this story is the growth of the genre of self-writing that provided a fertile, if still prescribed, channel for expressions of the religious experiences and identities of women during the latter decades of the seventeenth century.[95]

The traditional narrative has been that after the Cromwellian occupation the covenanting regime fell apart, riven by division and the loss of momentum and cohesiveness.[96] After the Restoration, political elites largely abandoned their commitment to the covenants, oaths that the majority of post-1660 Scots would not have had the opportunity to swear.[97] Accordingly, Alasdair Raffe has argued that because the term 'covenanter' has encouraged a misleading emphasis on the loudest, nonrepresentative voices of post-Restoration dissent, we ought to limit the use of the term to the years prior to 1660.[98] This is an important point. But I would suggest that if we want to make historiographical space to situate women in the covenanting movement, then we might need to decouple it from institutional power; as John Coffey put it, 'it was the conventicle rather than the committee that empowered the female sex.'[99] Militant women like Isobel Alison and Marion Harvie, executed for treason in Edinburgh in January 1681, self-consciously identified as covenanters, defending a decades-old religious movement with words, life and limb, and we ought to take these identities seriously.[100] Indeed, the experience of being a covenanter was, for most Scots, neither an expression of institutional power nor, conversely, resistance to

---

[93] Scott Spurlock, 'State, Politics, and Society in Scotland, 1637–1660', *The Oxford Handbook of the English Revolution*, 369.

[94] McDougall, 'Covenants and Covenanters in Scotland', 194.

[95] On the genre of Scottish self-writing, see David G. Mullan's *Narratives of the Religious Self in Early-Modern Scotland* (Aldershot: Ashgate, 2010).

[96] For a discussion of the resilience of covenanting ideology after the Restoration, see Neil McIntyre, 'Saints and Subverters: The Later Covenanters in Scotland, c. 1648–1682' (PhD diss., University of Strathclyde, 2016).

[97] Raffe, 'Who Were the Later Covenanters?', in Langley, ed., *The National Covenant in Scotland*, 203.

[98] Raffe, 'Who Were the Later Covenanters?', 203.

[99] Coffey, *Politics, Religion and the British Revolutions*, 102.

[100] Doak, 'Militant Women and "National" Community'.

institutions, but rather an invitation to the responsibility and community that the covenants had generated. Covenanting principles, far from static or staid, had always been flexible and dynamic, debated and negotiated within an evolving culture of dissent that was not only public, but fundamentally gendered.

Conclusion

This chapter is not about women as victims or women as revolutionaries. It is, instead, an account of worshipers, rioters, witches and wives, all finding their paths through the turmoil of the mid-seventeenth century, and the responses they elicited from men in power. Far from a definitive account, I hope it serves as an invitation for further inquiry into what our understanding of the covenanting period would look like if we explored it through the actions of – and reactions toward – women. In so doing, we should bear in mind that the relationships between Scottish men and women, be they kirk elders and female parishioners or covenanting ministers and their female allies, remained sites of 'patriarchal negotiation' and complexity.[101] The dramatic events of 1637–8 in many ways empowered women. Swearing the covenants created space for women and the lower orders to, as Yeoman put it, 'command respect, whilst traditional sources of external authority, such as the king, were castigated for their ungodly behaviour and even rebelled against'.[102] At the same time, while covenanting gave women space for protest and spiritual creativity, it also served to reinforce the patriarchal structures that made this space prescribed and conditional. Additionally, the disciplinary regime borne of the covenants had a disproportionate effect on women through its campaign against sexual sins and witchcraft. Despite the augmented role played by women in the burgeoning culture of dissent and the mutual respect and reliance between covenanting men and their female confidantes, the patriarchal equilibrium was never interrupted, only disrupted. As Judith Bennett observes, over the course of history patriarchal institutions 'have adapted remarkably well to the conflicts, contradictions, and confusions they produce'.[103] The early modern kirk was no exception.

And yet, this does not mean the female activism during the covenanting movement – and in the post-Restoration attempts to salvage it – had no lasting impact. The women at the prayerbook riots in 1637, who raised their hands the following year in defence of the 'true religion', who attended field conventicles and detailed their spiritual struggles in the post-Restoration period, did so in pursuit of further reformation. Their cause was not gender equality, but their

---

[101] Glaze, 'Women and Kirk Discipline', 127.
[102] Yeoman, 'Heart-work', 276.
[103] Bennett, *History Matters*, 80.

stories did inspire subsequent generations of Scottish women who wanted to see something of themselves in the history they encountered in their built environment. In 1992, a bronze sculpture by Merilyn Smith of Jenny Geddes's purported projectile, the 'Cutty Stool', was installed in St Giles' Cathedral in Edinburgh. It had been funded by and dedicated by some forty unnamed 'Scotswomen' who are immortalised in an inscription on the sculpture's base. Jenny Geddes may never have existed, but women's acts of resistance before, during and after the covenanting movement certainly did. Like many of the religious changes and challenges of the mid-seventeenth century, the politics and possibilities of the covenants opened new spaces, and revitalised old ones, in which female voices could be heard loud and clear. These voices echo still.

EIGHT

Emotion, Authority and Griefwork in the Spiritual Poetry of Lilias Skene

Sarah Dunnigan

Hee boud my will to bear his hand
And did rebook all fears
So mead me **feellingly** to know [my emphasis]
My need had reachd his ears
And that my frequent chastesments
Was tokens of his love[1]

Lilias Skene (1626/7–97) was a Quaker writer, prophet and preacher who was politically and spiritually active in the city of Aberdeen and its surrounding environment in the latter decades of the seventeenth century, a striking figure of dissent, resistance and rebellion in the contemporary devotional landscape as she agitated on behalf of imprisoned allies of the Religious Society of Friends.[2] As Roslyn Potter notes, '[t]hrough her poetry, her ministry and her radical actions, she upset the established balance of seventeenth century gender roles by challenging her male orthodox superiors within the Church of Scotland, or Scottish Kirk'.[3] Gordon DesBrisay draws attention to the way in which the eminent Scottish Quaker, Robert Barclay, introduced Skene to Elizabeth, Princess Palatinate: '"a woman of great experience and tenderness of heart who through great tribulations of body and mind hath attained the earnest of the Kingdom [of God]"', observing that whilst 'Quaker male prophets endured

---

[1] AUL, William Walker Papers, MS 2774, 58 [dated 1695]. All extracts from Skene's poetry are based on this text. For a fuller account of Skene's surviving corpus, see below, footnote 28, and references therein.
[2] See 'Lilias Skene, n. Gillespie', in *The New Biographical Dictionary of Scottish Women*, eds Elizabeth Ewan, Rose Pipes, Jane Rendall and Siân Reynolds (Edinburgh: Edinburgh University Press, 2018), 394.
[3] Roslyn Potter, 'Lilias Skene: Quaker poet and social activist in seventeenth-century Aberdeen' *[X]Position* 5 (2020): 1–4.

their share of bodily infirmities […] it was usually only women's health that was commented on'.[4]

Both comments illuminatingly intersect, implying a tension between Skene's fierce activism and a contemporary ideological culture which ascribed physical and (as an implied corollary) emotional fragility to women. Yet the extract above from Skene's lyric, composed two years before her death, suggests the possibility of a fruitful meeting-point between emotion and active faith – it is only through the agency of feeling that Skene, or rather her speaker, receives conviction of divine grace. Building on this strikingly recurrent allusion to the power of affect as the primary instrument of knowledge and understanding in Skene's poetry, this essay suggests that this corpus of lyric work – one of the most extensive in seventeenth-century Scottish women's writing[5] – forges a different kind of relationship between emotion, authority and gender. This is realised through an intricately expressive language of grief which enables Skene's speaker to assert, indeed reclaim, a distinctively expressive spiritual and emotional identity. Indeed, their nearness to, and intimacy with, Christ is, in part, attained through the latter's familiarity with the experience of grief: 'He was a man of sorrows and / Has wele aquent with greef'.[6]

Skene's Gaelic contemporary, the poet Sìleas na Ceapaich, lamented that '[s]mall wonder that I am covered with wounds and that they are repeatedly being burst open'; in relation to this, Kate Mathis and Joanna Martin comment that 'too much grief over too short a time is also damaging to the poet who must observe it'.[7] Whilst Sìleas's Catholic devotional context cannot be compared to Skene's Quakerism, the comment still provides a useful counterpoint, for this essay suggests that the poetry of Skene's latter decades does indeed evoke the healing and regenerative power of mourning. It adopts the term 'griefwork'[8]

---

[4] Gordon DesBrisay, 'Lilias Skene: A Quaker Poet and her "Cursed Self"', in *Woman and the Feminine in Medieval and Early Modern Scottish Writing*, eds Sarah M. Dunnigan, C. Marie Harker and Evelyn S. Newlyn (Basingstoke: Palgrave Macmillan, 2004), 162–77, at 172.

[5] On this subject, see Jane Stevenson, 'Reading, Writing and Gender in Early Modern Scotland', *The Seventeenth Century* 27 (2012): 335–74; Pamela B. Giles, 'Scottish Literary Women, 1560–1700' (PhD diss., University of Saskatchewan, Saskatoon, 2004).

[6] AUL, MS 2774, 55.

[7] Joanna Martin and Kate L. Mathis, 'Elegy and Commemorative Writing', in *The International Companion to Scottish Literature*, ed. Nicola Royan (Glasgow: Association for Scottish Literary Studies, 2018), 173–99, at 195. (Also for original Gaelic text; translation by Mathis.)

[8] The term, 'grief-work' as used in this essay describes the emotional affect, movement and agency perceived around expressions of despair and loss, but it was coined in the 1940s by the psychoanalyst Erich Lindemann, who analysed the symptomology of grief specifically in relation to bereavement; it influenced other renowned grief theorists, such as John Bowlby and Elizabeth Kubler-Ross, who described a process of active work and task-focused activities, each of which can last variably and non-linearly, in readjustment, acceptance and the formation of new relationships after loss. The conceptualisation of grief-work sits within the Freudian tradition as broadly understood [*Trauerarbeit*, mourning work]. There is obviously a huge theoretical and clinical literature on the subject but see, for example, Elizabeth Kubler-Ross and David Kessler,

from modern therapeutic grief theory in an attempt to evoke the sustained and resilient effort which can be perceived in Skene's lyrics both to comprehend, and to grow from, painful emotional experience. This is, in part, enabled by the belief-system of Skene's own chosen faith – its radical valuing of individual spiritual experience over conventional and institutional religious structures, and its notion of the 'Inner Light' – the light of Christ – which could be inwardly apprehended by every believer through processes of silence and stillness ('silent waiting').[9] In that respect, Quakerism offers Skene 'an emotional community'[10] which spiritually justifies retreat and exploration. Yet this essay suggests that one of the most salient and fascinating aspects of Skene's poetry is how it imaginatively uses vulnerability as a generative and healing point and, ultimately, as a means of intimate experiencing of the divine. DesBrisay notes significantly that 'Lilias was unusual among Quaker writers in admitting to spiritual struggles after her conversion: Friends routinely wrote of their despair prior to "convincement", but rarely committed subsequent doubts to paper'.[11]

This essay seeks to enlarge our understanding of this significant, yet still relatively critically neglected, early modern woman poet, suggesting that 'poetic energy', in Potter's terms, can be found in Skene's depictions of interiority – her emotional repertoire of pain – as well as 'when she is most politically engaged'. It also seeks to offer another perspective on what DesBrisay calls 'Lilias' wider effort toward self-abnegation', and the manifestation of extreme affect in her work ('my lothing self / And sence of miserie').[12] Rather than articulating what might be described as a 'future-oriented' grief (concerned, for example, with imminent death), the overwhelming preoccupation in Skene's poetry is with the sharpness and pain of immediate experience. Ultimately, the essay seeks to contribute to the growing body of scholarly work on emotions in medieval and early modern Scottish culture which builds on substantial scholarship on the history of emotions in the pre-modern period; to thinking about how 'affective relationships' in general are represented in early modern Scottish literary culture; and to opening up inquiry into how affect and emotion find imaginative embodiment in sixteenth- and seventeenth-century Scottish women's writing.[13]

On Grief and Grieving: Finding the Meaning of Grief Through the Five Stages of Loss (New York: Simon and Schuster, 2014); J. William Worden, *Grief Counselling and Grief Therapy*, 4th edn (London: Routledge, 2009).

[9] See further Stephen W. Angell, and Pink Dandelion, eds, *Early Quakers and Their Theological Thought, 1647–1723* (Cambridge: Cambridge University Press, 2015).

[10] Cf. Barbara Rosenwein, *Emotional Communities in the Early Middle Ages* (Ithaca: Cornell University Press, 2006).

[11] DesBrisay, 'Lilias Skene', 171.

[12] Potter, 'Lilias Skene', 3; DesBrisay, 'Lilias Skene', 168; AUL, MS 2774, 47 [dated 1691].

[13] There is an extensive body of scholarship on the history of early modern emotions from a variety of disciplinary and interdisciplinary perspectives but for a recent, comprehensive overview see Susan Broomhall and Andrew Lynch, eds, *A Cultural History of the Emotions in the Late Medieval, Reformation and Renaissance Age* (London: Bloomsbury, 2021); cf. also Barbara H. Rosenwein,

The essay begins, though, by acknowledging some of the broader cultural and literary contexts in which feminised expressions of grief take place in early modern Scotland.

* * *

Late medieval and early modern Scottish literature is full of grieving women – of voices and bodies gendered feminine who weep, lament and mourn. Across a wide range of artistic modes and genres, in both manuscript and print cultures, the female subject is imagined, or she imagines herself, in various expressive acts of grief. There are many illustrations from which to choose: for example, Robert Henryson's late fifteenth-century *Testament of Cresseid* carves out a formal rhetorical space for the titular heroine's death-lament; Mary Stuart laments the death of her first husband, François II, in a formal, funerary tribute; in sixteenth-century manuscript miscellanies, anonymous female voices articulate forms of abandonment, mostly by an earthly beloved; the court poet, Alexander Montgomerie, ventriloquises female elegy in the tripartite sonnet sequence, 'A Ladyis Lamentatione', with layers of spiritual and political resonance; the early seventeenth-century 'Lady Laudian's Lament', which has been ascribed to Lady Ann Ker, is a *momento mori* woven with a degree of ironic reflection.[14] This proliferation of grieving women, as it were, is not surprising, for it reflects far wider, deeply entrenched artistic and creative practices in classical and contemporary European culture which locate the feminine at the heart of expressive sadness – for example, classical lament and elegy [*planctus*]; Ovidian complaint; French

---

'Worrying about Emotions in History', *American Historical Review* 107, no. 3 (2002): 821–45; of particular relevance to the material discussed here, see Lisa Perfetti, ed., *The Representation of Women's Emotions in Early Modern Culture* (Tampere: University Press of Florida, 2005); Elisabeth Hodgson, *Grief and Women Writers in the English Renaissance* (Cambridge: Cambridge University Press, 2014); Juliana Schiesari, *The Gendering of Melancholia: Feminism, Psychoanalysis, and the Symbolics of Loss in Renaissance Literature* (Ithaca: Cornell University Press, 1992). On emotion, gender and family in premodern Scotland, see Elizabeth Ewan and Janay Nugent, eds, *Finding the Family in Medieval and Early Modern Scotland* (London: Routledge, 2008); Janay Nugent and Elizabeth Ewan, eds, *Children and Youth in Premodern Scotland* (Woodbridge: Boydell, 2015); Katie Barclay, *Love, Intimacy and Power: Marriage and Patriarchy in Scotland, 1650–1850* (Manchester: Manchester University Press, 2011).

[14] On female-voiced lyrics in early modern Scottish literature, see Evelyn S. Newlyn, 'A Methodology for Reading Against the Culture: Anonymous, Women Poets, and the Maitland Quarto Manuscript', in *Women and the Feminine*, 89–103; Sarah Dunnigan, 'Reclaiming the Language of Love and Desire in the Scottish Renaissance: Mary, Queen of Scots and the Late Sixteenth Century Female-voiced Love Lyric, c. 1567–86', in *Older Scots Literature*, ed. Sally Mapstone (Edinburgh: John Donald, 2005); Theo van Heijnsbergen, 'Masks of Revelation and the "Female" Tongues of Men: Montgomerie, Christian Lyndsay, and the Writing Game at the Scottish Renaissance Court', in *Literature, Letters and the Canonical in Early Modern Scotland*, eds Theo van Heijnsbergen and Nicola Royan (East Linton: Tuckwell Press, 2002), 69–89; Lucy R. Hinnie, 'Figuring the Feminine in the Bannatyne Manuscript (c. 1568)' (PhD diss., University of Edinburgh, 2018).

chanson d'aventure; Petrarchan lyric[15] – so it is not surprising, then, that this feminised grief corpus in early modern Scottish literary culture is full of echoes and reflections of this deeper legacy.

Although 'signes of a broken heart',[16] to use a phrase from one of Skene's own lyrics, are variously manifest, in their richly illuminating survey of elegy as a formal mode and genre in Gaelic tradition and vernacular Scots and English writing, Joanna Martin and Kate L. Mathis make a number of observations.[17] They point to the diversity and range of experiences which find mourning and elegiac expression: shared themes of public grief and erotic loss through bereavement or abandonment, noting a fascinating contrast in the mourning process between medieval and later sixteenth-century expressions, possibly fostered by the difference between Catholic and Protestant attitudes to grief. What emerges is a body of diversely expressive texts, ranging from the formal and prescriptive to the imaginatively hybrid, and moulded by a variety of social and religious contextual influences. Their essay alludes to the role of women writers in this culture of formal elegy but suggests that in terms of Lowland Scots vernacular poetic culture, elegy never takes root as a stable generic form. Rather, it is only in Gaelic literary culture that we find 'a significant number of women' creating formal elegy, and sufficient room for 'intensely personalised expressions of the effects of loss […] either catharsis or private record of the mourner's grief', attested by the earlier illustration from Sìleas na Ceapaich's allusion to her repeated emotional wounding.

And yet, whilst women may not explicitly compose formal elegy in early Scottish literary culture outside Gaelic tradition, the diverse modes of spiritual or devotional literature (where we find the most extensive surviving corpus of early modern Scottish women's writing) offer an alternative expressive mode for acts of mourning. This situates their work in deeper rooted traditions of spiritual and biblical lament whilst bridging outwards to these wider traditions of literary, cultural and mythic grieving women. These poetic acts of spiritual mourning by Skene, Melville and Mary variously use a language of emotion and affect to articulate an experience of extreme grief but also their various positions of marginality – social, political, religious. Skene and her devotional poetic predecessors – for example, Elizabeth Melville and Mary Stuart, despite their deep doctrinal and cultural differences – are fundamentally aligned in imaginatively speaking from a shared anguished position of abandonment by God. Skene's lyrics, for example, repeatedly express spiritual despair as loss, configured as various kinds of absence and desertion. This ranges from a plea

---

[15] On early modern female literary lament in general, see Lauren Berdant, 'The Female Complaint', *Social Text* 19/20 (1988): 237–59; Laurence Lipking, *Abandoned Women and Poetic Tradition* (Chicago: University of Chicago Press, 1988).

[16] AUL, MS 2774, 60.

[17] Martin and Mathis, 'Elegy and Commemorative Writing'.

for renewed intimacy which enfolds erotic and sacred language in ways which evoke the affective piety of late medieval devotional discourse – 'O lovely one come draw me neare / My distance from thee costs me deare' – to repeated echoes of Christ's lamentation on the cross (Matthew 27:46; Psalm 22): 'My God, my God, why hast thou me / Forsaken as denyed'.[18]

Here, though, is where a distinction between Skene and Melville's poetic mourning might suggestively be drawn. As we shall see shortly by means of detailed engagement with Skene's poetry, its 'grief-work' is active and creative – founded not just on a series of tropes of abandonment but on a dynamically introspective exploration of how grief can be endured, healed and transformed into a new, loving connection with the divine. In Melville's *Ane Godlie Dreame* – her most well-known, widely circulated printed text, and a visionary dream allegory articulating Calvinist doctrine – grief is also a generative and dynamic force but differently so from Skene's work.[19] Here, lamentation becomes an exemplary and inspirational experience, a means of building out towards others – fellow mourners with whom the speaker can construct community and solidarity, and ultimately the foundations of spiritual and political activism. This might be termed 'beneficial' grieving, and it is helpful to pause briefly on Melville's text in order to highlight how Skene's griefwork (however ultimately beneficial it, too, proves) operates in precisely the opposite way through an intense focus on the singularity and individuality of the grief experience.

Although the *Dreame*'s first printing did not explicitly attribute the poem to Melville, a sense of public witness is conveyed by means of the colophon, 'at the requeist of her freindis'.[20] In the first twelve stanzas, there is a striking emphasis on the significatory process of mourning, a vivid sense of griefwork on display: 'The twinkling teares aboundantlie ran down [...] / With siches and sobs as I did so lament [...]'.[21] This somatic distress is observed by the 'Angell bricht with visage schyning cleir' – the Christ figure who takes the dreamer on their pilgrimage. In this respect, the *Dreame*'s public, performative mourning

---

[18] AUL, MS 2774, 39; 54.

[19] All references to the *Dreame* are taken from Jamie Reid Baxter, ed., *Poems of Elizabeth Melville, Lady Culross* (Edinburgh: Solsequium, 2010), based on the 1603 edition printed in Edinburgh by Robert Charteris, 71–97. This edition also includes the spiritual lyric poetry from the Robert Bruce MS, New College Library, Edinburgh, which Reid Baxter attributes to Melville. For the purpose of this essay, I have chosen to focus on Melville's *Dreame* but there are potential further suggestive parallels between Skene's and Melville's lyric compositions. On Melville's writing and cultural contexts see, for example, Jamie Reid Baxter, 'Elizabeth Melville, Lady Culross: New light from Fife', IR 68 (2017): 38–77; Sarah C. E. Ross, *Women, Poetry, and Politics in Seventeenth-Century Britain* (Oxford: Oxford University Press, 2015); Rebecca Larouche, 'Elizabeth Melville and Her Friends: Seeing "Ane Godlie Dreame" through Political Lenses', *Clio: A Journal of Literature, History, and the Philosophy of History* 34, no. 3 (2005): 277–96.

[20] Reid Baxter, *Poems of Elizabeth Melville*, 71.

[21] Reid Baxter, *Poems of Elizabeth Melville*, 73, 75.

illustrates what Joanne Diaz notes in her study of early modern complaint: namely, that 'grief is lessened when imparted to others'.[22] This is also a precondition which underpins a great deal of therapeutic grief theory. In Melville's poem, the angel/Christ-figure receives their pain, and openly acknowledges that act of reciprocity: 'I heir thy sichs,/I sie thy twinkling teares,/Thou seimes to be in sum perplexitie'.[23] The simultaneous acts of disclosing grief, and the act of mourning being heard, seems to offer the beginning of emotional ease. In Melville's text, there is a finite power to the act of grieving ('mourning may not mend'), and only purposeful and concrete action can bring about the alleviation of distress. The dreamer's emotional and spiritual trajectory invests them with the authority to share, instruct and implore their community of the elect. By this point, too, mourning itself is redundant. Calvinist doctrine is arguably the single greatest element behind the 'restoration-oriented' process of Melville's text. Skene's poetic griefwork, to which we shall now turn, unfolds over sixty years later in entirely different spiritual and locational contexts. In contrast to Melville's narrative – authoritative, didactic, outwardly-focused – Skene's lyrics turn inwards with an intense concentration on the experience of affect itself. They constitute a non-linear exploration of emotional pain, this essay suggests, where intricate expressions of interiority distil the ebb and flow of grief feelings in striking and suggestive ways.

* * *

Skene's griefwork is situated within the larger corpus of her spiritual writing. It is therefore helpful to delineate briefly certain aspects of this – including some characteristics of her poetic discourse – before turning to its representation of affect. As noted earlier, Skene's lyric poetry survives in a single, non-authorial manuscript copy but it provides dating for almost all of the poems, and is arranged in a broadly linear chronology, valuably offering an opportunity to plot a trajectory within both her life and creative work.[24] The body of poems which contain the most intense expression of griefwork are those which date from the last decades of her life. This late period of in her creative work is marked by painful events, including spousal bereavement at the age of sixty-seven, but also a productivity: 'ten poems, one third of her total output in the last six

---

[22] Joanna Teresa Diaz, 'Grief as Medicine for Grief: Complaint poetry in early modern England, 1559–1609' (PhD diss., Evanston, Northwestern University, 2008), 8.
[23] Reid Baxter, *Poems of Elizabeth Melville*, 76.
[24] 'The lost manuscript of Lilias' verse that William Walker transcribed was begun on 12 February 1676 when poems from the previous eleven years were copied down and dated, preparatory to new poems being added' (DesBrisay, 'Lilias Skene', 164); for further information and context on the MS and Walker himself, see DesBrisay, 'Lilias Skene', 162, 164.

years of her life, starting in 1691'.[25] In that respect, Skene's work might be seen as the poetic equivalent of seventeenth-century Scottish women's spiritual 'life-writing' in prose which David Mullan has explored extensively.[26] The fragmentary lyric form evokes a comparable sense of the effort to find meaning and purpose to personal pain as part of the reflective ordering and configuration of a life within a spiritual framework. DesBrisay draws particular attention to the 'midlife crisis of faith that prompted her defection to Quakerism in 1666 [...] It was the pivotal event in a life subsequently understood in terms of a "before" and an "after".'[27] This profound moment of apotheosis and transition has a direct correlate in Skene's work in her poem, 'A Song of praise, when the Lord first revealed to me His mynd, that I should not joyne this Communion at Aberdeen 1666'.[28] There are other poems which are anchored to a specific occasion of significance in her Quaker community: for example, 'Upon the imprisonment off friends [freindes] for the Truthe at Montross the 8th of the 10th mo: 1671/72'. Here, the idea of collective solidarity and resistance is stressed: 'So must wee now for those who shall succeed / Goe as the needle throw before the thread / And that wee may prepare the way for those / Who follow...'.[29]

Significantly, this also suggests that there was a specific 'audience' or readership of Friends and Quaker associates for these poems, and implicates Skene – in ways similar to Melville – within a network of broader textual transmission amongst her religious community. DesBrisay suggests that Quakerism offered Skene both 'a liberating discourse to shape her thoughts and words, and a community of fellow writers to encourage and critique her work'.[30] Through it, and her own direct acts of political resistance – condemned as 'transgressions'

---

[25] DesBrisay, 'Lilias Skene', 172 ('By then, Lilias was [...] living simply with her daughter Anna and two female servants, preparing for her own death').

[26] David G. Mullan, ed., *Women's Life Writing in Early Modern Scotland: Writing the Evangelical Self, c. 1670–c. 1730* (Farnham: Ashgate, 2003).

[27] DesBrisay, 'Lilias Skene', 164.

[28] DesBrisay notes that 'communion was the most divisive issue separating Presbyterians and Episcopalians [...] Lilias became convinced that God required that she reject not just the tainted Episcopalian version of the sacrament, but the sacrament itself and the Church of Scotland with it' (DesBrisay, 'Lilias Skene', 165).

[29] AUL, MS 2774, 28 (1671/2). On seventeenth-century Quakerism in Scotland, see Gordon DesBrisay, 'Catholics, Quakers and Religious Persecution in Restoration Aberdeen', *IR* 47 (1996): 136–68; G. B. Burnet and W. H. Marwick, *The Story of Quakerism in Scotland, 1650–1950* (Cambridge: Lutterworth Press, 2007; reprint of 1952 edn). On Quakerism from a variety of historical, cultural and geographical perspectives, see Stephen Ward Angell, ed., *The Oxford Handbook of Quaker Studies* (Oxford: Oxford University Press, 2013), especially Robynne Rogers Healey, 'History of Quaker Faith and Practice: 1650–1808', 1–30. Cf. also Phyllis Mack's landmark study of gender and seventeenth-century spiritual activism, *Visionary Women, Ecstatic Prophecy in Seventeenth-Century England* (Berkeley: University of California Press, 1992).

[30] DesBrisay, 'Lilias Skene', 163.

by the Scottish Privy Council[31] – Skene publicly inhabited a position of conflict and defence. In one notable instance, a rhetorical challenge to one of the leading covenanting ministers, George Meldrum, 'Ane answerto a nameless authour of a little writ fill of mistakes and groundles challenges wth reflexiones upon truth, this nameles author is supposed to be G.M.', Skene assumes an explicitly adversarial position and self-justifying position: 'I answer all the threatenings breathed gainst me / The Lords my suretie shamd I cannot be / Thy calumnies & misreports I leave.'[32] This not only shows audacity and courage but places emphasis on the truthfulness of her own words, and thereby her chosen faith. Rhetorically, within a small but significant number of poems, there is a gesture towards a larger purpose and intent – 'communicat for the good of others'.[33] At least notionally in such poems, Skene offers herself as an exemplary figure – dispensing strength, or celebrating it within herself. In the poem entitled, 'Some things concerning freindes in Prison which came before me in the tyme off my sickness; to be delywered to them', Skene's speaker begins with a powerful exhortation:

> My friends stand fast, lett none affrayed be
> And in this winnowing season faint not yee
> But feell yourselves so fixed on the rock
> That present sufferings may not thence you knocke[34]

In the later griefwork poetry, as we shall see, there is strikingly far less attempt to centre her actions and feelings within an exemplary and, indeed, propehtic framework.

Skene's 'grief lyrics' voice the contradiction at the heart of all mourning poetry – namely, the compulsion to give expression to the complex range of affect or feeling which accompanies any experience of loss and which, almost inevitably, challenges the adequacy of language and aesthetic form to embody it. This can be mapped back to what Karen Weisman in her reading of formal elegy as a literary mode terms its 'point of vulnerability'. In that sense, elegy is a genre which comes undone in the very process of being created: 'the self-reflexivity of elegy begins to be taken as a point of vulnerability that deepens the challenge to find in it, if not a redemptive or recuperative forum, then an affirming aesthetic, in which even poems despairing of their own capacity for consolation, or even resolution, assert a value in their own production as

---

[31] DesBrisay, 'Catholics, Quakers and Religious Persecution', 162.
[32] AUL, MS 2774, 43.
[33] AUL, MS 2774, 16 ['Some lessons learned in the light of Jesus & the inward exercise of the soule, in the same also the communicat for the good of others'].
[34] AUL, MS 2774, 23 (1677).

aesthetic products'.³⁵ Skene's lyrics – though not conceived as formal elegies – exist in interesting tension with this assertion. On one level, as seemingly cathartic spiritual utterances (not explicitly addressed to an audience or community, as are some of her poems), they give the impression of immediacy and spontaneity as spiritual exercises and prayerful reflections on despair. On another level, the sense of humility so deep-rooted in Skene's work – as DesBrisay notes, borne out of a combination of Quaker philosophy and a sense of instinctive self-excoriation³⁶ – might suggest a resistance to any formal aesthetic shaping, and a wider, deep-seated Quaker unease about imaginative creation. Nancy Jiwon Cho, in her fascinating survey of the role of literature within Quaker cultures, notes that 'in the early years of the Society, there was little Quaker creative writing. For instance, prior to 1660, 'there was practically no Quaker verse printed'. When used, it was often as a prophetic rather than artistic medium.'³⁷

Yet Skene's lyrics are held together in lyrically taut and binding ways, a formal counterpoint to the emotional fracture and fragility voiced within them. Skene's subjects – sin, guilt, spiritual conflict, persecution, salvation, shaped and moulded through Quaker belief – are imagined in lyric forms which favour a kind of purity (arguably mirroring a wider Quaker preoccupation). Metrically and stanzaically simple on the whole, with a tendency towards shorter line lengths, they deploy end rhymes and aural patterning which stitch each poem together in cohesive and echoing ways:

> Heer is a heven, heer is the rest
> Much may be entert and posest […]³⁸

Another pervasive symbolic thread in Skene's poetry is that of light and darkness, shadow and illumination. Acts of seeing and perception are foregrounded, figuratively representing the desires underpinning her own spiritual journey, and invoke one of the most central and well-known metaphors of early Quaker discourse, the doctrine of the inner Light:

> Dispell all that obscures thy shyning light
> Make pure my heart & in it shyne more bright
> That I with clearness may distinctly see (p. 18)

---

[35] Karen Weisman, 'Introduction', *The Oxford Handbook of the Elegy*, ed. Weisman (Oxford: Oxford University Press, 2010), 5.
[36] DesBrisay, 'Lilias Skene', 174.
[37] Nancy Jiwon Cho, 'Literature', in Nancy Jiwon Cho, 'Literature', in *The Cambridge Companion to Quakerism*, eds Stephen W. Angell and Pink Dandelion (Cambridge: Cambridge University Press, 2018), 69–87.
[38] AUL, MS 2774, 44 (1693).

> Then from his face He puld away the vaile
> And from my understandinges eye the seale.[39]

In those lyrics which advocate on behalf of her persecuted faith, or offer solace and strength to Friends under duress, Skene has frequent recourse to the language of military conflict:

> Come all yee mightie men bring forth your shield
> Yee valiant ones appear now in the field
> All yee expect in warre gird on your thigh
> Your swords, so as in readiness yee be[40]

Roslyn Potter argues that this language of '"spiritual warfare"' 'reinforces the Quakers' spiritual and physical roles as members of a "gathered army"' and that '[a]ligning herself and her language with an image of "masculine" divine judgement is another way in which Skene's work […] subverts gendered conventions', differentiating it from 'spiritual verse by non-Quaker Scottish female poets'.[41] On one occasion, Skene's speaker asserts that '[t]he Battell is not myne but his / Who call'd me thereunto', characteristically disavowing her own agency in spiritual conflict whilst elsewhere she repeatedly asserts the desire to be 'a good souldear'.[42] Bound up with this militarised discourse is recurrent use of a language of subjugation and obedience which conceives spiritual development as a process of discipline and submission: 'That soule whom he [God] hath weaned/ And discplin'd'.[43] Yet the process of spiritual nurture is also experiential, enabled by retreat to a space of interiority which assigns value and authority to feeling itself. In the next section, we shall see how this is imaginatively felt and sensed in Skene's lyrics, and how it actively enables the work of growth and healing.

* * *

Skene's poetry is preoccupied with the experience, articulation and understanding of pain but it also seeks to erase it: 'So in my saull abound / That of all former heavand grief / No memory be found'.[44] This longing to be unburdened, however humanly comprehensible, strikes a paradox in the context of her poetry; for it is only in the act of expressing grief that Skene's speaker can move towards its annulment. However, it is that very process of 'speaking' grief, this

---

[39] AUL, MS 2774, 9.
[40] AUL, MS 2774, 25 (1677).
[41] Potter, 'Lilias Skene', 3.
[42] AUL, MS 2774, 38 (1674); 58 (1695).
[43] AUL, MS 2774, 15 (1674).
[44] AUL, MS 2774, 48 (1691).

essay suggests, which effects change – initiating the process of '[g]iving strength to the seed',[45] as one poem puts it, or discovering the light within. One lyric suggests that this process has its own momentum:

> Iff sorrow through temptations
> *Find accesse to the heart*
> Those errors as a current run
> So swift and swell as high
> They as an indentation turne
> And stopt they cannot be
> Untill the watters have run out[46]

The struggles of Skene's speaker are plural, evoked by terms which evoke the emotional weight borne by the speaker: 'burdens', 'temptationes', 'afflictions', 'tryalls'.[47] Skene depicts her struggles in concrete, embodied and visceral ways. This sense of physicality remains, even through a series of scripturally resonant metaphors: 'My night of trouble is dark & verie long /The waters verie deepe I'm come among / I feell no ground, I can discerne no shoares'.[48] Spiritual despair is also conveyed in terms of the inability to see and perceive, a 'clouding' which is both sensory and emotional.

Yet throughout these lyrics her body itself remains an expressive instrument, and affect is frequently corporeally imagined: 'Come cure my many bruses Lord'; she conceives herself as the 'selfe justifier' who needs 'slaine'.[49] There are graphic allusions to the violence divinely inflicted on her body:

> Yett never hitt me in the dark
> I saw the hand I knew the mark
> Which allwayes hit & never faill'd
> To wound that pairt was to be heal'd
> Through blowes & bruises, paine & smart,
> Thou cures the evils of my heart[50]

Skene's speaker masochistically submits to this violent chastisement because they understand it to serve a purpose – punishment and coercion is part of a

---

[45] AUL, MS 2774, 9 (1674).
[46] AUL, MS 2774, 16 (1677).
[47] AUL, MS 2774, 15 (1674); 46 (1691); 15 (1674).
[48] AUL, MS 2774, 32.
[49] AUL, MS 2774, 30, 31; cf. DesBrisay, 'Lilias Skene', 171, for contextual information on this poem, and in which he reads 'a longing for self-cancellation and reassurance that God is with her'.
[50] AUL, MS 2774, 35 (1673). As a counterpoint, expressions of physical support and nurture are occasionally used to define her relationship with God.

larger process of spiritual cleansing and renewal. The giving up of volition at this stage is a crucial part of Skene's journey to salvation and, in the extract below, a visible (stigmata-like) sign of pain: 'So in my hands, these woundes I beare'.[51] Alongside this violent, incarnational language of suffering, Skene's lyrics repeatedly give voice to the 'stuck' nature of her anguish – the repeated self-defeating enclosures and impasses in which despair becomes locked. Skene's speaker confesses to 'habituall' patterns of feeling, drawing on one of her staple metaphors of her experience as a voyage, a journey, but one without a clear linear destination. In certain moments, her lyrics articulate the fear that her 'travells' are never-ending.

> My soule had expectation
> I traveled have to find thy rest
> Now more than fortie yeares
> But have not fully it possest.[52]

At other times, Skene's articulation of grief is framed by a temporal tension – the conflict between a present which is straitened by despair and a conviction in a certain futurity that will see the end of that suffering: 'What was renewes, what is makes old'.[53]

The dominant psychic wound of Skene's later lyrics is the speaker's fear that they will never be fit for salvation or to receive God's grace. There is a deep, corrosive sense of inadequacy – 'My expectations faile me farr / My disapoyntment to many are'[54] – which manifests as a sense of 'self-failure':

> A principle of certaintie
> Long tyme I have professed
> And did beleeve in veritie
> A measure I possessed
> Now having lost it I conclude
> I have not waited till[55]

In contrast to other believers who harbour 'grieffe and fears' until knowing Christ, Skene's speaker implies a failure to withstand the 'waiting' process. Winding through these later poems is an implied sense of the 'unattainability' of the ideal spiritual self, ready to receive Christ, made in the full knowledge of

---

[51] AUL, MS 2774, 35 (1673).
[52] AUL, MS 2774, 33 (1681).
[53] AUL, MS 2774, 6 (1665).
[54] AUL, MS 2774, 36 (1673).
[55] AUL, MS 2774, 35 (1681).

the depth of their own failures: '[…] all this instabilitie / Was only on my syd.'[56] In this respect, the recognition and acknowledgement of grief comes from, and stays with, herself. This contrasts with the sharing and witnessing of pain in Melville's *Dreame* where the speaker directs their spiritual and emotional energy to the creation of an 'elect' community. To be sure, Skene's work does at times demonstrate the importance of relational networks in those poems on specific occasions (her conversion) or events (Friends' incarceration). Her speaker sometimes forges imaginative connections to other biblical figures (such as Mary Magdalene and Job); and one poem articulates a joyful litany of Quaker unity, a hymn to resistant strength within a persecuted minority – 'One lyffe, one love, one peace, on[e] joy, one way / One is our principle, our strenth our stay'.[57]

And yet estrangement from community – forms of solitude and withdrawal – are repeatedly emphasised in the later lyrics. Gordon DesBrisay identifies the central tension of Skene's poetry as a conflict between self and other: 'Lilias' salvation required that her lamentations to the Lord be heard by others. The dread she felt when He compelled her to speak out was compounded by the necessity that she somehow deny her own identity […] The price of saving her soul was losing her self'.[58] DesBrisay argues that a pivotal early moment in this conflict between 'individual and collective identities' was her original conversion to Quakerism. That experience as told by herself, arising through a direct and intimate connection with God, differs profoundly from the official account, a collective history, given by Friends: 'Quakers believed that individual inspiration could only occur within the context of a community of believers […] in her own tellings, Lilias aims to establish the authenticity of her religious experience and the authority she drew from it. Friends' account relays external circumstances, largely absent from Lilias' version'.[59]

Yet arguably Skene's later work also offers a counterpoint to this: a sense in which solitude, withdrawal, and inward retreat offer vital sources of renewal and transformation for Skene and, in fact, a consolidation of her Quaker faith. Repair and healing is enabled within her, through full engagement with, and contemplation of, pain – what this essay calls the process of 'griefwork'. Time and again, these lyrics strikingly emphasise the value, directness and primacy of 'experience'.

> This by experience I have tryed
> And very clearely seen […]
> Yett are my lessons more
> In weight & number they exceed

---

[56] AUL, MS 2774, 47 (1691).
[57] AUL, MS 2774, 30 ('Upon the imprisonment off freindes for the Truthe at Montross the 8th of the 10th mo: 1671/72').
[58] DesBrisay, 'Lilias Skene', 174.
[59] DesBrisay, 'Lilias Skene', 167.

> And are laid up in store
> Some of them memorable I
> Have by experience bought [...]
> Moreover I haue in the deeps
> Of my experience knowne [...]⁶⁰

Although erasure of pain is not always achieved within the compass of a single lyric, Skene's poetry still presents the process of interior retreat as valuable and regenerative in itself.

> Wherefore my chastened soule retire chastned
> Unto thy place of rest
> Lett no temptation come so neare
> Thy quyet to molest
> Abstract from all cease from desires
> Forbeare to have a will
> Wait till thou know what God requyres⁶¹

This locus of 'quyet' – of peace, repose and stillness – is accessed in part by relinquishing all volition and desire, and submitting instead to a process of patient waiting; although the phrasing is potentially ambiguous, elsewhere Skene's speaker describes this 'quyet' place as a form of paradise: 'Heer is a heven, heer is the rest'.⁶² This rest-filled place, as it were, opens up a sense of possibility for loving connection: 'For when my sick and weery flesh / Did seek rest *to be loved*' (my emphasis).⁶³ Crucially, Skene's lyrics imply that here – 'A room for quiet rest' (p. 41)⁶⁴ – is where the 'work' of inner repair can begin; this place of apparent stillness and passivity is, in fact, active and developmental, and a means of drawing closer to the divine.

Where Melville's *Dreame* generates spiritual authority by means of allegorical revelation, in Skene's lyric world that authority is only enabled by deep, experiential access to self; the knowledge which 'feeling' imparts; and emotional access to the divine:

> Then did I know by feeling
> What thow art oft reveeling
> That all my loss was gain

---

⁶⁰ AUL, MS 2774, 15 (1674); 16 (1677); 20 (1677).
⁶¹ AUL, MS 2774, 16 (1674).
⁶² AUL, MS 2774, 44.
⁶³ AUL, MS 2774, 55 (1695).
⁶⁴ AUL, MS 2774, 60.

> By bitternes and pain
> I had obtiened peace[65]

In Skene's poetry, affect itself is authoritative – a touchstone and source of knowledge which allows her speaker to know when she is distant from God, in her most fallen and sinful state, but also crucially to offer assurance of certainty, security and wholeness of being held in divine love. Skene's spirituality, then, works through an affective devotional mode, concentrated on sharp articulations of the experience of loss. And yet it is this very intricate, close and fascinating exploration of that loss that enables Skene's speaker to discover new meaning in the 'restoration-oriented' processes of nature, and organic patterns of dormancy and renewal.

> The lyffe of things not being bound
> So much to what appeareth
> As in the root and under ground
> It lurketh and retireth
> When flowres doe fade and leaves and fruit
> From everie tree doth fall
> The living substance in the root
> Remaines untoucht at all
> And each retirement of this sap
> A fresh spring issues in
> Which us of spirituall thinges a map
> Throw death lyffe doth begin.[66]

In this extract – from the collection's most spiritually optimistic poem, dated to 1683 – Skene's speaker draws on one of the other staple metaphors of early Quaker discourse, that of the Seed, to portray the growth of the soul as analogous to the organic nurture of plants. This analogy with natural process also encompasses the process of inward retreat which, this essay suggests, is so vital an element of Skene's poetic spirituality: 'in the root and under ground' is where renewal and repair happens. The 'living substance in the root' might be understood as the core experiential self which '[r]emaines untoucht' – whole, integrated and loving – despite the attenuations of pain and suffering ('When flowres doe fade and leaves and fruit/From everie tree doth fall …'). It powerfully evokes the efficacy of inner retreat expressed in a late poem: 'I inwardly reteered / Untill my way was cleered'.[67] In the context of two decades of articulating lyric

---

[65] AUL, MS 2774, 48 (1693).
[66] AUL, MS 2774, 40–1 (1683).
[67] AUL, MS 2774, 50 (1693).

pain, this hopeful gesture evokes ideas of access to the Inner Light within and of a 'clearing', in the sense of making space, for emotional renewal.

In conclusion, then, this essay has explored how Skene's lyric work imaginatively portrays grief and ultimately articulates a recuperative process of healing. Compared to the more definite, resolute trajectory of grief in Melville's poem, Skene's griefwork is spread out across a series of lyric fragments from her later creative period. Yet this repetitious voicing of pain in and of itself works towards its own resolution through interiority; a preoccupation with the value and immediacy of her own emotional experience; and emphasis on the power of feeling as a mode of knowledge. This is in part nurtured by Quaker practice and belief which bequeath Skene a particular 'emotional style'. Yet Skene's poetry portrays this dynamic emotional movement in searching and intricate ways. Unlike most Quaker poets in these decades (and it should be remembered that Skene's work belongs, in terms of Quaker literary expression, to a relatively early period), Skene gives voice to doubt. In returning time and again to her own personal fragility, she shifts the focus away from her place within the community of believers which is so vital to Quaker belief and practice. Imaginatively, Skene places herself in an interesting threshold position: both within and yet without the nourishing, supportive enclosure of that faith community. Given the frequent physical and emotional gendering of fragility in the early modern period as feminine, and DesBrisay's observation (noted in the essay's opening) that 'Quaker male prophets' rarely drew attention to their 'infirmities', Skene's poetry may seem to exemplify a conventional relationship between women, emotion and faith. Yet, as this essay has suggested, vulnerability is also seen as healing and regenerative in her work – the voice within Skene's poetry of doubt is singular and individual, hence distinctive within Quaker spiritual and creative practice in broader terms. But it also points the way forward to possible resolution: held within the boundaries of her distinctively short and rhythmic lyric forms, the raw and immediate expression of feeling enables Skene, using the essay's affect framework, to do therapeutic work. The deep encounter with feeling (her own) is what distinctively enables Skene to return to the light. In radical ways, perhaps, Skene's still relatively unknown poetry demonstrates how Fox's concept of 'the Truth in the Heart' can be reached by patiently re-imagining and reconfiguring all those 'signes of a broken heart'.[68]

---

[68] George Fox (1624–91), who founded the Religious Society of Friends; AUL, MS 2774, 60.

Part Three

Politics

NINE

Displaying Support for Women's Lineage: Late Medieval Seals and Family Identity

Rachel Meredith Davis[1]

Introduction

There is a group of seals used among three Scottish kinship groups descended from the Stewarts of Menteith and Abernethy that used an eagle displayed (upright with both wings, both legs, and tailfeathers outstretched) in the seal designs of members in the fourteenth and fifteenth centuries. The iconography was used as a 'supporter', meaning it supported the shields bearing the heraldry of the individual. An unusual iconography in the seals of medieval Scotland, the transmission of the eagle displayed supporter offers up significant insight into the role of gender, elite status and reputation in the formation and expression of elite identity in late medieval Scotland. The transmission of this iconography has not gone unnoticed by genealogists and heraldists.[2] However, what the eagle displayed supporter meant to the individuals that used it has challenged those interested in Scottish use of heritable insignia. In 2011, Bruce McAndrew argued that the genesis of the iconography found in

---

[1] This chapter is adapted from part of a chapter from my PhD thesis, although the emphasis on masculinity is a new thread of analysis. I have presented several versions of this paper over the years, which has shaped the present arguments. I am grateful to Dr Erin L. Jordan for her insightful questions and comments on an earlier version of this paper, presented at the International Medieval Congress in 2018. In the course of my PhD I amassed a debt of gratitude to my PhD supervisors, Professor Cordelia Beattie and Professor Steve Boardman, as well as my PhD examiners, Professor Katie Stevenson and Dr Rick Sowerby. Of course, like many other contributors to this volume, I am indebted to Professor Elizabeth Ewan, who has heard versions of this paper and the ideas that stemmed from my PhD research over the years. She has been a constant source of support and encouragement, championing early career researchers like me in women's and gender history in Scotland.

[2] Roger F. Pye, 'The Single Eagle Supporter in Scottish Armory', *Scottish Genealogist* 21, no. 1 (1974): 24; J. P. Ravilious, 'The Earls of Menteith: Alexander, Earl of Menteith and Sir Alexander Abernethy', *Scottish Genealogist* 57, no. 3 (2010): 131; Bruce McAndrew, 'The Single Eagle Supporter in Scottish Armory', *The Double Tressure: Journal of the Heraldry Society of Scotland* 34 (2011): 73.

later seals belonging to these kin groups was adapted from the Stewart earls of Menteith, the lineage of Alexander Abernethy's wife, Margaret, from which these later medieval kin groups traced their descent. McAndrew argued that this adaption of iconography from a female lineage was 'unusual', and likely owed to the particular circumstances of Abernethy's upbringing as a ward of the earl of Menteith.³ McAndrew's assumptions are symptomatic of wider issues within Scottish medieval historiography, where there is a continued privileging of male lineage and interests, rather than considering the more nuanced interplay of gender, status and reputation within the Scottish nobility.⁴

In this chapter, I argue that there is nothing 'unusual' about Abernethy's adoption of iconography associated with his wife's lineage. Cynthia J. Neville has observed that, in twelfth- and thirteenth-century Scotland, 'contemporary opinion vested so much authority in women as arbiters of family identity that it was not unusual for husbands to adopt the names and associations of wives whose prestige (and wealth) outstripped their own'.⁵ The concern of previous studies of the eagle displayed supporter has been to identify its origins. In doing so, they have overlooked the importance of women in these connections, and have missed the important role they played in the transference of the iconography. This case study offers significant insight into identity in late medieval Scotland and how men and women conceived of their elite status within the Scottish nobility.⁶ It shows the importance of female lineage amongst elite Scottish families rather than a prioritisation of male lineage, an assumption that persists in studies of chivalric culture.⁷ This chapter furthers the argument

---

³ McAndrew, 'The Single Eagle Supporter', 73.
⁴ Stephen Boardman has commented on a lack of consideration of elite women in politics during the period, see 'Lords and Women, Women as Lords: The career of Margaret Stewart, Countess of Angus and Mar, c. 1354–c. 1418', in *Kings, Lords and Men in Scotland and Britain, 1300–1625: Essays in Honour of Jenny Wormald*, eds Stephen Boardman and Julian Goodare (Edinburgh: Edinburgh University Press, 2014), 40.
⁵ Cynthia J. Neville, 'Women, Charters, and Land Ownership in Scotland, 1150–1350', *The Journal of Legal History* 26, no. 1 (2005): 30.
⁶ For a discussion of idealised masculinity in the seals of kings from the twelfth and thirteenth centuries see Cynthia Neville, 'Making a Manly Impression: The Image of Kingship on Scottish Royal Seals of the High Middle Ages', in *Nine Centuries of Man: Manhood and Masculinity in Scottish History*, eds Lynn Abrams and Elizabeth Ewan (Edinburgh: Edinburgh University Press, 2017), 101–21.
⁷ This argument is prevalent in recent studies of chivalry, see, for example, David Crouch, *The Chivalric Turn: Conduct and Hegemony in Europe before 1300* (Oxford: Oxford University Press, 2019), 305; Nigel Saul, *Chivalry in Medieval England* (Cambridge, MA: Harvard University Press, 2011), 270–82. It is worth noting that the body of scholarship on chivalry is extensive. This chapter references key works that are germane to the arguments at hand. Brigitte Bedos-Rezak suggested in 1990 a woman 'had no specific place in the heraldic grammar of her lineage' with regard to French seals. See, Brigitte Bedos-Rezak, 'Medieval Women in French Sigillographic Sources', in *Women and the Sources of Medieval History*, ed. Joel T. Rosenthal (Athens: University of Georgia Press, 1990), 6. For a discussion of previous interpretations of female use of heraldry, see Rachel Meredith Davis, 'Material Evidence? Re-approaching Elite Women's Seals and

that women's use of heraldry in seal design was not formulaic; rather, the seals within this group show a careful curation of identity, memory and power.[8] These findings bear similarities to those found in Scottish grave memorials and naming practices and furthers our understanding commemorative practices amongst Scots.[9] When considered through a lens of commemoration, we are able to access the personal elements of seals, which allow us to better understand the relationships between individuals within kin groups and their emotional ties to each other. The chapter provides a brief discussion of early uses of the iconography and Alexander Abernethy's adoption of iconography associated with his wife's lineage. It then discusses the meaning of the eagle displayed within the grammar of European heraldry before offering suggestions of its particular meaning to these kin groups. Ultimately, the chapter reveals the nuanced ways in which Scottish elites represented themselves to their peers and how iconographies of power and memory might be inherited from either male or female lineage, depending on status and reputation.

Alexander Abernethy, ward of Menteith

The eagle displayed supporter can be easily traced from the seal evidence of members of the Menteith family, attached to the 1290s homage rolls to Edward I (Figures 9.1, 9.2, 9.3 for variations of the eagle supporter).[10] Thus, it seems likely that Abernethy adapted his seal design to echo the seal design of his guardian and father-in-law. The marriage into the Menteith family would have resulted in an elevation in social status for the lord. It appears that

---

Charters', *PSAS* 150 (2021): 309. Sophie Harwood has also addressed the possibilities in studying women's heraldry, see 'Swans and Amazons: Penthesilea and the case for women's heraldry in medieval culture', *Medieval Journal* 7, no. 1 (2017): 61–87.

[8] My analysis uses extant seal impressions and seal casts. In the footnotes, I have noted, when possible, where original impressions are located. For a discussion of methodological approaches to these types of materials see Davis, 'Material Evidence?', 306–10.

[9] Katie Barclay, 'Emotional Lineages: Blood, Property, Family and Affection in Early Modern Scotland', in *Historicising Heritage and Emotions: The Affective Histories of Blood, Stone and Land*, ed. A. Marchant (New York: Routledge, 2019), 84–98; Matthew Hammond, ed., *Personal Names and Naming Practices in Medieval Scotland* (Woodbridge: Boydell Press, 2019), *passim*; Alice Louise Crook, *Personal Naming Practices in Early Modern Scotland: A Comparative Study of Eleven Parishes, 1680–1839* (PhD diss., University of Glasgow, 2016); Elizabeth Ritchie, 'Men and Place: Male Identity and the Meaning of Place in the Nineteenth-century Scottish Gàidhealtachd', *Genealogy* 4, no. 4 (2020): 97.

[10] TNA, SC13/C4. The cast of this seal, and the seals of Walter Steward, Alan Stewart of Menteith and Alexander Abernethy are used here in place of the original impression. The editors would like to thank Kevin Greig, Lyon Office Manager, Court of the Lord Lyon, for his kind assistance in locating and photographing Figure 9.1; TNA, SC13/S645; TNA, SC13/A4. The use of the eagle displayed iconography seems to be particular descendants of the earl of Menteith through this lineage. The arms of Alexander Menteith of Rusky, descended from John [Alan?] de Menteith, does not indicate a use of the eagle displayed in the *Bellenville Roll*; see Colin Campbell, 'Scottish Arms in the *Bellenville Roll*', *Scottish Genealogist* 25, no. 2 (1978): 45, no. 27.

Figure 9.1 Seal cast of Alexander, Earl of Menteith. © Lyon Office, the Court of the Lord Lyon, Edinburgh; by kind permission of the Lyon Office

Figure 9.2 Seal cast of Walter Steward. © Lyon Office, the Court of the Lord Lyon, Edinburgh; by kind permission of the Lyon Office

Figure 9.3 Seal cast of Alan Stewart of Menteith. © Lyon Office, the Court of the Lord Lyon, Edinburgh; by kind permission of the Lyon Office

Figure 9.4 Seal cast of Alexander Abernethy. © British Library Board

Abernethy adapted the eagle displayed supporter to assert his relationship to his wife's lineage and more closely align himself visually with the sigillographic representations of her family (Figure 9.4). His seal featured the eagle displayed supporter, bearing on its breast the arms of Abernethy – a lion debruised of a ribbon, bearing striking similarities to the earl of Menteith's seal.[11] The origin of the adaptation can be further evidenced in two ways. First, the heraldry of the collateral branch of Abernethy, the lords of Saltoun, did not use the eagle displayed supporter to exhibit the Abernethy arms, which suggests that the eagle

[11] TNA, E39/99/31; BL, Seal xlvii, 1090.

displayed supporter was not part of the iconography of earlier members of the Abernethy family.[12] Second, the contemporaneous seal of Margaret Brensesin, widow of William Abernethy, Alexander's uncle, features the Abernethy arms, but there is no iconographic eagle in her seal design.[13] Thus, the eagle displayed supporter was probably adapted from his father-in-law's (and perhaps his wife's) seal design.[14]

The circumstances of Abernethy's young life and wardship in the Menteith household are key to understanding why he adopted stylistic elements from the Stewarts of Menteith seals. The wardship of Abernethy's estates was awarded to Menteith at the February parliament at Scone in 1293.[15] At the same parliament, Abernethy's mother, Mary, Countess of Strathearn, was summoned to appear and testify to her son's rights to various landed holdings.[16] While the legislation dealt specifically with the wardship of the Abernethy estates, rather than the wardship of Abernethy's person, which were legally distinct in medieval laws governing wardship, the marriage of Abernethy to Margaret Stewart suggests a proximity of the Abernethy ward to the Stewarts of Menteith. The adaption of stylistic elements from the Stewarts of Menteith seal designs by Abernethy created a new articulation of Abernethy identity, combining elements from his marital family along with his heritable arms. Abernethy might have been motivated to re-invent his lineage and reputation. On 25 September 1288, Duncan, Earl of Fife, according to the *Chronicle of Lanercost*, was 'slaughtered on horseback by his own men and kinsfolk as he was travelling along the king's highway to Parliament'.[17] Andrew of Wyntoun's later *Original Chronicle of Scotland* also recorded the incident, citing Patrick Abernethy and Walter Percy as perpetrators of the crime, but naming William Abernethy as instigator.[18] There is evidence to suggest more Abernethy kinsmen were implicated in the crime, and Alexander Abernethy's father, Hugh, as the eldest, also had culpability for the actions of his younger brothers and a role in the murder. The date and circumstances of Hugh Abernethy's death are not entirely clear, but he died before 1293, when Alexander and his mother appeared at parliament to settle the wardship of the Abernethy estates, with the past tense used (*fuit*) to describe the countess of Strathearn's relationship to Hugh Abernethy.[19]

---

[12] George Abernethy of Saltoun's arms appear in the late fourteenth-century *Bellenville Roll*, with no appearance of an eagle displayed, see Campbell, 'Scottish Arms'.

[13] TNA, SC13/S661.

[14] Unfortunately, the seal of Mary Abernethy has not been located (yet – I remain optimistic!) and is not in Scottish seal catalogues.

[15] *RPS*, 1293/2/14.

[16] *RPS*, 1293/2/10.

[17] *Chron. Lanercost*, 59.

[18] *The Orygynale Cronykil of Scotland*, ed. David Laing, 3 vols (Edinburgh: Thomas and Archibald Constable, 1872). II: 323–4.

[19] *RPS*, 1293/2.

When Abernethy found himself a ward in the early 1290s, the reputation of the Abernethy kinship was damaged and his wardship and later marriage into the Stewarts of Menteith family presented him with the opportunity to re-brand himself as the heir of Abernethy married to a Stewart of Menteith. He acculturated symbols associated with his marital kin, which made him distinct from his Abernethy kinsmen, whose masculine and noble reputations might have been tarnished by the murder of the earl of Fife.

Multiple meanings? Iconography in European seals

The use of symbols in European sealing practice relied on what Brigitte Bedos-Rezak has termed a 'logic of sameness'.[20] That is, the visual display of an individual relied on the understanding by the contemporary audience of what that visual display meant.[21] The same can be said of heraldry as a specialised vocabulary understood by the European elite, with rules and regulations controlling how families could represent themselves.[22] Susan Crane has commented on the performance of self and the symbols with which 'power speaks to itself' in elite culture and the ways in which heraldry was a concise expression of this.[23] Thus, the meaning of this insignia only existed insofar as it was understood and accepted by other members of the European elite.[24] Therefore, we can establish what the eagle meant within the visual grammar of European heraldry. The eagle symbolised bravery for elites of medieval Europe, amongst other things.[25] According to the *Deidis of Armorie*, a late fifteenth-century heraldic manual and bestiary translated from French into Scots, the eagle was the royal bird, holding lordship over all birds.[26] The eagle had associations with the Roman Empire, and later, the Holy Roman Empire, and would have been understood as a symbol of power and chivalric reputation by European elites. The Scots manual emphasised the eagle's paramount place in the hierarchy of fowls, noting the crown and the bearer of it 'nocht to be born bot be a king', which underscored

---

[20] Brigitte Bedos-Rezak, *When Ego was Imago: Signs of Identity in the Middle Ages* (Leiden: Brill, 2011), 112–3.

[21] Elizabeth A. New, 'Biblical Imagery on Seals in Medieval England and Wales', in *Pourquoi les Sceaux? La sigillographie nouvel enjeu de l'histoire de l'art*, eds Marc Gil and Jean-Luc Chassel (Lille: Publications de l'Institut de recherches historiques du Septentrion, 2011), 466.

[22] Saul, *Chivalry*, 57; Maurice Keen, 'Introduction', in *Heraldry, Pageantry, and Social Display in Medieval England*, eds Peter Coss and Maurice Keen (Woodbridge: Boydell, 2002), 9. For discussions of heraldry and regulation in Europe, see Katie Stevenson, ed., *The Herald in Late Medieval Europe* (Woodbridge: Boydell, 2009), *passim*.

[23] Susan Crane, *The Performance of Self: Ritual, clothing, and identity during the Hundred Years War* (Philadelphia: University of Pennsylvania Press, 2002), 2.

[24] Davis, 'Material Evidence?', 308.

[25] Guy Cadogan Rothery, *Concise Encyclopedia of Heraldry* (London: Senate Books, 1994), 35.

[26] L. A. J. R. Houwen, ed., *The Deidis of Armorie: A Heraldic Treatise and Bestiary*, vol. 1 (Edinburgh: STS, 1994), 27.

the synthesis of lineage and behaviour in chivalric ideals.[27] Thus, the eagle was analogous to the lion in the pictorial vocabulary of power and prestige, representing idealised masculinity and lordship for elites.[28]

However, whether this image held further particular meaning for the Menteith/Abernethy families and their descendants is not immediately clear. With regards to Scottish armorial seals, McAndrew has argued that the eagle displayed 'is not a particularly common charge' within Scottish heraldry.[29] Indeed, it is not a common charge to appear in the *Scots Roll* or other contemporary armorial rolls from the continent featuring Scottish arms. While not common amongst Scots, the use of the iconography was common elsewhere in Europe – in Austria, Savoy, northern Italy, Normandy and Bavaria.[30] The uncommonness as an iconography used in Scottish heritable insignia makes it easier to trace the use amongst Scottish elites. The eagle displayed does appear as a heraldic charge (on a shield) associated with another Scottish family, Ramsay, which appears in the continental *Armorial of Gelre, Bellenville Roll* (both fourteenth century), and *Armorial de Berry* (1450–5).[31] It also appears in the later *Scots Roll* (c. 1490–1500) and is identified as the Ramsay arms.[32] Importantly, there are clear limitations to using armorial rolls as a means of tracing heraldic use, as they were compiled within a martial context, thus excluding women amongst their catalogues of heritable insignia of the elite of northwest Europe.[33] We must also note the difference in the use of the eagle displayed as an heraldic charge and that of supporter within the conventions of heraldry. McAndrew has argued that earlier seals belonging to the Menteith earls do not survive, although he posits it was an iconography used by the last ancient earl of Menteith, Murdach, suggesting this as the point of origin for the iconography.[34]

---

[27] *Deidis of Armorie*, vol. 1, 27. English: 'not to be born but to be a king'. McAndrew has commented on the similarity of the eagle displayed with the iconography of the Eastern Roman Empire and the German Empire. See Bruce A. McAndrew, *Scotland's Historic Heraldry* (Woodbridge: Boydell, 2006), 19.

[28] *Deidis of Armorie*, vol. 1, 27. For a general discussion of the meaning of the eagle in heraldry, see Rothery, *Concise Encyclopedia of Heraldry*, 35–48.

[29] McAndrew, *Scotland's Historic Heraldry*, 19.

[30] Rémy Cordonnier, '"Interpicturalité" Des Bestiaires Manuscrits et de l'iconographie Sigillaire: résultats d'une première enquête', in *Pourquoi les Sceaux?*, 493.

[31] Archibald Hamilton Dunbar, 'Fascimiles of the Scottish Coats of Arms Emblazoned in the"Armorial de Gelre"', *PSAS* 25 (1890): 16, page C; J. Storer Clouston, 'The Armorial de Berry (Scottish Section)', *PSAS* 25 (1890), plate VI, plate X; Campbell, 'Scottish Arms in the Bellenville Roll', 45, no. 26.

[32] Colin Campbell, *The Scots Roll: A Study of a Fifteenth-century Roll of Arms* (Edinburgh: Heraldry Society of Scotland, 1995).

[33] Jackson W. Armstrong has commented on fifteenth-century rolls of arms as having a 'primarily military significance', see Armstrong, 'The Development of the Office of Arms,' in *The Herald in Late Medieval Europe*, ed. Stevenson, 18.

[34] McAndrew, 'The Single Eagle Supporter', 74. Testing this argument further, the eagle displayed supporter cannot be traced in its connection to Menteith in armorial rolls, having consulted the following European armorial rolls: the *Armorial de Gelre, Armorial de Berry, Bellenville Armorial*

Although we cannot determine a further particular meaning for the Menteith lineage, we can understand the eagle supporter as an associated symbol that denoted status and chivalric reputation, which would have been understood via the European grammar of heritable insignia of the later middle ages. Thus, for both men and women belonging to the Menteith/Abernethy lineage, the eagle displayed supporter would have been understood as an iconography of power and noble reputation. When parsing the use of the eagle displayed by these Scottish kinship groups, we might also

Figure 9.5 Seal of Katherine Beaumont, Countess of Atholl. © TNA, Kew

consider whether the iconographic eagle displayed is also used as a stylistic means of featuring multiple seals, and the use of it within this kinship group might be compared to the composition of Katherine Beaumont, Countess of Atholl's contemporaneous seal (1359), which featured the eagle, bearing on each wing a shield (Figure 9.5).[35] The seal design is stylistically similar to the seals used by the countess of Angus and the countess of Ross. Thus, it may have been chosen originally as a fashionable means of displaying a shield or shields, with the understanding that the iconography carried additional meanings associated with good lordship and chivalric ideals, values that were universally shared by both men and women of the aristocracy. In summary, the eagle displayed supporter carried the meaning the eagle held with the grammar of heraldry, but it also gained meaning to the individuals using it within these kin groups over time, as it became an iconography associated with descent from the Abernethy/Menteith lineage, owing to its less frequent use within Scottish heraldry in the later middle ages.

Fourteenth- and fifteenth-century transference of the iconography

Maintenance of the eagle displayed supporter can be traced in the seal designs in female members of the Abernethy/Menteith, and later Angus and Ross/ MacDonald, families. The use of the iconography by men in these lineages is more haphazard, but it is worth discussing its use from the 1290s to the mid-fifteenth

and the *Scots Roll*, as well as R. R. Stodart's volumes that cover Scottish armorial bearings from 1370 to 1678, R. R. Stodart, *Scottish Arms*, 2 vols (Edinburgh: W. Paterson, 1881). This perhaps owes to the fact that it was not used as a charge on a coat of arms, but rather as a supporter of the shields.

[35] TNA, E42/494. She does not have a connection to the lineages discussed here.

century. The starting point for this 'female' transmission was the seal design of Margaret Stewart, Countess of Angus, the daughter of Alexander Abernethy and Margaret de Menteith, where the eagle displayed was used as the supporter of three shields.[36] As the eldest daughter and eventual female heir to the lordship of Abernethy, Margaret Stewart drew heavily on the stylistic elements of her father's seal. Until recently, her seal had been misidentified in Scottish seal catalogues as belonging to her granddaughter because of her use of the Stewart surname.[37] The use of her marital surname may have been a stylistic inheritance from her mother, who appeared as 'Margaret Abernethy' in surviving records, thereby using her husband's surname, rather than retaining of her natal surname, which was common practice in medieval and early modern Scotland.[38]

The use of the marital surname in her seal legend has led to arguments over which heraldry is present in the seal design as well. The seal design features an eagle displayed, bearing on its breast three shields. The centre shield is the most damaged, but appears to bear the arms of her martial family, the Stewarts of Bunkle – a fess chequy surmounted of a bend with three buckles.[39] The *dexter* shield bears the Abernethy arms and the *sinister* shield bears the Stewarts of Menteith arms. The placement of the arms of her marital kin indicates the elevation in status that the countess gained by marriage to John Stewart of Bunkle, who had been newly made the earl of Angus. However, the use of the arms of both her father and mother suggests the countess's continued tie to her natal lineages and the importance of both these kin groups to her identity as an elite woman. The associations were communicated visually, through the Abernethy arms and the eagle displayed supporter. The personal significance was reinforced by the text of the 1366 charter, which invoked the memory of her father. She issued it 'in good memory of Alexander Abernethy, lord of the same [*in bone memorie Alexandri Abernethi domini eiusdem*]'.[40] Significantly, the seal of her husband and the seal of her son, Thomas Stewart, while lords of Abernethy, did not employ either the eagle displayed supporter or the arms of Abernethy.[41]

---

[36] Original attached to NRS, GD190/3/68; BL, Seal xlvii. 1313.

[37] Davis, 'Material Evidence?', 305; John P. Ravilious and Andrew B. W. MacEwan identified it as belonging to the countess, see 'The Earls of Menteith', 130-39. This argument is echoed in McAndrew, 'The Single Eagle Supporter', 73.

[38] As J. P. Ravilious noted, she appears twice as 'Margaret Abernethy' in English records, see F. D. Blackley and G. Hermansen, *The Household Book of Queen Isabella of England, for the Fifth Regnal Year of Edward II, 8th July 1311 to 7th July, 1312* (Edmonton: University of Alberta Press, 1971), 156-7; 177. She also appears as Margaret Abernethy in a licence from Edward II to 'go to Scotland and treat with her friends for the recovery of her lands of her inheritance in Scotland', see H. C. Maxwell Lyte and J. G. Black, eds, *Calendar of Patent Rolls preserved in the Public Record Office: Edward II*, A.D. *1307-1327* (London: Eyre and Spottiswoode, 1894), 87 (membrane 32).

[39] McAndrew has argued the same, see 'The Single Eagle Supporter', 73.

[40] NRS, GD190/3/68.

[41] John Horne Stevenson and Marguerite Wood, *Scottish Heraldic Seals: Royal, Official, Ecclesiastical, Burghal, and Personal Seals* (Glasgow: Maclehose, 1940), III:602.

This suggests that the countess's use of the eagle displayed supporter visually referenced a relationship which was perhaps personally important rather than politically advantageous, as the iconography commemorated her deceased parents.

Use of the eagle displayed supporter in this way can be picked up again in the seal of her granddaughter, Margaret Stewart, Countess of Angus and Mar.[42] The appearance of the iconography in her seal could be a reference to her grandmother, but it is also worth noting that she used the title 'lady of Abernethy' in her charters.[43] Her seal design featured a standing female figure under a canopy,

Figure 9.6 Seal cast of Margaret Stewart, Countess of Angus and Mar. © Lyon Office, the Court of the Lord Lyon, Edinburgh; by kind permission of the Lyon Office

supporting a shield with each hand (Figure 9.6).[44] The *dexter* shield bears the arms of Mar, while the *sinister* shield bears the Stewarts of Bunkle arms. On each shield, an eagle is perched with its wings elevated, each holding the shield strap in its beak. Given that the arms present in the countess's seal did not assert a connection to the Abernethy lineage or lordship, the eagles can be read as an oblique reference to it, commemorating within the family circle an element of her grandmother's seal design. The visual reference in her seal to Abernethy via the iconographic eagles linked to her claim to the lordship asserted in her charters. Like her grandmother, her husband, the earl of Mar, did not adapt any iconography signifying the lordship of Abernethy, which, again, suggests that the lordship was not an important acquisition for the earl at the time of their marriage.[45] Unfortunately, there is no surviving seal of Margaret Stewart's son, George Douglas, first Douglas Earl of Angus. Moreover, the seal design of her grandson, William Douglas, makes no visual mention of his status as lord of Abernethy.[46] The seal design features a quartered shield, bearing the Angus and Douglas arms. The shield bears an escutcheon *en pretence* as well, but it's difficult to determine the exact arms. Like the use of the eagle displayed

---

[42] I have discussed the countess's use of heraldry before, see Davis, 'Material Evidence?', 313–15.

[43] She calls herself 'lady of Abernethy' in a number of documents, see, for example, William Fraser, ed., *Douglas Book* (Edinburgh: T. and A. Constable, 1885), vol. iii, 35–6 (no. 42): 50–1, no. 56.

[44] Seal of Margaret Stewart, Countess of Angus and Mar, attached to Durham Cathedral Archives, DCD Misc. Ch. 653 – (Durham Cathedral seal catalogue 2741); Stevenson and Wood, *Scottish Heraldic Seals*, III:602.

[45] Stevenson and Wood, *Scottish Heraldic Seals*, III:491–2.

[46] Seal of William Douglas, Earl of Angus, attached to Durham Cathedral Archives, DCD Misc. Ch. 795 – (Durham Cathedral seal catalogue 2799); Stevenson and Wood, *Scottish Heraldic Seals*, II:320.

Figure 9.7 Seal cast of George Douglas, Earl of Angus. © British Library Board

by Margaret Stewart, Countess of Angus, the use of the iconography by her granddaughter also suggests that it was of personal significance to the countess, rather than politically important.

The arms of Abernethy may have gained political significance by the mid-fifteenth century, as the Abernethy arms began to appear in the seal designs of the countess of Angus and Mar's descendants. The seal of George Douglas, fourth Douglas Earl of Angus feature the Abernethy arms in his seal design, asserting an affiliation to the lordship as well as the lineage of Abernethy (Figure 9.7).[47] The re-emergence of the arms of Abernethy in the seal design of the earl of Angus is perhaps indicative of the importance of Abernethy and its affiliation to Fife. Alan R. Borthwick has emphasised that the earl established himself at the royal court and benefitted from the fall of the Black Douglases in the 1450s.[48] Moncreiffe has suggested that after the executions of the Albany Stewarts, who held the earldom of Fife in 1425, the heirs to the lordship of Abernethy, the Red Douglases, were quick to 'establish themselves in the exercise of the hereditary prerogative of their kindred', which was the privilege of kingly inauguration. However, this is conjecture rather than an argument based on contemporary evidence.[49] The visual evidence of the seal design of George Douglas certainly asserted this affiliation to the Abernethy lineage, which may have had novel political advantage in in the mid-fifteenth century. Consequently, in this case the female heirs to the lordship of Abernethy mapped out the preservation of a visual link to the lineage through the use of the eagle displayed supporter in their seal designs.

The diffusion of the eagle displayed supporter to the Ross and MacDonald families came about through Abernethy's younger daughter, Mary. While a surviving seal of Mary has yet to be found to compare to the design of her older sister, the eagle displayed supporter appears in the seal design of her son Walter Leslie. Mary's son from her first marriage, Leslie changed his seal significantly in his lifetime following his marriage to Euphemia, Countess of Ross. Upon his

---

[47] BL, Seal xlvii, 1646.
[48] Alan R. Borthwick, 'Douglas, George, Fourth Earl of Angus, *c.*1417–1463', *ODNB*.
[49] Rupert Iain Moncreiffe, *The Law of Succession: Origins of the Law of Succession to Arms and Dignities in Scotland*, ed. Jackson W. Armstrong (Edinburgh: John Donald, 2010), 225. The contemporary evidence to support Moncreiffe's supposition is meagre. There is no mention of James III's inaugurator in the sixteenth-century Asloan MS, see, Asloan MS, I:230. For a discussion of the coronation of James III and wider context, see Norman MacDougall, *James III: A Political Study* (Edinburgh: John Donald, 1982), 51.

marriage, he adapted the eagle displayed supporter, which bore on its breast the quartered arms of Leslie – on a bend three buckles – and Ross – three lions rampant (Figure 9.8).[50] The seal design of Euphemia, his wife, bears striking similarities to the seal design of Leslie's aunt, the countess of Angus. It features an eagle displayed supporter, bearing on its breast three shields (Figure 9.9).[51] The central shield bore the arms of Ross, with the *dexter* shield bearing the arms of Buchan – three garbs – and the *sinister* shield bearing the arms of Leslie. The resemblance of the countess's and Leslie's seal design may owe to Leslie's close relationship to the Angus household, where he served during the 1350s, and his aunt, the countess of Angus. However, his adoption of the eagle displayed supporter came later.[52] The visual display of an affiliation to Abernethy cannot be traced in the charters of these individuals, owing to the fact that they did not hold the lordship of Abernethy. In this instance, the assertion of membership of the lineage exists 'independently of the document', to borrow Elizabeth New's articulation of her findings on Welsh seals.[53] The marshalling of Leslie's arms alongside the adoption of the eagle displayed supporter and the Leslie surname by the countess of Ross suggests an integration of the Leslie and Ross lineages, and the eagle displayed supporter gained an association with Ross through the couple.

Figure 9.8 Seal cast of Walter Leslie, Lord of Ross (1371). © NRS

Figure 9.9 Seal cast of Euphemia Leslie, Countess of Ross. © National Records of Scotland

---

[50] NRS, RH17/1, no. 497 (drawer 20). I have analysed the countess's seal before, Davis, 'Material Evidence?', 315–17.
[51] NRS, RH17/1, no. 499 (drawer no. 20).
[52] Stephen Boardman comments on Walter's service in the household of his kinsman, Thomas Stewart, see Stephen Boardman, 'Leslie, Sir Walter, Lord of Ross (d.1382)', *ODNB*.
[53] Elizabeth New, 'Lleision ap Morgan Makes an Impression: Seals and the Study of Medieval Wales', *Welsh Historical Review* 26, no. 3 (2013): 332.

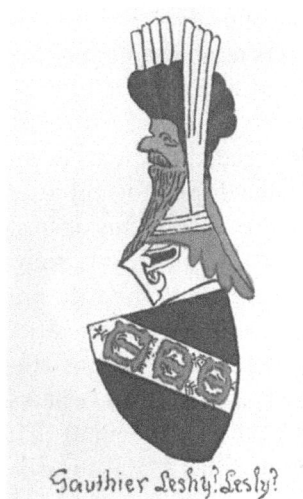

Figure 9.10 The arms and crest of Walter Leslie. © PSAS

Figure 9.11 Seal cast of Walter Leslie (1367), © NRS

As stated above, Leslie's seal changed significantly during his lifetime, and was used contextually depending on his activities as Sir Walter Leslie and as Walter Leslie, Lord of Ross. Leslie altered his heraldic device and seal design to incorporate the prestigious estates and lineage of his wife. His pre-marital arms appear in the *Armorial of Gelre* the *Bellenville Roll*, as well as in a Laing seal cast, featuring the straightforward arms of Leslie (Figures 9.10 and 9.11).[54] While his later design retained primacy of his natal lineages, by placing the Leslie arms in the first and fourth quadrant of the shield, the adoption of the Ross arms as well as the increased size of his seal underscores how the high status of his wife was 'absorbed' by him through marriage and reflected in his representational identity.[55] The adoption of his wife's arms and the adaptation of his seal to reflect his status as 'Lord of Ross' was visually reinforced and validated the title employed by Leslie in the text of the charters dealing with Ross estates.[56] Having spent time in the countess of Angus's household in the 1350s, he might have associated the eagle supporter with comital office, adapting it as a commemoration of that lineage upon his elevation in status as husband of the countess of Ross. Returning to the meaning of the eagle as a symbol that idealised masculine values of good lordship, this may have been an attractive iconography for

---

[54] Dunbar, '"Armorial de Gelre"', 20 (plate II); Campbell, 'Bellenville Roll', 37 (no. 2); NRS, Seal casts, matrices, and detached seals, RH17/1, no. 493 (drawer 20).

[55] For discussions on seal size and rank, see John A. McEwan, 'Does Size Matter? Seals in England and Wales, ca.1200–1500', in *A Companion to Seals in the Middle Ages*, ed. Laura J. Whatley (Leiden: Brill, 2019), 103–25; Jörg Peltzer, 'Making an Impression: Seals as Signifiers of Individual and Collective Rank in the Upper Aristocracy in England and the Empire in the Thirteenth and Fourteenth Centuries', in *Seals and Their Context in the Middle Ages*, ed. Philipp Schofield (Oxford: Oxbow Books, 2015), 63–4.

[56] Peter Coss, *The Lady in Medieval England, 1000–1500* (Stroud: Sutton, 2000), 39.

the lord of Ross to adopt not only to signal his familial connections, but to also emphasise his chivalric and noble reputation. This offers us an example of the ways in which chivalric reputation, elite status and gender intersected in the construction of masculine identity.

The circumstances by which the countess of Ross succeeded to the earldom in the 1360s might also explain her adoption of the eagle displayed supporter in her seal design. Her father had entailed the earldom in 1350 to his nearest male heir, his brother Hugh Ross.[57] Countess Euphemia used the royal favour afforded by her marriage to Leslie to advance her own rights to the earldom of Ross and gain the ability to exercise power in the region she considered her birthright. Her first husband, Leslie, was a favourite of David II and his crusader reputation brought prestige to their marriage. They both reaped benefits from their relationship. Euphemia was disinherited by the male entail that her father had put in place in 1350 after her brother died in 1357. Thus, she and her father had a strained relationship. Significantly, her father also had a troubled relationship with David II.[58] Leslie's position as a favourite of the royal court worked to the couple's advantage with David II re-granting the earldom to Euphemia and her husband while her father, the earl, was still living, and entailing the patrimony to the children produced in their marriage.[59] In addition to this, David II granted the couple other estates in the later 1360s.[60] The evidence of their marriage suggests a partnership, with the two of them appearing jointly in these royal grants.

The grants of the 1360s, however, were contested by the earl of Ross. Her father challenged her succession after David II's death, arguing that he had been coerced into resigning the earldom to his daughter and son-in-law.[61] Importantly, the rights of Euphemia and Leslie were not reversed by Robert II.[62] The countess subsequently invoked her filial relationship and status as female heir and referred to herself as the 'daughter and heir of William, former Earl of Ross' (*Eufamea domina de Rosse filia et heres Willelmi quondam comitis de Rosse*), which glossed over any dispute over the succession that may have occurred in the decades before and legitimised her succession through the assertion of her as the inheritor of Ross.[63] While the texts of her charters might have

---

[57] NRS, J. & F. Anderson Collection, GD297/163.
[58] R. W. Munro and Jean Munro, 'Ross Family (*per. c.*1215–*c.*1415)', *ODNB*.
[59] Joseph Robertson, ed., *Antiquities of the Shires of Aberdeen and Banff* (Aberdeen: Spalding Club), II:386–7.
[60] The couple received the barony of New Forest in Dumfries and the thanages of Kincardine, Aberluthnott, Fettercairn and Aberchirder in the later 1360s. See, *RMS*, vol. 1, 87, no. 258; *RMS*, vol. 1, 118–19, no. 338; *RMS*, vol. 1, 119, no. 339.
[61] NRS, J. & F. Anderson Collection, GD297/193; a transcription of the charter can be found in Robertson, ed., *Antiquities of the Shires of Aberdeen and Banff*, II:387–9.
[62] Boardman, *The Early Stewart Kings*, 47.
[63] Robertson, ed., *Antiquities of the Shires of Aberdeen and Banff*, II:389–90.

downplayed the tumultuous succession to her estates, her seal might be read differently. We might interpret the seal design of the countess, which used iconography associated with Leslie's maternal family, as an effort to break with any associated iconography from the earlier Ross earls. While she continued to use the Ross arms, she also visually referenced her Leslie husband, a crusader hero, through the inclusion of his arms. The partnership of the couple in the managing of the Ross estates is borne out in their seals as well. The visual similarities between the two suggest this. The use of the eagle displayed supporter and the Leslie arms created a new identity for the Ross family, producing a new imagery representing the Leslie earls of Ross.

The integration of the eagle displayed as a heraldic charge rather than a supporter can be traced in the sigillographic representations of Mary Leslie, Countess of Ross and Lady of the Isles, her husband, Donald, Lord of the Isles, and their descendants. The seal design of the countess features a standing female figure under a canopy, supporting a shield in each hand.[64] The shields present in the countess's seal are also less distinct. A galley surmounted of an eagle displayed – representing the modified arms of lordship of the Isles – can be seen in the *dexter* position, with the Ross arms, while indistinct, represented in the *sinister*. The modified arms of the lordship of the Isles are the clearest example of how considerations of status, reputation and power in late medieval Scotland affected identity constructions among noble elites rather than a simple privileging of male lineage and patrilineal descent. The seal design of Donald, Lord of the Isles, while also damaged, reflects the adaption of the eagle displayed into the arms of the lordship of the Isles (Figure 9.12).[65] The permanent change of the MacDonald arms provides visual evidence of the aspirations of the MacDonald family in mainland Scotland and shows that the affiliation with Ross, Leslie and Abernethy was permanently absorbed

Figure 9.12 Seal cast of Donald, Lord of the Isles. © Lyon Office, the Court of the Lord Lyon, Edinburgh

---

[64] BL, Seal xlvii, 1511. Scottish seal catalogues as well Walter de Gray Birch's catalogue of seal casts in the British Museum, describe the countess's shields as resting on the back of a dragon. While the seal cast does show a high relief of something below the shields, the presence of a dragon in the seal design is not apparent. It seems that this description is an error in the cataloguing process. For a discussion of issues with accuracy in antiquarian seal catalogues, see Davis, 'Material Evidence?', 305.

[65] Stevenson and Wood, *Scottish Heraldic Seals*, III:483.

Figure 9.13 Seal cast of Alexander, Earl of Ross and Lord of the Isles. © Lyon Office, the Court of the Lord Lyon, Edinburgh

Figure 9.14 Seal cast of John, Earl of Ross and Lord of the Isles. © Lyon Office, the Court of the Lord Lyon, Edinburgh

into the heraldry and ambitions of the marital kin of Mary Leslie (see the seal of her son and grandson, John, Figures 9.13 and 9.14).[66] Just like with the use of the iconography in the seals of Mary's mother and father, assertions of affiliation to the Abernethy lineage cannot be traced in the language of her charters. However, the use of the eagle displayed provided a visual reference to this lineage and descent through the younger female heir of Mary de Menteith and Alexander Abernethy.

Conclusion

The eagle displayed supporter, a heraldic symbol that denoted good lordship and chivalric reputation, was transferred through the Stewarts of Menteith/Abernethy lineage, gaining a particular meaning through its subsequent use in the later fourteenth and fifteenth centuries which was maintained and asserted by women affiliated with this lineage. The adaptation of the iconography by the Ross/Leslie and MacDonald families visually continued an affiliation to the Abernethy/Menteith family. Its absorption into the arms of the lordship of the Isles underscores the interests and ambitions of the individuals using the iconography in their sigillographic representations. Use throughout the fourteenth century seems to suggest that it was a stylistic inheritance, which provided a visual shorthand within the wider family circle of an individual's link to the Menteith/Abernethy lineage. These personal links gave way to political strategy as it was adopted and absorbed into the sigillographic renderings of later descendants of this kindred. The stylistic inheritance of the eagle displayed supporter, as traced through these seals shows the ways in which the visual vocabulary of sealing iconography could be used to commemorate personal links, as well as rights and claims to lineage and estates. The chapter has

[66] Stevenson and Wood, *Scottish Heraldic Seals*, III:483.

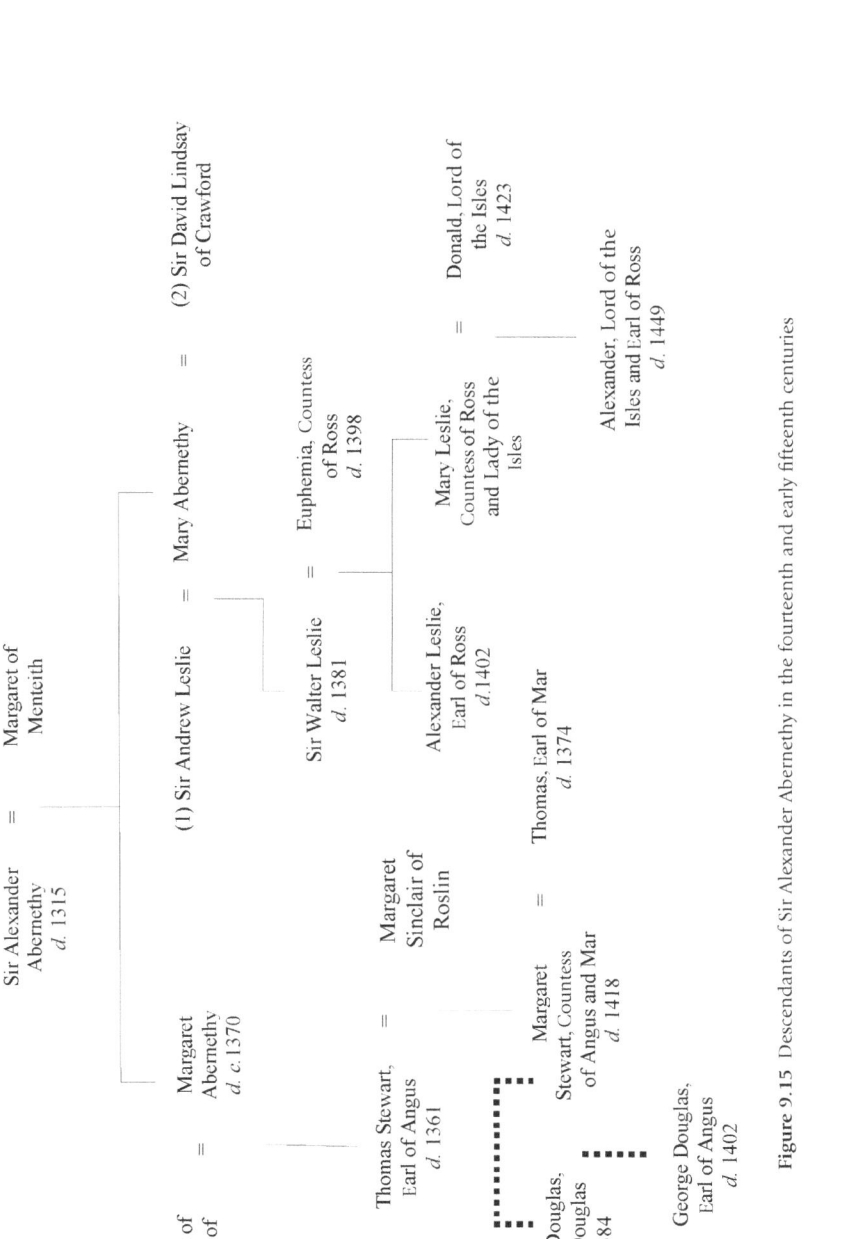

Figure 9.15 Descendants of Sir Alexander Abernethy in the fourteenth and early fifteenth centuries

demonstrated that female use of heritable insignia continues to be a rich vein of further research into identity construction, as women's deployment of heraldry was far from formulaic, suggesting the potential of further gendered analysis of seals in Scotland and north-west Europe.[67]

Similarly, the study of men's use of heraldry is another avenue for further research where the assumptions regarding the preference for agnatic lineage might be tested. This case study of the use of the eagle displayed supporter shows the nuanced ways in which female lineages might be promoted when they led to an increase in status and privileges for the men that married 'up', which aligns with and builds on the findings that Cynthia Neville has made on earlier medieval material. The implications of men's willingness to adopt the symbols of their spouses' lineages, and thereby gaining the associative benefits of them, suggest that the supremacy of male lineage was perhaps not as fixed as we might assume in late medieval Scotland, nor in medieval European society more generally. This raises questions about seal iconography that we might associate as markers of masculinity or femininity. Instead, we might consider these markers as iconographies of power, reputation and lineage, which men and women employed if they were situationally advantageous to the expression of their elite status. In the case of its use by the countess of Angus and her granddaughter we also find the commemorative and personal significance of heritable insignia. These men and women were quick to acculturate an iconography that signalled an elevation in status, rather than follow any supposed fixed formulae in elite identity construction. The use of the eagle displayed within these kin groups shows that men and women were quick to adapt the symbolic trappings of lineage in order to lay claim to political legitimacy, landed resources and elite privileges.

[67] Davis, 'Material Evidence?', 321.

TEN

Another Damsel in Distress? Katherine Beaumont, a Disinherited Noblewoman in Fourteenth-century Scotland

Iain A. MacInnes and Morvern French

On 30 November 1335 Katherine Beaumont, disinherited Countess of Atholl, entered Lochindorb Castle, an island fortress in the Scottish Highlands.[1] On the same day, her husband, David Strathbogie, claimant to the earldom of Atholl, was killed at the Battle of Culblean against the forces of Andrew Murray, the Bruce guardian of Scotland.[2] Katherine remained at Lochindorb until 15 July 1336, during which period she was besieged by Murray's troops before being rescued by those of King Edward III of England.[3] Modern historians of Edward have described his rescue of Katherine as a great chivalric exploit, yet the event is not well represented in the medieval chronicle narrative.[4] Indeed, little is known about Katherine at all in comparison to other besieged noblewomen during the 1330s, whose deeds were recorded far better. This chapter will reconsider Katherine Beaumont by discussing her time in Scotland and contextualising her experience alongside that of other women active in the Second Scottish War of Independence (1332–57). It will also compare Katherine's experience with historic and literary tropes to more fully understand depictions of this brief but important facet of the Anglo-Scottish conflict and Katherine's role in it.

---

[1] TNA, London, SC8/13/611.
[2] Alasdair Ross, 'Men for all Seasons? The Strathbogie Earls of Atholl and the Wars of Independence, c. 1290–c. 1335. Part 2', *Northern Scotland* 21, no. 1 (2001): 1–15; W. Douglas Simpson, 'The Campaign and Battle of Culblean, AD 1335', *PSAS* 64 (1930): 201–11.
[3] G. W. S. Barrow, 'The Wood of Stronkalter: A Note on the Relief of Lochindorb Castle by Edward III in 1336', *SHR* 46, no. 141 (1967): 77–9; Iain A. MacInnes, '"To subject the north of the country to his rule": Edward III and the "Lochindorb Chevauchée" of 1336', *Northern Scotland* 3, no. 1 (2012): 16–31.
[4] A. E. Prince, 'The Strength of English Armies in the Reign of Edward III', *English Historical Review* 46, no. 183 (1931): 353–71, at 358; Ian Mortimer, *The Perfect King: The Life of Edward III, Father of the English Nation* (London: Vintage, 2008), 130; Richard Barber, *Edward III and the Triumph of England: The Battle of Crécy and the Order of the Garter* (London: Penguin, 2014), 106; W. Mark Ormrod, *Edward III* (New Haven: Yale University Press, 2011), 173.

Katherine Beaumont's experience of war

The countess of Atholl's experience of war in Scotland was closely tied to the events of the Second Scottish War of Independence and her husband's participation in them.[5] The Disinherited – individuals and families who had lost lands because of opposition to King Robert I during the First War (1296–1328) – returned to Scotland in August 1332. Led by Edward Balliol, they won early victories, including a large-scale battle at Dupplin Moor near Perth, and Balliol was crowned King of Scots. The Bruce Scots, who supported the young King David II, were successful in mounting opposition over the winter of 1332–3, chasing Balliol from Scotland. The Disinherited returned the following year and besieged Berwick-upon-Tweed, this time with the support of Edward III. Battlefield victory at Halidon Hill in 1333 resulted in the division of much of Scotland amongst the Disinherited, after which only a few castles remained in Bruce hands.[6]

Balliol made Strathbogie his lieutenant in the north of Scotland. In the words of Andrew of Wyntoun's chronicle, Strathbogie went 'Attour þe Month, and all þe land, / [That] Jhone the Cummyn had quhile in hand / He sesit till him as of fee; / And þare a wele lang tyme duelt he.'[7] Strathbogie was heir through his mother, Joan, to the lands of John Comyn of Badenoch, the claimant to the throne whom Robert Bruce killed in 1306. These lands were principally in Badenoch and Lochaber, potentially providing him with a strong foothold in the north and west.[8] Success in convincing the local people to support him and Balliol may have made this region sufficiently safe for Katherine to travel north and join him, and it was only during the period from around mid-1333 onwards that this would have been feasible.[9] Strathbogie's active involvement in these early war years, and Katherine's prior location in England, mean that she likely conceived their son, David, after her arrival in Scotland, and the young Strathbogie heir was probably born in Scotland, at the earliest in around May 1334.[10]

---

[5] Iain A. MacInnes, *Scotland's Second War of Independence* (Woodbridge: Boydell, 2016), ch. 1.
[6] Ross, 'Men for all Seasons? […] Part 2', 6.
[7] *Chron. Wyntoun*, VI:38.
[8] Alan Young, 'Comyn, Sir John, Lord of Badenoch (d. 1306), magnate,' *ODNB*; Ross, 'Men for all Seasons? […] Part 2', 4–8.
[9] Morvern French and Iain A. MacInnes, 'Katherine Beaumont, Countess of Atholl, and the Second Scottish War of Independence (*c.* 1327–*c.* 1336)', *SHR* 102, 3: no. 260 (2023), 333–66.
[10] Although generally thought to have been born c. 1332, the *inquisitions post mortem* held for David Strathbogie suggest a birth date of 1334. Fiona Watson, 'Strathbogie, David, styled tenth earl of Atholl (d. 1326), magnate and soldier', *ODNB*; *Calendar of Inquisitions Post Mortem* (London: HMSO, 1904–), vii, Edward III (1327–1336), no. 713; French and MacInnes, 'Katherine Beaumont', 341–2.

Katherine was a new mother, at the age of around nineteen years, in a kingdom actively at war. In Scotland she may have resided and given birth in one of Strathbogie's northern castles.[11] This would have put her within the heart of Strathbogie's recaptured domains, and in territory to which she could feasibly lay claim herself. Katherine too was a scion of the Comyns, through her mother, Alice, and residual support for the family may have been extended to her as much as it was to Strathbogie.[12] Her location would also have given her access to spiritual support during and after her pregnancy, possibly at Kinloss or Coupar Angus abbeys, both dedicated to the Virgin Mary. The needs of the mother before and after birth, and the ceremony and festivities around the event, required a secure and comfortable location.[13] Finding and remaining in such a location may not have been easy.[14] The recommencement of Bruce counter-offences in 1334 caused unrest, while in-fighting amongst the Disinherited brought disunity and stymied the possibility of organised resistance to the Bruce Scots. Strathbogie retreated to Lochindorb, in the northern part of his domains, perhaps hoping that its apparent security would protect his wife and son.[15] Soon, however, Strathbogie was in flight from John Randolph, Earl of Moray, who caught Strathbogie in Lochaber and forced his surrender on 27 September.[16] Strathbogie's submission was not a one-sided affair, and

---

[11] These may have included Blair, Inverlochy, Lochindorb and Ruthven, or an alternative location could have been at the Atholl *caput* of Rait (Logierait). G. W. S. Barrow, 'Badenoch and Strathspey, 1130-1312: 1. Secular and Political', *Northern Scotland* 8 (1988): 1-15, at 8-9; French and MacInnes, 'Katherine Beaumont'.

[12] Alan Young, *Robert the Bruce's Rivals: The Comyns, 1212-1314* (East Linton: Tuckwell Press, 1997), 206.

[13] Elite medieval women attended mass before retiring to their chambers around one month ahead of childbirth, remaining for at least one month afterwards. Their retinues of female allies attended during and after pregnancy and labour, controlling access to the chambers and assisting with the birth. After the child's baptism, Katherine would have undergone a purification ceremony followed by feasting. Nicholas Orme, *Medieval Children* (New Haven: Yale University Press, 2001), 19-21; Rachel M. Delman, 'Gendered Viewing: Childbirth and female authority in the residence of Alice Chaucer, Duchess of Suffolk, at Ewelme, Oxfordshire', *Journal of Medieval History* 45, no. 2 (2019): 181-203, at 184; Becky R. Lee, 'The Purification of Women after Childbirth: A Window onto Medieval Perceptions of Women', *Florilegium* 14 (1995-6): 43-55; Gail McMurray Gibson, 'Scene and Obscene: Seeing and Performing Late medieval childbirth', *Journal of Medieval and Early Modern Studies* 29, no. 1 (1999): 7-24.

[14] Ross, 'Men for all Seasons? [...] Part 2', 4. More work on the Strathbogies and their control of northern Scotland in this period is planned as this research develops further.

[15] *Chron. Fordun*, 349; *Chron. Wyntoun*, VI:24; *Chron. Bower*, VII:95; *Scalacronica, 1272-1363*, ed. Andy King (Woodbridge: Surtees Society, 2019) [hereafter *Scalacronica*], 116-17; *Adae Murimuth continuatio chronicarum. Robertus de Avesbury de gestis mirabilibus regis Edwardi Tertii*, ed. E. M. Thompson (London: Rolls Series, 1889) [hereafter *Chron. Murimuth*], 72-3; 'Annales Paulini', in *Chronicles of the Reigns of Edward I and Edward II*, ed. W. Stubbs (London: Rolls Series, 1882-3), I:362; *Chronica Monasterii de Melsa*, ed. E. A. Bond (London: Rolls Series, 1868), II:372.

[16] *Chron. Fordun*, 349; *Chron. Wyntoun*, vi, 47-9; *Scalacronica*, 118-19; Ranald Nicholson, *Edward III and the Scots: The formative years of a military career, 1327-1335* (London: Oxford University Press, 1965), 172.

he was granted several territories and the constableship of Scotland to win him over to the Bruce side. Strathbogie was left in charge in the north to 'maynteyn weile þat cuntre', which 'qwhil he Scottis was sa did he'.[17] From a position of adversity, then, by around October 1334 the couple found themselves in an advantageous situation as new members of the Bruce party.[18]

The Strathbogies remained in Bruce allegiance until summer 1335, when a two-pronged English invasion forced many former Disinherited to seek the mercy of the two Edwards. Strathbogie negotiated his surrender, but once again did so from a position of power and was made their lieutenant of Scotland.[19] He returned to significant action in the north, concluding with his siege of Kildrummy Castle, defended by Christina Bruce.[20] Christina's husband, Andrew Murray, along with William Douglas and Earl Patrick of March gathered an army and rode north to the castle's relief. Not awaiting their arrival, Strathbogie withdrew and fought the Bruce Scots at Culblean (Mar) on St Andrew's Day 1335, when he was killed. Bruce forces later besieged Lochindorb, in which Katherine was resident. She was not, however, there prior to Culblean.[21] She may have been with her husband, perhaps even at the siege of Kildrummy, and only sent away at the approach of Bruce forces.[22]

Following Strathbogie's death, Katherine was left to defend the island fortress of Lochindorb and her young son from Bruce attack, remaining there

---

[17] Ross, 'Men for all Seasons? [...] Part 2': 6–9; James A. Robertson, *Comitatus de Atholia: The Earldom of Atholl, Its Boundaries Stated, also the Extent therein of the Possessions of the Family of De Atholia and their Descendants, the Robertsons* (Edinburgh: Murray and Gibb, 1860), 9–10; *Chron. Wyntoun*, VI:49.

[18] Katherine appears to have lost some of her support network at this time, including her mother, as well as wives of Strathbogie retainers who also fled Scotland. See French and MacInnes, 'Katherine Beaumont', 347–8. In a future article we will consider the network of women around Katherine when she was in Scotland.

[19] 'Robertus de Avesbury de gestis mirabilibus regis Edwardi Tertii', in *Adae Murimuth continuatio chronicarum. Robertus de Avesbury de gestis mirabilibus regis Edwardi Tertii*, ed. E. M. Thompson (London: Rolls Series, 1889) [hereafter *Chron. Avesbury*], 298–302; *Chron. Bower*, VII:103.

[20] Morvern French, 'Christina Bruce and Her Defence of Kildrummy Castle', *Royal Studies Journal* 7, no. 1 (2020): 22–38.

[21] Katherine's petition to Edward III in c. 1348 for compensation for her costs during the Lochindorb siege states that she entered Lochindorb on St Andrew's Day 1335, the same date as Culblean (TNA, SC8/13/611).

[22] Such a possibility may be borne out by Barbour's example of the Bruce women joining Robert I and their husbands in the period around the Methven campaign in 1306. John Barbour, *The Bruce*, ed. A. A. M. Duncan (Edinburgh: Canongate Books, 1997), 106. See also James M. Blythe, 'Women in the Military: Scholastic Arguments and Medieval Images of Female Warriors', *History of Political Thought* 22, no. 2 (2001): 242–69; Elizabeth den Hartog, '"Defending the castle like a man": On Belligerent Medieval Ladies', *Virtus* 27 (2020): 79–98, at 87; Linda A. McMillin, 'Women on the Walls: Women and Warfare in the Catalan Grand Chronicles', *Catalan Review* 3, no. 1 (1989): 123–36; Patricia Skinner, 'Gender and Memory in Medieval Italy', in *Medieval Memories: Men, Women and the Past, 700–1300*, ed. Elisabeth van Houts (Abingdon: Routledge, 2013), 36–52; Simpson, 'Battle of Culblean', 204.

until rescued by Edward III in July 1336.²³ However, the siege may not have been as active as is perhaps assumed.²⁴ After the Battle of Culblean, Bruce forces mopped up residual Balliol support, and sporadic truces interrupted wartime activity.²⁵ Furthermore, severe weather may have affected besiegers and besieged, with extensive snowfall denying the attackers the chance of offensive efforts and cutting off supplies to the defenders.²⁶ A more active siege appears to have begun following the expiry of the most recent truce in May 1336.²⁷ There was a siege camp on the shore of the loch, and underwater archaeology has discovered stone balls on the loch bed that may have been projectiles fired at the walls.²⁸ Between May and July 1336, then, Katherine experienced the full force of a Bruce siege and was required to act in defence of Lochindorb until her rescue.

This reconstruction of Katherine's time in Scotland suggests an active role in the war, even before the siege. As an Englishwoman, a member of the Disinherited, and the mother of a young son, Katherine may appear to hold a unique position in the conflict. Nonetheless, she shared some experiences with female Bruce adherents who also played prominent roles in the war. They include Christian Cheyne, Lady Seton, who contributed to the defence of Berwick-upon-Tweed in 1333 through encouraging words rather than deeds. Christina Bruce made 'stout and manly resistens' against Strathbogie at Kildrummy. And 'Black Agnes' Randolph, Countess of Dunbar, led a defence of Dunbar that was comically paralleled with the womanly responsibility to

---

²³ For the nature and defensibility of Lochindorb, see Iain Anderson and Piers Dixon, 'Inverlochy and Lochindorb Castles – A Comparative Study', *Architectural Heritage* 22 (2011): 1–17, at 16.
²⁴ French and MacInnes, 'Katherine Beaumont', 349–58.
²⁵ French and MacInnes, 'Katherine Beaumont', 352–3. *Rotuli Scotiæ in Turri Londinensi et in domo capitulari Westmonasteriensi asservati* (London: Record Commission, 1814–1819), i, 384–8, 391, 397, 410; *Foedera, Conventiones, Litterae et Cuiscunque Generis Acta Publica*, ed. T. Rymer (London, 1816–69), II, ii, 930–1, 933.
²⁶ French and MacInnes, 'Katherine Beaumont', 354–5. Irish evidence indicates significant snowfall across the winter of 1335–6, and the 1330s were a period of climatic change in Scotland. *The Annals of Clonmacnoise*, ed. Denis Murphy (Dublin: University Press, 1896), 290; *The Annals of Connacht*, ed. A. Martin Freeman (Dublin: Dublin Institute for Advanced Studies, 1944), 275; Richard Oram, '"The Worst Disaster Suffered by the People of Scotland in Recorded History": Climate Change, Dearth and Pathogens in the Long 14th Century', *PSAS* 144 (2014): 223–44; Richard Oram and W. Paul Adderley, 'Lordship and Environmental Change in Central Highland Scotland, c. 1300–c. 1400', *Journal of the North Atlantic* 1, no. 1 (2008): 74–84.
²⁷ *Chron. Lanercost*, 296–8; *The Chronicle of Walter of Guisborough, previously edited as the Chronicle of Walter of Hemingford or Hemingburgh*, ed. H. Rothwell (London: Camden Society, 1957) [hereafter *Chron. Hemingburgh*], 311.
²⁸ *Original Letters Illustrative of English History*, ed. Henry Ellis, third series, 3 vols (London: Bentley, 1846) [hereafter *Original Letters*], I:35; *The Wars of Edward III: Sources and Interpretations*, ed. Clifford J. Rogers (Woodbridge: Boydell and Brewer, 1999), 49; *Chron. Wyntoun*, VI:75. Five stone shots have been recovered. Nicholas Dixon and Barrie Andrian, 'The Scottish Trust for Underwater Archaeology, Lochindorb Survey, August 1993' (Edinburgh: STUA, 1994), 6.

maintain the home.²⁹ Katherine Beaumont was clearly not alone in defending a castle in this conflict. Where she differed is in being a Disinherited, as opposed to a Bruce, noblewoman, but even here, her presence in Scotland was not unique. Her mother, Alice Comyn, Countess of Buchan, was besieged at Dundarg Castle (Buchan) alongside her father, Henry Beaumont, and some of her siblings in 1334.³⁰ Others include Mary de Monthermer, Countess of Fife, and her daughter, Isabella, who were captured when Bruce forces took Perth in 1332.³¹ Eve Mowbray and one of her daughters were captured at Cumbernauld Castle when it fell to English forces following a siege in 1335.³² And Philippa and Margaret Mowbray, also daughters of Eve, experienced the war first-hand: Philippa fled Scotland with her husband after his surrender to the Bruce Scots, and Margaret was potentially one of Katherine Beaumont's ladies-in-waiting at Lochindorb.³³ Such examples demonstrate that many women physically experienced this conflict. While not all were involved in leading the defence of fortresses, their location in Scotland during a period of active and ongoing war nevertheless reinforces their importance.

Katherine Beaumont as a besieged noblewoman

While Katherine's experience was not unique, it remains to compare it to those of other besieged noblewomen. A nineteenth-century historian speculated that she mournfully 'looked out from her iron-stanchioned chamber window' to survey the besiegers and their siege engines, from the 'the gloom and solitude' of her location.³⁴ More recent scholars have suggested that within castles ladies remained enclosed, segregated and secluded in the most private spaces most

---

[29] Elizabeth Ewan, 'The Dangers of Manly Women: Late Medieval Perceptions of Female Heroism in Scotland's Second War of Independence', in *Woman and the Feminine in Medieval and Early Modern Writing*, eds Sarah M. Dunnigan, C. Marie Harker and Evelyn S. Newlyn (Basingstoke: Palgrave Macmillan, 2004), 3–18; Nicola Royan, 'Some Conspicuous Women in the Original Chronicle, Scotichronicon and Scotorum Historia', *IR* 59, no. 2 (Autumn 2008): 131–44, at 134–9; French, 'Christina Bruce', 22–38; Cynthia Neville, 'Bruce, Christian', in *The New Biographical Dictionary of Scottish Women*, eds Elizabeth Ewan, Rose Pipes, Jane Rendall and Siân Reynolds (Edinburgh: Edinburgh University Press, 2018), 55–6; Fiona Watson, 'Bruce, Christian (d. 1356)', *ODNB*.

[30] The Beaumonts left Scotland under safe conduct, provided to Henry 'with his wife, children, and whole household [*tota familia*]'. *Chron. Fordun*, 349; *Chron. Bower*, VII:95, 119.

[31] *Chron. Bower*, VII:83.

[32] *Chronicon Henrici Knighton*, ed. J. R. Lumby (London: Rolls Series, 1895–1899), [hereafter *Chron. Knighton*] I:473; Nicholson, *Edward III and the Scots*, 206.

[33] BL, Cotton Nero C VIII, 268r; *Calendar of Documents relating to Scotland*, ed. J. Bain (Edinburgh: H.M. General Register House, 1881–8), III: no. 1174; John H. Fisher, *John Gower, Moral Philosopher and Friend of Chaucer* (New York: New York University Press, 1964), 41–4.

[34] George Bain, *History of Nairnshire* (Nairn: Nairnshire Telegraph, 1893), 146–7.

or all of the time and were 'confined to their towers'.³⁵ However, although space was to a certain extent divided by gender, 'the practice of space in the Middle Ages was never homogeneous, but always in flux, and depended on how its attributes were defined at the time and disseminated by the historical agents'.³⁶ In this scenario – that of a prominent widowed noblewoman leading the defence of a castle – Katherine's position as an authority figure and her own agency override our gendered expectations of how she would use that space.³⁷ The visibility of women within castles' public spaces was an essential aspect of the exercise of lordship, particularly in the absence of a male castellan:

> The visibility of women in the day-to-day running of the castle and the consequent importance for the maintenance of authority is highlighted in times of war. [...] How they used space and commanded their men at arms at such times could determine whether the castle fell or withstood the siege. For women to be effective in these situations, they needed to be known and trusted by the wider castle household, including their men at arms.³⁸

Katherine's contemporary, Christina Bruce, fulfilled this need for recognition during the siege of Kildrummy Castle, personally organising her men in its defence.³⁹ From at least May 1336, Katherine likely had to perform a similar role. Indeed, her claim for compensation from Edward III for 'leading the defence of Lochindorb' demonstrates her active engagement.⁴⁰

It is unlikely that Katherine lived in seclusion in her private chamber at Lochindorb since her status required a household of administrators, clerics, military staff, ladies-in-waiting, nurses for the infant David, laundresses and kitchen staff, all of which she was required to manage. She is likely to have been prominently visible in the hall that once stood on the western side of

---

³⁵ Roberta Gilchrist, 'Medieval Bodies in the Material World: Gender, stigma and the body', in *Framing Medieval Bodies*, eds Sarah Kay and Miri Rubin (Manchester: Manchester University Press, 1994), 43–61, at 51–5. See also Roberta Gilchrist, *Gender and Archaeology: Contesting the Past* (London: Routledge, 1999), 116, 120, 123–5, 128–39; Amanda Richardson, 'Gender and Space in English Royal Palaces c.1160–c.1547: A Study in Access Analysis and Imagery', *Medieval Archaeology* 47, no. 1 (2003): 131–65, at 137–46; Jean-Marie Kauth, 'Barred Windows and Uncaged Birds: The enclosure of woman in Chrétien de Troyes and Marie de France', *Medieval Feminist Forum* 46, no. 2 (2010): 34–67, at 37–8.
³⁶ Barbara A. Hanawalt and Michal Kobialka, 'Introduction', in *Medieval Practices of Space*, eds Barbara A. Hanawalt and Michal Kobialka (Minneapolis: University of Minnesota Press, 2000), x.
³⁷ Allan Gavin Rutherford, 'A Social Interpretation of the Castle in Scotland' (PhD diss., University of Glasgow, 1998), 346; Katherine Weikert, *Authority, Gender and Space in the Anglo-Norman World, 900–1200* (Woodbridge: Boydell, 2020), 147.
³⁸ Leonie V. Hicks, 'Magnificent Entrances and Undignified Exits: Chronicling the Symbolism of Castle Space in Normandy', *Journal of Medieval History* 35, no. 1 (2009): 52–69, at 60.
³⁹ *Chron. Wyntoun*, VI:60–1.
⁴⁰ TNA, SC8/13/611.

the courtyard, or in one of the two chambers that were located on the eastern side and at the north-west corner. The simple layout of the castle, known from surviving stone remains, indicates that access to the hall or chambers was easily achieved, and so the lady or lord of the castle would have been spatially accessible, probably via extra-mural stairs within the courtyard.[41] This prominent visibility would have been a key factor in imbuing the staff and garrison of the castle with a sense of collective effort as they dealt with the repercussions of Bruce siege weaponry employed against the walls. Modern legend suggests that damage to the ruins can be traced directly to the effects of such attacks.[42] Increasingly serious shortages of food, hay for animals, and other materials would also have had a cumulative effect as the Bruce encirclement denied resupply to the besieged. When relieved in July 1336, Katherine noted that 'for everyone in the castle there no longer remained any victuals, except for one cask of wine of little or no worth, and two bushels of grain; and they did not have any straw or cloaks or anything else on which they could lie down or take their rest'.[43]

Katherine may have provided encouragement to her troops in such circumstances. As a comparison, Sybil, wife of Robert Bordet, took control of Tarragona in Spain c. 1124–5 while her husband was away, and

> every night she put on a hauberk like a soldier and, carrying a rod in her hand, mounted onto the battlements, patrolled the circuit of the walls, kept the guards on the alert, and encouraged everyone with good counsel to be on the alert for the enemy's stratagems.[44]

This account was intended to inspire admiration for Sybil, who was not stepping into a manly role but fulfilling a womanly one: that of household manager and visible leader.[45] Katherine too may have occupied a prominent position on Lochindorb's defences, which are thought to have constituted, on the east and part of the north side, a tall wall only a few steps from the water's edge, forming an outer court guarded on the east by a gateway protected by a portcullis.[46]

---

[41] Anderson and Dixon, 'Inverlochy and Lochindorb Castles', 11; for plans see 5–6, ills 3–4. Access analysis can suggest the relationship between spaces within the castle and the ease or difficulty, the latter indicating a higher level of seclusion, of accessing particular spaces. At Lochindorb further, less permanent, structures may have existed within the courtyard.

[42] Joseph Taylor, *Edward I of England in the North of Scotland* (Elgin: Robert Jeans, 1858), 224; W. G. Stewart, *Lectures on the Mountains; or, The Highlands and Highlanders of Strathspey and Badenoch as they were and as they are*, second series (London: Saunders, Otley and Co., 1860), 123–4.

[43] *The Wars of Edward III*, ed. Rogers, 48–9.

[44] *The Ecclesiastical History of Orderic Vitalis*, ed. and trans. M. Chibnall, 6 vols (Oxford: Clarendon Press, 1969–80), VI:404–5.

[45] Hicks, 'Magnificent Entrances and Undignified Exits', 61.

[46] Anderson and Dixon, 'Inverlochy and Lochindorb Castles', 5–6, ills 3–4; John Gifford, *Highlands and Islands*, Buildings of Scotland series (London: Pevsner Architectural Guides, 1992), 95.

Although likely prominent within the castle, Katherine's position was more secluded within the wider landscape and the lordship of Badenoch, to which Strathbogie had laid claim. Possession of the island castle indicated a position of authority on her part, as '[a] sign of authority is the ability to go where others cannot'.[47] Murray's siege was an attempt to challenge that authority by claiming access to the same symbolic space.[48] Although unsuccessful in taking the castle, his troops' encirclement not only prevented its resupply but also prevented Katherine from carrying out, on behalf of her son, the full functions of lordship such as administering justice and collecting rents, which in peacetime would have taken place within the hall of the castle.[49] Katherine was thus denied the full use of the space and spent 400 marks, without any funds incoming, on defensive expenses which likely included the payment of wages to the garrison.[50]

Chroniclers did not, however, record Katherine's actions in positive terms. Indeed, in several English sources she receives little mention at all. Most ignore the events of 1336 altogether, while others describe Edward III's ride north without mentioning Lochindorb.[51] Only two English chronicles include the events of the siege, only one of which, Thomas Gray's *Scalacronica*, mentions Katherine's presence specifically.[52] This absence may be a result of several factors. Events in Scotland may have lost their appeal to writers in England once chroniclers were writing about English success in the Hundred Years War. Medieval misogyny may also have played a part. Despite women fulfilling roles

---

[47] Rutherford, 'A Social Interpretation of the Castle in Scotland', 40.

[48] Rutherford, 'A Social Interpretation of the Castle in Scotland', 41; Amanda Flather, *Gender and Space in Early Modern England* (Woodbridge: Boydell, 2007), 8.

[49] Rutherford, 'A Social Interpretation of the Castle in Scotland', 196; Matthew Johnson, *Behind the Castle Gate: From Medieval to Renaissance* (London and New York: Routledge, 2002), 78.

[50] TNA, SC8/13/611.

[51] *The Chronicle of Geoffrey le Baker*, ed. David Preest and Richard Barber (Woodbridge: Boydell and Brewer, 2012), 52; *Chron. Avesbury*, 298–302; *Polychronicon Ranulphi Higden monachi Cestrensis; Together with the English Translations of John Trevisa and of an Unknown Writer of the Fifteenth Century*, eds C. Babington and J. R. Lumby (London: Rolls Series, 1865–6), VIII:332–3; *The Brut, or Chronicles of England*, ed. F. W. D. Brie (London: Early English Text Society, 1906–8), 292. See also the *Long Anglo-Norman Prose Brut* (BL, Cotton MS Tiberius A VI, 185r); *Historia Roffensis of William of Dene*, BL, Cotton Faustina B V, 78r; 'Gesta Edwardi de Carnarvan, auctore Canonico Bridlingtoniensi, cum continuatione A.D. 1377', in *The Chronicles of the Reigns of Edward I and Edward II*, ed. W. Stubbs, ii (London: Rolls Series, 1883), 128; *Annales Paulini*, 365; *Chron. Murimuth*, 77; *Chron. Knighton*, I:477; *Gesta Scotorum contra Anglicos*, Reigate, Parish Church of St Mary Cranston Library, Item 1117, 279v–279r; Lambeth Palace Library, London, MS 99, 205r; *Chron. Hemingburgh*, 311–12; Thomas Walsingham, *Historia Anglicana*, ed. H. T. Riley (London: Rolls Series, 1863–4), I:197; *The Anonimalle Chronicle, 1333 to 1381*, ed. V. H. Galbraith (Manchester: Manchester University Press, 1927), 7; Kirkstall Abbey Long Chronicle, University of Oxford, Bodleian Library, Laud Misc. 722, 79r; *Chron. Lanercost*, 298.

[52] Corpus Christi College, Cambridge, MS 281, *Parker Library On the Web: Manuscripts in the Parker Library at Corpus Christi College, Cambridge*, https://parker.stanford.edu/parker/catalog/wd305nz9008; *Scalacronica*, 122–3.

as castle defenders in some instances, male chroniclers may have minimised Katherine's activities and instead amplified Edward's chivalric endeavours. Chroniclers may also have been put off discussing the events at Lochindorb because they brought to mind those depicted in French propaganda about Edward and his alleged rape of the countess of Salisbury. The French tale did, after all, revolve around the king rescuing an English countess from Scottish siege in a northern location, before sexually assaulting her. The parallels to Katherine's rescue may have been too close for comfort.[53] The most detailed English account involving Katherine Beaumont is not a chronicle at all, but a newsletter, dated 3 August 1336, presumably relaying information from the king himself.[54] It recorded the day-to-day progression of the campaign, including Edward's rescue of Katherine; her thanking the king, in the third person, for his rescue; and the state that the defenders were reduced to as a result of lack of supplies. She was not, however, afforded direct speech in her own words, and the reported dialogue reflects well on the king's actions rather than on Katherine's.

Scottish chroniclers provided more detail on events at Lochindorb, but with little information about Katherine Beaumont specifically. Like their English counterparts, they may have been aware of tales of the English king's sexual misconduct and connections to this event, but baulked at repeating scurrilous popular stories in their own works.[55] They also emphasised Andrew Murray's success in avoiding being overtaken by English forces. In Wyntoun's work, Murray was the hero despite his failure to capture the castle and being forced to retreat. The episode provides a conclusion to events from 1335 when Murray rode to the rescue of his besieged wife, Christina Bruce, at Kildrummy. Additionally, and like the Lanercost chronicler's depiction of Agnes Dunbar, which portrayed her negatively as lacking sisterly affection when faced with the execution of her captive brother, Scottish writers had no reason to be positive about Katherine Beaumont.[56] Wyntoun referred to a number of 'ladyis, þat ware lufly' at Lochindorb, including Katherine herself.[57] This contrasts markedly with his description of Christina Bruce, whose resistance he praised as

---

[53] Antonia Gransden, 'The Alleged Rape by Edward III of the Countess of Salisbury', *English Historical Review* 87, no. 343 (1972): 333–44; French and MacInnes, 'Katherine Beaumont', 358–65.

[54] *Original Letters*, i, 33–9; *The Wars of Edward III*, ed. Rogers, 48–9.

[55] French and MacInnes, 'Katherine Beaumont', 365. Jelle Haemers, 'Filthy and Indecent Words: Insults, Defamation, and Urban Politics in the Southern Low Countries, 1300–1550', in *The Voices of the People in Late Medieval Europe: Communication and Popular Politics*, eds Jan Dumolyn, Jelle Haemers, Hipólito Rafael Oliva Herrer and Vincent Challet (Turnhout: Brepols, 2014), 247–67, at 262; Laura Slater, 'Rumour and Reputation Management in Fourteenth-Century England: Isabella of France in Text and Image', *Journal of Medieval History* 47, no. 2 (2021): 1–36, at 4.

[56] *Chron. Lanercost*, 314.

[57] *Chron. Wyntoun*, VI:74. Katherine's ladies-in-waiting would have formed the 'company of women' that oversaw and assisted the countess with the birth of her child. Lee, 'Purification of Women', 48–9; Delman, 'Gendered Viewing', 186–7.

'stout and manly'.[58] Although Christina fulfilled her womanly role as protector of the household, Wyntoun also depicted her as a capable defender. It may be that Christina used the public castle spaces more effectively, perhaps visibly on the defences, allowing her actions to be described as 'manly'.[59] Christina's age – in her early forties at least – would have granted her greater experience and perhaps confidence than Katherine, enabling her to be a more successful leader. Christina was perhaps dealt with more generously by a Scottish source that saw her actions as a patriotic defence by a sister of Robert I. In comparison, Katherine, the English wife of the Disinherited David Strathbogie, an individual crafted into a bogeyman by Scottish sources, received far less recognition of her military and leadership capabilities.[60]

Similar influences may be seen in the absence of chronicle comment about Katherine as a mother. After the relief of Lochindorb, Fordun indicated that Edward III 'brought away the wife and the heir of David Earl of Athol', but his is the only work to record the presence of the son.[61] Protection of the young Atholl heir would have been an essential part of Katherine's role during the siege and, in this case, she succeeded. Nothing was made of the theme of motherhood in chronicle accounts of the siege, however, in opposition to accounts of Lady Seton and Agnes Randolph in which images of motherhood were employed in depictions of their castle defence. Lady Seton subverted the ideal of a woman who protected her family, and specifically her children, by convincing her husband not to surrender Berwick even though their captive son was threatened with execution. However, she also demonstrated her willingness to fulfil her womanly duty by providing further sons for her husband.[62] In Bower's description of Agnes Randolph's defence of Dunbar, he also used birthing imagery. The earl of Salisbury deployed a wheeled wooden platform with soldiers hidden beneath, called a 'sow':

> At this the countess Black Annot shouted in a strong voice, saying 'Montague, Montague, beware for your sow will farrow [give birth to piglets]!' With that, she caused an ingenious machine inside the castle to be drawn back for discharging a missile, and a large heavy stone [...] struck the sow fiercely like lightning and dashed the heads of many inside to pieces.[63]

---

[58] *Chron. Wyntoun*, VI:60.
[59] See Tadhg O'Keeffe, 'Concepts of "Castle" and the Construction of Identity in Medieval and Post-Medieval Ireland', *Irish Geography* 34, no. 1 (2001): 69–88, at 77.
[60] *Chron. Bower*, VII:115; *Chron. Wyntoun*, VI:58–60, 62; *Chron. Fordun*, 351.
[61] *Chron. Fordun*, 352. In a later period, Boece wrote that Katherine was at Lochindorb with 'all [Strathbogie's] barnis', suggesting the possibility that David was not an only child. Hector Boece, *Buik of the Chronicles of Scotland*, ed. William B. Turnbull, iii (London: Rolls Series, 1858), 334.
[62] *Chron. Wyntoun*, VI:9; Ewan, 'The Dangers of Manly Women', 5–6.
[63] *Chron. Bower*, VII:129; Ewan, 'The Dangers of Manly Women', 8.

As noted by Elizabeth Ewan, such birthing imagery called attention to the protagonist's womanhood, but it is wholly absent in accounts of Katherine Beaumont.[64]

Neither was her motherhood explicitly linked to a common medieval association between the lady of a castle and the castle itself. With its enclosed spaces, it was a metaphor for the feminine ideal, and the presence of a lord's wife and heir symbolised the stability of a hierarchical, patriarchal society: 'When one violates the lady, one violates the castle and, thus, one violates the social order represented by the castle/lady.'[65] The perpetuation of lineage depended on the inviolability of women's spaces, so to invade them – from the domestic sphere to the wider estate – threatened a lady's reputation and, by extension, the authority of her male family.[66] The protection of a woman's chastity or fidelity by an enclosing structure was linked in medieval thought to her own containment and protection of her child within the womb.[67] There was also a link between the defence of a castle and the production of children. The word 'enceinte' came to mean both a castle enclosed by walls and 'pregnant'.[68] In such an interpretation, Lochindorb physically represented Katherine's role as wife and mother: an important link in the chain of what was intended to be a reinstated Strathbogie line. Defence of the castle was, literally, the defence of a future inheritance to be achieved through Katherine. That pro-Bruce Scottish chroniclers did not emphasise this element is unsurprising, given they saw Strathbogie's claims as illegitimate. Similar absence from English sources may relate to hesitancy over the episode, especially because of the metaphorical connection between sieges and the violation of a woman or of female space. Again, it may have been too problematic to recount at a time when French propaganda accused the English king of sexually violating a noblewoman.

Even the contemporary account provided by Edward III was not wholly positive in its depiction of Katherine. Its mention of the poverty of supply at the castle reflects poorly on her womanly, and aristocratic, responsibility to provide for her household. Indeed, without Edward's rescue, the castle would

---

[64] Ewan, 'The Dangers of Manly Women', 8.
[65] Susan E. Murray, 'Women and Castles in Geoffrey of Monmouth and Malory', *Arthuriana* 13, no. 1 (2003): 17–41, at 18.
[66] Rachel M. Delman, 'The Queen's House before the Queen's House: Margaret of Anjou and Greenwich Palace, 1447–1453', *Royal Studies Journal* 8, no. 2 (2021): 6–25, at 23–4.
[67] Murray, 'Women and Castles', 19–20; Gilchrist, 'Medieval Bodies in the Material World', 57; Gilchrist, *Gender and Archaeology*, 139–40; Kauth, 'Barred Windows and Uncaged Birds', 42–3, 52. Female chastity and fertility were related to other enclosed spaces including the garden or *hortus conclusus*: Karen Dempsey, 'Tending the "Contested" Castle Garden: Sowing Seeds of Feminist Thought', *Cambridge Archaeological Journal* 31, no. 2 (2021): 265–79, at 266–7. In contrast, women occupying liminal or public spaces could be considered improper: Diane Wolfthal, *In and Out of the Marital Bed: Seeing Sex in Renaissance Europe* (New Haven and London: Yale University Press, 2010), chs 3, 5.
[68] Delman, 'Gendered Viewing', 197.

likely have fallen. Medieval opinion held that, although women's mental and physical weakness should have prevented their participation in warfare, they were to exercise authority within their own homes by providing for members of the household and guests.[69] Such ideas found their way into more comedic depictions of women at war. Margaret of Beverley, serving in the defence of Jerusalem in 1187, wore a cooking pot as a helmet.[70] Matilda de Braose, wife of a Welsh marcher lord, is said to have 'boasted that she had so many cheeses that if a hundred of the most vigorous men in England were besieged in a castle, they could defend themselves with her cheeses for a month'.[71] And Agnes Randolph provided supplies to her besiegers as a mocking reflection of their own lack of provender.[72] In contrast, lack of provisions appears to have been Katherine's principal weakness. The closeness of the siege and the harsh winter may have denied the garrison any chance to replenish its stores. Indeed, the dearth of supplies for Edward's own forces in July 1336 suggests that foodstuffs were difficult to acquire.[73] The king's account was likely intended to emphasise his own bravery and success, saving Katherine and her garrison from Bruce attack and potential starvation, but it did little to recognise her bravery and determination in the face of such difficulties, or the reality of her experience over the preceding months. Katherine is both voiceless, in that she does not speak directly in any account, and condemned by the words attributed to her in the newsletter. Coupled with a lack of any description of her efforts in the castle's defence, Katherine was rendered inert in accounts of the siege of Lochindorb, in contrast to the various Bruce noblewomen similarly besieged in the same decade.

Conclusion

The example of Katherine Beaumont provides a different perspective on the experience of women in this period. Although her circumstances appear similar to those of other women who have been the subjects of earlier studies, Katherine stands out as a young woman whose role as defender was complicated by her

---

[69] Blythe, 'Women in the Military', 261–4, 267–8.
[70] 'Thomas of Froidmont: The Adventures of Margaret of Beverly, A Woman Crusader', in *Crusades: A Source Reader*, eds S. J. Allen and E. Amt (Toronto: University of Toronto Press, 2014), 204; Helen J. Nicholson, '"La demoiselle del chastel": Women's Role in the Defence and Functioning of Castles in Medieval Writing from the Twelfth to the Fourteenth Centuries', in *Crusader Landscapes in the Medieval Levant: The Archaeology and History of the Latin East*, eds Micaela Sinibaldi, Kevin J. Lewis, Balázs Major and Jennifer A. Thompson (Cardiff: University of Wales Press, 2016), 387–402, at 388; Susan Signe Morrison, *A Medieval Woman's Companion: Women's Lives in the European Middle Ages* (Oxford: Oxbow Books, 2016), 76.
[71] *Histoire des ducs de Normandie et des rois d'Angleterre*, ed. Francisque Michel (Paris, 1840), 111–12; Nicholson, '"La demoiselle del chastel"', 389.
[72] *Liber Pluscardensis*, ed. Felix J. H. Skene, 2 vols (Edinburgh: William Paterson, 1877), II:216.
[73] *The Wars of Edward III*, ed. Rogers, 49.

castle's location, the difficulty of resupply, and the presence of her young son. Conversely, she may be representative of a larger number of women not yet studied who found themselves in a similar position. These women were, or were married to, members of the Disinherited party, returning or traveling to Scotland in search of lost inheritances. With early successes, they may have had some ability to make good on their claims and may even have been welcomed back to their ancestral lands. Consequently, Katherine may be more representative than she at first appears. She may have had more success than most in Scotland due to her husband's significance in Scottish affairs: a significance that ensured that her stay, though brief, revolved around the principal events of the day. It also brought unwanted attention when she found herself besieged within Lochindorb Castle, far from support, and alone as a new widow. While chronicle and record evidence is insufficient to fully understand her experiences and activities during this siege, the discussion here suggests some possibilities and proposes that she is likely to have shared similar responsibilities to the better-known Bruce women. Ultimately, there remains some mystery about Katherine. Despite her importance within this conflict, and Edward III's own detailed account of his rescue of the 'damsel in distress', her time in Scotland was not well served in the chronicle narrative. This may be a result of several causes, not least of which is her position on the 'wrong side', ensuring that later pro-Bruce/Stewart writers avoided positive comment about her. English chroniclers may have avoided discussing her at all because of scandalous gossip about Edward III. Nonetheless, Katherine Beaumont is a fascinating figure who deserves greater study, and who may yet emerge more fully from the shadows to allow detailed analysis of her activities and experience during this period of conflict.

ELEVEN

Negotiating Youth, Old Age and Manhood: A Comparative Approach to Late Medieval Scottish Kingship

Lucinda H. S. Dean[1]

While the web of his life was still in the early stages, it was the Lord's wish to sacrifice him with a shortening of the normal course of life. Before he could grow to the elderly stages, death ran ahead and snatched him inopportunely …[2]

By mentioning both 'early stages' and 'elderly stages' of life in the account of James I's death in 1437, the fifteenth-century chronicler Walter Bower implies that James – then aged forty-four years – was at a mid-point of life and certainly not elderly. Similarly, when recording the death of forty-seven-year-old David II (d. 1371), Bower states that death 'brought to an end under its fatal law a king who was scarcely approaching mature manhood'.[3] In these statements, Bower may have been harnessing associations with the stages of life for a specific dramatic effect: to emphasise the great loss to the kingdom that occurred when these kings were snatched away in their prime. Nonetheless, these declarations also illustrate how medieval and early modern contemporaries in Scotland, as elsewhere, divided life into distinct stages.[4] Corrine T. Field and Nicholas Syrett have suggested that many historians tend to discuss age as a 'neutral marker of identity without investigating its meaning …', and, in so doing, have potentially missed important opportunities to better understand past societies.[5] They argue

---

[1] The author offers thanks to Jane Dawson, the anonymous reviewers, and attendees of the University of Edinburgh's Scottish History seminar (October 2022) for their helpful comments, and the editorial team for managing a supportive process of workshopping and chapter swapping.
[2] *Chron. Bower*, 8:302–3.
[3] *Chron. Bower*, 7:360–1.
[4] Alexandra Shepard, *Meanings of Manhood in Early Modern England* (Oxford: Oxford University Press, 2003), 21–3, 54–8; *Ratis Raving and Other Moral and Religious Pieces in Prose and Verse (from Cambridge University MS KK.I.)*, ed. J. Rawson Lumby (London: Early English Text Society, 1890), lines 1104–1745.
[5] Corrine T. Field and Nicholas Syrett, 'Chronological Age: A Useful Category of Historical Analysis', *American Historical Review* 125, no. 2 (April 2020): 371–84, at 375.

that, as societies across most temporal and geographical boundaries divide life into chronological stages and associate these stages with roles in society, '[t]hese life stages have structured how human societies function'.[6] With Field and Syrett's suggestions in mind, this chapter positions age and life stages at the centre of a discussion about manhood and kingship. Taking the 'early' and 'elderly' stages of life as a particular focus, it identifies examples of when, how and why contemporary and near-contemporary chronicle and narrative history writers refer to age in relation to late medieval royal men. Using these examples, in conjunction with a fifteenth-century didactic poem, it analyses age-related expectations and the interplay with contemporary understandings of manhood to build on existing scholarship about elite male experience in late medieval Scotland.[7] By drawing on theories about the hierarchy of masculinities, this discussion will also pose questions about how threats to the hegemonic masculine status of a king, especially from members of his own family, might shed new light on power and how it was performed.[8]

Recognising the importance of age and life stages in the Scottish context, Janay Nugent and Elizabeth Ewan sought to address a specific lacuna within the Scottish historiography when they instigated the collection of essays *Children and Youth in Premodern Scotland*, published in 2015.[9] This study sits in a wider body of scholarship illustrating the potential value of exploring pre-modern childhood and youth in pre-modern Europe, particularly in relation to gendered identity and experience.[10] Most recently, and particularly relevant for this

---

[6] Field and Syrett, 'Chronological Age': 374.

[7] Cynthia Neville, 'Making a Manly Impression: The Image of Kingship on Scottish Royal Seals of the High Middle Ages', and Sergi Mainer, 'Contrasting Kingly and Knightly Masculinities in Barbour's Bruce', in *Nine Centuries of Man: Manhood and Masculinity in Scottish History*, ed. Lynn Abrams and Elizabeth Ewan (Edinburgh: Edinburgh University Press, 2017), 101–41; Caitlin T. Holton, '"With A Vertu and Leawté": Masculine Relationships in Medieval Scotland' (MA diss., University of Guelph, 2011); Caitlin T. Holton, 'Masculine Identity in Medieval Scotland: Gender, ethnicity, and regionality' (PhD diss., University of Guelph, 2017).

[8] This is one of a few foundation-laying studies in the development of a broader research project focused on kingship and manhood in pre-modern Scotland by the author, see also: Lucinda H. S. Dean, '"Richesse in Fassone and in Fairness": Marriage, Manhood and Sartorial Splendour for Sixteenth-century Scottish Kings', *SHR* 100, no. 3 (December 2021): 378–96; 'Reaching the Estate of Manhood: A Case Study of James V of Scotland' (forthcoming). An early version of the latter (given at Centre for History, UHI, 2017) is accessible online, accessed March 3, 2020: https://www.youtube.com/watch?v=RUakt04ftZk&t=102s.

[9] Janay Nugent and Elizabeth Ewan, 'Introduction: Adding Age and Generation as a Category of Historical Analysis', in *Children and Youth in Premodern Scotland*, eds Elizabeth Ewan and Janay Nugent (Woodbridge: Boydell, 2015), 1–12.

[10] For example, Nicholas Orme has provided groundbreaking explorations of medieval childhood, including *Medieval Children* (New Haven: Yale University Press, 2001) and *Tudor Children* (New Haven: Yale University Press, 2023). There is also a growing body of work on youth, see Kim M. Phillips, *Medieval Maidens: Young Women and Gender, 1270–1540* (Manchester: Manchester University Press, 2003); Shepard, *Meanings of Manhood*, 93–126; Elizabeth Currie, *Fashion and Masculinity in Renaissance Florence* (London: Bloomsbury, 2016), ch. 6: 'Youth, Fashion, and

chapter, Emily Ward has drawn Scotland's high medieval boy kings, such as Alexander III, into wider European comparisons of the continuity and change in notions of maturity.[11] Alexandra Shepard argued in 2003 that there was a dearth of work on pre-modern old age, particularly where ageing intersects with issues of masculinity.[12] While this is arguably still the case in relation to medieval Scotland, recent work for early modern Scotland and Europe more broadly demonstrates a growing interest and focus on old age and masculinity.[13] The study of pre-modern manhood is also an area ripe for research in a Scottish context, as Lynn Abrams and Ewan stated: 'Men are everywhere in narratives of Scotland's past, but at the same time they are nowhere.'[14] For example, the majority of studies on late medieval Scottish monarchs take a political approach that engages little with socio-cultural issues like gender, leaving many questions to be asked about gendered experiences of men and the impact of these on the wider historical narrative.[15] Katherine J. Lewis suggests this too is

Desire', 109–27; Benjamin B. Roberts, *Sex, Drugs and Rock 'n' Roll in the Dutch Golden Age* (Amsterdam: Amsterdam University Press, 2017); Elizabeth S. Cohen and Margaret Reeves, eds, *The Youth of Early Modern Women* (Amsterdam: Amsterdam University Press, 2018).

[11] Emily J. Ward, 'Child Kingship and Notions of (Im)maturity in Northwest Europe, 1050–1262', *Anglo-Norman Studies* 40 (2018): 197–212.

[12] Shepard, *Meanings of Manhood*, 215–17.

[13] In Scottish scholarship, some examples include Chris Langley's work on the impact of old age on ministers in seventeenth- and eighteenth-century Scotland, while Katie Barclay's work on marriage and ageing complicates the idea of life stages as static and considers the experience of ageing and changing relationships of married couples. See Chris R. Langley, 'Clerical Old Age and the Forming of Rites of Passage in Early Modern Scotland', *Studies in Church History* 59 (2023): 244–64; Katie Barclay, 'Intimacy and the Life Cycle in the Marital Relationships of the Scottish Elite during the Long Eighteenth Century', *WHR* 20, no. 2 (2011): 189–206. Examples of broader European scholarship include: Erin J. Campbell, ed., *Growing Old in Early Modern Europe: Cultural Representations* (London: Routledge, 2006); Anthony Ellis, *Old Age, Masculinity, and Early Modern Drama: Comic Elders on the Italian and Shakespearean Stage* (London: Routledge, 2009); Erik Spindler, 'Youth and Old Age in Late Medieval London', *London Journal: A Review of Metropolitan Society in the Past and Present* 36, no. 1 (2011): 1–22, esp. 10–19; Cynthia Skenazi, *Aging Gracefully in the Renaissance: Stories of Later Life from Petrarch to Montaigne* (Leiden: Brill, 2013); Will Rogers, *Writing Old Age and Impairments in Late Medieval England* (Leeds: ARC Humanities Press, 2021); Thijs Porck, 'The Ages of Man and the Ages of Woman in Early Medieval England: From Bede to Byrhtferth of Ramsay and the *Tractus de quaternario*', in *Early Medieval English Life Courses: Cultural-Historical Perspectives*, eds Thijs Porck and Harriet Soper (Leiden: Brill, 2022), 17–46; Amie Bolissian, 'Masculine Old Women or Feminine Old Men? Rethinking Gender and the Ageing Body in Early Modern English Medicine', *Gender and History* 35, no. 2 (July 2023): 408–42.

[14] Quote from: Lynn Abrams and Elizabeth Ewan, 'Introduction', in *Nine Centuries of Man*, 1–20, at 2.

[15] Many of the monographs of Scottish kings were published in the 1990s and early 2000s, when gender was not a mainstream concern in Scottish historiography, and even works on Mary Queen of Scots side-stepped the issue of gender, see Anna Groundwater, 'Afterward: What Now?', in Jenny Wormald, *Mary Queen of Scots: A Study in Failure* (1988, rev. ed. Edinburgh: John Donald, 2017), 211–21. Newer works on Mary have taken a gendered approach, see Retha M. Warnicke, *Mary Queen of Scots* (London: Routledge, 2006); Kristen Post Walton, *Catholic Queen, Protestant Patriarchy: Mary Queen of Scots and the Politics of Gender and Religion* (London: Routledge, 2006).

quite common across scholarship more widely.[16] Originating from women's and then gender history, the study of masculinity often takes a history from below approach that excludes, sometimes explicitly, elite and royal men.[17] However, a growing body of work, primarily from scholars of English history, is reaping wide-reaching rewards in terms of generating new understanding by turning a gendered lens upon pre-modern kingship.[18] Within this scholarship, two strands have been particularly influential upon the approach taken in this chapter: the importance of looking at the language contemporaries chose to use and the apparent synergies with Raewyn W. Connell's influential theories about stratified system of masculinities when looking at kingship through a gendered lens.

As Fletcher has illustrated, analysing the language around aspects of manhood offers a means of identifying 'unspoken, commonplace ideas of a society' that can better facilitate gendered analysis of actions and rhetoric.[19] To this end, the intention here is to examine complementary primary source materials: a fifteenth-century advice poem known as 'Ratis Raving' used alongside contemporary and near-contemporary chronicles and sixteenth-century histories recording the actions of kings. 'Ratis Raving' is a poem of over 1,800 lines that offers didactic advice in a father-to-son style typical across Europe in the

However, more recent publications or revised editions on Scottish male monarchs are still quite traditionally political, see Christine McGladdery, *James II*, rev. ed. (1990, repr. Edinburgh: John Donald, 2015); Norman Reid, *Alexander III, First Among Equals* (Edinburgh: John Donald, 2019); Ken Emond, *The Minority of James V: Scotland in Europe, 1513–1528* (Edinburgh: John Donald, 2019); Richard Oram, *David I, King of Scots, 1124–1153* (Edinburgh: John Donald, 2020). The exceptions include chapters in Abrams and Ewan's *Nine Centuries of Man*: see Neville, 'Making a Manly Impression', 101–21; Mainer, 'Contrasting Kingly and Knightly Masculinities in Barbour's Bruce', 122–41.

[16] Katherine J. Lewis, *Kingship and Masculinity in Late Medieval England* (Abingdon: Routledge, 2013), 9.

[17] For example, see Dawn M. Hadley, 'Introduction', in *Masculinity in Medieval Europe*, ed. Dawn M. Hadley (repr. Abingdon and New York: Routledge, 2014), 1–18, at 3; Derek G. Neal, *The Masculine Self in Late Medieval England* (Chicago: University of Chicago Press, 2008), 6–7.

[18] W. Mark Ormrod, 'Monarchy, Martyrdom and Masculinity: England in the later middle ages', in *Holiness and Masculinity in the Middle Ages*, eds Patricia H. Cullum and Katherine J. Lewis (Cardiff: University of Wales Press, 2004), 174–91; Christopher Fletcher, 'Manhood and Politics in the Reign of Richard II', *Past and Present* 189, no. 1 (November 2005): 3–39; Christopher Fletcher, *Richard II: Manhood, Youth and Politics, 1377–99* (Oxford: Oxford University Press, 2008); Christopher Fletcher, 'Manhood, Kingship and the Public in Late Medieval England', *Edad Media Revista de Historia* 13 (2012): 123–42; Lewis, *Kingship and Masculinity*; Emma Levitt, 'The Construction of High Status Masculinity through the Tournament and Martial Activity in the Later Middle Ages' (PhD diss., University of Huddersfield, 2017); Hélder Carvalhal, 'Kingship and Masculinity in Renaissance Portugal (Fifteenth and Sixteenth Centuries)', in *The Routledge History of Monarchy: New perspectives on rulers and rulership*, ed. Elena Woodacre et al. (Abingdon: Routledge, 2019), 300–13; Emma Levitt, 'Tiltyard Friendships and Bonds of Loyalty in the Reign of Edward IV', in *Loyalty to the Monarchy in Late Medieval and Early Modern Britain, c.1400–1688*, eds Matthew Ward and Matthew Hefferan (Basingstoke: Palgrave Macmillan, 2020), 15–36.

[19] Fletcher, 'Manhood and Politics', 3–39; Fletcher, *Richard II*.

late medieval and early modern period.[20] Found within a collection of poetry and other didactic texts, the poem has been reproduced in printed format with introductory information about authorship and manuscript dating, but has otherwise been surprisingly neglected.[21] While the poem does not discuss Scottish rulers specifically, it does include an extensive commentary – over 600 lines – on age as associated with seven life stages: the first four stages covering childhood and youth, the fifth exploring the 'perfect' age, and the last two discussing old age. Notably, the poem also uses the term 'eild' (age) for stages of life that encompassed a range of years that was not always fixed, showing the fluidity of age as a concept in the medieval past; as Field and Syrett argue, 'age was less a fact than it was a negotiation'.[22] These sections on the 'eilds' of man offer unparalleled near-contemporary reflections on the expectations and challenges of each stage of life from the hand of a Scottish writer, so providing a framework (along with legal texts) for analysing the statements identified in the chronicle and history writing employed herein. The chronicle texts used are Walter Bower's *Scotichronicon* (1440s) and the vernacular poetic chronicle of Andrew of Wyntoun (1420s).[23] The challenges with the chronicle and narrative record of late medieval Scotland are well known, including partisan favouring of particular dynasties or individuals, overt moralising by clerics about secular activities and reliance on no longer extant texts.[24] However, these challenges can be used to the advantage of this study when seeking Fletcher's 'unspoken, commonplace ideas of a society'.[25] Additionally, although written significantly after the fact, a number of sixteenth-century commentators have also been consulted to reflect on how such discussions about age are modified, and why,

---

[20] *Ratis Raving*, lines 1104–1745. For fuller introduction about dating and authorship of the poem, see *Ratis Raving and Other Early Scots Poems on Morals*, ed. R. Girvan (Edinburgh: William Blackwood and Sons, 1939), xx–xxii, xxxii–lxxiv, 1–51. The reproductions of the poems are very similar and line numbers are the same.

[21] Sarah Dunnigan, 'Sons and Daughters, "Young Wyfis" and "Barnis": Lyric, Gender, and the Imagining of Youth in the Maitland Manuscripts', in *Children and Youth in Premodern Scotland*, 187–204, at 190. A full gendered analysis of this poem would be a very worthwhile task and is one the author is keen to undertake in the future.

[22] Field and Syrett, 'Chronological Age', 374–9, quote at 377.

[23] *Chron. Bower*, *Chron. Wyntoun*. *Gesta Annalia II* was also consulted but makes surprisingly few references to age in relation to the kings being researched: *Chron. Fordun*.

[24] Examples of work on Scottish chronicle tradition: Stephen Boardman, 'Chronicle Propaganda in Fourteenth-Century Scotland: Robert the Steward, John Fordun, and the "Anonymous Chronicle"', *SHR* 76, no. 201 (April 1997): 23–43; Dauvit Broun, 'A New Look at Gesta Annalia Attributed to John of Fordun', in *Church, Chronicle and Learning in Medieval and Early Renaissance Scotland: Essays Presented to Donald Watt on the Occasion of the Completion of Bower's Scotichronicon*, ed. Barbara E. Crawford (Edinburgh: Mercat Press, 1999), 9–30; John J. McGavin, *Theatricality and Narrative in Medieval and Early Modern Scotland* (Farnham: Ashgate, 2007); McGladdery, *James II*, 209–53.

[25] Fletcher, 'Manhood and Politics', 3–39; Fletcher, *Richard II*.

in later decades.²⁶ Here then, these sources are being used to understand contemporary expectations and associations around age, as well as how and why such expectations and associations were incorporated into a dialogue about royal men over time.

The ideal medieval king was an embodiment of the perfect balance of masculine ideals; no one was his equal and all others (men and women) were subordinate to him, with most being complicit in their subordination to maintain the gendered social hierarchy. Lewis argues that this situation echoes Raewyn W. Connell's sociological theories about the existence of a range of interdependent masculine identities.²⁷ These interdependent identities – including hegemonic, complicit, subversive and alternate – functioned within a hierarchy in which the hegemonic masculinity was the dominant or 'culturally exalted' expression of manhood in a specific society or place.²⁸ While this masculine hierarchy was not fixed, and a constant performative effort was required to maintain the necessary 'observably and palpably' dominant position, many medieval kings came to the throne at a significant disadvantage as children, youths or older men.²⁹ This was a significant issue in late medieval and early modern Scotland. To provide a balance of youthful and older royal figures, the examples herein refer to the reigns of David II and the early Stewart monarchs. By considering royal men, and their interactions with others, in the 'early' and 'elderly' periods of life, this chapter engages with those instances when manhood was often at its most vulnerable and thus where hegemonic status was most open to challenge, often from those who should have maintained complicity with their subordinate position.

Youth

Janay Nugent stated that youth was a 'complex, conflicting and kaleidoscopically shifting concept', but the liminality of this life stage between childhood and adulthood was consistent in accounts from later medieval and early modern

---

[26] John Mair, *A History of Greater Britain*, trans. and ed. Archibald Constable and Æneas J. G. Mackay (Edinburgh: University of Edinburgh Press, 1892) [hereafter *Mair's History*]; Hector Boece, *The Chronicles of Scotland Compiled by Hector Boece, Translated into Scots by John Bellenden, 1531*, ed. Edith Batho and H. Winifred Husbands, 2 vols (Edinburgh and London: William Blackwood and Sons, 1941) [hereafter *Belleden's Boece*]; George Buchanan, *The History of Scotland*, trans and ed. James Aikman, 4 vols (Glasgow: Blackie, Fullerton and Co., 1827) [hereafter *Buchanan's History*].

[27] Lewis, *Kingship and Masculinity*, 34–5. For a helpful article that explores complicit masculinity, specifically the ways those of middling rank utilised this system to their advantage, see: Kim Phillips, 'Masculinities and the Medieval English Sumptuary Laws', *Gender and History* 19, no. 1 (April 2007): 22–42.

[28] Raewyn W. Connell and J. W. Messerschmidt, 'Hegemonic Masculinity: Rethinking the Concept', *Gender and Society* 19, no. 6 (December 2005): 829–59.

[29] Lewis, *Kingship and Masculinity*, 35.

Europe.³⁰ There were legal frameworks in Scotland, as elsewhere, that sought to define a specific age at which a child became a youth, or a youth became an adult.³¹ In a sixteenth-century collection of common law, the *Practicks of Sir James Balfour of Pittendreich*, three pertinent ages emerge for boys and men: fourteen (the age at which tutorage may end and a boy could legally marry), twenty-one (the legal age at which a man could inherit property and title, often known as the 'perfite' or perfect age) and twenty-five (the youngest age that a man was considered of 'sufficient judgement and qualiteis' to tutor younger people and the age by which kings of Scots should have enacted the act of revocation to undo grants of their minority).³² However, the fifteenth and sixteenth centuries saw kings of Scots claiming their majority (or others doing so on their behalf) at a range of ages, including twelve, sixteen and nineteen. As Amy Blakeway has demonstrated, while laws existed to provide a framework for reaching adulthood, in reality there was fluidity around when a man (or king) reached adulthood, how this related to an ability to rule, and whether these things were synonymous with one another.³³

The author of 'Ratis Raving' divided childhood and youth into four different 'eild': the first age (one to three years), the second age (three to seven), the third age (seven to fifteen) and the fourth age (fifteen to thirty).³⁴ The transitional years at the end of the third age and start of the fourth included all the ages noted in the legal definitions around the transition toward adulthood and thus constituted the liminal period that equated to pre-modern adolescence. In 'Ratis Raving', and elsewhere in Europe, youth or adolescence also continued to thirty, so it is important to disaggregate what constituted adolescence from our modern preconceptions.³⁵ The poem relays the contradictions of

---

³⁰ Janay Nugent, 'Concepts of Youth', in *A Cultural History of Youth in the Renaissance*, ed. Lucy Underwood (New York: Bloomsbury, 2023), 11–30, at 11.

³¹ Ward argues that there was a shift in the central middle ages, between eleventh and thirteenth centuries, that saw a desire to 'legally define' maturity in Scotland and beyond: Ward, 'Child Kingship and Notions of (Im)maturity', 197–211, esp. 198.

³² Note that these ages are gender specific and there were different important ages for females; for example, Roman law permitted marriage for a girl from twelve. James Balfour, *Practicks of Sir James Balfour of Pittendreich: Reproduced from printed edition of 1754*, ed. P. G. B. McNeill, 2 vols (Edinburgh: Stair Society, 1962), 1: 8–13, 114–21, quote at 118. See also Amy Blakeway, *Regency in Sixteenth-Century Scotland* (Woodbridge: Boydell, 2015), 73–88.

³³ Blakeway, *Regency*, 74. Initially, this chapter sought to incorporate an analysis of the perfect age, but the subject is worthy of a separate article and the author intends to pursue this separately in the future.

³⁴ *Ratis Raving*, lines 1112–1411.

³⁵ For further on definitions and debates about adolescence in pre-modern times, see Deborah Youngs, *The Life Cycle in Western Europe, c. 1300–c. 1500* (Manchester: Manchester University Press, 2006), 96–125; Rachel E. Moss, 'An Orchard, A Lover and Three Bastards: The Formation of Adult Male Identity in a Fifteenth-Century Family', in *What is Masculinity? Historical Dynamics from Antiquity to the Contemporary World*, eds John H. Arnold and Sean Brady (Basingstoke: Palgrave Macmillan, 2013), 226–44.

this age: it was filled with jollity, activity, opportunity and vigour, but also rife with temptations, particularly of a sexual nature. It was also a time when a youth was expected to undertake the work of a man to demonstrate 'quhe[th]er [th]ow to wyce or vertew draw'.[36] Chronicle accounts recording the activities of fourteenth- and fifteenth-century Scottish princes and monarchs echo the conflicting possibilities and challenges of this liminal age. Several characteristics associated with youth are particularly apparent: proving manly worth, spurning wise advice, forming homosocial bonds, testing the hegemony, the transformative nature of age and acceptance of good council in reaching the 'perfeccione/ Of resone' associated with full adult manhood.[37]

Comparing the language used by Andrew of Wyntoun and Bower in discussions about David II and his nephew, Robert the Steward, who was around eight years older than David, illustrates how chroniclers relayed royal men's efforts to undertake the 'work of men' to prove their worth, as described in 'Ratis Raving'. For Robert the Steward, the years of David's absence in France – where the young king was sent for safety between 1334 and 1341 – was a transformative period.[38] Robert was approximately sixteen or seventeen years old at the time of David's departure.[39] Both Bower and Wyntoun indicate that, initially, Robert was 'withoutin weire/ Off eild he past nocht xvii yere' and was hidden at the family estate of Rothesay for safety.[40] That he was 'without war' indicates that Robert was not deemed experienced or indeed manly at this stage. Medieval advice suggested noble youths should begin to train for war between twelve and fourteen, and ideally begin their military career around eighteen; in reality young nobles, and even kings, were active in war much earlier, but reaching seventeen 'without war' would not have been unusual.[41] With the support of good advice from combat-ready supporters, whose ages are difficult to determine, Robert rallied men to him in the following year as he 'was beginning to grow into a young man'.[42] This is reminiscent of associations in 'Ratis Raving' between the fourth age and activities through which youths could demonstrate their progression towards adulthood. By 1339, during the siege of Perth under Robert's command, he was described by Wyntoun as having taken 'worthi war

---

[36] *Ratis Raving*, lines 1274–1411, quote line 1344.
[37] *Ratis Raving*, lines 1412–17.
[38] *Ratis Raving*, lines 1274–1411, quote at lines, 1336–43.
[39] Robert the Steward's date of birth is not known explicitly, but it was in 1316: Stephen Boardman, *The Early Stewart Kings: Robert II and Robert III, 1371–1406* (East Linton: Tuckwell Press, 1996), 3–4. Bower states that he was fifteen, but Wyntoun's suggestion of age is closer to the known year of birth.
[40] *Chron. Bower*, 8:96–7; *Chron. Wyntoun*, 6:26–7.
[41] Youngs, *The Life Cycle*, 107–8.
[42] *Chron. Bower*, 7:104–5.

to feycht the feylde', which points to the transformative possibilities of this period of youth.[43]

David II, in comparison, returned to Scotland from France in 1341 – after an absence of eight years – as a youth of seventeen, and was, like Robert had been at the same age, 'without weire'. David's absence while his peers proved their valour, vigour and manhood on the battlefields of the Second Wars of Independence meant that he had arguably missed critical developmental and bonding opportunities.[44] It is perhaps unsurprising then that some of David's first actions on returning to Scotland in 1341 were raids into English territories, which Michael Penman notably describes as 'David's initial blooding in the art of war'.[45] If David II's return to Scotland saw him 'yarnyt for to se feychtynge', as Wyntoun's chronicle suggests, an explanation for his yearning to fight can be further nuanced by considering issues of age and hegemonic status in the masculine hierarchy.[46] As a young man in the fourth age, David II's actions were indicative of a young man seeking to prove himself capable of the tasks expected of his station.[47] In a country beset with persistent fighting for nearly half a century, the measure of any man – particularly the king – was rooted in his martial prowess. Yet David's youth and absence, while others such as the Steward had opportunities to prove themselves, put him at a disadvantage in terms of demonstrating his hegemonic position atop the masculine hierarchy of Scotland's male elite and left him impatient to prove his worth.

David II and David, Duke of Rothesay and heir to Robert III, present interesting case studies where the issue of advice, and from whom it should be taken, arises for young men nearing the cusp of legal manhood at twenty-one. Following David's return from France, Wyntoun's commentary laments the fact that the king spent too much time '[l]ustynge, dawnssynge and playinge', but he also associates this with David's 'waxyn' or growing up and the fact that 'he was yonge' (David would have been between seventeen and twenty-two).[48] Wyntoun's tone and choice of words suggest a tacit acceptance of the raucous behaviour of young men. However, Bower associates this behaviour, and the keeping of youthful company, with 'the king's inadvertence or negligence not to say vacillating behaviour' that caused discord among his nobility during the years following his return to Scotland.[49] David's youthful eagerness to prove his worth on the battlefield was also firmly tied to the defeat of the Scots at Neville's Cross in 1346 by both chroniclers, but Bower squarely placed the fault

---

[43] *Chron. Wyntoun*, 6:124–5.
[44] Boardman, *Early Stewart Kings*, 1–10; Michael Penman, *David II* (Edinburgh: John Donald, 2005), 53–75.
[45] Penman, *David II*, 85.
[46] *Chron. Wyntoun*, 6:170–1.
[47] *Ratis Raving*, lines 1274–1411.
[48] *Chron. Wyntoun*, 6:161.
[49] *Chron. Bower*, 7:150–7.

on poor advice from youthful flatterers and his account of events is followed by a moralising chapter in which the advice of older men was advocated.[50] The difference between Wyntoun and Bower's record is even more stark for David, Duke of Rothesay, whose frequent involvement 'in unruly games and trivial sports' in his early twenties led to the appointing of councillors to support the young duke in his role as lieutenant of the realm.[51] Rothesay remains 'sweet and virtuous; young and fair' until his murder, aged twenty-three, according to Wyntoun, but for Bower, the 'spurning of his council of honourable men' following the death of the steadying force of his mother, Queen Annabella, was the decision that sealed his fate.[52]

Wyntoun and Bower were both older clerical men so their variable approaches to young men and youthful behaviour were likely linked instead to audience, sponsors and political allegiance. The critique around Rothesay and the narrative of his murder is almost absent from Wyntoun. This has been connected to the chronicler's sponsor, Sir John Wemyss, being a tenant of the man accused of orchestrating the murder, Robert, Earl of Fife and Duke of Albany.[53] It is the subtler differences – that between tacit acceptance of youthful misbehaviour and shifting the blame to 'youthful council' and 'spurning wise council' – which speak to audience and purpose. History and advice are woven together in Wyntoun's verses, but they were also written in vernacular Scots for the entertainment of a growing literate population of secular minor gentry. Bower's history was written with a more particular audience in mind: a minor king nearing the end of the third age of 'Ratis Raving' (seven to fifteen).[54] Subsequent narrative histories written during the minority-ridden sixteenth century – such as Hector Boece, his translator Bellenden and George Buchanan – use Bower's narrative of Rothesay as a basis to pin an increasingly exaggerated narrative of the prince's failings in the 'lust and insolence' of youth.[55] Their more draconian accusations appear rooted in the anxieties of their own era and their active efforts to offer advice to youthful kings coming of age. From those who explained youthful misdemeanours as expected behaviour to those who firmly criticised them, these chronicles and histories reveal a commonly held appreciation of the instability of the years prior to maturing into adult manhood. The fact that most of them sought out others to blame for these youthful misadventures also allowed them to speak about associations

---

[50] *Chron. Bower*, 7:253–61; *Chron. Wyntoun*, 6:170–1.
[51] *Chron. Bower*, 8:38–9.
[52] *Chron. Wyntoun*, 6:357–8; *Chron. Bower*, 8:38–9.
[53] Caroline Edington, 'Wyntoun, Andrew, c. 1350–1422', *ODNB*.
[54] Edington, 'Wyntoun, Andrew, c. 1350–1422'; D. E. R. Watt, 'Bower [Bowmaker], Walter, 1385–1449', *ODNB*.
[55] *Belleden's Boece*, 361; *Buchanan's History*, 2:170–1.

between youth and misadventure through poor choices and advice, rather than directly criticise the monarch.

That these royal youths chose to surround themselves with men of similar age and 'spurn' older counsel, as described in these narratives, is perhaps unsurprising if the situation is filtered through a gendered lens considering both homosocial bonding and the masculine hierarchy. For example, Bower hangs David II's early overconfidence on surrounding himself with 'knights and armed men in the flower of youth' when making raids on northern England.[56] These actions can be easily situated in the context of homosocial bonding with peers: a critical aspect of developing manly identity, an important facet of moving from childhood to manhood and something David II missed out on during his absence in France.[57] The importance of creating and nurturing bonds between children and young men of the same generation is recognisable in the actions of adult kings seeking to foster these relations from an early age. A good example of this can be found at the baptism of James I's twin sons, James and Alexander, in 1430. At this event, the king created six knights who were sons of notable elites and all of 'tender' years to provide 'fellow-soldiers' for his sons.[58] The period of youth, and particularly once young men reached the prominent ages in law – like twenty-one – was also one in which testing the hierarchy and offering alternate hegemonic ideals or subverting the hierarchy was a natural step.[59] Stephen Boardman indicates that the 'council of honourable men' spurned by David, Duke of Rothesay, was headed by the duke of Albany, Rothesay's uncle, who was then in his fifties – a man nearing the end of his prime, even entering into early old age.[60] Thus, Rothesay's youthful efforts to shake off this council's control can also be situated within his own progression towards manhood. After at least four or five years of being politically active, it is unsurprising he was eager to pursue his own path and frustrated by the older men's continued efforts to control him.[61]

The shift from youth into manhood was recognised as an opportunity for transformation even in one receiving criticism for youthly misbehaviour, poor choices or questionable activities. For David II, who was previously chastised for youthful lusting and an eagerness to fight that led to disastrous results, Wyntoun notes a specific turning point in the 1360s, when David: 'Fra [th]an

---

[56] *Chron. Bower*, 7:150–3.
[57] For example, see P. J. P Goldberg, 'Masters and Men in Late Medieval England', in *Masculinity in Medieval Europe*, 56–70; Shepard, *Meanings of Manhood*, 93–126.
[58] *Chron. Bower*, 8:262–3.
[59] Shepard, *Meanings of Manhood*, 93–126, passim; William M. Aird, 'Frustrated Masculinity: The Relationship between William the Conqueror and his Eldest Son', in *Masculinity in Medieval Europe*, 39–55.
[60] Boardman, *Early Stewart Kings*, 224–5.
[61] See a comparison in study of Robert Curthose, eldest son of William the Conqueror: Aird, 'Frustrated Masculinity', 39–55.

his lande ryolte/ He led, and rewllyt in equyte/... And syne his parliament at Scoyne/ Qwhar al walde be delyuerit sone./ He was al manly, war and wysse'.[62]

The king was then nearing forty years old. An even more striking example of this recognition was recorded for Alexander Stewart, Earl of Mar and illegitimate son of Robert III's brother, who Bower indicated 'changed into another kind of man' from a youthful wild leader of caterans to a wealthy adult man of renowned character.[63] The amendments made by sixteenth-century history writers – building upon Bower's fifteenth-century chronicle and those of his continuators – offer interesting insights into associations with age and the redemptive qualities of accepting good advice. John Mair associated Mar's shift in character explicitly with the earl reaching the age of thirty.[64] George Buchanan amends the narrative to relate Mar's character shift to prudently putting aside the 'bad advice of wicked associates' of his youth and seeking 'good counsel' as an adult, enabling him an opportunity to alter his reputation.[65] With this amendment Buchanan linked advancing age and the ending of youth to a period when a man was more open to hear the voices of good counsel and thus reach the 'perfeccione/ Of resone'.[66] Writing in the later sixteenth century during the minority and youth of his former tutee James VI, with the express intention of providing exemplars for him, Buchanan was likely influenced by hopes and fears as James traversed his youth and was seen by many to have fallen under the spell of Esme Stewart.[67] The transition to full manhood was not always connected to a specific numerical age, which illustrates the potentially dramatic effect of advice on the recipient's maturity and the malleability of age and life stages among chronicle and history writers.

Old age

If youth and the ascent to the man's estate presented a variety of challenges for pre-modern men, the period that followed the age of the 'perfeccione of ressone' potentially posed as many challenges for those lucky (or unlucky) enough to reach it. While the issue of old age was not one faced by many of the late medieval Stewart monarchs, the founder of the dynasty, Robert II, and

---

[62] *Chron. Wyntoun*, 6:170–1, 253 (in MS Cotton version only).
[63] *Chron. Bower*, 8:292–3. See also: *Mair's History*, 363–4; *Buchanan's History*, 2:101.
[64] *Mair's History*, 363–4.
[65] *Buchanan's History*, 2:101.
[66] *Ratis Raving*, lines 1412–17.
[67] D. M. Abbott, 'Buchanan, George', *ODNB*; Roderick J. Lyall, 'James VI and the Sixteenth-Century Cultural Crisis', in *The Reign of James VI*, eds Julian Goodare and Michael Lynch (Edinburgh: John Donald, 2000), 55–70, at 59–62; Amy Blakeway, 'James VI and James Douglas, Earl of Morton'; Steven Reid, 'Of bairns and bearded men: James VI and the Ruthven Raid', in *James VI and Noble Power in Scotland, 1578–1603*, eds Miles Kerr-Peterson and Steven J. Reid (Abingdon: Routledge, 2017), 12–31, 37–9.

his son, Robert III, did not become kings until significantly later than their fiftieth year. Older age, as with youth, was subdivided by the author of 'Ratis Raving' into distinct periods: the sixth 'eild' ranged from fifty to seventy or eighty and featured preparation for death, but also continued to hold distinct possibilities in terms of wisdom and opulence; whereas, once into the seventh or final 'eild', at seventy or eighty, there was 'lytill es of lyking ... / ... And falyeis al perfeccione'.[68] Youngs' synthesising of the broader European context demonstrates that the author of 'Ratis Raving' was not alone in this demarcation of two periods of old age, with other commentators such as Dante making similar suggestions.[69] As with youth, the age at which a man was deemed old varied and there were common contradictions found in old age. Wisdom, good counsel and experience were some of the primary virtues associated with older men, such as the advisors spurned by David, Duke of Rothesay, but this stage was also marked by mental and physical weaknesses associated with ageing that posed a real threat to retaining position within the masculine hierarchy.[70] These conflicting understandings around ageing, and indeed physical disability, are quickly apparent in both 'Ratis Raving' and the commentators recording Scotland's early Stewart rulers.

The old age of Robert II and the infirmity in ageing of Robert III feature prominently in the modern historiography considering the political machinations of the early Stewart dynasty.[71] However, the manner in which old age and infirmity were discussed by contemporaries, how these experiences of ageing linked to issues of manhood and the hegemonic hierarchy, and the variability of impact of old age on different individuals are all matters ripe for further analysis. The contradictions of old age are clear from 'Ratis Raving': the age could be 'stable, co[v]atous and swere [lazy or reluctant]' and one that 'yarnis gretly the assent/ Of conseil and awaysment', with potential to ascend to the role of wise counsellor.[72] Comparing descriptions of old age across the three of Robert II's sons – Robert III (c. 1337–1406), Robert, Duke of Albany (c. 1340–1420), and Walter Stewart, Earl of Atholl (c. early 1360–1437) – throws up quite stark differences between the way that old age is characterised within a group of

---

[68] *Ratis Raving*, lines 1569–1745.
[69] Youngs, *The Life Cycle*, 163–5. Pat Thane suggests that sixty to seventy was seen as a pivotal threshold throughout history: 'Old Age in the European Culture: A Significant Presence from Antiquity to the Present', *American Historical Review* 125, no. 2 (April 2020): 385–95.
[70] Youngs, *The Life Cycle*, 165–73; Shepard, *Meanings of Manhood*, 214–45; Stephen R. Smith, 'Growing Old in Early Stuart England', *Albion* 8, no. 2 (1976): 125–41; Skenazi, *Aging Gracefully in the Renaissance*, esp. 15–97.
[71] Boardman offers the most comprehensive study, see *The Early Stewart Kings*. See also a new approach considering this period of one of corporate rulership: Shayna Devlin, '"Whatever the World Admires in a Prince" – Robert Stewart, Duke of Albany: Power, Politics, and Family in Late Medieval Scotland' (PhD diss., University of Guelph, 2019).
[72] *Ratis Raving*, lines 1603, 1636–7, 1668–9.

siblings, offering an interesting example of the complexities of this older age where men could profit or suffer.

Robert III is presented by Bower's *Scotichronicon* as a man in the 'decrepit aige' by the early 1400s when his actual age (in his early to mid-sixties) placed him firmly in the first of 'Ratis Raving's two stages of old age.[73] Bower conveys a sense of recognition of the impact of the ageing process upon Robert's abilities and the depression caused by feeling redundant in his manly capacities in caring and providing for, as well as controlling, his sons and his kingdom.[74] This is achieved through brief but incremental comments and vignettes, including 'the weak and decrepit king' having to write to his brother, Albany, to regain control of his eldest son, Rothesay, and the ageing king's background role in ongoing battles with England while Albany, as governor, leads the way.[75] The concluding event was the capture of his younger son James, following the death of the elder David, following which Bower states: 'his [Robert III's] spirit failed directly, the strength of his body dwindled, his face grew pale, and in his grief he ate no more food until he breathed out his spirit to his creator'.[76] Later continuators, such as Bellenden's translation of Hector Boece's history, further developed the narrative to suggest that in his final days Robert III wrote a begging letter to James's captor, Henry IV of England, and pleaded his case with direct reference to having 'fallin in decrepit aige'.[77] These narrative authors may have sought to emphasise the desperate position of the realm, with an ageing king and an absent young heir, through manipulating the accumulative impact of ageing and the king's deterioration for dramatic effect. Yet, for this to have had an impact, it indicates that such narratives were rooted in commonly shared fears about ageing and the problems it could bring.

Robert III's brother, Robert Earl of Fife and Duke of Albany, by contrast, flourished in old age. Albany was already in his late sixties at Robert III's death, when he was reappointed as governor during the absence of his nephew, James I, and he died around his eightieth year. Chronicle descriptions offer no suggestions of weakness, rather his ageing is linked to virtues of old age, particularly wisdom: 'his wisdom provided the ornament of nearly all the virtues, so that his discourse whether delivered in the highest councils ... or elsewhere was always seasoned with wit and charm'.[78] For Albany, old age was the period when he was at the undisputed pinnacle of the hegemonic hierarchy in terms of age, status and fatherhood. For the youngest son of Robert II, Walter

---

[73] *Chron. Bower*, 8:38–9.
[74] Shepard discusses the challenges faced by older men where their ability to continue as the provider and head of household was undermined in older age, see *Meanings of Manhood*, 231–45.
[75] *Chron. Bower*, 8:38–9, 44–5, 52–55.
[76] *Chron. Bower*, 8:63.
[77] *Bellenden's Boece*, 367.
[78] *Chron. Bower*, 8:132–5.

Stewart, Earl of Atholl, the frustration of not achieving manly goals is described in quite a different manner. Bower states that he was 'a man grown old in a life of evil-doing', which Mair adapts in the following century as 'a man grown old in wickedness' as he tried and failed to seek the kingship for himself.[79] Though Atholl was in his mid-late seventies when executed for involvement in the murder of his nephew, there were no suggestions that this failure was through any incapacities directly associated with old age. For Mair, it was his inability to achieve his desired goals that affected the manner in which he aged. Men could, then, both thrive and fail once past the 'perfeccion of ressone'. Old age was – like youth – a period when masculinity was at its most fragile, and this was particularly so where young or adult men stood hungry for their time to shine.

The complexities of Robert II's extended family and the competition between brothers show recognisable similarities to English royal case studies of Robert Curthose, son of William the Conqueror, and the future Henry V, son of Henry IV. In these cases, an older father – who was 'first' of his dynasty – perceived a threat from a competent son reaching adulthood, and then, threatened by the eldest's successes and achievements, favoured younger sons to punish the potential challenger to the king's manhood and hegemonic status.[80] In late fourteenth- and early fifteenth-century Scotland, these frustrations were arguably further exaggerated by the ages of the fathers and sons. Whereas Robert Curthose and the future Henry V were young men in the fourth age of 'Ratis Raving' – so between fifteen and thirty – Robert II's two eldest sons were already in their thirties when their father became king in 1371 and both were in their forties before they sought to subvert the hierarchical masculine order through direct challenge.

John, Earl of Carrick and the future Robert III, initially tested the hierarchy, perhaps expressing frustrations around his progression towards manhood, by gravitating towards David II, the ruling king who organised Carrick's wedding and looked to leapfrog Robert the Steward for the younger generation.[81] Robert II's accession in 1371 confirmed Carrick's position as heir, but Carrick was already a married man in his thirties with his own children.[82] In 1384, now nearing forty-seven, he utilised parliament to manoeuvre himself into the position of lieutenant of the realm and temporarily imprisoned his father in 1388.[83] Aged a little under seventy years old by then, Robert II's own position

---

[79] *Mair's History*, 364–5. On Walter, Earl of Atholl, see: Michael Brown, '"That Old Serpent and Ancient of Evil Days": Walter, Earl of Atholl and the Death of James I', *SHR* 71, no. 191/2 (April–October 1992): 23–45.

[80] Aird, 'Frustrated Masculinity', 39–55; Lewis, *Kingship and Masculinity*, 67–83.

[81] Boardman, *The Early Stewart Kings*, 22; Penman, *David II*, 348.

[82] Boardman states that Robert III (formerly John, Earl of Carrick) was fifty-three years old at his accession in 1390, which would suggest that he was born in c. 1337 and aged about thirty-four in 1371. See *The Early Stewart Kings*, 174.

[83] Devlin, 'Whatever the World Admires in a Prince', 58–62.

in the hegemony was severely challenged and fears about his own masculine identity may have led him to attempt to manipulate the situation in manner that would punish his eldest son. Carrick's injury acquired at the Battle of Otterburn (1388) was clearly referred to in the parliament records as the reason for his removal from power.[84] Physical incapacity in an age where the knightly warrior was a prominent feature of the hegemonic masculine idea was an obvious challenge for the incumbent ruler seeking to mirror this ideal, and Carrick's lameness is later declared as the root of disorder in the realm more generally by Bower: 'the king, being bodily infirm, had no grip anywhere'.[85] However, Carrick's injuries may have proven a pertinent excuse for his old father, Robert II, frustrated by Carrick's successes and direct challenges to his own waning manhood, to promote a younger favoured son.

When commenting on the installation of Robert, Earl of Fife and Duke of Albany, as lieutenant in place of Robert II (due to his age) and his elder brother (due to physical injury) in 1388, Mair's sixteenth-century commentary pauses to insert a unique discussion of this situation. Although his commentary shows little effort to favour Robert II, he states that he saw no reason why an old man could not rule as wisely as a young one, nor why 'bodily infirmity' should be a 'hindrance to his exercise of the duties of a king' as long as it was 'unaccompanied by any infirmity of the mind'.[86] He concludes that the bestowal of the 'regency' upon a younger son could do nothing but 'run the risk of having two rival kings within the state'.[87] Mair's reflections are sensible. The removal of one brother – who had briefly been given (or taken) a prominent, much sought after position – and installation of the second younger son could easily sow seeds of discord.[88] Indeed, Mair's interpretation of this situation, and the potential issues it could cause, may have been inspired by the murder of James III, which occurred in his own lifetime and followed an uprising using the king's heir as a figurehead following the king favouring a younger brother.[89] Shayna Devlin suggests that Robert II divided power between himself and his sons, particularly Robert, Earl of Fife, as a form of corporate monarchy to stabilise power and extend the reach of the crown's power.[90] However, Carrick's challenge to his father and the subsequent promotion of Robert, Earl of Fife, illuminate the complexities for an older ruler trying to manage a brood of adult

---

[84] RPS, 1388/12/1.
[85] Chron. Bower, 8:62–3.
[86] Mair's History, 329.
[87] Mair's History, 329.
[88] For other examples, see: Aird, 'Frustrated Masculinity', 39–55; Lewis, Kingship and Masculinity, 67–83.
[89] Norman Macdougall, James III: A Political Study (Edinburgh: John Donald, 1982), 306–7, 313–14, 326–9.
[90] Devlin, 'Whatever the World Admires in a Prince', 43–58.

male children, particularly as these children sought to define their own position in the hierarchy at the expense of their father's masculine identity.

Conclusion

Caitlin Holton has argued that manhood might have been observably different from both boyhood and womanhood, but 'medieval men could not rest secure' for proving one's position in the masculine hierarchy was an ongoing project.[91] Threats to gendered positionality were even more prominent in those liminal periods as men came of age and moved towards older years. Age and manhood were frequently put in a dialogue with one another. Writers from the late fourteenth to the sixteenth centuries drew upon widespread associations with age and manly qualities to praise or criticise royal men without making direct attacks on kingship as an institution. An analysis of how chronicles and histories treat age and gender when considering Scottish kings provides evidence for the rich potential awaiting a gendered exploration of male monarchs in pre-modern Scotland. Did age make a man? The answer to this question is not straightforward. Age was a fluid concept and just one facet of 'reaching the estate of manhood'. Association with the liminal ages or stages of life – youth and old age – certainly affected how men were perceived. As kings were expected to be an embodiment of ideal manhood and take a hegemonic position in the masculine hierarchy, age had a very real destabilising effect as the examples of frustrated masculinity in youth, adulthood and old age herein can attest. Recognising that kings had to fit into the expectations of manhood understood broadly within society, and so could be judged as other men by the same yardstick but were also not always as easily forgiven for behaving in the manner expected of their age or life stage, offers historians new insights into both the monarchs themselves and the world they inhabited. This reveals the value in considering age and life stages as a category of historical analysis in the Scottish context.

---

[91] Holton, 'Masculine Identity in Medieval Scotland', 30–1.

TWELVE

Sons and Daughters, Mothers and Mercenaries: Agency and Agenda in the Cross-North Channel Context, c. 1550–c. 1600

Alison Cathcart

Within the field of late medieval and early modern Scottish history, both in Lowland and Highland society, most studies of women have focused on the elite and often on individuals. These studies have nuanced our appreciation of women's roles in wider society, whether as wife, mother, foster-mother, widow, guardian, confidante or as heiress to an estate or title, and in different contexts, whether political, legal or economic.[1] While recent research has argued that we need to move beyond viewing women who exerted power or authority as 'exceptional', there is also a need to reconsider women whose agency has been either marginalised or condemned because it transcended the bounds of what was regarded as appropriate behaviour for a woman.[2] Such has been the fate of Agnes Campbell and her daughter Finola (or 'Iníon Dubh') MacDonald, two women born into the elite of Highland clan society and subsequently married into two of the most powerful Irish kindreds in Ulster in 1569.[3] As Gaelic women they operated within a cross-North Channel world which, in the latter

---

[1] The correspondence of Kathrine Ruthven was highlighted in Jane Dawson, ed., *Campbell Letters, 1559–1583*, SHS, series V, vol. 10 (Edinburgh, 1997), 22–7; for other studies of noble women see Ruth Grant, 'Politicking Jacobean Women: Lady Ferniehirst, the Countess of Arran and the Countess of Huntly, c. 1580–1603', in *Women in Scotland, c. 1100–c. 1750*, eds Elizabeth Ewan and Maureen M. Meikle (East Linton: Tuckwell Press, 1999), 95–111; Steve Boardman, 'Lords and Women, Women as Lords: The Career of Margaret Stewart, Countess of Angus and Mar, c. 1354–c. 1418', in *Kings, Lords and Men in Scotland and Britain, 1300–1625: Essays in Honour of Jenny Wormald*, eds Steve Boardman and Julian Goodare (Edinburgh: Edinburgh University Press, 2014), 37–58. There is a wealth of literature on the topic within wider European and English historiography.

[2] Heather J. Tanner, Laura L. Gathagan and Lois L. Huneycutt, 'Introduction', in *Medieval Elite Women and the Exercise of Power, 1100–1400*, ed. Heather J. Tanner (Cham: Palgrave Macmillan, 2019), 1–18.

[3] There are various spellings of her name, which means 'dark/black maiden' but see Emmett O'Byrne, 'MacDonnell (Nic Dhomhnaill), Fiona (Fionnghuala) ('Iníon Dubh')', *DIB*. I would like to thank a former undergraduate student of mine, Rebecca MacKay, for bringing to my attention the need for further study of these two women.

half of the sixteenth century, saw significant military activity.[4] This was a result of reinvigorated English efforts to impose authority across Ireland and subdue ongoing resistance to English governance there.

Ulster was regarded as the most problematic part of Ireland and the far northwest of the province, a region incorporating the lordships of the O'Neills of Tyrone and the O'Donnells of Tyrconnell, was largely unchartered territory for the English. Regular reinforcements were sent to bolster the English army in Ireland and the Lord Deputy, the English representative in Ireland, undertook expeditions by land and sea in efforts to deal with ongoing unrest across the north. The need on the part of Irish lords for an additional supply of fighting men, both in their local rivalries and in efforts to repel English encroachment, saw regular recruitment of men from the western Highlands and Isles of Scotland. This developed into a sustained mercenary trade which frustrated English efforts to pacify the north of Ireland. Scottish mercenaries also came as marriage dowries, as was the case for both Agnes and Finola. But while there has been some attention paid to both these women, largely because of the impact their cross-channel marriages had on Ulster politics for subsequent decades, they have not been the focus of sustained attention.[5] This chapter aims to add to our understanding of Agnes and Finola as wives and mothers, but also to examine their agency and agenda within the wider cross-channel mercenary trade of the later sixteenth century.[6] In doing so it will consider how

---

[4] For the long-standing links across the North Channel see Colin Breen, 'Maritime Connections: Landscape and Lordship along the Gaelic Atlantic Seaboard of Scotland and the North of Ireland During the Middle Ages', Maritime Communities of the North Atlantic Arc in the Early Modern Period, *Journal of the North Atlantic* 12 (2019): 3–15. For the wider cross-channel context and military activity see Alison Cathcart, *Plantations by Land and Sea: North Channel communities of the Atlantic Archipelago, c. 1550–1625* (Oxford: Peter Lang, 2021); Gerald A. Hayes-McCoy, *Scots Mercenary Forces in Ireland (1565–1603): An Account of their Service during that Period and of the Reaction of their Activities on Scottish Affairs, and of the Effect of their Presence in Ireland, Together with an Examination of the Gallóglaigh or Galloglass* (Dublin: Edmund Burke Pub., 1937; reprinted 1996).

[5] For the importance of their marriages see Jane Dawson, *The Politics of Religion in the Age of Mary, Queen of Scots: The Earl of Argyll and the Struggle for Britain and Ireland* (Cambridge: Cambridge University Press, 2002), 155–65, 168–9, 199–208. For a lovely, but brief, discussion of Finola see Katharine Simms, *Gaelic Ulster in the Middle Ages: History, Culture, and Society* (Four Courts Press: Dublin, 2020), 443–45; see also Cathcart, *Plantations by Land and Sea*, 108–18; Andrea Knox, '"Barbarous and Pestiferous Women": Female Criminality, Violence and Aggression in Sixteenth- and Seventeenth-Century Scotland and Ireland', in *Twisted Sisters. Women, Crime and Deviance in Scotland since 1400*, eds Yvonne Galloway Brown and Rona Ferguson (East Linton: Tuckwell Press, 2002), 13–31, at 22–4.

[6] Notwithstanding the helpful discussion of agency as being associated with 'soft' power and thus gendered and subordinate (see Theresa Earenfight, 'A Lifetime of Power: Beyond Binaries of Gender', in *Medieval Elite Women*, ed. Tanner, 271–93, especially 276–7), this chapter adopts a neutral definition of agency as an action or a person who acts to produce a particular result (see *OED*).

they were perceived by contemporaries and how they have been portrayed in the subsequent historiography.[7]

* * *

As a daughter of Colin Campbell, third earl of Argyll, and thus sister to the fourth earl and aunt to the fifth earl, Agnes was a significant player in the marriage market.[8] Throughout her life, however, her influence extended well beyond this thanks to her Campbell lineage, her own political astuteness and her desire to secure her sons' inheritance. As a daughter of the Campbell chief and the earl of Argyll she would have had a good education, but her upbringing at court meant she was fluent in both English and French, linguistic skills that would serve her well in later negotiations with the English. She had a brief first marriage to James Stewart of Bute that ended in annulment but it would be her marriage in 1545 to James MacDonald of Dunivaig and the Glens that would determine the rest of her life.[9] Although likely that the fourth earl, her brother, arranged this marriage it brought Agnes into the world of MacDonald cross-channel activity.[10] Through marriage the MacDonalds had established a presence in the Glens of Antrim by the turn of the fifteenth century; by the mid-sixteenth century, although the English crown did not recognise MacDonald claims to these lands, the Glens were fully incorporated into the wider clan estate. During the 1550s and 1560s James and his younger brother, Sorley Boy, were active in Ulster, regularly crossing the channel and expanding MacDonald influence east into Clandeboy and west into the Route.[11] During these decades Agnes had little direct involvement with Irish politics but bore her husband five

---

[7] Although not her own field of expertise, Elizabeth Ewan has long sought to shed light on the role of women in Scottish Gaelic society. Domhnall Uilleam Stiùbhart, 'Woman and Gender in the Early Modern Western Gaidhealtachd', in *Women in Scotland*, eds Ewan and Meikle, 233–49; Alison Cathcart, '"Inressyng of Kyndnes, and Renewing off thair Blud": The Family, Kinship and Clan Policy in Sixteenth-Century Scottish Gaeldom', in *Finding the Family in Medieval and Early Modern Scotland*, eds Elizabeth Ewan and Janay Nugent (Aldershot: Ashgate, 2008), 127–38; Anne Frater, 'Clann and Clan: Children of the Gaelic nobility, c. 1500–c. 1800', in *Children and Youth in Premodern Scotland*, eds Janay Nugent and Elizabeth Ewan (Woodbridge: Boydell, 2015), 89–103; Janay Nugent, '"Your Louing Childe and Foster": The Fostering of Archie Campbell of Argyll, 1633–39', in *Children and Youth in Premodern Scotland*, eds Nugent and Ewan, 47–64.

[8] Dawson, *Politics of Religion*, 62, for the significance of Campbell women and their marriages. For a discussion of family and marriage in a wider early modern Scottish context see Keith M. Brown, *Noble Society in Scotland: Wealth, Family and Culture, from Reformation to Revolution* (Edinburgh: Edinburgh University Press, reprinted 2004), 113–77.

[9] Dawson, *Politics of Religion*, 81.

[10] The marriage enabled Argyll to re-establish relations with the Clan Donald, which had been threatened by the recent rebellion in 1545 (on which see Alison Cathcart, 'The Forgotten '45: Donald Dubh's rebellion in an archipelagic context', *SHR* 91: 2, no. 232 (2012): 239–64) and, arguably, consolidate his role as broker in the cross-channel mercenary trade.

[11] Colin Breen, *Dunluce Castle* (Dublin: Four Courts Press, 2012), 63–82.

children – three sons: Archibald, Angus and Donald Gorm, and two daughters: Katherine and Finola.[12]

James's death in 1565 transformed Agnes's situation and her subsequent marriage to Turlough Luineach O'Neill, head of the powerful O'Neill kindred, which brought her directly into Ulster politics, is regarded as having been arranged by her nephew, the fifth earl of Argyll. This is an understandable interpretation in the light of the 1560s' context but it overlooks Agnes's own agency in regards to any future marriage.[13] In November 1568 she told the Lord Deputy of Ireland, Sir Henry Sidney, that she was

> willeng to matche w[i]t[h] some great man of this countrie birthe at the Quenes appointment, So as she and hers might enioye that inherita[u]nce that her husband and her auncestoures by the nombers of vii lynallie in dissent had occupied.[14]

Agnes's own agenda here is too readily overlooked. She sought a union that would offer leverage in Ulster advantageous to her sons. Utilising her own marriage as a bargaining tool, Agnes pushed for MacDonald claims of possession to be acknowledged by the English through formal land grant. She reinforced this negotiation with a threat, telling Sidney, if she 'coulde not haue ... at the Quenes hands' a grant of the lands her late husband possessed then 'as lange as there were any of the Clandonnelles alive they woolde neu[er] cease p[ro]seqution of that title w[i]t[h] all the force they coulde.'[15] Even if Argyll had brokered the marriage between Agnes and Turlough, Agnes was pursuing an agenda in the interests of, and on behalf of, her MacDonald sons in Ulster.

In that respect, the agenda of Finola, daughter of Agnes and James MacDonald, was no different. At the same time her mother was married to Turlough Luineach O'Neill, Finola was married to Hugh McManus O'Donnell, head of the O'Donnell kindred and lord of Tyrconnell. Like her mother, Finola brought with her a dowry of Scottish mercenaries which would have been welcomed by her husband who was facing significant internal unrest in his lordship. The marriages of 1569, that established a Campbell–MacDonald–O'Neill–O'Donnell axis across Ulster, secured for O'Donnell a steady supply of mercenaries which in turn bolstered his authority within his kindred and his lordship. His wife was crucial in both regards and Finola spent her life supporting her O'Donnell husband as lord of Tyrconnell and securing the succession of their eldest son, Red Hugh (or Hugh Roe), who was subsequently

---

[12] Helen Coburn Walshe, 'Campbell, Lady Agnes (d. in or after 1590), noblewoman', *ODNB*.
[13] Dawson, *Politics of Religion*, 163; Cathcart, *Plantations by Land and Sea*, 109–10.
[14] TNA, SPO, 1509–1714: Part II: The Tudors: Henry VIII to Elizabeth I, 1509–1603: State Papers Foreign: Ireland, Scotland, Borders and Registers of the Privy Council, 63/26 folios 71–2.
[15] SPO, 63/26 folio 72.

inaugurated in May 1592.[16] Like so many noble wives and mothers, although often absent from the sources, Finola was closely involved in the affairs of the lordship and this went hand-in-hand with the affairs of her immediate family.[17] Finola worked constantly to strengthen Red Hugh's position as heir and, in order to secure her son's succession, she utilised ancient Irish prophecy regarding Aodh Eangach, an 'expected deliverer who would drive the English out of Ireland'.[18] Associated with earlier O'Donnell lords, Finola recognised its potency if connected to her son, both in terms of his position in the lordship and his later role in opposing the English.[19] Indeed, during the Nine Years War (1593–1603) the English were aware of the prophecy, and of Finola's role in promoting it.[20] It was, the English asserted, by her 'forward meanes' that her son, Red Hugh, hoped:

> to be fully asisted out of Scotland to effect and to bringe to passe some old devised p[ro]phesie w[hi]ch flieth amongst them in noe smale request, importeinge that when two hughes lawfully and im[m]ediatly succeede ech other as Odonells, beinge soe formally and ceremoniuslie created, according the cuntreis custome the last hugh shall (fursooth) be a monarch in Ireland, and oght banish thence all forrein nations and conquerors.[21]

Negotiating marriages and working to protect the interests of the family was acceptable female behaviour and many noble wives and mothers were active participants in pursuing strategic alliances that benefitted their husbands and children. But in the turbulent North Channel context of the later sixteenth century this often saw Agnes and Finola act in ways that transgressed the norms

---

[16] Alongside Red Hugh, the marriage produced at least six other children: Ruari (who would succeed his brother), Manus, Caffar, Nuala, Margaret and Mary. Hugh McManus also had a number of other, older children from previous relationships. Darren McGettigan, *Red Hugh O'Donnell and the Nine Years War* (Dublin: Four Courts Press, 2005), 39, comments that 'these children were regarded as illegitimate'. If that was the case, it is evidence of the extent to which Irish lords recognised the need for a legitimate male heir to satisfy English law as established through the 'surrender and regrant' policy. However, under Irish custom illegitimacy would not have prevented other sons of Hugh McManus from succeeding him. Red Hugh succeeded his father, as opposed to an older half-brother, because of the efforts of his mother, Finola.

[17] Grant, 'Politicking Jacobean Women', 95–6; Jennifer C. Ward, 'Noblewomen, Family, and Identity in Later Medieval Europe', in *Nobles and Nobility in Medieval Europe*, ed. Anne J. Duggan (Woodbridge: Boydell, 2000), 246–62, especially 256–7.

[18] McGettigan, *Red Hugh O'Donnell*, 42. See also Thomas Finan, 'Prophecies of the Expected Deliverer in Thirteenth- and Fourteenth-Century Irish Bardic Poetry', *New Hibernia Review* 6, no. 3 (2002): 113–24.

[19] *Annála Connacht*, 1537. Accessed 10 October 2022 via University College Cork CELT Project: ucc.ie/en/research-sites/celt/. See also Simms, *Gaelic Ulster*, 444.

[20] Michael Newton, 'Prophecy and Cultural Conflict in Gaelic Tradition', *Scottish Studies* 35 (2007–10): 144–73, at 152, argues that, 'in capable hands [prophecy] can provide a framework in which to express contemporary events, or to resist or justify the status quo'.

[21] SPO, 63/170, 31v.

of what was acceptable for females at that time: recruiting and controlling mercenaries, while also taking action perceived to be 'unnatural' for a woman in order to defend the interests of their sons.

Both women were involved in the cross-channel mercenary trade, recruiting and suppling their husbands and sons with much needed military reinforcements. Agnes's husband, Turlough Luineach, relied heavily on his wife and the Scottish mercenaries she could recruit for him to bolster his position but, when seeking to come to terms with the English, peace was conditional on his cessation of such recruitment. Agnes did not recruit mercenaries solely for her husband; she was keen to see ongoing involvement of the Scots in Ulster on behalf of her sons. This was necessary to maintain the MacDonald stronghold in the lands of the Glens and further east in the Route, and it is important to recognise Agnes's role during this time.[22] Her husband, O'Neill, and Sorley Boy MacDonald, were at times allies and, at other times, enemies. This constantly changing political landscape was compounded by the death of the fifth earl of Argyll and the succession of his brother, Colin, sixth earl, who, it has been suggested, was less interested both in Ulster politics and in the alliance with the O'Neills. Despite the sixth earl being 'willing to loosen his connections with the O'Neills', it has been argued that '[o]nly Argyll could supply the necessary galleys to transport a large ... army to Ulster'.[23] But this does not hold up. The MacDonalds were a maritime kindred and for centuries had maintained a presence in the north of Ireland, crossing regularly between Kintyre, Islay and Antrim.[24] The Campbells were not the only maritime power in the west of Scotland and Angus MacDonald, eldest son of Agnes and James, would have had the galleys needed to transport mercenaries as required. Indeed, that the sixth earl was less personally involved in Ireland may have given Agnes more direct leverage over the mercenary trade and it needs to be considered that it was Agnes, not Sorley Boy nor the sixth earl, who was really calling the shots regarding the movement of Scottish Highlanders across the North Channel and who was controlling them in Ireland.[25]

It is too easy to assume that it was the male members of the Clan Donald who had the real power and the lack of agency afforded to Agnes in relation to

---

[22] Cathcart, *Plantations by Land and Sea*, 97–121.
[23] J. Michael Hill, *Fire and Sword: Sorley Boy MacDonnell and the rise of Clan Ian Mor, 1538–90* (London: Athlone Press, 1993), 172–3.
[24] Cathcart, *Plantations by Land and Sea*, 114–21.
[25] Hill, *Fire and Sword*, 176, argues that while Agnes 'may have Argyll's consent for Turlough to import more mercenaries ... there was no doubt that Sorley would control them once they arrived'. He cites a letter of April 1579 from Hugh O'Donnell of Tyrconnell informing the Lord Deputy of Turlough Luineach's hosting to the west of Lough Foyle. Turlough was accompanied 'with the most parte of the Galloglasses of the McDonnells'. The lack of standardisation of the use of MacDonnells and MacDonalds, referring to the Irish and Scottish branches respectively, means it should not be taken at face value that Sorley Boy was in control of the Scots. See SPO, 63/66, folio 170 for O'Donnell's letter.

the mercenary trade is telling. Given the examples of women who could and did fulfil the role of military leader, it is time to consider Agnes's agency and influence more carefully.[26] English contemporaries referred to Agnes's movement back and forth to Scotland in order to recruit men and also her ability to deny her husband the reinforcements he needed.[27] But Agnes's agency is not so well acknowledged in the historiography. While Hill acknowledges Agnes was a conduit for 'the flow of mercenaries' into Ulster, he does not consider that Agnes herself might command the force while there.[28] Perhaps this is understandable given the absence of definitive evidence but the evidence for Finola's agency in recruiting and commanding mercenaries is more compelling. Orchestrating the supply of mercenaries necessary to pursue her agenda was vital for Finola, a role widely acknowledged by contemporaries.[29]

In May 1587 Lord Deputy Sir John Perrot described Finola as 'agreate bringer in of Scottes' and various reports the previous year referred to her going to Scotland 'to the intente to draw thence great companies of men'.[30] The 'xvi C Skotes' who accompanied her arrival into Lough Foyle in September 1586 would have aided her at a time when she was fully involved in O'Donnell affairs on account of her husband's ill-health in the late 1580s.[31] Although useful to Hugh McManus in securing Tyrconnell, it would appear that these Scots remained under the command of Finola. Shortly after her son, Red Hugh, was inaugurated as 'the O'Donnell' in 1592, steps were taken to reconcile him with the Lord Deputy Sir William Fitzwilliam. As part of the agreement reached on 2 August 1592 Red Hugh agreed to 'put away all strangers that are not of Tirconnell' – a direct reference to his Scottish mercenaries – 'except some xl or l[tie] to attend vpon yo[u]r mother'.[32] And, while Finola recruited mercenaries for her husband and son when they needed them, she could also prevent their arrival when not required. In 1599, Red Hugh laid siege to Cullooney Castle where Donough O'Connor, Lord of Lower Connacht, had positioned

---

[26] Simms, *Gaelic Ulster*, 441–50; Emmett O'Byrne, 'O'Malley, Gráinne (Grace) ('Granuaile')', *DIB*; accessed 27 January 2023; Katrin E. Sjursen, 'Pirate, Traitor, Wife: Jeanne of Belleville and the Categories of Fourteenth-Century French Noblemen', in *Medieval Elite Women*, ed. Tanner, 135–56; Estelle Paranque, 'Isabel Clara Eugenia, Governor of the Spanish Netherlands: Trade, Politics, and Warfare, Ruling like a King, 1621–1633', in *Colonisation, Piracy, and Trade in Early Modern Europe: The Roles of Powerful Women and Queens*, eds Estelle Paranque, Nate Probasco and Claire Jowitt (Cham: Palgrave Macmillan, 2017), 73–93.

[27] SPO, 63/30, folio 72; SPO 63/32, folio 48; SPO 63/38, folio 102. That the English asserted Agnes had 'caryed awaye w[i]th her into Scotlande the strongest part of the Scottes' also points to their belief in the influence she had over her husband as well as the mercenary trade.

[28] Hill, *Fire and Sword*, 172.

[29] SPO, 63/34, folio 42. As early as September 1571 the Privy Council was informed that 'Odonnells wyf is gone into Scotland to hire Skottes'.

[30] SPO, 63/129, folio 134; SPO, 63/124, folio 147.

[31] SPO, 63/126, folio 86v; McGettigan, *Red Hugh O'Donnell*, 39.

[32] SPO, 63/166/folio 122; McGettigan, *Red Hugh O'Donnell*, 61, states this was 'some ninety or one hundred' but the manuscript clearly states forty to fifty.

himself, and who was supported by the English in their efforts to counter O'Donnell. With her son unable to muster sufficient reinforcements to withstand O'Connor, Finola went to recruit more forces in Scotland. During the two months she was away, however, Red Hugh was victorious, defeating the English and gaining O'Connor's submission. O'Donnell sent word to his mother to 'stay' the mercenaries, which she did, instead returning in January 1600 with a, no doubt very welcome, supply of gunpowder.[33]

Lughaidh O'Clery, biographer of Red Hugh, stated that Finola 'had many troops from Scotland, and some of the Irish at her call and under her control, in her hire and pay constantly'.[34] That the mercenaries were under Finola's command, as well as forming her personal bodyguard, is also suggested by her reliance on them in pursuing her own agenda: that of furthering the political ambitions of her husband and son, both of whom had to contend with challenges to their position. In the late 1580s, no doubt exploiting his illness at this time, O'Donnell faced opposition within his lordship.[35] These threats to the stability of the lordship and the position of her husband were taken seriously by Finola, especially as her son, Red Hugh, had been captured by the English the previous year and she was well aware of the wider repercussions of the situation.[36] '[D]etermined to ensure the succession of her own eldest-born', Finola took action that resulted in the English description of her as 'a crewel bloody woman'.[37] The annals record that one rival, Hugh O'Gallagher, was 'killed by Ineenduv' on account that he was shot at 'with darts and bullets, until … left … lifeless' by her Scottish mercenaries, an act that was 'done for her'.[38] Two years later, in 1590, Finola similarly dealt with another rival, Donnell O'Donnell, who was '[a cause of] great anguish and sickness of mind' to her.[39] She gathered all the men of Tyrconnell loyal to her husband along with 'a great number of Scots' to counter the forces of Donnell, killing him in the process. In doing so she effectively eliminated the rivals of both her husband and her son, using her Scottish mercenaries, who 'were constantly in her service and pay, and … in attendance on her in every place', for her own ends.[40]

---

[33] SPO, 63/205, folio 341; SPO, 63/207, 29v. Nevertheless, a supply of gunpower at this time would have been welcome, see Cathcart, *Plantations by Land and Sea*, 193–5.

[34] *Beatha Aodha Ruiadh ui Dhomhnaill. The life of Hugh Roe O'Donnell, prince of Tirconnell (1586–1602)*, by Lughaidh O'Clery, ed. Rev. Denis Murphy (Dublin: Fallon, 1895), 41.

[35] *AFM*, V, 1588 [1867–1869, 1873].

[36] *Beatha Aodha Ruiadh ui Dhomhnaill*, 7–13.

[37] Simms, *Gaelic Ulster*, 444; SPO, 63/170, 31v.

[38] *AFM*, V, 1588 [1873] notes that Hugh had killed Finola's brother, Alexander, adding that 'she had many other causes of enmity towards him; and it was sickness of heart and anguish of mind to her that revenge was not taken of him for his pride and arrogance'.

[39] *AFM*, VI, 1590 [1891].

[40] *AFM*, V, 1588 [1873]; *AFM*, VI, 1590 [1889–91]. 'The Scots discharged a shower of arrows from their elastic bows, by which they pierced and wounded great numbers and, among the rest, the

Following these events, Finola continued to work towards securing her son's succession and, soon after Red Hugh's escape from imprisonment in Dublin and return to Tyrconnell, his father decided 'to resign his lordship to his son'.[41] The annals record the resignation was 'the resolution which O'Donnell came to (as he felt his own feebleness and great age)' and that it was 'universally applauded by all'.[42] No doubt Hugh McManus was unwell but there is no mention in the annals of the influence Finola might have brought to bear on this decision. In contrast, Simms argues that it was Finola's 'military strength and determination' that enabled her to 'force through her husband's resignation … and the inauguration of her son'.[43] She was present with her husband and many of the leading men of Tyrconnell who gathered at Kilmacrennan for the inauguration.[44] O'Clery noted her attendance, stating:

> It was an advantage that she came to the gathering, for she was the head of advice and counsel of the Cinel Conaill, and though she was slow and very deliberate and much praised for her womanly qualities, she had the heart of a hero and the soul of a soldier, inasmuch as she exhorted in every way each one that she was acquainted with, and her husband especially, to avenge his injuries and wrongs on each according to his deserts.[45]

Given he was the biographer of her son, it is perhaps unsurprising that O'Clery would convey a very positive image of Finola, while the concerns of the Four Masters would have been to portray the O'Donnell lords, and their wives, in a good light.[46] But O'Clery, while praising her for her 'womanly qualities', also highlighted her courage and military capability, qualities more associated with men, alongside her role in giving advice.[47] Such views, however, stand in stark contrast to the comments by English observers and indeed by historians. One modern biography refers to her 'machinations' while a contemporary

---

son of O'Donnell himself, who … was slain at Doire-leathan'. See also McGettigan, *Red Hugh O'Donnell*, 46; Simms, *Gaelic Ulster*, 444.

[41] See *AFM*, VI, 1592 [1913–1927], *Beatha Aodha Ruiadh ui Dhomhnaill*, 13–39, recounts his escape and journey home, a journey that cost him his two big toes on account of frostbite. For the inauguration see *AFM*, VI, 1592 [1929]; *Beatha Aodha Ruiadh ui Dhomhnaill*, 41–3.

[42] *AFM*, VI, 1592 [1929].

[43] Simms, *Gaelic Ulster*, 444.

[44] *AFM*, VI, 1592 [1929]; *Beatha Aodha Ruiadh ui Dhomhnaill*, 43. The resignation of the lordship by Hugh McManus to his son 'was universally applauded by all', or at least all those who attended for the annals also note the 'great number … who did not come hither, through spite and malice'.

[45] *Beatha Aodha Ruiadh ui Dhomhnaill*, 39–41.

[46] Edel Bhreathnach and Bernadette Cunningham, eds, *Writing Irish History: The Four Masters and their World* (Dublin: Wordwell, 2007), 20–3, 29–30.

[47] Elizabeth Ewan, 'The Dangers of Manly Women: Late medieval perceptions of female heroism in Scotland's Second War of Independence', in *Woman and the Feminine in Medieval and Early Modern Scottish Writing*, eds Sarah M. Dunnigan, C. Marie Harker and Evelyn S. Newlyn (New York: Palgrave Macmillan, 2004), 3–18, at 4.

study of Red Hugh refers to Finola 'luring' her son's rival, Hugh O'Gallagher, to his murder.[48] Such negative views echo those of the English observers who knew that Finola had 'comitted sondrie murthers' in her elimination of individuals who threatened the position of her son. For the English, involvement in the mercenary trade was one matter, but ordering the removal of rivals was quite another. This was violent behaviour, and Finola was far from a passive bystander in activity that transgressed the norms of what was acceptable for a woman.[49] Yet such was the reality of the world that both Finola and Agnes operated in and survival of the family demanded such action.

While advancing the claims of her late husband and her sons, and as wife to Turlough Luineach O'Neill, Agnes needed to balance MacDonald interests with those of O'Neill – and very probably Campbell ones too. She also had to contend with periods of O'Neill–O'Donnell hostility which would have placed pressure on her relationship with her daughter, Finola, as wife of O'Donnell.[50] Holding all these competing factions in tension required strong negotiating skills on her part. In addition, Agnes was involved in parleys with various members of the English administration during the 1570s and 1580s as, on several occasions, Turlough Luineach sent Agnes to Newry to treat for peace with the English. This was partly due to his own ill-health but also because O'Neill recognised his wife's skills in such matters.[51] From the English perspective she was an amenable go-between and often they described Agnes in favourable terms: 'a wyse and a cyvell woman and ... an ernest instrument of peace', 'a very nobell wysse woman' and 'a contynuall good instr[u]m[e]nt' who 'dutyfully uses her self to further the queens maiestie service every waye as if she weare a natural borne subiecte'.[52] Evidently Agnes made an impression on Sir Francis Walsingham who sought to 'p[ro]cure ... some sute ... of hir ma[jes]tie' for her, while the queen herself appears to have shown Agnes favour by sending her a gown.[53] While the English viewed Agnes as the more educated and more civil of the married couple, that Agnes was involved in negotiating peace between the

---

[48] O'Byrne, 'MacDonnell (Nic Dhomhnaill), Fiona (Fionnghuala) ('Iníon Dubh')', *DIB*; McGettigan, *Red Hugh O'Donnell*, 51. To be sure, it is very likely that this is what happened, although AFM, V, 1588 [1873], using more neutral language, states that O'Gallagher 'happened to be coming up ... towards the place that she was at'.

[49] Anne-Marie Kilday, "Angels with Dirty Faces': Violent Women in Early Modern Scotland', in *Female Transgression in Early Modern Britain: Literary and Historical Explorations*, eds Richard Hillman and Pauline Ruberry-Blanc (Ashgate: Farnham, 2014), 141–62, at 142–3.

[50] SPO, 63/87, folio 77 which mentions Agnes and Finola being 'in messadge betwene' their husbands, then on either side of Lough Foyle, 'but their message came to noe effecte'.

[51] SPO, 63/65, 46r.

[52] SPO, 63/52, folios 135–6; SPO, 63/53, 167v; SPO, 63/65, 46r.

[53] SPO, 63/59, folio100; SPO, 63/60, folio 143; SPO, 63/63, folio 16; SPO, 63/65, 46r. Given Agnes resided far from courtly life it is hard to appreciate what she might have thought of such a gift, especially as, from the English perspective, it was a gift to 'contynewe him [her husband] in quyett'.

English and her husband was due to her realistic appreciation of the situation in Ulster and her political astuteness.

Agnes clearly impressed many of the English who encountered her, either with her education or, as is more likely, because she far exceeded any expectations they might have had concerning the widow of James MacDonald who was a key player in the mercenary trade that frustrated effective English governance of Ulster. Their pre-conceived ideas were challenged when they met a well-educated and politically aware woman, although contemporaries preferred to comment on aspects of Agnes's character that were acceptable for a female: she was 'very well spoken, of great modesty, good nature, parentage, and disposition'.[54] Some English contemporaries were concerned with Agnes's influence over her husband; while this may have been concern about the subversion of natural order it was also a concern regarding the repercussions of such influence for the situation in Ulster.[55] Recent historiography, however, is more damning of Agnes's actions, referring to her 'machinations on behalf of her sons'.[56] No doubt on occasion Agnes was duplicitous in her negotiations with the English, at times declaring that visits back to Scotland were not to bring 'hither Scottes and other straungers' into Ireland when, in fact, that is almost certainly what she was doing.[57] But it is likely that all parties involved in Ulster at this time were, on occasion, somewhat economic with the truth, especially when so much was at stake. In the end, a few years before her death in 1590, Agnes realised her aims. While in 1586 Sorley Boy was made denizen and granted the lands of the Route, her son Angus became a tenant of the English crown holding the Glens of Antrim, albeit from his uncle.[58] To that end, she had been a significant figure in Ulster for over two decades and saw her sons' claim to land there finally acknowledged.[59]

Finola too realised her aims of both protecting the position of her husband and the inheritance of her son, securing his succession to the lordship in 1592.

---

[54] Hill, *Fire and Sword*, 174.
[55] SPO, 63/35, folio117.
[56] Hill, *Fire and Sword*, 174.
[57] SPO, 63/105, folio 0209.
[58] SPO, 63/112, folio 41 XII for the September 1584 agreement resulting from a 'humble sute ... made unto us ... by the Ladie Agnes Cambell wife to Turloghe Lennoghe Onele, mother to ... Donell Gorme'. In this Donnell Gorm promised 'alwaies to serve against Sauerlie Bwoy and anie other forraine Scott' – a clause that made it unworkable; see Ciaran Brady, 'East Ulster, the MacDonalds and the Provincial Strategies of Hugh O'Neill, Earl of Tyrone, 1585–1603', in *Scotland the Ulster Plantations: Explorations in the British settlements of Stuart Ireland*, eds William P. Kelly and John R. Young (Dublin: Four Courts Press, 2009), 41–61, at 48–9. SPO, 63/118, folio 115; J. S. Brewer and William Bullen, eds, *Calendar of Carew Manuscripts, Preserved in the Archiepiscopal Library at Lambeth, 1515–1624*, 6 vols (London: Longman & Co., 1867–73), II, nos 611, 614.
[59] She had done so while preventing the Clan Donald from tearing itself apart – at least during her lifetime. The two branches would become increasingly more hostile to one another after 1590.

Doing so entailed her direct involvement in recruiting mercenaries and also in the murder of rival claimants to the lordship that brought condemnation from the English. But in contrast to her mother Agnes, who the English preferred to negotiate with rather than her O'Neill husband, English sources often refer to Finola as 'the Scottishe woman'.[60] If the English regarded the Scottish Agnes as more preferable to her Irish O'Neill husband it suggests a hierarchy of civility, with the Irish as most uncivilised, English as most civilised, and the Scots somewhere in between. But the English commentators suggest that the Irish looked down on Finola because of her Scottishness, thus positing a different perspective.[61] Indeed, that Red Hugh was 'meer Scottish', suggested the English, was the reason for the 'hatred borne unto hym by his owne contryfolke and kyndred'.[62] Given the extent of intermarriage between kindreds across this North Channel world, the description of Finola and Red Hugh as being 'mere' Scottish is more likely a reflection of English concerns rather than Irish ones as such views are not supported either by Irish contemporaries or Finola's actions.[63] The comments of English were not simply critical and derogatory, but they sought to 'other' both mother and son on account of their Scottish blood. No doubt some of this 'othering' resulted from Finola's role in the recruitment of Scottish mercenaries for her son, then involved in fighting alongside Hugh O'Neill, second earl of Tryone, against the English in the Nine Years War.[64] The ongoing recruitment of mercenary forces had long been the proverbial thorn in the English side, but in the 1590s it strengthened the Irish lords and threatened English dominance across Ulster. Finola's influential position in being able to provide such aid for her son when necessary was recognised fully by the English.[65]

Conclusion

Political activity by women in Ireland was 'both disturbing and threatening'.[66] Indeed William Palmer has argued that Englishmen readily blamed the wives (or other female associates) of Irish men for initiating rebellion, dominating them or giving them poor (that is, anti-English) advice. The intersection of gender

---

[60] SPO, 63/139, 78v.
[61] SPO, 63/139, 79r.
[62] SPO, 63/202/1, 127v; SPO, 62/303, 127v; SPO, 63/204, 75r. See also the comments made by Lord Deputy Sir William Fitzwilliam in his report: SPO, 63/139, 78v–79r.
[63] S. J. Connolly, *Contested Island: Ireland 1460–1630* (Oxford: Oxford University Press, 2007), 46, 46 n.99.
[64] Hiram Morgan, *Tyrone's Rebellion: The outbreak of the Nine Years War in Tudor Ireland* (Woodbridge: Boydell, reprinted 1999).
[65] SPO, 63/205, 184v; SPO, 63/205, 341v. She was also able to prevent the Scots coming when it would have been inconvenient.
[66] William Palmer, 'Gender, Violence, and Rebellion in Tudor and Early Stuart Ireland', *Sixteenth Century Ireland* 23, no.4 (1992): 699–712, at 700.

and ethnicity, therefore, saw Irish women judged harshly. When Finola burned 'O donells castle and haull of Dunnegall' the English acknowledged this was 'don[e] for pollecie ... least yt shold be ... a holt for a garrizou[n] to lye there'.[67] She was not given credit for military strategy or tactics but readily condemned for behaviour not considered appropriate for a female, and also behaviour that contributed to resistance to English authority. Her role in giving orders for, or overseeing the murders of, rival claimants for the O'Donnell lordship brought further condemnation. That Finola moved beyond the boundaries of what was perceived to be acceptable female behaviour by English contemporaries meant she was viewed with suspicion and contempt. Her relentless support, both in terms of military reinforcements and propaganda, for her son and his involvement in the rebellion against English authority in Ireland ultimately saw her 'othered'. In comparison, her mother Agnes was viewed in a different light, preferred to her Irish husband and largely regarded as a moderating influence on him. The English viewed Agnes as counselling Turlough Luineach towards peace; Finola was encouraging her son in rebellion against the English.

As daughters, wives and mothers, both women pursued the interests of their sons in Ulster. In doing so, they recruited and commanded mercenary forces, counselled and advised husbands and sons and maintained their own agendas in the face of rivals.[68] Both women operated within the complex world of Ulster politics in the latter decades of the sixteenth century; they shaped that cross-channel mercenary world and shaped Ulster – a world largely controlled by men. It may have been acceptable to the English for their queen to command armies and to project masculine or military characteristics, but it was not acceptable for Agnes or Finola to do so.[69] That is understandable given that the forces Agnes and Finola recruited and commanded were often used to resist the English presence in Ulster. While contemporaries may have disliked this military role, they still recognised it. In contrast, historians either have tended to overlook this agency on the part of women, too readily assuming that the mercenary trade was controlled by men; or have interpreted the actions of Agnes and Finola rather subjectively, referring to their 'machinations'.[70] We need to acknowledge the agency of women and the actions they took in pursuit of their individual agendas. Across Europe, a 'mother's care' for her son included 'ensuring his inheritance' so the actions of Agnes and Finola should

---

[67] SPO, 63/141, folio 64.

[68] We know that Turlough Luineach valued the counsel she provided. In 1579 it was commented that he 'diskloside his mynde ... in the p[re]sence of the la[dy] his wife' (SPO, 63/69, folio 0039).

[69] Elizabeth I's speech at Tilbury on the eve of the Spanish Armada in 1588, BL, Harley 6798, folio 87.

[70] McGettigan, *Red Hugh O'Donnell*, 51; Palmer, 'Gender, Violence, and Rebellion', 702 wrote that Finola was 'charged' with causing the murder of rivals, almost suggesting that this was not true.

not be seen as exceptional.[71] The world they inhabited demanded actions and behaviours of these women beyond what was considered appropriate but that does not mean they should be ignored. As such, rather than assume the mercenary trade was brokered by men, this chapter suggests a reconsideration of the military role of women both within lordships and in the mercenary trade that operated across the North Channel during the later sixteenth century. While the evidence may be limited at times, a wider body of scholarship is increasingly re-evaluating the military roles of women within late medieval and early modern society. We need to move beyond binaries of gender, beyond what is considered appropriate or acceptable behaviours for women, and consider female agency and agenda in the context within which they lived.

---

[71] Ward, 'Noblewomen, Family, and Identity', 256–7.

Conclusion
New Vistas and the Future for Scottish Gender History

Cathryn Spence, Janay Nugent and Mairi Cowan

This volume draws to a close with Alison Cathcart's study of two women whose political and familial influence crossed the waters of the North Channel to bridge a divide between Scotland and Ireland. Like that chapter, so too has this collection sought to cross a (slightly larger!) body of water to help bridge another type of divide – bringing together scholars from both sides of an ocean, in multiple disciplines and at all career stages – to show the connections and possibilities in the field of Scottish medieval and early modern gender history.

When we issued our call for papers for this volume, we were motivated by a desire both to honour Elizabeth Ewan as an esteemed mentor and to chart the development of Scottish gender history in the medieval and early modern periods. Professor Ewan's influence on this evolving field is undeniable, and this collection illustrates the importance of her work.

The response to the project was immediate, overwhelmingly positive and enthusiastic as we drew together scholars of medieval and early modern Scotland. These contributors hold positions in academic, heritage and governmental sectors in Britain, the United States and Canada, with research backgrounds in archaeology, material culture, literature, as well as public, political, economic and social history. Aside from their connection to Elizabeth Ewan, two elements unite these scholars and their chapters for this volume. One is an interest in gender history. Some contributors identify first and foremost as gender historians, while others are scholars who are open to the possibilities offered by engaging with gender history. The second element is the excitement they bring to this project. Without exception, the scholars in this group have been collegial and giving, coming together not only to create the edited volume you hold in your hands or see on your screen, but also to nurture a community of historians. This collection serves as an example to continue Professor Ewan's legacy, reflecting the type of scholar and tone of scholarship inspired by Elizabeth Ewan and her career: engaged, supportive and creative.

Inspired by Elizabeth Ewan's example, contributors to this volume examine the intersection of place, faith and politics with gender to present new and varied ways of understanding events and people in Scottish history. The study of gender has revealed the ubiquity of power structures and the need to remain attentive to questions of power in any study of the past. Gender itself is not simple, however. It is simultaneously empowering and constricting. Historians in this volume tease out such ambiguities, contradictions and uncertainties, making them visible and proving their significance.

Growing out of this collection are some additional opportunities for engagement with broader theoretical approaches. One obvious avenue of continued expansion is masculinity studies. Often, studies of gender are concerned primarily with the experiences of women, and more research is needed on the experiences of men as gendered individuals. Much of the canon of Scottish history has focused on the events and people – mainly men – that formed and transformed the nation at the level of high politics. Beyond the largely urban, Lowland world of masculine-centred political culture, considerations within Scotland of how power and gender were experienced in the Highlands compared to the Lowlands, urban versus rural spaces, and in Gaelic and Scots communities would all add greatly to our understanding of Scottish history.

Other exciting theoretical approaches that could open up new questions are founded in critical studies. For example, critical race theory could help historians identify and assess the contributions of a greater diversity of people to Scottish history, help clarify Scotland's role in colonial projects including the British empire, and add to histories of the Scottish diaspora. There is also scope for more queer pre-modern history. As the records of Scotland have shown themselves so rich for other aspects of gender history, these issues too deserve greater research and discussion.

Finally, a deeper and broader engagement with historiographies beyond Scotland could be integral to future research. Medieval and early modern Scots showed themselves willing and able to engage actively with people and ideas that lay beyond their borders, and gender historians should be similarly unafraid to explore and interrogate ideas far and wide as a way of broadening Scottish historiography, enriching other historiographies and maintaining the continued dynamism of the field.

There remains much more still to explore and examine. Fortunately, the field is home to a dynamic and dedicated community of scholars, eager to embark upon new areas and questions even as they continue to investigate more traditional aspects of medieval, early modern and gender studies. Much as Elizabeth Ewan has inspired contributors in this collection, so we hope that this collection will inspire the next generation to study gender as a way of giving voice to those who are often underrepresented in the literature to provide us with a greater understanding of Scotland's past.

Bibliography

Archival sources

Aberdeen University Library
William Walker Papers, MS 2774, 1695.

Bodleian Library
Kirkstall Abbey Long Chronicle, Laud Misc. 722.

The British Library
Cotton Nero C VIII.
Elizabeth I speech. Harley 6798.
Historia Roffensis of William of Dene, Cotton Faustina B V.
Laing Casts.
Long Anglo-Norman Prose Brut, Cotton MS Tiberius A VI.
Seals xlvii.

Corpus Christi College, Parker Library
MS 281, Manuscripts in the Parker Library at Corpus Christi College, Cambridge, https://parker.stanford.edu/parker/catalog/wd305nz9008.

Court of the Lord Lyon, Edinburgh
Stevenson and Wood Casts.

Durham Cathedral Archives, Durham University Library, Archives, and Special Collections, Durham
Medieval Seals (Scottish Private Seals).
Miscellaneous Charters 1–999.

Glasgow City Archives
Glasgow's Burgh Court, Court Book. 1657–1659, B1/1/vol. 5.
Glasgow's Burgh Diet, Diet Book. 1670–1673, B B1/1/vol. 7.

Lambeth Palace Library, London
MS 99.

The National Archives, Kew
E39, Exchequer: Treasury of Receipt: Scottish Documents.
E42, Exchequer: Treasury of Receipt: Ancient Deeds, Series AS.
SC13, Scots Seals Mainly from Homages to Edward I.
QFA1/19, Index to Seals: Personal equestrian (owner on horseback). Personal Armorial: Women (coat of arms).

The National Archives, London
The National Archives Currency Converter: 1270–2017, https://www.nationalarchives.gov.uk/currency/.
SC 8/13/611.
SPO, State Papers Foreign: Ireland, Scotland, Borders and Registers of the Privy Council.
SPO, 1509–1714. Part II: The Tudors: Henry VIII to Elizabeth I, 1509–1603.

National Library of Scotland, Edinburgh
Adv. Ms. 33.7.26, Sir James Balfour's Letters, 1630–43.
Blaeu's Atlas. 1654, https://maps.nls.uk/atlas/blaeu.
Adv. 32.4.7 – 'Πρόνοια. Providentia. Divina Providentia in Rebus Humanis. Divine Providence in humane affaires. A collection of providential passages antient and modern foreign and domestick by Master James Fraser Minister At Kirkhill. Written Anno 1678'.
NLS Charters
Relatio Incarcerationis et Martyrii P Ioannis Ogilbei Natione Scoti e Societate Jesus, APS. 2.78.23.
Wodrow MSS, folio 32, 'Petition of the Honest Women of Edinburgh'.

National Records of Scotland, Edinburgh
CH2/550/1-2, Glasgow Kirk Session Records.
CH2/171/1, 2, 31, 32A-B, 33, 35, Glasgow Presbytery Records.
CH2/751/2, Ayr Kirk Session Records.
GD93, Papers of the Munro Family of Foulis.
GD190, Papers of the Smythe Family of Methven, Perthshire.
GD297, J.&F. Anderson Collection.
JC2/13, High Court Book of Adjournal, 24 December 1669–1 Aug 1673.
JC6/8, High Court Minute Book, 1 June 1669–27 January 1673.
JC26/37, High Court Process Papers, 1670.
RH17/1, Seal casts, matrices, and detached seals.

Parish Church of St Mary Cranston Library
Gesta Scotorum contra Anglicos, Reigate, Item 1117.

Perth Museum and Art Gallery
Perth Museum accession register ('pencil' register).
PMAG Archive 38, *LASP Letter Book 1785–1893*.
PMAG Archive 39, *LASP Minute Book 1827–1897*.
PMAG Archive 43, *LASP List of MSS & Objects Donated 1784–1892*.

Signet Library
MS 20, Lawyer's Handbook (c. 1643).

Printed primary sources

Adae Murimuth Continuatio Chronicarum. Robertus de Avesbury de gestis mirabilibus regis Edwardi Tertii, edited by E. M. Thompson. London: Rolls Series, 1889.

Adamson, Henry. *The Muses Threnodie or Mirthful Mournings on the Death of Mr Gall* ... Perth: James Cant, 1638; 1774 edition.

Annála Connacht. University College Cork CELT Project.

Annála Rioghachta Éireann: Annals of the Kingdom of Ireland by the Four Masters, from the Earliest Period to the year 1616, edited and translated by J. O'Donovan. Second edition, 7 vols. Dublin: Hodges, Smith & Co., 1856.

'Annales Paulini'. In *Chronicles of the Reigns of Edward I and Edward II*, edited by W. Stubbs. London: Rolls Series, 1882–3.

Annals of Clonmacnoise, edited by Denis Murphy. Dublin: University Press, 1896.

Annals of Connacht, edited by A. Martin Freeman. Dublin: Dublin Institute for Advanced Studies, 1944.

Anonimalle Chronicle, 1333 to 1381, edited by V. H. Galbraith. Manchester: Manchester University Press, 1927.

Asloan Manuscript, edited by W. A. Craigie. 2 vols. Edinburgh, 1923–5.

Baillie, Robert. *The Letters and Journals of Robert Baillie*, edited by David Laing. 3 vols. Edinburgh: Bannatyne Club, 1841–2.

Balcanquhall, Walter. *A Large Declaration Concerning the Late Tumults in Scotland*. London, 1639.

Balfour, James. *Practicks of Sir James Balfour of Pittendreich: Reproduced from Printed Edition of 1754*, edited by P. G. B. McNeill. 2 vols. Edinburgh: Stair Society, 1962.

Bannatyne, Richard. *Memorials of Transactions in Scotland*, edited by Robert Pitcairn. Edinburgh: Bannatyne Club, 1836.

Barbour, John. *The Bruce*, edited by A. A. M. Duncan. Edinburgh: Canongate Books, 1997.

Beatha Aodha Ruaidh ui Dhomhnaill. *The Life of Hugh Roe O'Donnell, Prince of Tirconnell (1586–1602)*, edited by Lughaidh O'Clery and Rev. Denis Murphy. Dublin: Fallon, 1895.

Birch, W. de G. *Catalogue of Seals in the Department of Manuscripts in the British Museum*, vol. iv. London: British Museum, 1895.

Boece, Hector. *Buik of the Chronicles of Scotland*, edited by William B. Turnbull, iii. London: Rolls Series, 1858.

Boece, Hector. *The Chronicles of Scotland*, translated by John Bellenden, 1531; edited by Edith Batho and H. Winifred Husbands. 2 vols. Edinburgh and London: William Blackwood and Sons, 1941.

Bower, Walter. *Scotichronicon*, edited by D. E. R. Watt. 9 vols. Aberdeen and Edinburgh: University of Aberdeen Press, 1987–98.

Brut or Chronicles of England, edited by F. W. D. Brie. London: Early English Text Society, 1906–8.

Buchanan, George. *De Maria Scotorum Regina*. Critical hypertext edition by Dana F. Sutton, 2001.

Buchanan, George. *The History of Scotland*, translated and edited by James Aikman. 4 vols. Glasgow: Blackie, Fullerton and Co., 1827.

Buchanan, George. *Vernacular Writings*, edited by P. Hume Brown. STS 26, 1892.

Burne, Nicol. *Disputation in Catholic Tractates of the Sixteenth Century*, edited by T. Law. STS, 1901.

Calendar of Carew Manuscripts, Preserved in the Archiepiscopal Library at Lambeth, 1515–1624, edited by J. S. Brewer and William Bullen. 6 vols. London: Longman & Co., 1867–73.

Calendar of Documents Relating to Scotland, edited by J. Bain. Edinburgh: H. M. General Register House, 1881–8.

Calendar of Entries in the Papal Registers Relating to Great Britain and Ireland: Papal Letters, edited by W. H. Bliss. London, 1896.

Calendar of Inquisitions Post Mortem. London: HMSO, 1904–.
Calendar of Patent Rolls Preserved in the Public Record Office: Edward II, A.D. *1307–1327*, edited by H. C. Maxwell Lyte and J. G. Black London, 1894.
Calendar of State Papers, Foreign Series of the Reign of Edward, Mary and Elizabeth, edited by J. Stevenson et al. London, 1861–1950.
Calendar of State Papers Relating to Scotland and Mary, Queen of Scots, edited by J. Bain et al. Edinburgh, 1898–1969.
Calendar of State Papers, Venice, edited by R. Brown and G. Cavendish Bentinck. London, 1890.
Charters and Documents Relating to the Collegiate Church and Hospital of the Holy Trinity and the Trinity Hospital, Edinburgh, AD *1460–1661*, edited by J. D. Marwick (SBRS, 1871).
Charters and Other Documents Relating to the City of Glasgow, 1175–1649, edited by J. D. Marwick. 2 vols. Glasgow: SBRS, 1917.
Chronica Monasterii de Melsa, edited by E. A. Bond. London: Rolls Series, 1868.
Chronicle of Geoffrey le Baker, edited by David Preest and Richard Barber. Woodbridge: Boydell and Brewer, 2012.
Chronicle of Lanercost, 1272–1346, translated by Herbert Maxwell. Glasgow: MacLehose, 1913.
Chronicle of Perth: A Register of Remarkable Occurrences, Chiefly Connected with that City, from the year 1210 to 1688, edited by John Maitland. Edinburgh: Maitland Club, 1831.
Chronicle of Walter of Guisborough, Previously Edited as the Chronicle of Walter of Hemingford or Hemingburgh, edited by H. Rothwell. London: Camden Society, 1957.
Chronicon Henrici Knighton, edited by J. R. Lumby. London: Rolls Series, 1895–9.
Clouston, J. Storer. 'The Amorial de Berry (Scottish Section)'. *PSAS* 72 (1938): 84–114.
Collace, Jean. 'Some Short Remembrances of the Lord's Kindness to me and his Work on my Soul, for my own use'. In *Women's Life Writing in Early Modern Scotland: Writing the Evangelical Self, c. 1670–1730*, edited by David Mullan, 95–135. Aldershot: Ashgate, 2003.
Collace, Katharine. 'Memoirs or Spiritual Exercises of Mistress Ross'. In *Women's Life Writing in Early Modern Scotland: Writing the Evangelical Self, c. 1670–1730*, edited by David Mullan, 95–135. Aldershot: Ashgate, 2003.
Craig, Thomas. *The Jus Feudale; With an Appendix Containing the Books of the Feus; A Translation by Right Honourable James Avon Clyde*. 2 vols. Edinburgh, 1934.
Cranstoun, James, ed. *Satirical Poems of the Time of the Reformation*. 2 vols. STS old ser. Edinburgh, 1891–3.
Dalrymple, James. *The Institutions of the Law of Scotland: Deduced from its Originals, and Collated with the Civil, Canon, and Feudal Laws, and with the Customs of Neighboring Nations: in IV Books* (Edinburgh, 1693).
Dawson, Jane, ed. *Clan Campbell Letters, 1559–1583*. SHS, 5th ser. 10. Edinburgh, 1997.
Decisions of the Court of Session, from Its Institution until the Separation of the Court into Two Divisions in the Year 1808, Digested under Proper Heads, in the Form of a Dictionary, edited by William Morison. 42 vols. Edinburgh: Printed for Archibald Constable, 1801–11.
Deidis of Armorie: A Heraldic Treatise and Bestiary, edited and translated by L. A. J. R. Houwen. 2 vols. Edinburgh: STS, 1994.
Diary of Mr John Lamont of Newton, 1649–1671. Edinburgh: Maitland Club, 1830.
Douglas Book, vol. iii, edited by William Fraser. Edinburgh, 1885.
Dunbar, Archibald Hamilton. 'Facsimiles of the Scottish Coats of Arms Emblazoned in the "Armorial de Gelre"'. *PSAS* 25 (1890), 9–22.
Duncan, William James, ed. *Miscellaneous Papers Principally Illustrative of Events in the Reigns of Queen Mary and King James VI*. Glasgow: Edward Khull, 1834.
Ecclesiastical History of Orderic Vitalis, edited and translated by Marjorie Chibnall. 6 vols. Oxford: Clarendon Press, 1969–80.
Extracts from the Records of the Burgh of Edinburgh, 1642–1655, edited by Marguerite Wood. Edinburgh: Oliver and Boyd, 1938.

Extracts from the Records of the Burgh of Glasgow, 1573–1642, edited by J. D. Marwick. 2 vols. Glasgow: SBRS, 1914.

Foedera, Conventiones, Litterae et Cuisunque Generis Acta Publica, edited by T. Rymer. London, 1816–69.

Fordun, John. *Chronicle of the Scottish Nation*, translated and edited by William F. Skene. Edinburgh: Edmonston and Douglas, 1872.

'Gesta Edwardi de Carnarvan, auctore Canonico Bridlingtoniensi, cum continuatione A.D. 1377'. In *The Chronicles of the Reigns of Edward I and Edward II*, ii, edited by W. Stubbs. London: Rolls Series, 1883.

[Hickes, George]. *Ravillac Redivivus: Being a Narrative of the Late Tryal of Mr. James Mitchel a Conventicle-preacher, who was Executed the 18th of January last, for an Attempt which he made on the Sacred Person of the Archbishop of St. Andrews. To which is Annexed, an Account of the Tryal of that Most Wicked Pharisee Major Thomas Weir, who was Executed for Adultery, Incest and Bestiality*. London, 1678.

Histoire des Ducs de Normandie et des Rois d'Angleterre, edited by Francisque Michel. Paris, 1840.

Historical Manuscripts Commission 6th Report, 'Moray MSS'. London, 1877.

Hope's Major Practicks, 1608–1633, edited by James Avon Clyde. 2 vols. Edinburgh, 1937–8.

Household Book of Queen Isabella of England, for the Fifth Regnal Year of Edward II, 8th July 1311 to 7th July 1312, edited by F. D. Blackley and G. Hermansen. Edmonton: University of Alberta Press, 1971.

Jacobus de Voragine, *The Golden Legend: Readings on the Saints*, translated by William Granger Ryan. Princeton: Princeton University Press, 1993.

John Knox's History of the Reformation in Scotland. 2 vols, edited by W. C. Dickinson. Edinburgh, 1949.

Journals of Sir John Lauder, Lord Fountainhall, with his Observations on Public Affairs and Other Memoranda, 1665–1676, edited by Donald Crawford. Edinburgh: SHS, 1900.

Kirkton, James. *A History of the Church of Scotland, 1660–1679*, edited by Ralph Stewart. Lewiston: Edwin Mellen, 1992.

Knox, John. *History of the Reformation in Scotland*, edited by W. C. Dickinson, 2 vols. Edinburgh, 1949.

Laing, Henry. *Descriptive Catalogue of Impressions from Ancient Scottish Seals*. Edinburgh, 1850.

Lauderdale Papers, edited by Osmund Airy. 3 vols. London, 1884.

Leslie, Henry. *A Treatise of the Authority of the Church*. London, 1639.

Liber Pluscardensis, edited by Felix J. H. Skene. 2 vols. Edinburgh: William Paterson, 1877.

Lindesay of Pitscottie, Robert. *The Historie and Chronicles of Scotland*, edited by A. J. G. Mackay. 3 vols. STS, 1899–1911.

MacDonald, William Rae. *Scottish Armorial Seals*. Edinburgh, 1904.

Mair, John. *A History of Greater Britain*, translated and edited by Archibald Constable and Æneas J. G. Mackay. Edinburgh: University of Edinburgh Press, 1892.

Marwick, J. D., ed. *Charters and Documents Relating to the Collegiate Church and Hospital of the Holy Trinity and the Trinity Hospital, Edinburgh, AD 1460–1661*. SBRS, 1871.

Miscellaneous Papers Principally Illustrative of Events in the Reigns of Queen Mary and King James VI, edited by W. J. Duncan. Glasgow: Maitland Club, 1834.

Narratives of Scottish Catholics under Mary Stuart and James VI, edited by William Forbes-Leith. Edinburgh: Paterson, 1889.

Original Letters Illustrative of English History, edited by Henry Ellis. Third series, 3 vols. London: Bentley, 1846.

Paterson, Ninian. *The Fanatick Indulgence Granted Anno 1679*. Edinburgh, 1683.

'People of Medieval Scotland, 1093–1371', https://www.poms.ac.uk.

Pitcairn, Robert, ed. *Ancient Criminal Trials in Scotland from 1488 to 1624*. 3 vols. Edinburgh, 1833.

Place Names of Fife, https://fife-placenames.glasgow.ac.uk.

Polychronicon Ranulphi Higden Monachi Cestrensis; Together with the English Translations of John Trevisa and of an Unknown Writer of the Fifteenth Century, edited by C. Babington and J. R. Lumby. London: Rolls Series, 1865–6.

Practicks of Sir James Balfour of Pittendreich, edited by Peter McNeill. 2 vols. Edinburgh: Stair Society, 1962–3.

Protocol Book of Mr Gilbert Grote, 1552–1753, edited by William Angus. Edinburgh: SRS, 1914.

Ratis Raving and Other Early Scots Poems on Morals, edited by R. Girvan. Edinburgh: William Blackwood and Sons, 1939.

Ratis Raving and Other Moral and Religious Pieces in Prose and Verse (from Cambridge University MS KK.I.), edited by J. Rawson Lumby. London: Early English Text Society, 1890.

Records of the Commissions of the General Assemblies of the Church of Scotland, 1650, vol. 2, edited by Alexander F. Mitchell and James Christie. Edinburgh, 1892.

Records of Inverness Burgh Court Books: 1556–86, edited by William Mackay and Herbert C. Boyd. Aberdeen: New Spalding Club, 1911.

Records of the Parliaments of Scotland to 1707, edited by Keith M. Brown, et al. St Andrews, 2008, http://www.rps.ac.uk.

Records of the Proceedings of the Justiciary Court Edinburgh, 1661–1678, edited by W. G. Scott-Moncrieff. 2 vols. Edinburgh: SHS, 1905.

Red Book of Menteith, vol. ii, edited by William Fraser. Edinburgh, 1880.

Regiam Maiestatem: The Earliest Known Version, edited by John Reuben Davies with Alice Taylor. Edinburgh: Stair Society, 2022.

Register of the Great Seal of Scotland, 1306–1424, edited by John Maitland Thomson et al. Edinburgh, 1882–1914.

Register of Marriages for the Parish of Edinburgh, 1595–1700, edited by Henry Paton. Edinburgh: SRS, 1905.

Register of the Privy Council of Scotland, edited by Peter Hume Brown, series 1–3. Edinburgh, 1881–1933.

Registrum Magni Sigilli Regum Scotorum / The Register of the Great Seal of Scotland, edited by John Maitland Thomson et al. 11 vols. Edinburgh: Register House, 1897–1912.

Robertson, Joseph, ed. *Topography and Antiquities in the Shires of Aberdeen and Banff*. 4 vols. Aberdeen, 1869.

'Robertus de Avesbury de Gestis Mirabilibus Regis Edwardi Tertii'. In *Adae Murimuth Continuatio Chronicarum. Robertus de Avesbury de Gestis Mirabilibus Regis Edwardi Tertii*, edited by E. M. Thompson. London: Rolls Series, 1889.

Roll of Edinburgh Burgesses and Guild-Brethren, 1406–1700, edited by Charles B. Boog Watson. Edinburgh: SRS, 1929.

Rose, Alexander. *A Sermon Preached Before the Right Honourable the Lords Commissioners of His Majesties Most Honourable Privy Council*. Glasgow, 1684.

Rotuli Scaccarii Regum Scotorum / Exchequer Rolls of Scotland, edited by G. Burnee. Edinburgh: H. M. Register House, 1882.

Rotuli Scotiæ in Turri Londinensi et in Domo Capitulari Westmonasteriensi Asservati. London: Record Commission, 1814–19.

Row, William. *The Life of Mr Robert Blair*, edited by Thomas M'Crie. Edinburgh 1848.

Scalacronica, 1272–1363, edited by Andy King. Woodbridge: Surtees Society, 2019.

Sinclair, George. *Satan's Invisible World Discovered*. Edinburgh, 1685.

Spottiswoode, John. *A True Relation of the Proceedings Against John Ogilvie, A Jesuit in Ancient Criminal Trials of Scotland*, edited by Robert Pitcairn, vol. 3, part 1, 330–53. Edinburgh: Bannatyne Club, 1833.

Spottiswoode, John. *History of the Church of Scotland*, edited by M. Russell. 3 vols. Edinburgh: Spottiswoode Society, 1847–51.

Stevenson, John Horne and Marguerite Wood. *Scottish Heraldic Seals: Royal, Official, Ecclesiastical, Burghal, and Personal Seals*. Glasgow, 1940.

Stevenson, J., ed. *The History of Mary Stewart by Claude Nau*. Edinburgh: William Paterson, 1883.
Taylor, Alice, ed. *The Laws of Medieval Scotland: Legal Compilations from the Thirteenth and Fourteenth Centuries*. Edinburgh: Stair Society, 2019.
'Thomas of Froidmont: The Adventures of Margaret of Beverly, a Woman Crusader'. In *Crusades: A Source Reader*, edited by S. J. Allen and E. Amt. Toronto: University of Toronto Press, 2014.
Thomson, T., ed. *A Diurnal of Remarkable Occurrent …* Edinburgh: Bannatyne Club, 1833.
Thomson, T., ed. *Memoirs of his own Life. By Sir James Melville of Halhill*. Edinburgh: Bannatyne Club, 1827.
Thomson, T., ed. *Registrum Honoris de Morton*. Edinburgh: Bannatyne Club, 1853.
Tourist's Hand-Book to Perth and Neighbourhood, with Historical Notanda, Civil & Ecclesiastical. Perth: James Dewar & Son, 1848.
Walsingham, Thomas. *Historia Anglicana*, edited by H. T. Riley. London: Rolls Series, 1863–4.
Wars of Edward III: Sources and Interpretations, edited by Clifford J. Rogers. Woodbridge: Boydell, 1999.
Wyntoun, Andrew. *The Original Chronicles of Andrew of Wyntoun*, edited by F. J. Amours. 6 vols. Edinburgh and London: William Blackwood and Sons, 1903–14.
Wyntoun, Andrew. *The Orygynale Cronykil of Scotland*, edited by David Laing. 3 vols. Edinburgh, 1872.

Secondary sources

Abrams, Lynn. 'Gendering the Agenda'. In *Gender in Scottish History Since 1700*, edited by Lynn Abrams, Eleanor Gordon, Deborah Simonton and Eileen Janes Yeo, 1–16. Edinburgh: Edinburgh University Press, 2006.
Abrams, Lynn and Elizabeth Ewan, eds. *Nine Centuries of Man: Manhood and Masculinities in Scottish History*. Edinburgh: Edinburgh University Press, 2017.
Aird, William M. 'Frustrated Masculinity: The Relationship Between William the Conqueror and his Eldest Son'. In *Masculinity in Medieval Europe*, edited by Dawn M. Hadley, 39–55. Reprint. Abingdon: Routledge, 2014.
Allen, Aaron. *Building Early Modern Edinburgh: A Social History of Craftwork and Incorporation*. Edinburgh: Edinburgh University Press, 2018.
Amato, Joseph A. *Everyday Life: How the Ordinary became Extraordinary*. London: Reaktion Books, 2016.
Amato, Joseph A. *On Foot: A History of Walking*. New York: New York University, 2004.
Anderson, Iain and Piers Dixon. 'Inverlochy and Lochindorb Castles – A Comparative Study'. *Architectural Heritage* 22 (2011): 1–17.
Anderson, James. *The Ladies of the Covenant: Memoirs of Distinguished Scottish Female Characters, Embracing the Period of the Covenant and the Persecution*. Glasgow: Blackie and Son, 1851.
Angell, Stephen Ward, ed. *The Oxford Handbook of Quaker Studies*. Oxford: Oxford University Press, 2013.
Angell, Stephen W. and Pink Dandelion, eds. *Early Quakers and Their Theological Thought, 1647–1723*. Cambridge: Cambridge University Press, 2015.
Armstrong, Robert and Tadhg O'Hannrachain, eds. *Insular Christianity: Alternative Models of the Church in Britain and Ireland, c. 1570–c. 1700*. Manchester: Manchester University Press, 2013.
Bailey, Joanne. 'Favoured or Oppressed? Married Women, Property and "Coverture" in England, 1660–1800'. *Continuity & Change* 17, no. 3 (2002): 351–72.
Bailey, Michael D. 'Concern over Superstition in Late Medieval Europe'. *Past & Present* Supplement 3 (2008): 115–33.
Bain, George. *History of Nairnshire*. Nairn: Nairnshire Telegraph, 1893.
Barber, Richard. *Edward III and the Triumph of England: The Battle of Crécy and the Order of the Garter*. London: Penguin, 2014.

Barclay, Katie. *Caritas: Neighbourly Love and the Early Modern Self*. Oxford: Oxford University Press, 2021.

Barclay, Katie. 'Emotional Lineages: Blood, Property, Family and Affection in Early Modern Scotland'. In *Historicising Heritage and Emotions: The Affective Histories of Blood, Stone and Land*, edited by. A. Marchant, 84–98. New York: Routledge, 2019.

Barclay, Katie. 'Intimacy and the Life Cycle in the Marital Relationships of the Scottish Elite during the Long Eighteenth Century'. *WHR* 20, no. 2 (2011): 189–206.

Barclay, Katie. *Love, Intimacy and Power: Marriage and Patriarchy in Scotland, 1650–1850*. Manchester: Manchester University Press, 2011.

Barclay, Katie and Rosalind Carr. 'Women, Love, and Power in Enlightenment Scotland'. *WHR* 27, no. 2 (2018): 176–98.

Barclay, Katie, Tanya Cheadle and Eleanor Gordon, 'The State of Scottish History: Gender'. *SHR* 92, Supplement: no. 234 (2013): 83–107.

Barclay, Katie and Emily Ireland. 'The Household as a Space of the Law'. *Law and History* 7, no. 2 (2021): 98–126.

Barclay, Katie and Rebecca Mason. 'Scottish Women's and Gender History and Women Historians in Scotland: Past, Present and Future Directions'. *SHR* 102, 2, no. 259 (August 2023): 187–210.

Barnes, Ishbel C. M. *Janet Kennedy, Royal Mistress: Marriage and Divorce at the Courts of James IV and V*. Edinburgh: John Donald, 2007.

Barrett, T. H. 'Superstition and its Others in Han China'. *Past & Present* Supplement 3 (2008): 95–114.

Barrow, G. W. S. 'Badenoch and Strathspey, 1130–1312: Secular and Political'. *Northern Scotland* 8 (1988): 1–15.

Barrow, G. W. S. *Robert Bruce: And the Community of the Realm of Scotland*. Edinburgh: Edinburgh University Press, 2005.

Barrow, G. W. S. 'The Wood of Stronkalter: A Note on the Relief of Lochindorb Castle by Edward III in 1336'. *SHR* 46, no. 141 (1967): 77–9.

Bawcutt, Priscilla. '"Holy Words for Healing": Some Early Scottish Charms and their Ancient Religious Roots'. In *Literature and Religion in Late Medieval and Early Modern Scotland*, edited by Luuk Houwen, 127–44. Leuven, Belgium: Peeters, 2012.

Beattie, Cordelia. 'Living as a Single Person: Marital Status, Performance and the Law in Late Medieval England'. *WHR* 17, no. 3 (2008): 327–40.

Beattie, Cordelia and Cathryn Spence. 'Married Women, Testaments and Property in Sixteenth-century Scotland'. *SHR* 102, no. 258 (2023): 1–33.

Beattie, Cordelia and Matthew Frank Stevens, eds. *Married Women and the Law in Premodern Northwest Europe*. Woodbridge: Boydell, 2013.

Bedos-Rezak, Brigitte. 'Medieval Women in French Sigillographic Sources'. In *Women and the Sources of Medieval History*, edited by Joel T. Rosenthal, 1–36. Athens: University of Georgia Press, 1990.

Bedos-Rezak, Brigitte. *When Ego was Imago: Signs of Identity in the Middle Ages*. Leiden: Brill, 2011.

Bennett, Judith. *History Matters: Patriarchy and the Challenge of Feminism*. Philadelphia: University of Pennsylvania Press, 2010.

Berdant, Lauren. 'The Female Complaint'. *Social Text* 19/20 (1988): 237–59.

Bhreathnach, Edel and Bernadette Cunningham, eds. *Writing Irish History: The Four Masters and their World*. Dublin: Wordwell, 2007.

Bitel, Lisa M. and Felice Lifshitz, eds. *Gender and Christianity in Medieval Europe*. Philadelphia: University of Pennsylvania Press, 2008.

Blakeway, Amy. 'James VI and James Douglas, Earl of Morton'. In *James VI and Noble Power in Scotland, 1578–1603*, edited by Miles Kerr-Peterson and Steven J. Reid, 12–31. Abingdon: Routledge, 2017.

Blakeway, Amy. *Regency in Sixteenth-Century Scotland*. Woodbridge: Boydell, 2015.
Blakeway, Amy. 'The Response to the Regent Moray's Assassination'. *SHR* 88 (2009): 9–33.
Blythe, James M. 'Women in the Military: Scholastic Arguments and Medieval Images of Female Warriors'. *History of Political Thought* 22, no. 2 (2001): 242–69.
Boardman, Stephen. 'Chronicle Propaganda in Fourteenth-Century Scotland: Robert the Steward, John Fordun, and the "Anonymous Chronicle"'. *SHR* 76, no. 201 (April 1997): 23–43.
Boardman, Stephen. 'Lords and Women, Women as Lords: The Career of Margaret Stewart, Countess of Angus and Mar, c. 1354–c. 1418'. In *Kings, Lords and Men in Scotland and Britain, 1300–1625: Essays in Honour of Jenny Wormald*, edited by Steve Boardman and Julian Goodare, 37–58. Edinburgh: Edinburgh University Press, 2014.
Boardman, Stephen. *The Campbells, 1250–1513*. Edinburgh: John Donald, 2006.
Boardman, Stephen. *The Early Stewart Kings: Robert II and Robert III, 1371–1406*. East Linton: Tuckwell Press, 1996.
Bolissian, Amie. 'Masculine Old Women or Feminine Old Men? Rethinking Gender and the Ageing Body in Early Modern English Medicine'. *Gender & History* 35, no. 2 (July 2023): 408–42.
Bowden, Hugh. 'Before Superstition and After: Theophrastus and Plutarch on *Desidaimonia*'. *Past & Present* Supplement 3 (2008): 56–71.
Bowie, Karin. *Public Opinion in Early Modern Scotland, 1560–1707*. Cambridge: Cambridge University Press, 2020.
Brady, Ciaran. 'East Ulster, the MacDonalds and the Provincial Strategies of Hugh O'Neill, Earl of Tyrone, 1585–1603'. In *Scotland the Ulster Plantations: Explorations in the British Settlements of Stuart Ireland*, edited by William P. Kelly and John R. Young, 41–61. Dublin: Four Courts Press, 2009.
Breen, Colin. *Dunluce Castle*. Dublin: Four Courts Press, 2012.
Breen, Colin. 'Maritime Connections: Landscape and Lordship along the Gaelic Atlantic Seaboard of Scotland and the North of Ireland during the Middle Ages'. *Journal of the North Atlantic* Special vol. 12 (2019): 3–15.
Brock, Michelle D. 'Keeping the Covenant in Cromwellian Scotland'. *SHR* 99 (2020): 392–411.
Brock, Michelle D. *Satan and the Scots: The Devil in Post-Reformation Scotland, c. 1560–1700*. Farnham: Ashgate, 2016.
Brock, Michelle D. '"The Man Will Shame Me": Women, Sex and Kirk Discipline during the Cromwellian Occupation'. *Scottish Church History* 51, no. 2 (2022): 133–56.
Brooks, Christopher. *Lawyers, Litigation and English Society since 1450*. London: Hambledon Continuum, 1998.
Broomhall, Susan and Andrew Lynch, eds. *A Cultural History of Emotions in the Late Medieval, Reformation and Renaissance Age*. London: Bloomsbury, 2021.
Brotherstone, Terry, Deborah Simonton and Oonagh Walsh, eds. *Gendering Scottish History: An International Approach*. Glasgow: Cruithne Press, 1999.
Broun, Dauvit. 'A New Look at Gesta Annalia Attributed to John of Fordun'. In *Church, Chronicle and Learning in Medieval and Early Renaissance Scotland: Essays Presented to Donald Watt on the Occasion of the Completion of Bower's Scotichronicon*, edited by Barbara E. Crawford, 9–30. Edinburgh: Mercat Press, 1999.
Brown, Callum G. 'Rotavating the Kailyard: Re-imagining the Scottish "Meenister" in Discourse and the Parish State since 1707'. In *Anticlericalism in Britain, c. 1500–1914*, edited by Nigel Aston and Matthew Cragoe, 138–58. Stroud: Sutton, 2001.
Brown, Helen Sarah. 'Lay Piety in Later Medieval Lothian, c. 1306–c. 1513'. PhD diss., University of Edinburgh, 2007.
Brown, Keith M. *Kingdom or Province? Scotland and the Regal Union, 1603–1715*. London: Macmillan, 1992.
Brown, Keith M. *Noble Society in Scotland: Wealth, Family and Culture from the Reformation to Revolution*. Edinburgh: Edinburgh University Press, 2003.

Brown, Michael. '"That Old Serpent and Ancient of Evil Days": Walter, Earl of Atholl and the Death of James I'. *SHR* 71, no. 191/2 (April–October 1992): 23–45.

Brown, Michael and Katie Stevenson, eds. *Medieval St Andrews: Church Cult, City*. Woodbridge: Boydell, 2017.

Brown, William Eric. *John Ogilvie: An Account of his Life and Death with a Translation of the Documents Relating Thereto*. London: Burns Oates and Washbourne, 1925.

Brubaker, Leslie and Julia M. H. Smith, eds. *Gender in the Early Medieval World: East and West, 300–900*. Cambridge: Cambridge University Press, 2004.

Burnet, George B. and William H. Marwick. *The Story of Quakerism in Scotland, 1650–1950*. Cambridge: Lutterworth Press, 2007; reprint of 1952 edn.

Burns, Ryan. 'Enforcing Uniformity: Kirk Sessions and Catholics in Early Modern Scotland, 1560–1650'. *IR* 69, no. 2 (2018): 111–30.

Burns, Ryan. 'Gender, Resistance and Conformity in Early Modern Scotland, 1560–1650'. *IRSS* 44 (2020): 57–84.

Butler, Sara M. and Krista J. Kesselring, eds. *Crossing Borders: Boundaries and Margins in Medieval and Early Modern Britain: Essays in Honour of Cynthia J. Neville*. Leiden: Brill, 2018.

Bynum, Caroline Walker. 'Are Things "Indifferent"? How Objects Change our Understanding of Religious History'. *German History* 34, no. 1 (2016): 88–112.

Bynum, Caroline Walker. *Christian Materiality: An Essay on Religion in Late Medieval Europe*. New York: Zane Books, 2011.

Campbell, Colin. 'Scottish Arms in the Bellenville Roll'. *Scottish Genealogist* 25, vol. 2 (1978): 33–52.

Campbell, Colin. *The Scots Roll: A Study of a Fifteenth-century Roll of Arms*. Edinburgh: Heraldry Society of Scotland, 1995.

Campbell, Erin J., ed. *Growing Old in Early Modern Europe: Cultural Representations*. London: Routledge, 2006.

Campbell, J., Elizabeth Ewan and Heather Parker, eds. *Shaping Scottish Identities: Gender, Nation and the Worlds Beyond*. Guelph: Centre for Scottish Studies, 2011.

Carpenter, Sarah. 'Performing Diplomacies: The 1560s Court Entertainments of Mary Queen of Scots'. *SHR* 82 (2003): 194–225.

Carr, Daniel J. 'Are Equity and Law in Scotland Fused, Separate or Intertwined?' In *Equity and Law: Fusion and Fission*, edited by John C. P. Goldberg, Henry E. Smith and P. G. Turner, 179–200. New York: Cambridge University Press, 2019.

Carr, Rosalind. *Gender and Enlightenment Culture in Eighteenth-Century Scotland*. Edinburgh: Edinburgh University Press, 2014.

Carvalhal, Hélder. 'Kingship and Masculinity in Renaissance Portugal (Fifteenth and Sixteenth Centuries)'. In *The Routledge History of Monarchy: New Perspectives on Rulers and Rulership*, edited by Elena Woodacre, Lucinda H. S. Dean, Chris Jones, Russel E. Martin and Zita Rohr, 300–13. Abingdon: Routledge, 2019.

Cathcart, Alison. '"Inressyng of kyndnes, and renewing off thair blud": The Family, Kinship and Clan Policy in Sixteenth-century Scottish Gaeldom'. In *Finding the Family in Medieval and Early Modern Scotland*, edited by Elizabeth Ewan and Janay Nugent, 127–38. Aldershot: Ashgate, 2008.

Cathcart, Alison. *Plantations by Land and Sea: North Channel Communities of the Atlantic Archipelago, c. 1550–1625*. Oxford: Peter Lang, 2021.

Cathcart, Alison. 'The Forgotten '45: Donald Dubh's Rebellion in an Archipelagic Context'. *SHR* 91, 2, no. 232 (2012): 239–64.

Cho, Nancy Jiwon. 'Literature.' In *The Cambridge Companion to Quakerism*, edited by Stephen W. Angell and Pink Dandelion, 69–87. Cambridge: Cambridge University Press, 2018.

Clark, Nia. 'Re-imagining Mary, Queen of Scots in Contemporary Scottish Women's Writing'. In *The Afterlife of Mary, Queen of Scots*, edited by Steven J. Reid, Chapter 9. Edinburgh: Edinburgh University Press, 2024.

Coffey, John. *Politics, Religion and the British Revolutions: The Mind of Samuel Rutherford.* Cambridge: Cambridge University Press, 1997.

Cohen, Elizabeth S. and Margaret Reeves, eds. *The Youth of Early Modern Women.* Amsterdam: Amsterdam University Press, 2018.

Collins, Thomas. *Martyr in Scotland: The Life and Times of John Ogilvie.* New York: Macmillan, 1955.

Connell, Raewyn W. and J. W. Messerschmidt. 'Hegemonic Masculinity: Rethinking the Concept'. *Gender and Society* 19, no. 6 (December 2005): 829–59.

Connolly, Sean J. *Contested Island: Ireland, 1460–1630.* Oxford: Oxford University Press, 2007.

Cordonnier, Rémy. '"Interpicturalité" des bestiaires manuscrits et de l'iconographie sigillaire: résultats d'une première enquête'. In *Pourquoi les sceaux? La sigillographie nouvel enjeu de l'histoire de l'art,* edited by Marc Gil and Jean-Luc Chassel, 469–95. Lille: Publications de l'Institut de Recherches Historiques du Septentrion, 2011.

Cornell, Harriet, 'Gender, Sex and Social Control: East Lothian, 1610–1640'. PhD diss., University of Edinburgh, 2012.

Coss, Peter. *The Lady in Medieval England, 1000–1500.* Stroud: Sutton, 2000.

Coutts, Winifred. *The Business of the College of Justice in 1600: How it Reflects the Economic and Social Life of Scots Men and Women,* vol. 50. Edinburgh: Stair Society, 2003.

Cowan, Mairi. *Death, Life, and Religious Change in Scottish Towns, c. 1350–1560.* Manchester: Manchester University Press, 2013.

Cowan, Mairi and Laura E. Walkling. 'A "gret cradil of stait": Growing up with the Court of James IV.' In *Children and Youth in Premodern Scotland,* edited by Janay Nugent and Elizabeth Ewan, 5–31. Woodbridge: Boydell, 2015.

Cowan, Samuel. *The Ancient Capital of Scotland: The Story of Perth from the Invasion of Agricola to the Passing of the Reform Bill,* 2 vols. London: Simpkin, Marshall, Hamilton and Kent, 1904.

Cowan, Sharon, Chloë Kennedy and Vanessa E. Munro, eds. *Scottish Feminist Judgments: (Re)creating Law from the Outside In.* Oxford: Hart Publishing, 2019.

Craig, Carys J., Joseph F. Turcotte and Rosemary J. Coombe. 'What's Feminist about Open Access? A Relational Approach to Copyright in the Academy'. *feminists@law* 1, no. 1 (2011): 1–35.

Crane, Susan. *The Performance of Self: Ritual, Clothing, and Identity during the Hundred Years War.* Philadelphia: University of Pennsylvania Press, 2002.

Craun, Edwin D., ed. *The Hands of the Tongue: Essays on Deviant Speech.* Kalamazoo: Medieval Institute Publications, 2007.

Crenshaw, Kimberlé. 'Demarginalizing the Intersection of Race and Sex: A Black Feminist Critique of Antidiscrimination Doctrine, Feminist Theory and Antiracist Politics'. *University of Chicago Legal Forum* 139 (1989): 139–67.

Crenshaw, Kimberlé. *On Intersectionality: Essential Writings.* New York: New Press, 2017.

Crook, Alice Louise. 'Personal Naming Practices in Early Modern Scotland: A Comparative Study of Eleven Parishes, 1680–1839'. PhD diss., University of Glasgow, 2016.

Crouch, David. *The Chivalric Turn: Conduct and Hegemony in Europe before 1300.* Oxford: Oxford University Press, 2019.

Currie, Elizabeth. *Fashion and Masculinity in Renaissance Florence.* London: Bloomsbury, 2016.

Davies, John Reuben with Alice Taylor, *Regiam Maiestatem: The Earliest Known Version.* Edinburgh: Stair Society, 2022.

Davis, Natalie Zemon. *Women on the Margins: Three Seventeenth-century Lives.* Cambridge, MA: Harvard University Press, 1995.

Davis, Rachel Meredith. 'Elite Women and Power in Late Medieval Scotland, 1296–1458'. PhD diss., University of Edinburgh, 2020.

Davis, Rachel Meredith. 'Material Evidence? Re-approaching Elite Women's Seals and Charters in Late Medieval Scotland'. *PSAS* 150 (2021): 301–26.

Dawson, Jane. *John Knox.* New Haven: Yale University Press, 2015.

Dawson, Jane. 'The Noble and the Bastard: The Earl of Argyll and the Law of Divorce in Reformation

Scotland'. In *Sixteenth-Century Scotland: Essays in Honour of Michael Lynch*, edited by Julian Goodare and Alasdair A. MacDonald, 147–68. Leiden: Brill, 2008.

Dawson, Jane. *The Politics of Religion in the Age of Mary, Queen of Scots: The Earl of Argyll and the Struggle for Britain and Ireland*. Cambridge: Cambridge University Press, 2002.

Dawson, Jane. *Scotland Re-Formed, 1488–1587*. Edinburgh: Edinburgh University Press, 2007.

Daybell, James, Kit Heyam, Svante Norrhem and Emma Severinsson. 'Gendering Objects at the V&A and Vasa Museums'. *Museum International* 72, no. 102 (2020): 106–17.

Dean, Lucinda H. S. 'In the Absence of an Adult Monarch: Ceremonial Representations of Authority by Marie de Guise, 1543–1558.' In *Medieval and Early Modern Representations of Authority in Scotland and the British Isles*, edited by Katherine Buchanan, Lucinda H. S. Dean and Michael A. Penman, 143–62. London: Routledge, 2016.

Dean, Lucinda H. S. 'Reaching the Estate of Manhood: A Case Study of James V of Scotland'. Forthcoming.

Dean, Lucinda H. S. '"Richesse in Fassone and in Fairness": Marriage, Manhood and Sartorial Splendour for Sixteenth-century Scottish Kings'. *SHR* 100, no. 3 (December 2021): 378–96.

Delman, Rachel M. 'Gendered Viewing: Childbirth and Female Authority in the Residence of Alice Chaucer, Duchess of Suffolk, at Ewelme, Oxfordshire'. *Journal of Medieval History* 45, no. 2 (2019): 181–203.

Delman, Rachel M. 'Mary of Guelders and the Architecture of Queenship in Fifteenth-Century Scotland'. *SHR* 102, no. 2 (2023): 211–31.

Delman, Rachel M. 'The Queen's House before the Queen's House: Margaret of Anjou and Greenwich Palace, 1447–1453'. *Royal Studies Journal* 8, no. 2 (2021): 6–25.

Delman, Rachel M. 'Women and Materiality in Medieval and Early Modern Scotland Symposium Report'. Women's History Network. https://womenshistorynetwork.org/women-and-materiality-in-medieval-and-early-modern-scotland-symposium-report/.

Dempsey, Karen. 'Tending the "Contested" Castle Garden: Sowing Seeds of Feminist Thought'. *Cambridge Archaeological Journal* 31, no. 2 (2021): 265–79.

Dempsey, Karen, Roberta Gilchrist, Jeremey Ashbee, Stefan Sagrott and Samantha Stones. 'Beyond the Martial Façade: Gender, Heritage and Medieval Castles'. *International Journal of Heritage Studies* 26, no. 4 (2019): 352–69.

den Hartog, Elizabeth. '"Defending the Castle Like a Man": On Belligerent Medieval Ladies'. *Virtus* 27 (2020): 79–98.

DesBrisay, Gordon. 'Aberdeen and the Dutch Atlantic: Women and Woolens in the Seventeenth Century'. In *Women in Port: Gendering Communities, Economies, and Social Networks in Atlantic Port Cities, 1500–1800*, edited by Douglas Catterall and Jodi Campbell. Leiden: Brill, 2012.

DesBrisay, Gordon. 'Catholics, Quakers and Religious Persecution in Restoration Aberdeen'. *IR* 47 (1996): 136–68.

DesBrisay, Gordon. 'Lilias Skene: A Quaker Poet and her "cursed self"'. In *Woman and the Feminine in Medieval and Early Modern Scottish Writing*, edited by Sarah M. Dunnigan, C. Marie Harker and Evelyn S. Newlyn, 162–77. Basingstoke: Palgrave Macmillan, 2004.

DesBrisay, Gordon. 'Twisted by Definition: Women under Godly Discipline in Seventeenth-century Scottish Towns'. In *Twisted Sisters: Women, Crime and Deviance in Scotland Since 1400*, edited by Yvonne Galloway Brown and Rhona Ferguson, 137–52. East Linton: Tuckwell Press, 2002.

DesBrisay, Gordon and Karen Sander Thomson. 'Crediting Wives: Married Women and Debt Litigation in the Seventeenth Century'. In *Finding the Family in Medieval and Early Modern Scotland*, edited by Elizabeth Ewan and Janay Nugent, 85–98. Aldershot: Ashgate, 2008.

Deufel, Nicole. 'Telling her Story of War: Challenging Gender Bias at Culloden Battlefield Visitor Centre'. *Historical Reflections/Réflexions Historiques* 37, no. 2 (2011): 72–89.

Devlin, Shayna. '"Whatever the World Admires in a Prince". Robert Stewart, Duke of Albany: Power, Politics, and Family in Late Medieval Scotland'. PhD diss., University of Guelph, 2019.

Dictionary of Irish Biography. 2009. https://www.dib.ie/biography/.

Dictionary of the Older Scottish Tongue. www.dsl.ac.uk.

Diaz, Joanna Teresa. 'Grief as Medicine for Grief: Complaint Poetry in Early Modern England, 1559–1609'. PhD diss., Evanston, Northwestern University, 2008.

Dike, Catherine. *Walking Sticks*. Aylesbury: Shire Publications, 1990.

Dixon, Nicholas and Barrie Andrian. 'The Scottish Trust for Underwater Archaeology, Lochindorb Survey, August 1993'. Edinburgh: STUA, 1994.

Doak, Laura. 'Militant Women and "National" Community: The Execution of Isabel Alison and Marion Harvie, 1681'. *Journal of the Northern Renaissance* 12 (2021).

Donaldson, Gordon. *All the Queen's Men: Power and Politics in Mary Stewart's Scotland*. New York: St Martin's Press, 1983.

Donaldson, Gordon. *The First Trial of Mary, Queen of Scots*. London: B. T. Batsford, 1969.

Doran, Susan, ed. *Elizabeth and Mary: Royal Cousins, Rival Queens*. London: BL, 2021.

Duffy, Eamon. *The Stripping of the Altars: Traditional Religion in England, 1400–1580*, 2nd ed. New Haven: Yale University Press, 2005.

Dunbar, Linda J. *Reforming the Scottish Church: John Winram (c. 1492–1582) and the Example of Fife*. Aldershot: Ashgate, 2002.

Duncan, A. A. M. *Scotland: The Making of the Kingdom*. Edinburgh: Mercat Press, 1975, 1992.

Dunnigan, Sarah. 'Reclaiming the Language of Love and Desire in the Scottish Renaissance: Mary, Queen of Scots and the Late Sixteenth-century Female-voiced Love Lyric, c. 1567–86'. In *Older Scots Literature*, edited by Sally Mapstone. Edinburgh: John Donald, 2005.

Dunnigan, Sarah. 'Sons and Daughters, "young wyfis" and "barnis": Lyric, Gender, and the Imagining of Youth in the Maitland Manuscripts'. In *Children and Youth in Premodern Scotland*, edited by Janay Nugent and Elizabeth Ewan, 187–204. Woodbridge: Boydell, 2015.

Dunnigan, Sarah and Elizabeth Ewan, guest eds. '"Transformative Disorder": Scotland 1550–1650'. *Renaissance and Reformation* 30, no. 4 (Fall 2006/7).

Dunnigan, Sarah M., C. Marie Harker and Evelyn S. Newlyn, eds. *Woman and the Feminine in Medieval and Early Modern Writing*. Basingstoke: Palgrave Macmillan, 2004.

Durfournaud, Nicole. 'Between Parental Power and Marital Authority: How Merchant Women Stood the Test of Customary Laws in Brittany in the Sixteenth to Seventeenth Centuries'. In *Gender, Law and Economic Well-Being in Europe from the Fifteenth to the Nineteenth Century: North Versus South?*, edited by Anna Bellavitis and Beatrice Zucca Micheletto, 47–6. London: Routledge, 2018.

Durkan, John. 'John Ogilvie's Glasgow Associates'. *IR* 21 (1970): 153–70.

Dye, Sierra. 'To Converse with the Devil? Speech, Sexuality, and Witchcraft in Early Modern Scotland'. *IRSS* 37 (2012): 9–40.

Dye, Sierra, Elizabeth Ewan and Heather Parker, eds. *Gender and Mobility in Scotland and Abroad*. Guelph: Centre for Scottish Studies, 2018.

Earenfight, Theresa, 'A Lifetime of Power: Beyond Binaries of Gender'. In *Medieval Elite Women and the Exercise of Power, 1100–1400*, edited by Heather J. Tanner, 271–93. Cham: Palgrave Macmillan, 2019.

Edinburgh City Council. City Development Department. 'Pre-1750 Buildings in Edinburgh Old Town Conservation Area'.

Edinburgh City Council. Finance and Resources Committee, 'Trinity Apse, Edinburgh – Proposed New Lease: Meeting Thursday 12th August 2021'.

Edwards, Valerie J., George W. Holden, Vincent J. Felitti and Robert F. Anda. 'Relationship Between Multiple Forms of Childhood Maltreatment and Adult Mental Health in Community Respondents: Results from the Adverse Childhood Experiences Study'. *American Journal of Psychiatry* 160 (2003): 1453–60.

Ellis, Anthony. *Old Age, Masculinity, and Early Modern Drama: Comic Elders on the Italian and Shakespearean Stage*. London: Routledge, 2009.

Emond, Ken. *The Minority of James V: Scotland in Europe, 1513–1528*. Edinburgh: John Donald, 2019.

Erickson, Amy L. 'Mistresses and Marriage: Or, a Short History of the Mrs'. *History Workshop Journal* 78 (Autumn 2014): 39–57.

Erickson, Amy L. *Women and Property in Early Modern England*. London: Routledge, 1993.

Ewan, Elizabeth. 'A Land Fit for Heroines? The Biographical Dictionary of Scottish Women'. *JSHS* 26 (2006): 1–13.

Ewan, Elizabeth. 'A New Trumpet? The History of Women in Scotland, 1300–1700'. *History Compass* 7, no. 2 (2009): 431–46.

Ewan, Elizabeth. 'A Realm of One's Own? The Place of Medieval and Early Modern Women in Scottish History'. In *Gendering Scottish History: An International Approach*, edited by Terry Brotherstone, Deborah Simonton and Oonagh Walsh, 19–36. Glasgow: Cruithne Press, 1999.

Ewan, Elizabeth. 'Alison Rough: A Woman's Life and Death in Sixteenth-century Edinburgh'. *Women's History Magazine* 45 (Autumn 2003): 4–13.

Ewan, Elizabeth. 'An Urban Community: The Crafts in Thirteenth-century Aberdeen'. In *Medieval Scotland: Crown, Lordship and Community*, edited by Alexander Grant and Keith J. Stringer, 156–73. Edinburgh: Edinburgh University Press, 1993.

Ewan, Elizabeth. 'Beyond Borders and Boundaries: The Use of Banishment in Sixteenth-century Scottish towns'. In *Crossing Borders: Boundaries and Margins in Late Medieval and Early Modern Britain*, edited by Sarah M. Butler and Krista J. Kesselring, 237–57. Leiden: Brill, 2018.

Ewan, Elizabeth. 'Crime or Culture? Women and Daily Life in Late Medieval Scotland'. In *Twisted Sisters: Women, Crime and Deviance in Scotland since 1400*, edited by Yvonne Brown and Rona Ferguson, 117–36. East Linton: Tuckwell Press, 2002.

Ewan, Elizabeth. 'Disorderly Damsels? Women and Interpersonal Violence in Pre-Reformation Scotland'. *SHR* 89, no. 228 (2010): 153–71.

Ewan, Elizabeth. 'Family, Gender and Lifecycle in Late Medieval Scotland'. In *A Companion to Late Medieval Scotland*, edited by Andy King. Leiden: Brill, forthcoming.

Ewan, Elizabeth. 'For Whatever Ales Ye: Women as Consumers and Producers in Scottish Medieval Towns'. In *Women in Scotland, c. 1100–c. 1750*, edited by Elizabeth Ewan and Maureen L. Meikle, 125–35. East Linton: Tuckwell Press, 1999.

Ewan, Elizabeth. 'Gendering the Reformation'. In *A Companion to the Reformation in Scotland, c. 1525–1638*, edited by William Ian P. Hazlett, 511–41. Leiden: Brill, 2021.

Ewan, Elizabeth. '"Hamperit in ane Honeycamb": Sights, Sounds and Smells in the Medieval Town'. In *Everyday Life in Medieval Scotland*, edited by E. J. Cowan and Lizanne Henderson, 109–44. Edinburgh: Edinburgh University Press, 2011.

Ewan, Elizabeth. 'Impatient Griseldas: Women and the Perpetration of Violence in Sixteenth-century Glasgow'. *Florilegium* 29 (2011): 149–68.

Ewan, Elizabeth. 'Late Medieval Scotland: A Study in Contrasts'. In *A Companion to Medieval Scottish Poetry*, edited by P. Bawcutt and J. Hadley-Williams, 19–33. Woodbridge: Boydell, 2006.

Ewan, Elizabeth. 'Living in the Late Medieval Town of St Andrews'. In *Medieval St Andrews: Church, Cult, City*, edited by Michael Brown and Katie Stevenson, 117–40. Woodbridge: Boydell, 2017.

Ewan, Elizabeth. '"Many Injurious Words": Defamation and Gender in Late Medieval Scotland'. In *History, Literature and Music in Scotland, 700–1560*, edited by R. Andrew McDonald, 163–86. Toronto: University of Toronto Press, 2002.

Ewan, Elizabeth. 'Mistresses of Themselves: Domestic Servants and By-employments in Sixteenth-century Scotland'. In *Domestic Service and the Formation of European Identity: Understanding the Globalization of Domestic Work, 16th–21st centuries*, edited by A. Fauve-Chamoux, 411–33. Bern: Peter Lang, 2004.

Ewan, Elizabeth. 'Mons Meg and Merchant Meg: Women in Late Medieval Edinburgh'. In *Freedom and Authority: Scotland, c. 1050–c. 1650*, edited by D. Ditchburn and T. Brotherstone, 131–42. East Linton: Tuckwell Press, 1999.

Ewan, Elizabeth. 'Protocol Books and Towns in Medieval Scotland'. In *La Diplomatique urbaine en europe du moyen age*, edited by W. Prevenier and T. de Hemptinne, 143–56. Ghent: Garant, 2000.

Ewan, Elizabeth. 'Schooling in the Towns, c. 1400–c. 1560'. In *The Edinburgh History of Education in Scotland*, edited by Robert Anderson, Mark Freeman and Lindsay Paterson, 39–56. Edinburgh: Edinburgh University Press, 2015.

Ewan, Elizabeth. 'Scottish Burghs'. In *Atlas of Scottish History to 1707*, edited by Peter G. B. McNeill and Hector L. MacQueen, 231–7. Edinburgh: The Scottish Medievalists and the Department of Geography, University of Edinburgh, 1996.

Ewan, Elizabeth. 'Scottish Portias: Women in the Courts in Mediaeval Scottish Towns'. *Journal of the Canadian Historical Association* 3, no. 1 (1992): 27–43.

Ewan, Elizabeth. 'The Age of Bon-Accord: Aberdeen in the Fourteenth Century'. In *New Light on Medieval Aberdeen*, edited by John S. Smith, 228–44. Aberdeen: Aberdeen University Press, 1985.

Ewan, Elizabeth. 'The Community of the Burgh in the Fourteenth Century'. In *The Scottish Medieval Town*, edited by Michael Lynch et al., 32–45. Edinburgh: John Donald Press, 1988.

Ewan, Elizabeth. 'The Dangers of Manly Women: Late Medieval Perceptions of Female Heroism in Scotland's Second War of Independence'. In *Woman and the Feminine in Medieval and Early Modern Writing*, edited by Sarah M. Dunnigan, C. Marie Harker and Evelyn S. Newlyn, 3–18. Basingstoke: Palgrave Macmillan, 2004.

Ewan, Elizabeth. 'The Early Modern Family'. In *The Oxford Handbook of Modern Scottish History*, edited by T. M. Devine and Jenny Wormald, 268–84. Oxford: Oxford University Press, 2012.

Ewan, Elizabeth. 'The Female Character: Early Scots Literature as a Source for the History of Scottish Medieval Women'. *ACTA* 16 (1993 for 1989): 29–38.

Ewan, Elizabeth. '"To the Longer Liver": Provisions for the Dissolution of the Marital Economy in Scotland, 1470–1550'. In *The Marital Economy in Scandinavia and Britain, 1400–1900*, edited by Maria Ågren and Amy Louise Erickson, 191–206. Aldershot: Ashgate, 2005.

Ewan, Elizabeth. '"Tongue, You Lied": The Role of the Tongue in Rituals of Public Penance in Medieval Scotland'. In *The Hands of the Tongue*, edited by Edwin D. Craun, 115–36. Kalamazoo: Medieval Institute Publications, 2007.

Ewan, Elizabeth. 'Town and Hinterland in Medieval Scotland'. In *The Pre-Industrial Cities and Technology Reader*, edited by Colin Chant and David Goodman, 125–8. London: Routledge, 1999.

Ewan, Elizabeth. 'Townlife and Trade'. In *Scotland: The Making and Unmaking of the Kingdom, c. 1100–c. 1707*, edited by Bob Harris and Alan R. MacDonald, 1–38. Dundee: Dundee University Press, 2006.

Ewan, Elizabeth. *Townlife in Fourteenth-century Scotland*. Edinburgh: Edinburgh University Press, 1990.

Ewan, Elizabeth. 'Women and the Biographies of Nations: *The Biographical Dictionary of Scottish Women*'. In *True Biographies of Nations? The Cultural Journeys of Dictionaries of Biography*, edited by Karen Fox, 119–37. Canberra: Australian National University Press, 2019.

Ewan, Elizabeth. 'Women's History in Scotland: Towards an Agenda'. *IR* 46, no. 2 (Autumn 1995): 155–64.

Ewan, Elizabeth and Gordon DesBrisay, 'Life in the Two Towns, 1100–1800'. In *Aberdeen Before 1800*, edited by E. P. Dennison et al., 44–70. East Linton: Tuckwell Press, 2002.

Ewan, Elizabeth, Sue Innes, Siân Reynolds and Rose Pipes, eds. *The Biographical Dictionary of Scottish Women*. Edinburgh: Edinburgh University Press, 2006; paperback edition, 2007.

Ewan, Elizabeth and Maureen M. Meikle, eds. *Women in Scotland, c. 1100–c. 1750*. East Linton: Tuckwell Press, 1999.

Ewan, Elizabeth and Janay Nugent, eds. *Finding the Family in Medieval and Early Modern Scotland*. Aldershot: Ashgate, 2008.

Ewan, Elizabeth and Heather Parker. 'Surveying Scottish Studies in Canada'. *IRSS* 24 (2009): 139–54.

Ewan, Elizabeth, Rose Pipes, Jane Rendall and Siân Reynolds, eds. *The New Biographical Dictionary of Scottish Women*, 2nd edition. Edinburgh: Edinburgh University Press, 2018.

Ewan, Elizabeth and S. Rigby. 'Government, Power and Authority, 1300-1540'. In vol. 3 of *Cambridge Urban History of Britain*, edited by D. M. Palliser, 291-312. Cambridge: Cambridge University Press, 2000.

Falconer, J. R. D. *Crime and Community in Reformation Scotland: Negotiating Power in a Burgh Society.* London: Pickering and Chatto, 2013.

Fawcett, R. *St John's Kirk of Perth*. Perth: Friends of St John's Kirk, 1987.

Field, Corrine T. and Nicholas Syrett. 'Chronological Age: A Useful Category of Historical Analysis'. *American Historical Review* 125, no. 2 (April 2020): 371-84.

Finan, Thomas. 'Prophecies of the Expected Deliverer in Thirteenth- and Fourteenth-century Irish Bardic Poetry'. *New Hibernia Review* 6, no.3 (2002): 113-24.

Finlay, John. 'The Lower Branch of the Legal Profession in Early Modern Scotland'. *Edinburgh Law Review* 11, no. 1 (2007): 31-61.

Finlay, John. 'Women and Legal Representation in Early Sixteenth-century Scotland'. In *Women in Scotland, c. 1100-c. 1750*, edited by Elizabeth Ewan and Maureen M. Meikle, 165-75. East Linton: Tuckwell Press, 1999.

Finn, Margot. 'Women, Consumption and Coverture in England, c. 1760-1860'. *Historical Journal* 39, no. 3 (1996): 703-22.

Fisher, John H. *John Gower, Moral Philosopher and Friend of Chaucer*. New York: New York University Press, 1964.

Fitch, Audrey-Beth. *The Search for Salvation: Lay Faith in Scotland, 1480-1560*, edited by Elizabeth Ewan. Edinburgh: John Donald, 2009.

Fittis, Robert Scott. *Ecclesiastical Annals of Perth to the Period of the Reformation*. Perth and Edinburgh: Gemmel & Cowan, 1885.

Flather, Amanda. *Gender and Space in Early Modern England*. Woodbridge: Boydell, 2007.

Fleming, Alexander and Roger A. Mason, eds. *Scotland and the Flemish People*. Edinburgh: Birlinn, 2019.

Fletcher, Christopher. 'Manhood and Politics in the Reign of Richard II'. *Past & Present* 189, no. 1 (November 2005): 3-39.

Fletcher, Christopher. 'Manhood, Kingship and the Public in Late Medieval England'. *Edad Media Revista de Historia* 13 (2012): 123-42.

Fletcher, Christopher. *Richard II: Manhood, Youth and Politics, 1377-99*. Oxford: Oxford University Press, 2008.

Forte, A. D. M. 'Some Aspects of the Law of Marriage in Scotland: 1500-1700'. *Marriage and Property: Women and Marital Customs in History*, edited by Elizabeth Craik, 104-18. Aberdeen: Aberdeen University Press, 1984; 1991.

Foucault, Michel. *Discipline and Punish: The Birth of the Prison*. Translated by Alan Sheridan. New York: Random House, 1979.

Franklin, Julie et al. 'The Development of Candlemaker Row, Edinburgh, from the 11th to the 20th Centuries: Excavations at Greyfriars Kirkhouse'. *Scottish Archaeological Internet Reports* 71 (2017): 1-35.

Frater, Anne. 'Clann and Clan: Children of the Gaelic nobility, c. 1500-c. 1800'. In *Children and Youth in Premodern Scotland*, edited by Janay Nugent and Elizabeth Ewan, 89-103. Woodbridge: Boydell, 2015.

French, Morvern. 'Christina Bruce and her Defence of Kildrummy Castle'. *Royal Studies Journal* 7, no. 1 (2020): 22-38.

French, Morvern and Iain A. MacInnes. 'Katherine Beaumont, Countess of Atholl, and the Second Scottish War of Independence (c. 1327-c. 1336). *SHR* 102, 3: no. 260 (2023): 333-66.

French, Morvern and Iain A. MacInnes. 'Katherine Beaumont, Part 1: Her Early Life and the Second Scottish War of Independence'. Forthcoming.

Furgol, Edward. 'The Scottish Itinerary of Mary Queen of Scots, 1542-8 and 1561-8'. *PSAS* 117 (1987), 219-31, fiche 1; C1-D6.

Gaimster, David R. M. and Roberta Gilchrist, eds. *The Archaeology of Reformation, 1480–1580*. Leeds: Maney Publishing, 2003.

Gibson, Gail McMurray. 'Scene and Obscene: Seeing and Performing Late Medieval Childbirth'. *Journal of Medieval and Early Modern Studies* 29, no. 1 (1999): 7–24.

Gibson, A. J. S. and T. C. Smout. *Prices, Food and Wages in Scotland, 1550–1780*. Cambridge: Cambridge University Press, 1995.

Gifford, John. *Highlands and Islands, The Buildings of Scotland Series*. London: Pevsner Architectural Guides, 1992.

Gilchrist, Roberta. *Gender and Archaeology: Contesting the Past*. London: Routledge, 1999.

Gilchrist, Roberta. 'Medieval Bodies in the Material World: Gender, Stigma and the Body'. In *Framing Medieval Bodies*, edited by Sarah Kay and Miri Rubin, 43–61. Manchester: Manchester University Press, 1994.

Gilchrist, Roberta. 'The Materiality of Medieval Heirlooms: From Biographical to Sacred Objects'. In *Mobility, Meaning and the Transformations of Things*, edited by Hans Peter Hahn and Hadas Weiss, 170–82. Oxford: Oxbow Books, 2013.

Giles, Pamela B. 'Scottish Literary Women, 1560–1700'. PhD diss., University of Saskatchewan, 2004.

Giorgi, Rosa. *Saints in Art*. Los Angeles: J. Paul Getty Museum, 2003.

Glasgow Women's Library. https://womenslibrary.org.uk/.

Glaze, Alice. 'Women and Kirk Discipline: Prosecution, Negotiation, and the Limits of Control'. *JSHS* 36, no. 2 (2016): 125–42.

Glover, Katharine. *Elite Women and Polite Society in Eighteenth-Century Scotland*. Woodbridge: Boydell, 2011.

Goatman, Paul. 'Exemplary Deterrent or Theatre of Martyrdom?: John Ogilvie's Execution and the Community of Glasgow'. *Journal of Jesuit Studies* 7, no. 1 (2020): 47–66.

Goatman, Paul. 'Religious Tolerance and Intolerance in Jacobean Scotland: The Case of Archibald Hegate Revisited'. *IR* 67, no. 2 (2016): 159–81.

Godfrey, Mark, 'Royal Councils, Law Courts and Governance: The Role of Litigation in Early Modern Scotland'. In *Rechtsgeschichte heute: Religion und Politik in der Geschichte des Rechts – Schlaglichter einer Ringvorlesung*, edited by N. Jansen and P. Oestmann, 77–94. Tübingen: Mohr Siebeck, 2014.

Goldberg, P. J. P. 'Masters and Men in Late Medieval England'. In *Masculinity in Medieval Europe*, edited by Dawn M. Hadley, 56–70. Reprint. Abingdon and New York: Routledge, 2014.

Goodare, Julian. 'How Archbishop Spottiswoode Became an Episcopalian'. *Renaissance and Reformation* 30, no. 4 (2006): 83–103.

Goodare, Julian. *State and Society in Early Modern Scotland*. Oxford: Oxford University Press, 1999.

Goodare, Julian. 'The Scottish Witchcraft Panic of 1597'. In *The Scottish Witch-Hunt in Context*, edited by Julian Goodare, 51–72. Manchester: Manchester University Press, 2002.

Goodare, Julian, ed. *The Scottish Witch-Hunt in Context*. Manchester: Manchester University Press, 2002.

Goodare, Julian. 'Women and the Witch-Hunt in Scotland'. *Social History* 23, no. 3 (October 1998): 288–308.

Goodare, Julian, Lauren Martin, Joyce Miller and Louise Yeoman. 'The Survey of Scottish Witchcraft'. http://www.shca.ed.ac.uk/witches/.

Gordon, Richard. '*Superstitio*, Superstition and Religious Repression in the Late Roman Republic and Principate (100 BCE–300 CE)', *Past & Present* Supplement 3 (2008): 72–94.

Graham, Michael F. *The Uses of Reform: 'Godly Discipline' and Popular Behaviour in Scotland and Beyond, 1560–1610*. Leiden: Brill, 1996.

Gransden, Antonia. 'The Alleged Rape by Edward III of the Countess of Salisbury'. *English Historical Review* 87, no. 343 (1972): 333–44.

Grant, Ruth. 'Politicking Jacobean Women: Lady Ferniehirst, the Countess of Arran and the Countess of Huntly, c. 1580–1603'. In *Women in Scotland, c. 1100–c. 1750*, edited by Elizabeth Ewan and Maureen M. Meikle, 95–111. East Linton: Tuckwell Press, 1999.

Green, Thomas. *Consistorial Decisions of the Commissaries of Edinburgh, 1564 to 1576/7*. Edinburgh: Edinburgh University Press, 2014.

Green, Thomas M. *The Spiritual Jurisdiction in Reformation Scotland: A Legal History*. Edinburgh: Edinburgh University Press, 2019.

Guthrie, Charles J. 'The Traditional Belief in John Knox's House at the Netherbow Vindicated'. *PSAS* 33 (1899): 249–73.

Hadley, Dawn M. 'Introduction'. In *Masculinity in Medieval Europe*, edited by Dawn M. Hadley, 1–18. Reprint. Abingdon and New York: Routledge, 2014.

Hadley, Dawn M., ed. *Masculinity in Medieval Europe*. London: Routledge, 1999.

Haemers, Jelle. 'Filthy and Indecent Words: Insults, Defamation, and Urban Politics in the Southern Low Countries, 1300–1550'. In *The Voices of the People in Late Medieval Europe: Communication and Popular Politics*, edited by Jan Dumolyn, Jelle Haemers, Hipólito Rafael, Oliva Herrer and Vincent Challet, 247–67. Turnhout: Brepols, 2014.

Hall, Mark. A. 'An Ivory Knife Handle from the High Street, Perth, Scotland: Consuming Ritual in a Medieval Burgh'. *Medieval Archaeology* XLV (2001): 169–88.

Hall, Mark. A. 'Burgh Mentalities, a Town-in-the country Case Study of Perth, Scotland'. In *Town and Country in the Middle Ages – Contrasts and Interconnections, 1100–1500*, edited by Kate Giles and Christopher Dyer, 211–28. Leeds: Leeds Society for Medieval Archaeology, 2005.

Hall, Mark. A. 'Crossing the Pilgrimage Landscape: Some Thoughts on a Holy Rood Reliquary from the River Tay at Carpow, Perth & Kinross, Scotland'. In *Beyond Pilgrim Souvenirs and Secular Badges: Essays in Honour of Brian Spencer*, edited by Sarah Blick, 75–91. Oxford: Oxbow, 2007.

Hall, Mark. A. 'Money Isn't Everything: The Cultural Life of Coins in the Medieval European Town of Perth, Scotland'. *Journal of Social Archaeology* 12, no. 1 (February 2012): 72–91.

Hall, Mark. A. 'Of Holy Men and Heroes: The Cult of Saints in Medieval Perthshire'. *IR* 56, no. 1 (Spring 2005): 60–87.

Hall, Mark. A. 'Status, Magic and Belief: Exploring Identity through Dress Accessories and Other Amulets in Medieval Scotland: A Perthshire Case Study'. *SHR* 100.3, no. 254 (December 2021): 469–92.

Hall, Mark. A. 'The Cult of Saints in Medieval Perth: Everyday Ritual and the Materiality of Belief'. *Journal of Material Culture* 16, no. 1 (March 2011): 80–104.

Hall, Mark. A. 'Wo/men Only? Marian Devotion in Medieval Perth'. In *The Cult of Saints and the Virgin Mary in Medieval Scotland*, edited by Steve Boardman and Eila Williamson, 105–24. Woodbridge: Boydell, 2010.

Hall, Mark A. and D. D. R. Owen. 'A Tristram and Iseult Mirror-case from Perth: Reflections on the Production and Consumption of Romance Culture'. *Tayside and Fife Archaeological Journal* 4 (1998): 150–65.

Hamilton, Sarah and Andrew Spicer, eds. *Defining the Holy: Sacred Space in Medieval and Early Modern Europe*. Aldershot: Ashgate, 2005.

Hammond, Matthew, ed. *Personal Names and Naming Practices in Medieval Scotland*. Woodbridge: Boydell, 2019.

Hanawalt, Barbara A. and Michal Kobialka. 'Introduction'. In *Medieval Practices of Space*, edited by Barbara A. Hanawalt and Michal Kobialka, ix–xviii. Minneapolis: University of Minnesota Press, 2000.

Hannay, R. K. 'The Coffin in the Wall'. *SHR* 15, no. 58 (1918): 156–8.

Harris, Barbara. *Aristocratic Women and the Fabric of Piety, 1450–1550*. Amsterdam: Amsterdam University Press, 2018.

Harris, Barbara. *English Aristocratic Women, 1450–1550*. Oxford: Oxford University Press, 2002.

Harris, Tim. *Restoration: Charles II and his Kingdoms, 1660–1685*. London: Penguin, 2005.

Harrison, Jill. 'Fresh Perspectives on Hugo van der Goes' Portrait of Margaret of Denmark and the Trinity Altarpiece'. *Court Historian* 24, no. 2 (2019): 120–37.

Harrison, John G. 'Women and the Branks in Stirling, c. 1600 to c. 1730'. *Scottish Economic and Social History* 18, no. 2 (1998): 114–31.

Harwood, Sophie. 'Swans and Amazons: Penthesilea and the Case for Women's Heraldry in Medieval Culture'. *Medieval Journal* 7, no. 1 (2017): 61–87.

Hay Fleming, David. *Mary Queen of Scots*. London: Hodder and Stoughton, 1898.

Hayden, Dolores. 'Making Women's History Visible in the Urban Landscape'. *City and Society* 10, no. 1 (1998): 9–20.

Hayes-McCoy, Gerald A. *Scots Mercenary Forces in Ireland (1565–1603): An Account of their Service During that Period and of the Reaction of their Activities on Scottish Affairs, and of the Effect of their Presence in Ireland, together with an Examination of the Gallóglaigh or Galloglass*. Dublin: Edmund Burke, 1937; reprinted 1996.

Hazlett, Ian, ed. *A Companion to the Reformation in Scotland, ca. 1525–1638*. Leiden: Brill, 2022.

Henderson, Lizanne. *Witchcraft and Folk Belief in the Age of Enlightenment: Scotland, 1670–1740*. Basingstoke: Palgrave Macmillan, 2016.

Hendrix, Scott. H. and Susan C. Karant-Nunn, eds. *Masculinity in the Reformation Era*. Kirksville, MO: Truman State University Press, 2008.

Herbst, Katrin, ed. *Martin Luther: Treasures of the Reformation*. Halle: Landesamt für Denkmalpflege und Archäologie Sachsen-Anhalt & Sandstein Verlag, 2016.

Hicks, Leonie V. 'Magnificent Entrances and Undignified Exits: Chronicling the Symbolism of Castle Space in Normandy'. *Journal of Medieval History* 35, no. 1 (2009): 52–69.

Higgitt, John. *'Imageis Maid With Mennis Hand': Saints, Images, Belief and Identity in Later Medieval Scotland*. Whithorn: Friends of the Whithorn Trust, 2003.

Hill, J. Michael. *Fire and Sword: Sorley Boy MacDonnell and the Rise of Clan Ian Mor, 1538–90*. London: Athlone Press, 1993.

Hinnie, Lucy R. 'Figuring the Feminine in the Bannatyne Manuscript (c. 1568)'. PhD diss., University of Edinburgh, 2018.

Historic Environment Scotland. 'Another Record-Breaking Year for Scottish Heritage Sites'.

Historic Environment Scotland. 'New Exhibition Officially Opens at Edinburgh Castle'. Last modified November 15, 2018.

Historic Environment Scotland. 'What is a Listing? Categories of Listing' History of the Project and the Time: Licoricia of Winchester. Accessed 20 February 2023. History Workshop Online. www.historyworkshop.org.uk.

Hodgson, Elisabeth. *Grief and Women Writers in the English Renaissance*. Cambridge: Cambridge University Press, 2014.

Hodson, Laura. '"I Expected … Something": Imagination, Legend, and History in TripAdvisor Reviews of Tintagel Castle'. *Journal of Heritage Tourism* 15, no. 4 (2020): 410–23.

Holton, Caitlin T. 'Masculine Identity in Medieval Scotland: Gender, Ethnicity, and Regionality'. PhD diss., University of Guelph, 2017.

Holton, Caitlin T. '"With A Vertu and Leawté": Masculine Relationships in Medieval Scotland'. MA diss., University of Guelph, 2011.

Hood, Nathan C. J. 'Corporate Conversion Ceremonies: The Presentation and Reception of the National Covenant'. In *The National Covenant in Scotland, 1638–1689*, edited by Chris Langley, 21–38. Woodbridge: Boydell, 2020.

Hooper, Stephen. 'A Cross-Cultural Theory of Relics: On Understanding Religion, Bodies, Artefacts, Images and Art'. *World Art* 4, no. 2 (2014): 175–207.

Hooper, Stephen. 'Bodies, Artefacts and Images: A Cross-cultural Theory of Relics'. In *Matter of Faith: An Interdisciplinary Study of Relics and Relic Veneration in the Medieval Period*, edited by James Robinson, Lloyd de Beer and Anna Harnden, 190–9. London: British Museum, 2014.

Houston, R. A. 'The Composition and Distribution of the Legal Profession, and the Use of Law in Britain and Ireland, c. 1500–c. 1850'. *Legal History Review* 86 (2018): 123–56.

Hufton, Olwen. 'Altruism and Reciprocity: The Early Jesuits and their Female Patrons'. *Renaissance Studies* 15, no. 3 (2001): 328–53.

Hughes, Ann. *Gender and the English Revolution*. London: Routledge, 2011.

Hughes, Ann. '"Gender Trouble": Women's Agency and Gender Relations in the English Revolution'. In *The Oxford Handbook of the English Revolution*, edited by Michael J. Braddick, 347–62. Oxford: Oxford University Press, 2015.

Hughes, Paula. 'Witch-Hunting in Scotland, 1649–1650'. In *Scottish Witches and Witch-Hunters*, edited by Julian Goodare, 85–102. London: Palgrave, 2013.

Innes, Matthew. 'Keeping it in the Family: Women and Aristocratic Memory, 700–1200'. In *Medieval Memories: Men, Women and the Past, 700–1300*, edited by Elisabeth M. C. van Houtts, 17–35. Harlow: Longman, 2001.

Ireland, Emily. 'Re-examining the Presumption: Coverture and "legal impossibilities" in Early Modern English Criminal Law'. *Journal of Legal History* 43, no. 2 (2022): 187–209.

Johnson, Matthew. *Behind the Castle Gate: From Medieval to Renaissance*. New York: Routledge, 2002.

Kaplan, Debra. 'Women and Worth: Female Access to Property in Early Modern Urban Jewish Communities'. In *Leo Baeck Institute Year Book* 55, no. 1 (2010): 93–113.

Karant-Nunn, Susan. *The Reformation of Ritual: An Interpretation of Early Modern Germany*. New York: Routledge, 1997.

Karras, Ruth Mazo. 'Thomas Aquinas's Chastity Belt: Clerical Masculinity in Medieval Europe'. In *Gender and Christianity in Medieval Europe*, edited by Lisa M. Bitel and Felice Lifshitz, 52–67. Philadelphia: University of Pennsylvania Press, 2008.

Kauth, Jean-Marie. 'Barred Windows and Uncaged Birds: The Enclosure of Woman in Chrétien de Troyes and Marie de France'. *Medieval Feminist Forum* 46, no. 2 (2010): 34–67.

Keen, Maurice. 'Introduction'. In *Heraldry, Pageantry, and Social Display in Medieval England*, edited by Peter Coss and Maurice Keen, 1–16. Woodbridge: Boydell, 2002.

Kennedy, Allan. '"A Heavy Yock Uppon Their Necks": Covenanting Government in the Northern Highlands, 1638–1651'. *JSHS* 30, no. 2 (2010): 93–112.

Kiernan, V. G. 'A Banner with a Strange Device: The Later Covenanters'. In *Covenant, Charter, and Party: Traditions of Revolt and Protest in Modern Scottish History*, edited by Terry Brotherstone, 25–49. Aberdeen: Aberdeen University Press, 1989.

Kilday, Anne-Marie. '"Angels with dirty faces": Violent Women in Early Modern Scotland'. In *Female Transgression in Early Modern Britain: Literary and Historical Explorations*, edited by Richard Hillman and Pauline Ruberry-Blanc, 141–62. Ashgate: Farnham, 2014.

Kimble, Sara L. and Marion Röwekamp. 'Introduction: Legal Cultures and Communities of Female Protest in Modern European History, 1860–1960s'. In *New Perspectives on European Women's Legal History*, edited by Sara L. Kimble and Marion Röwekamp, 1–24. London: Routledge, 2016.

Knox, Andrea. '"Barbarous and Pestiferous Women": Female Criminality, Violence and Aggression in Sixteenth- and Seventeenth-century Scotland and Ireland'. In *Twisted Sisters: Women, Crime and Deviance in Scotland since 1400*, edited by Yvonne Galloway Brown and Rona Ferguson, 13–31. East Linton: Tuckwell Press, 2002.

Korpiola, Mia. 'A Litigating Widow and Wife in Early Modern Sweden: Lady Elin Johansdotter [Månesköld] and her family circle'. In *Litigating Women: Gender and Justice in Europe, c.1300–c.1800*, edited by Teresa Phipps and Deborah Youngs, 173–92. London: Routledge, 2022.

Kubler-Ross, Elizabeth and David Kessler, *On Grief and Grieving: Finding the Meaning of Grief through the Five Stages of Loss*. New York: Simon & Schuster, 2014.

Langley, Chris R. 'Anticlericalism in Early Modern Scotland?'. In *The Clergy in Early Modern Scotland*, edited by Chris R. Langley, Catherine E. McMillan and Russell Newton, 89–107. Woodbridge: Boydell, 2021.

Langley, Chris R. 'Clergy Widows in Early Modern Scotland'. *Scottish Church History* 51, no. 2 (2022): 111–32.
Langley, Chris R. 'Clerical Old Age and the Forming of Rites of Passage in Early Modern Scotland'. *Studies in Church History* 59 (2023): 244–64.
Langley, Chris R., ed. *The National Covenant in Scotland, 1638–1689*. Woodbridge: Boydell, 2020.
Langley, Chris R., Catherine E. McMillan and Russell Newton, eds. *The Clergy in Early Modern Scotland*. Woodbridge: Boydell, 2021.
Lanzinger, Margareth and Janine Maegraith. 'Women Negotiating Wealth: Gender, Law and Arbitration in Early Modern Southern Tyrol'. In *Litigating Women: Gender and Justice in Europe, 1100–1750*, edited by Teresa Phipps and Deborah Youngs, 152–72. London: Routledge, 2022.
Lanzinger, Margareth, Janine Maegraith, Siglinde Clementi, Ellinor Forster and Christian Hagen, eds. *Negotiations of Gender and Property through Legal Regimes (14th–19th Century): Stipulating, Litigating, Mediating*. Leiden: Brill, 2021.
Laqueur, Thomas W. 'Crowds, Carnival and the State in English Executions, 1604–1868'. In *The First Modern Society: Essays in English History in Honour of Lawrence Stone*, edited by A. L. Beier, David Cannadine and James M. Rosenheim, 305–55. Cambridge: Cambridge University Press, 1989.
Larner, Christina. *Enemies of God: The Witch-hunt in Scotland*. Baltimore: Johns Hopkins University Press, 1981.
Larouche, Rebecca. 'Elizabeth Melville and Her Friends: Seeing "ane godlie dreame" through Political Lenses'. *Clio* 34, no. 3 (2005): 277–96.
Lawson, John Parker. *The Book of Perth*. Edinburgh: Thomas G. Stevenson, 1847.
Lee, Becky R. 'The Purification of Women after Childbirth: A Window onto Medieval Perceptions of Women'. *Florilegium* 14 (1995–6): 43–55.
Leneman, Leah. *Living in Atholl: A Social History of the Estates, 1685–1785*. Edinburgh: Edinburgh University Press, 1986.
Leonard, Amy E. and Karen L. Nelson, eds. *Masculinities, Violence, Childhood: Attending to Early Modern Women – and Men*. Newark: University of Delaware Press, 2000.
Levack, Brian. *Witch-hunting in Scotland: Law, Politics and Religion*. New York: Routledge, 2008.
Levitt, Emma. 'Tiltyard Friendships and Bonds of Loyalty in the Reign of Edward IV'. In *Loyalty to the Monarchy in Late Medieval and Early Modern Britain, c. 1400–1688*, edited by Matthew Ward and Matthew Hefferan, 15–36. Basingstoke: Palgrave Macmillan, 2020.
Levitt, Emma. 'The Construction of High Status Masculinity through the Tournament and Martial Activity in the Later Middle Ages'. PhD diss., University of Huddersfield, 2017.
Lewis, Katherine J. *Kingship and Masculinity in Late Medieval England*. Abingdon: Routledge, 2013.
Lifschitz, Felice. 'Gender Trouble in Paradise: The Case of the Liturgical Virgo'. In *Images of Medieval Sanctity: Essays in Honour of Gary Dickson*, edited by Debra Higgs Strickland, 25–39. Leiden: Brill, 2007.
Lifschitz, Felice. 'Priestly Women, Virginal Men'. In *Gender and Christianity in Medieval Europe*, edited by Lisa M. Bitel and Felice Lifshitz, 87–102. Philadelphia: University of Pennsylvania Press, 2008.
Lindsay, Alison. '"This Fair Lady, in her Laces": Margaret Howie Strang Hall, the First Woman in Scotland to Try to Become a Lawyer'. *WHR* 29, no. 4 (2019): 555–62.
Lipking, Laurence. *Abandoned Women and Poetic Tradition*. Chicago: University of Chicago Press, 1988.
Lyall, Roderick J. 'James VI and the Sixteenth-Century Cultural Crisis'. In *The Reign of James VI*, edited by Julian Goodare and Michael Lynch, 55–70. Edinburgh: John Donald, 2000.
Lynch, Michael. *Edinburgh and the Reformation*. Edinburgh: John Donald, 1981.
Lynch, Michael. 'Queen Mary's Triumph: The Baptismal Celebrations at Stirling in December 1566'. *SHR* 69 (1990): 1–21.
McAndrew, Bruce A. *Scotland's Historic Heraldry*. Woodbridge: Boydell, 2006.

McAndrew, Bruce A. 'The Single Eagle Supporter in Scottish Armory'. *The Double Tressure: Journal of the Heraldry Society of Scotland* 34 (2011): 72–6.

McClain, Lisa. 'On a Mission: Priests, Jesuits, "Jesuitresses," and Catholic Missionary Efforts in Tudor-Stuart England'. *The Catholic Historical Review* 101, no. 3 (2015): 437–62.

McDonald, R. Andrew, ed. *History, Literature, and Music in Scotland, 700–1560*. Toronto: University of Toronto Press, 2016.

Macdonald, Stuart and Daniel MacLeod, eds. *Keeping the Kirk: Scottish Religion at Home and in the Diaspora*. Guelph: Guelph Centre for Scottish Studies, 2014.

McDougall, Jamie Murdoch. 'Covenants and Covenanters in Scotland, 1638–1679'. PhD diss., University of Glasgow, 2017.

MacDougall, Norman. *James III: A Political Study*. Edinburgh: John Donald, 1982.

McEwan, John A. 'Does Size Matter? Seals in England and Wales, ca. 1200–1500'. In *A Companion to Seals in the Middle Ages*, edited by Laura J. Whatley, 103–25. Leiden: Brill, 2019.

McGavin, John J. *Theatricality and Narrative in Medieval and Early Modern Scotland*. Farnham: Ashgate, 2007.

McGettigan, Darren. *Red Hugh O'Donnell and the Nine Years War*. Dublin: Four Courts Press, 2005.

McGladdery, Christine. *James II*. Edinburgh: John Donald, 1990; revised and reprinted Edinburgh: John Donald, 2015.

McInally, Tom. *The Sixth Scottish University: The Scots Colleges Abroad, 1575 to 1799*. Leiden: Brill, 2012.

MacInnnes, Allan I. *Charles I and the Making of the Covenanting Movement, 1625–1621*. Edinburgh: John Donald, 1991.

MacInnes, Iain A. *Scotland's Second War of Independence*. Woodbridge: Boydell, 2016.

MacInnes, Iain A. '"To Subject the North of the Country to his Rule": Edward III and the "Lochindorb Chevauchée" of 1336'. *Northern Scotland* 3, no. 1 (2012): 16–31.

MacIntosh, Marjorie K. 'The Benefits and Drawbacks of Femme Sole Status in England'. *Journal of British Studies* 44 (2005): 410–38.

McIntyre, Neil. 'Saints and Subverters: The Later Covenanters in Scotland, c. 1648–1682'. PhD diss., University of Strathclyde, 2016.

MacLeod, Daniel. 'Declining His Majesty's Authority: Treason Revisited in the Case of John Ogilvie'. In *Scotland's Long Reformation: New Perspectives on Scottish Religion, c. 1500–c. 1660*, edited by John McCallum, 179–201. St Andrews Studies in Reformation History, 1. Leiden: Brill, 2016.

MacLeod, Daniel. 'Making Time Protestant in Early-Modern Glasgow'. *Reformation and Renaissance Review* 20, no. 2 (2018): 168–84.

MacLeod, Daniel. 'Servants to St Mungo'. PhD diss., University of Guelph, 2014.

MacLeod, Daniel. 'Their Own Parish Kirk: Sacramental Spaces and Jurisdictional Jealousy in Early Modern Glasgow'. In *Where Mortal and Immortal Meet: Essays in Celebration of the 85th Anniversary of The Society of Friends of Glasgow Cathedral*, edited by Andrew G. Ralston, 182–97. Eugene: Wipf and Stock, 2021.

McMillan, Catherine. '"Scho Refuseit Altogidder to Heir His Voce": Women and Catholic Recusancy in North East Scotland, 1560–1610'. *Scottish Church History* 45, no. 1 (2016): 36–48.

McMillin, Linda A. 'Women on the Walls: Women and Warfare in the Catalan Grand Chronicles'. *Catalan Review* 3, no. 1 (1989): 123–36.

McNamee, Colm. *The Wars of the Bruces: Scotland, England and Ireland, 1306–1328*. East Linton: Tuckwell Press, 1997.

McNulty, Claire. 'The Experience of Discipline in Parish Communities in Edinburgh, Scotland, 1638–1651'. PhD diss., Queen's University Belfast, 2021.

McRoberts, David. 'A Sixteenth-Century Picture of St Bartholomew from Perth'. *IR* 10, no. 2 (1959): 281–6.

McRoberts, David. 'Material Destruction Caused by the Scottish Reformation'. In *Essays on the Scottish Reformation, 1513–1625*, edited by David McRoberts, 415–62. Glasgow: Burns, 1962.

McSeveney, Alan James. 'Non-Conforming Presbyterian Women in Restoration Scotland: 1660–1679'. PhD diss., University of Strathclyde, 2005.

Mack, Phyllis. *Visionary Women: Estatic Prophecy in Seventeenth-century England*. Berkeley: University of California Press, 1992.

Mainer, Sergi. 'Contrasting Kingly and Knightly Masculinities in Barbour's Bruce'. In *Nine Centuries of Man: Manhood and Masculinity in Scottish History*, edited by Lynn Abrams and Elizabeth Ewan, 122–41. Edinburgh: Edinburgh University Press, 2017.

Mann, Alastair. *The Scottish Book Trade: Print Commerce and Print Control in Early Modern Scotland*. East Lothian: Tuckwell Press, 2000.

Markus, Gilbert. 'Dewars and Relics in Scotland: Some Clarifications and Questions'. *IR* 60, no. 2 (2009): 95–144.

Marshall, Rosalind K. *Queen Mary's Women: Female Relatives, Servants, Friends and Enemies of Mary, Queen of Scots*. Edinburgh: John Donald, 2006.

Marshall, Rosalind K. *Virgins and Viragos: A History of Women in Scotland from 1080–1980*. Chicago: Chicago Academy, 1983.

Martin, Joanna and Kate L. Mathis, 'Elegy and Commemorative Writing'. In *The International Companion to Scottish Literature*, edited by Nicola Royan, 173–99. Glasgow: Association for Scottish Literary Studies, 2018.

Mason, Rebecca. 'Property Over Patriarchy?: Remarried Women as Litigants in the Courts of Seventeenth-century Glasgow'. In *Litigating Women: Gender and Justice in Europe, 1100–1750*, edited by Teresa Phipps and Deborah Youngs, 133–51. London: Routledge, 2022.

Mason, Rebecca. 'Women, Marital Status and Law: The Marital Spectrum in Seventeenth-Century Glasgow'. *Journal of British Studies* 58, no. 4 (2019): 787–804.

Meikle, Maureen. *A British Frontier?: Lairds and Gentlemen in the Eastern Borders, 1540–1603*. East Linton: Tuckwell Press, 2004.

Meikle, Maureen. 'Victims, Viragos and Vamps: Women of the Sixteenth-century Anglo-Scottish Frontier'. In *Government, Religion and Society in Northern England, c. 1000–1700*, edited by John C. Appleby and Paul Dalton, 172–84. Gloucester: Alan Sutton, 1997.

Meller, Harald, ed. *Fundsache Luther: Archäologen auf den spuren des Reformators*, Stuttgart: Theiss Verlag, 2008.

Mijnheer, Christina Louise and Jordan Robert Gamble. 'Value Co-creation at Heritage Visitor Attractions: A Case Study of Gladstone's Land'. *Tourism Management Perspectives* (2019): 1–12.

Miller, Robert. 'Where did John Knox Live in Edinburgh? And the Legend of "John Knox's House"'. *PSAS* 33 (1899): 80–115.

Mitchison, Rosalind. *Life in Scotland*. London: Batsford, 1978.

Moncreiffe, Rupert Iain. *The Law of Succession: Origins of the Law of Succession to Arms and Dignities in Scotland*, edited by Jackson W. Armstrong. Edinburgh: John Donald, 2010.

Moore, Lindsay. 'Women, Property, and the Law in the Anglo-American World, 1630–1700'. *Early American Studies: An Interdisciplinary Journal* 14, no. 3 (Summer 2016): 537–67.

Moore, Lindsay, *Women Before the Court: Law and Patriarchy in the Anglo-American World, 1600–1800*. Manchester: Manchester University Press, 2019.

Morgan, Hiram. *Tyrone's Rebellion: The Outbreak of the Nine Years War in Tudor Ireland*. Woodbridge: Boydell, reprinted 1999.

Morrison, Susan Signe. *A Medieval Woman's Companion: Women's Lives in the European Middle Ages*. Oxford: Oxbow Books, 2016.

Mortimer, Ian. *The Perfect King: The Life of Edward III, Father of the English Nation*. London: Vintage, 2008.

Moss, Rachel E. 'An Orchard, A Lover and Three Bastards: The Formation of Adult Male Identity in a Fifteenth-century Family'. In *What is Masculinity? Historical Dynamics from Antiquity to the Contemporary World*, edited by John H. Arnold and Sean Brady, 226–44. Basingstoke: Palgrave Macmillan, 2013.

Muir, Edward. *Ritual in Early Modern Europe*, 2nd edition. Cambridge: Cambridge University Press, 2005.

Muldrew, Craig. '"A Mutual Assent of Her Mind"? Women, Debt, Litigation and Contract in Early Modern England'. *History Workshop Journal* 55 (2003): 47–71.

Mullan, David G. *Narratives of the Religious Self in Early-Modern Scotland*. Aldershot: Ashgate, 2010.

Mullan, David G. 'Women in Scottish Divinity, c. 1590–1640'. In *Women in Scotland, c. 1100–c. 1750*, edited by Elizabeth Ewan and Maureen M. Meikle, 29–41. East Linton: Tuckwell Press, 1999.

Mullan, David G. *Women's Life Writing in Early Modern Scotland: Writing the Evangelical Self, c. 1670–c. 1730*. Farnham: Ashgate, 2003.

Mullett, Michael. *The Catholic Reformation*. New York: Routledge, 1999.

Murray, Jacqueline. 'One Flesh, Two Sexes, Three Genders?'. In *Gender and Christianity in Medieval Europe*, edited by Lisa M. Bitel and Felice Lifshitz, 34–51. Philadelphia: University of Pennsylvania Press, 2008.

Murray, Susan E. 'Women and Castles in Geoffrey of Monmouth and Malory'. *Arthuriana* 13, no. 1 (2003): 17–41.

Neal, Derek G. *The Masculine Self in Late Medieval England*. Chicago: University of Chicago Press, 2008.

Nebelsick, L. D. '"Es Sey Hieour Etwo ein Sepulcrum Gewesen": Martin Luther and the Sixteenth-century Beginnings of Archaeological Research in Central Europe and Scandinavia'. In *Martin Luther and the Reformation*, edited by Anne-Simone Rous, 290–301. Halle: Landesamt für Denkmalpflege und Archäologie Sachsen-Anhalt & Sandstein Verlag, 2008.

Neville, Cynthia. *Land, Law and People in Medieval Scotland*. Edinburgh: Edinburgh University Press, 2010.

Neville, Cynthia. 'Making a Manly Impression: The Image of Kingship on Scottish Royal Seals of the High Middle Ages'. In *Nine Centuries of Man: Manhood and Masculinity in Scottish History*, edited by Lynn Abrams and Elizabeth Ewan, 101–21. Edinburgh: Edinburgh University Press, 2017.

Neville, Cynthia J. 'Women, Charters, and Land Ownership in Scotland, 1150–1350'. *Journal of Legal History* 26, no. 1 (2005): 25–54.

New, Elizabeth. 'Biblical Imagery on Seals in Medieval England and Wales'. In *Pourquoi les Sceaux? La Sigillographie nouvel enjeu de l'histoire de l'art*, edited by Marc Gil and Jean-Luc Chassel, 451–68. Lille: Publications de l'Institut de recherches historiques du Septentrion, 2011.

New, Elizabeth. 'Lleision ap Morgan Makes an Impression: Seals and the Study of Medieval Wales'. *Welsh Historical Review* 26, no. 3 (2013): 327–50.

Newlyn, Evelyn S. 'A Methodology for Reading Against the Culture: Anonymous, Women Poets, and the Maitland Quarto Manuscript'. In *Woman and the Feminine in Medieval and Early Modern Scottish Writing*, edited by Sarah M. Dunnigan, C. Marie Harker and Evelyn S. Newlyn, 89–103. Basingstoke: Palgrave Macmillan, 2004.

Newton, Michael. 'Prophecy and Cultural Conflict in Gaelic Tradition'. *Scottish Studies* 35 (2007–10): 144–73.

Nicholson, Helen J. '"La demoiselle del chastel": Women's Role in the Defence and Functioning of Castles in Medieval Writing from the Twelfth to the Fourteenth Centuries'. In *Crusader Landscapes in the Medieval Levant: The Archaeology and History of the Latin East*, edited by Micaela Sinibaldi, Kevin J. Lewis, Balázs Major and Jennifer A. Thompson, 387–402. Cardiff: University of Wales Press, 2016.

Nicholson, Ranald. *Edward III and the Scots: The Formative Years of a Military Career, 1327–1335*. London: Oxford University Press, 1965.

Nugent, Janay. 'Concepts of Youth'. In *A Cultural History of Youth in the Renaissance*, edited by Lucy Underwood. New York: Bloomsbury, 2023.

Nugent, Janay. '"None must meddle betuenne man and wife": Assessing Family and the Fluidity of Public and Private in Early Modern Scotland'. *Journal of Family History* 35 (2010): 219–31.

Nugent, Janay. 'Reformed Masculinity: Ministers, Fathers and Male Heads of Households, 1560–1660'. In *Nine Centuries of Man: Manhood and Masculinities in Scottish History*, edited by Elizabeth Ewan and Lynn Abrams, 39–54. Edinburgh: Edinburgh University Press, 2017.

Nugent, Janay. '"The Mistresse of the Family Hath a Special Hand": Family, Women, Mothers and the Establishment of a "godly community of Scots"'. In *Keeping the Kirk: Scottish Religion at Home and in the Diaspora*, edited by Stuart Macdonald and Daniel MacLeod, 39–62. Guelph: Guelph Centre for Scottish Studies, 2014.

Nugent, Janay. '"Your louing childe and foster": The Fostering of Archie Campbell of Argyll, 1633–39'. In *Children and Youth in Premodern Scotland*, edited by Janay Nugent and Elizabeth Ewan, 47–64. Woodbridge: Boydell, 2015.

Nugent, Janay and Elizabeth Ewan, eds. *Children and Youth in Premodern Scotland*. Woodbridge: Boydell, 2015.

Nugent, Janay and Elizabeth Ewan. 'Introduction: Adding Age and Generation as a Category of Historical Analysis'. In *Children and Youth in Pre-Modern Scotland*, edited by Janay Nugent and Elizabeth Ewan, 1–12. Woodbridge: Boydell, 2016.

Oberman, Heiko. 'Anticlericalism as an Agent of Change'. In *Anticlericalism in Late Medieval and Early Modern Europe*, edited by Peter A. Dykema and Heiko Oberman, ix–xi. Leiden: Brill, 1994.

O'Keeffe, Tadhg. 'Concepts of "Castle" and the Construction of Identity in Medieval and Post-Medieval Ireland'. *Irish Geography* 34, no. 1 (2001): 69–88.

Oram, Richard. *David I, King of Scots, 1124–1153*. Edinburgh: John Donald, 2020.

Oram, Richard. '"The Worst Disaster Suffered by the People of Scotland in Recorded History": Climate Change, Dearth and Pathogens in the Long 14th Century'. *PSAS* 144 (2014): 223–44.

Oram, Richard and W. Paul Adderley. 'Lordship and Environmental Change in Central Highland Scotland, c. 1300–c. 1400'. *Journal of the North Atlantic* 1, no. 1 (2008): 74–84.

Orme, Nicholas. *Medieval Children*. New Haven: Yale University Press, 2001.

Orme, Nicholas. 'Monarchy, Martyrdom and Masculinity: England in the Later Middle Ages'. In *Holiness and Masculinity in the Middle Ages*, edited by Patricia H. Cullum and Katherine J. Lewis, 174–91. Cardiff: University of Wales Press, 2004.

Orme, Nicholas. *Tudor Children*. New Haven: Yale University Press, 2023.

Ormrod, W. Mark. *Edward III*. New Haven: Yale University Press, 2011.

Oxford Dictionary of National Biography. Oxford: Oxford University Press, 2004.

Ozment, Steven. *When Fathers Ruled: Family Life in Reformation Europe*. Cambridge, MA: Harvard University Press, 1983.

Palmer, William. 'Gender, Violence, and Rebellion in Tudor and Early Stuart Ireland'. *Sixteenth Century Ireland* 23, no. 4 (1992): 699–712.

Paranque, Estelle. 'Isabel Clara Eugenia, Governor of the Spanish Netherlands: Trade, Politics, and Warfare, Ruling like a King, 1621–1633'. In *Colonisation, Piracy, and Trade in Early Modern Europe: The Roles of Powerful Women and Queens*, edited by Estelle Paranque, Nate Probasco and Claire Jowitt, 73–93. Cham: Palgrave Macmillan, 2017.

Parker, Heather. '"At thair perfect age": Elite Child Betrothal and Parental Control, 1430–1560'. In *Children and Youth in Premodern Scotland*, edited by Janay Nugent and Elizabeth Ewan, 173–86. Woodbridge: Boydell, 2015.

Parker, Heather. '"In all gudly haste": The Formation of Marriage in Scotland, c. 1350–1600'. PhD diss., University of Guelph, 2012.

Parlett, Graham, John Fletcher and Chris Cooper. 'The Impact of Tourism on the Old Town of Edinburgh'. *Tourism Management* 16, no. 5 (1995): 355–60.

Paton, G. H. Campbell. 'Husband and Wife: Property Rights and Relationships'. In *An Introduction to Scottish Legal History*, 99–115. Edinburgh: Stair Society, 1958.

Pearce, Michael. 'The Jewels Mary, Queen of Scots, Left Behind', 2016. https://www.academia.edu/37587900/The_jewels_Mary_Queen_of_Scots_left_behind.

Peltzer, Jörg. 'Making an Impression: Seals as Signifiers of Individual and Collective Rank in the

Upper Aristocracy in England and the Empire in the Thirteenth and Fourteenth Centuries'. In *Seals and Their Context in the Middle Ages*, edited by Philipp Schofield. Oxford: Oxbow Books, 2015.

Penman, Michael. *David II*. Edinburgh: John Donald, 2005.

Penman, Michael. *The Scottish Civil War: The Bruces & the Balliols & the War for Control of Scotland, 1286–1356*. Charleston: Tempus Publishing, 2002.

Perfetti. Lisa, ed. *The Representation of Women's Emotions in Early Modern Culture*. Tampere: University Press of Florida, 2005.

Peters, Christine. *Women in Early Modern Britain, 1450–1640: Social History in Perspective*. Basingstoke: Palgrave Macmillan, 2003.

Phillips, Kim. 'Masculinities and the Medieval English Sumptuary Laws'. *Gender & History* 19, no. 1 (April 2007): 22–42.

Phillips, Kim. *Medieval Maidens: Young Women and Gender, 1270–1540*. Manchester: Manchester University Press, 2003.

Phipps, Teresa and Deborah Youngs, eds. *Litigating Women: Gender and Justice in Europe, 1100–1750*. London: Routledge, 2022.

Porck, Thijs. 'The Ages of Man and the Ages of Woman in Early Medieval England: From Bede to Byrhtferth of Ramsay and the Tractus de quaternario'. In *Early Medieval English Life Courses: Cultural-historical Perspectives*, edited by Thijs Porck and Harriet Soper, 17–46. Leiden: Brill, 2022.

Post Walton, Kristen. *Catholic Queen, Protestant Patriarchy: Mary Queen of Scots and the Politics of Gender and Religion*. London: Routledge, 2006.

Potoczny, Méline. 'Report on the Representation of Women in Historic Environment Scotland's Guidebooks and Statements of Significance'. Unpublished report, Historic Environment Scotland, 2022.

Potter, Roslyn. 'Lilias Skene: Quaker Poet and Social Activist in Seventeenth-century Aberdeen'. *[X]Position* 5 (2020): 1–4.

Prince, A. E. 'The Strength of English Armies in the Reign of Edward III'. *English Historical Review* 46, no. 183 (1931): 353–71.

Purdie, Rhiannon and Emily Wingfield, eds. *Six Scottish Courtly and Chivalric Poems Including Squyer Meldrum*. Kalamazoo: Medieval Institute Publications, 2018.

Pye, Roger F. 'The Single Eagle Supporter in Scottish Armory'. *Scottish Genealogist* 21, no. 1 (1974).

Raffe, Alasdair. 'Female Authority and Lay Activism in Scottish Presbyterianism, 1660–1740'. In *Religion and Women in Britain, c. 1660–1760*, edited by Sarah Apetrei and Hannah Smith, 59–74. Farnham: Ashgate, 2014.

Raffe, Alasdair. *The Culture of Controversy: Religious Arguments in Scotland, 1660–1714*. Woodbridge: Boydell, 2012.

Raffe, Alasdair. 'Who Were the Later Covenanters?' In *The National Covenant in Scotland, 1638–1689*, edited by Chris R. Langley. Woodbridge: Boydell, 2020, 197–214.

Ravilious, J. P. 'The Earls of Menteith: Alexander, Earl of Menteith and Sir Alexander Abernethy'. *Scottish Genealogist* 57, no. 3 (2010).

Reid, Norman. *Alexander III, First Among Equals*. Edinburgh: John Donald, 2019.

Reid, Steven. 'Of Bairns and Bearded Men: James VI and the Ruthven Raid'. In *James VI and Noble Power in Scotland, 1578–1603*, edited by Miles Kerr-Peterson and Steven J. Reid, 32–55. Abingdon: Routledge, 2017.

Reid, Steven, ed. *The Afterlife of Mary, Queen of Scots*. Edinburgh: Edinburgh University Press, 2024.

Reid Baxter, Jamie. 'Elizabeth Melville, Lady Culross: New Light from Fife'. *IR* 68 (2017): 38–77.

Reid Baxter, Jamie, ed. *Poems of Elizabeth Melville, Lady Culross*. Edinburgh: Solsequium, 2010.

'Reviving the Trinity Network'. https://blogs.ed.ac.uk/trinitynetwork/the-trinity-network-who-are-we/.

Rhodes, Bess. *Riches and Reform: Ecclesiastical Wealth in St Andrews, c. 1520–1580*. Leiden: Brill, 2019.

Richardson, Amanda. 'Gender and Space in English Royal Palaces, c. 1160–c. 1547: A Study in Access Analysis and Imagery'. *Medieval Archaeology* 47, no. 1 (2003): 131–65.

Ritchie, Elizabeth. 'Men and Place: Male Identity and the Meaning of Place in the Nineteenth-century Scottish Gàidhealtachd'. *Genealogy* 4, no. 4 (2020): 97.

Roberts, Alasdair. 'The Role of Women in Scottish Catholic Survival'. *SHR* 70, no. 190, part 2 (October 1991): 129–50.

Roberts, Benjamin B. *Sex, Drugs and Rock 'n' Roll in the Dutch Golden Age*. Amsterdam: Amsterdam University Press, 2017.

Robertson, James A. *Comitatus de Atholia: The Earldom of Atholl; Its Boundaries Stated, also the Extent Therein of the Possessions of the Family of De Atholia and their Descendants, the Robertsons*. Edinburgh: Murray and Gibb, 1860.

Rogers, Will. *Writing Old Age and Impairments in Late Medieval England*. Leeds: ARC Humanities Press, 2021.

Roper, Lyndal. *Oedipus and the Devil: Witchcraft, Sexuality and Religion in Early Modern Europe*. London: Routledge, 1994.

Roper, Lyndal. *The Holy Household: Women and Morals in Reformation Augsburg*, Oxford: Clarendon Press, 1989.

Rosenwein, Barbara. *Emotional Communities in the Early Middle Ages*. Ithaca: Cornell University Press, 2006.

Rosenwein, Barbara. 'Worrying about Emotions in History', *American Historical Review* 107, no. 3 (2002): 821–45.

Ross, Alasdair. 'Men for all Seasons? The Strathbogie Earls of Atholl and the Wars of Independence, c. 1290–c. 1335. Part 2'. *Northern Scotland* 21, no. 1 (2001): 1–15.

Ross, Sarah C. E. *Women, Poetry, and Politics in Seventeenth-Century Britain*. Oxford: Oxford University Press, 2015.

Ross, Thomas and G. Baldwin Brown. 'The Magdalen Chapel, Cowgate, Edinburgh'. *The Book of the Old Edinburgh Club*, vol. 8 (1916): 1–78.

Rothery, Guy Cadogan. *Concise Encyclopedia of Heraldry*. London: Senate Books, 1994.

Rous, Anne-Simone, ed. *Martin Luther and the Reformation/Treasure of the Reformation*. Halle: Landesamt für Denkmalpflege und Archäologie Sachsen-Anhalt & Sandstein Verlag, 2016.

Rowlands, Allison. '"Superstition", Magic and Clerical Polemic in Seventeenth-Century Germany'. *Past & Present* Supplement 3 (2008): 157–77.

Royan, Nicola. 'Some Conspicuous Women in the Original Chronicle, Scotichronicon and Scotorum Historia'. *IR* 59, no. 2 (Autumn 2008): 131–44.

Rublack, Ulinka. 'Grapho-Relics: Lutheranism and the Materialization of the Word'. *Past & Present* Supplement 5 (2010): 144–66.

Rutherford, Allan Gavin. 'A Social Interpretation of the Castle in Scotland'. PhD diss., University of Glasgow, 1998.

Sanderson, Margaret H. B. *A Kindly Place? Living in Sixteenth-Century Scotland*. East Linton: Tuckwell Press, 2002.

Sanderson, Margaret H. B. *Cardinal of Scotland: David Beaton, c. 1494–1546*. Edinburgh: John Donald, 2001.

Sanderson, Margaret H. B. 'Catholic Recusancy in Scotland in the Sixteenth Century'. *IR* 21 (Autumn 1970): 87–107.

Sanderson, Margaret H. B. *Mary Stewart's People*. Edinburgh: Mercat Press, 1987.

Saul, Nigel. *Chivalry in Medieval England*. Cambridge, MA: Harvard University Press, 2011.

Schiesari, Juliana. *The Gendering of Melancholia: Feminism, Psychoanalysis, and the Symbolics of Loss in Renaissance Literature*. Ithaca: Cornell University Press, 1992.

Scott, Joan W. 'Gender: A Useful Category of Historical Analysis'. *American Historical Review* 91, no. 5 (1986): 1053–75.

Scribner, Robert. 'Incombustible Luther: The Image of the Reformer in Early Modern Germany'. *Past & Present* 110 (February 1986): 38–68.

Scottish Studies Foundation: Undergraduate Scholarship to Honour Professor Elizabeth Ewan.

Sellar, David. 'The Family'. In *A History of Everyday Life in Medieval Scotland*, edited by Edward J. Cowan and Lizanne Henderson, 89–108. Edinburgh: Edinburgh University Press, 2011.

Settimini Elena. 'Women's Representation and Participation in UNESCO Heritage Discourse'. *International Journal of Heritage Studies* 27, no. 1 (2021): 1–15.

Shepard, Alexandra. *Meanings of Manhood in Early Modern England*. Oxford: Oxford University Press, 2003.

Sheridan, Sara. 'Where are the Women? A Guide to an Imagined Scotland'. Edinburgh: Historic Environment Scotland, 2019.

Simmonds, Gemma. 'Women Jesuits?' In *Cambridge Companion to the Jesuits*, edited by Thomas Worcester, 120–35. Cambridge: Cambridge University Press, 2008.

Simms, Katharine. *Gaelic Ulster in the Middle Ages: History, Culture, and Society*. Dublin: Four Courts Press: 2020.

Simonton, Deborah. 'Community of Goods, Coverture and Capability in Britain: Scotland versus England'. In *Gender, Law and Economic Well-Being in Europe from the Fifteenth to the Nineteenth Century: North versus South?*, edited by Anna Bellavitis and Beatrice Zucca Micheletto, 31–46. London: Routledge, 2018.

Simpson, Andrew R. C. and Adelyn Wilson, eds. *Scottish Legal History: Volume one, 1100–1707*. Edinburgh: Edinburgh University Press, 2017.

Simpson, W. Douglas. 'The Campaign and Battle of Culblean, AD 1335'. *PSAS* 64 (1930): 201–11.

Sjursen, Katrin E. 'Pirate, Traitor, Wife: Jeanne of Belleville and the Categories of Fourteenth-century French Noblemen'. In *Medieval Elite Women and the Exercise of Power, 1100–1400*, edited by Heather J. Tanner, 135–56. Cham: Palgrave Macmillan, 2019.

Skenazi, Cynthia. *Aging Gracefully in the Renaissance: Stories of Later Life from Petrarch to Montaigne*. Leiden: Brill, 2013.

Skinner, Patricia. 'Gender and Memory in Medieval Italy'. In *Medieval Memories: Men, Women and the Past, 700–1300*, edited by Elisabeth van Houts, 36–52. Abingdon: Routledge, 2013.

Slater, Laura. 'Rumour and Reputation Management in Fourteenth-Century England: Isabella of France in Text and Image'. *Journal of Medieval History* 47, no. 2 (2021): 1–36.

Smith, Laurajane. 'Heritage, Gender and Identity'. In *The Ashgate Research Companion to Heritage and Identity*, edited by Brian Graham and Peter Howard, 159–178. Abingdon: Routledge, 2008.

Smith, M. Q. 'Medieval Chandeliers in Britain and their Symbolism'. *The Connoisseur* 190 (1975): 266–71.

Smith, S. A. A. and Allan Knight, eds. *The Religion of Fools? Superstition Past and Present. Past & Present* Supplement 3 (2008).

Smith, Stephen R. 'Growing Old in Early Stuart England'. *Albion* 8, no. 2 (1976): 125–41.

Spence, Cathryn, '"By her own mouth speaking": Women's Authoritative Voices in Early Modern Wills and Testaments'. *SHR* 102, no. 2 (2023): 273–89.

Spence, Cathryn. 'Negotiating the Economy: Gender, Status, and Debt Litigation in the Burgh Courts of Early Modern Scotland'. In *Crossing Borders: Boundaries and Margins in Medieval and Early Modern Britain: Essays in Honour of Cynthia J. Neville*, edited by Sara Butler and Krista J. Kesselring, 174–92. Leiden: Brill, 2018.

Spence, Cathryn. *Women, Credit, and Debt in Early Modern Scotland*. Manchester: Manchester University Press, 2016.

Spicer, Andrew. '"Accommodating of Thame Selfis to Heir the Worde": Preaching, Pews and Reformed Worship in Scotland, 1560–1638'. *History* 88, no. 291 (2003): 405–22.

Spicer, Andrew. 'Adiaphora, Luther and the Material Culture of Worship'. *Studies in Church History* 56 (2020): 246–72.

Spicer, Andrew. '"God Hath Put Such Secretes in Nature": Conventicles, Consecrations and the Concept of the Sacred in Post-Reformation Scotland'. In *Sacred Space in Early Modern Europe*, edited by Will Coster and Andrew Spicer, 81–103. Cambridge: Cambridge University Press, 2005.

Spicer, Andrew. 'Iconoclasm and Adaptation: The Reformation of the Churches in Scotland and the Netherlands'. In *The Archaeology of the Reformation, 1480–1580*, edited by David R. M. Gaimster and Roberta Gilchrist, 29–43. Leeds: Maney Publishing, 2003.

Spicer, Andrew. 'The Scottish Reformation and Church Architecture, 1560–ca. 1638'. In *A Companion to the Reformation in Scotland, ca. 1525–1638*, edited by Ian Hazlett, 313–42. Leiden: Brill, 2022.

Spilman, Frances. *The Twelve: Lives and Legends of the Apostles*. New York: Lulu.com, 2017.

Spindler, Erik. 'Youth and Old Age in Late Medieval London'. *London Journal: A Review of Metropolitan Society in the Past and Present* 36, no. 1 (2011): 1–22.

Spurlock, R. Scott. *Cromwell and Scotland: Conquest and Religion, 1650–1660*. Edinburgh: John Donald, 2007.

Spurlock, R. Scott. '"I do disdain both Ecclesiasticke and Politick Popery": Lay Catholic Identity in Early Modern Scotland'. *Records of the Scottish Church History Society* 38 (2008): 5–22.

Spurlock, R. Scott. 'State, Politics, and Society in Scotland, 1637–1660'. *The Oxford Handbook of the English Revolution*, edited by Michael J. Braddick, 363–78. Oxford: Oxford University Press, 2015.

Spurlock, R. Scott. 'The Laity and the Structure of the Catholic Church in Early Modern Scotland'. In *Insular Christianity: Alternative Models of the Church in Britain and Ireland, c. 1570–c. 1700*, edited by Robert Armstrong and Tadhg O'Hannrachain, 231–51. Manchester: Manchester University Press, 2013.

Stevenson, David. 'Deposition of Ministers in the Church of Scotland under the Covenanters, 1638–1651'. *Church History* 44, no. 3 (September 1975): 321–35.

Stevenson, David. *King or Covenant? Voices from the Civil War*. East Linton: Tuckwell Press, 1996.

Stevenson, David. 'Major Weir: A Justified Sinner?'. *Scottish Studies* 16 (1972): 161–73.

Stevenson, David. *Union, Revolution, and Religion in 17th-Century Scotland*. Aldershot: Variorum, 1997.

Stevenson, Jane. 'Reading, Writing and Gender in Early Modern Scotland'. *Seventeenth Century* 27 (2012): 335–74.

Stevenson, Katie, ed. *The Herald in Late Medieval Europe*. Woodbridge: Boydell, 2009.

Stevenson, Seonaid and Maria Fletcher. 'A Century of Women in the Scottish Legal Profession'. In *Law and Justice: A Collection of Essays in Memory of Professor Ian Willock*, edited by Eamon P. H. Keane and Peter Robson. Vancouver: Fairleigh Dickinson University Press, 2023.

Stewart, Laura A. M. 'Authority, Agency and the Reception of the Scottish National Covenant of 1638'. In *Insular Christianity: Alternative Models of the Church in Britain and Ireland, c. 1570–1700*, edited by Robert Armstrong and Tadhg Ó hAnnracháin, 88–106. Manchester: Manchester University Press, 2013.

Stewart, Laura A. M. 'Contesting Reformation: Truth-telling, the Female Voice, and the Gendering of Political Polemic in Early Modern Scotland'. *Huntington Library Quarterly* 84, no. 4 (Winter 2021): 717–43.

Stewart, Laura A. M. *Rethinking the Scottish Revolution: Covenanted Scotland, 1637–1651*. Oxford: Oxford University Press, 2016.

Stewart, W. G. *Lectures on the Mountains; or, the Highlands and Highlanders of Strathspey and Badenoch as they Were and as they Are*, Second Series. London: Saunders, Otley and Co., 1860.

Stiùbhart, Domhnall Uilleam. 'Woman and Gender in the Early Modern Western Gaidhealtachd'. In *Women in Scotland, c. 1100–c. 1750*, edited by Elizabeth Ewan and Maureen M. Meikle, 233–49. East Linton: Tuckwell Press, 1999.

Stretton, Tim. 'Law, Property and Litigation'. In *The Routledge History of Women in Early Modern Europe*, edited by Amanda Capern, 199–216. London: Routledge, 2019.

Stretton, Tim. *Marital Litigation in the Court of Requests, 1542–1642*. Cambridge: Cambridge University Press, 2008.
Stretton, Tim. 'The Legal Identity of Married Women in England and Europe 1500–1700'. In *Europa Und Seine Regionen: 2000*, edited by Jahre Rechtsgeschichte, Andreas Bauer and Karl H. L. Welker, 309–22. Cologne: Bohlau Verlag, 2007.
Stretton, Tim. *Women Waging Law in Elizabethan England*. Cambridge: Cambridge University Press, 1998.
Stretton, Tim and Krista Kesselring, eds. *Married Women and the Law: Coverture in England and the Common Law World*. Montreal and Kingston: McGill-Queen's University Press, 2013.
Swanson, Robert. 'Medieval Anticlericalism: Terms and Conditions'. *History of Religions* 61, no. 1 (2021): 6–29.
Tanner, Heather J., Laura L. Gathagan and Lois L. Huneycutt. 'Introduction'. In *Medieval Elite Women and the Exercise of Power, 1100–1400*, edited by Heather J. Tanner, 1–18. Cham: Palgrave Macmillan, 2019.
Taylor, Alice, ed., *The Laws of Medieval Scotland: Legal Compilations from the Thirteenth and Fourteenth Centuries*, Edinburgh: Edinburgh University Press, 2019.
Taylor, Joseph. *Edward I of England in the North of Scotland*. Elgin: Robert Jeans, 1858.
Taylor, Simon and Gilbert Márkus. *The Place-Names of Fife*. Donnington: Shaun Tyas, 2010.
Thane, Pat. 'Old Age in the European Culture: A Significant Presence from Antiquity to the Present'. *American Historical Review* 125, no. 2 (April 2020): 385–95.
Thomas, Andrea. '"Dragonis baith and dowis ay in double forme": Women at the Court of James V, 1513–1542.' In *Women in Scotland, c. 1100–c. 1750*, edited by Elizabeth Ewan and Maureen Meikle, 83–94. East Linton: Tuckwell Press, 1999.
Todd, Margo. *The Culture of Protestantism in Early Modern Scotland*. New Haven: Yale University Press, 2002.
Tripadvisor, Reviews. https://www.tripadvisor.co.uk/Attraction_Review.
van Heijnsbergen, Theo. 'Advice to a Princess: The Literary Articulation of a Religious, Political and Cultural Programme for Mary, Queen of Scots.' In *Sixteenth-Century Scotland: Essays in Honour of Michael Lynch*, edited by Julian Goodare and Alasdair A. Macdonald, 99–122. Leiden: Brill, 2008.
van Heijnsbergen, Theo. 'Masks of Revelation and the "Female" Tongues of Men: Montgomerie, Christian Lyndsay, and the Writing Game at the Scottish Renaissance Court'. In *Literature, Letters and the Canonical in Early Modern Scotland*, edited by Theo van Heijnsbergen and Nicola Royan, 69–89. East Linton: Tuckwell Press, 2002.
van Houtts, Elisabet M. C. *Memory and Gender in Medieval Europe, 900–1200*. London: Macmillan, 1999.
Verschuur, Mary. *A Noble and Potent Lady: Katherine Campbell, Countess of Crawford*. Abertay History Society no. 46. Dundee, 2006.
Walker, David. *A Legal History of Scotland: The Seventeenth Century*. Edinburgh, T. &. T. Clark, 1996.
Walker, Rose. 'Images of Royal and Aristocratic Burial in Northern Spain, c. 950–c. 1250'. In *Medieval Memories*, edited by Elisabeth Van-Houts, 150–72. Harlow: Longman, 2000.
Walsham, Alexandra. 'Domesticating the Reformation: Material Culture, Memory, and Confessional Identity in Early Modern England'. *Renaissance Quarterly* 69, no. 2 (2016): 566–616.
Walsham, Alexandra. 'Recycling the Sacred: Material Culture and Cultural Memory after the English Reformation'. *Church History* 86, no. 4 (2017): 112–54.
Walsham, Alexandra, ed. *Past & Present* Supplement 5 – *Relics and Remains* (2010).
Walsham, Alexandra. 'Skeletons in the Cupboard: Relics after the English Reformation', *Past & Present* Supplement 5 – *Relics and Remains* (2010): 121–43.
Ward, Emily J. 'Child Kingship and Notions of (Im)maturity in Northwest Europe, 1050–1262'. *Anglo-Norman Studies* 40 (2018): 197–212.
Ward, Jennifer C. 'Noblewomen, Family, and Identity in Later Medieval Europe'. In *Nobles and Nobility in Medieval Europe*, edited by Anne J. Duggan, 246–62. Woodbridge: Boydell, 2000.

Warner, Marina. *Alone of All Her Sex: The Myth and Cult of the Virgin Mary*. London: Weidenfeld & Nicolson, 1976.

Warnicke, Retha M. *Mary Queen of Scots*. London: Routledge, 2006.

Weikert, Katherine. *Authority, Gender and Space in the Anglo-Norman World, 900–1200*. Woodbridge: Boydell, 2020.

Weisman, Karen, ed. *The Oxford Handbook of the Elegy*. Oxford: Oxford University Press, 2010.

'Where are the Statues of Scots Women'? *The Scotsman*. Last modified January 23, 2016.

Wiesner-Hanks, Merry E., ed. *Challenging Women's Agency and Activism in Early Modernity*. Amsterdam: Amsterdam University Press, 2021.

Wiesner-Hanks, Merry E. *Women and Gender in Early Modern Europe*. Cambridge: Cambridge University Press, 1993.

Wilson, Daniel. 'St Ninian's Suburb, and the Collegiate Church of the Holy Trinity, founded at Edinburgh by Queen Mary of Gueldres, the Widow of James II, in 1462'. *PSAS* 18 (1884): 128–70.

Wolfthal, Diane. *In and Out of the Marital Bed: Seeing Sex in Renaissance Europe*. New Haven and London: Yale University Press, 2010.

Worden, J. William. *Grief Counselling and Grief Therapy*, 4th edition. London: Routledge, 2009.

Wormald, Jenny. *Court, Kirk and Community: Scotland, 1470–1625*. Toronto: University of Toronto Press, 1981.

Wormald, Jenny. *Mary, Queen of Scots: A Study in Failure*. London: George Philip, 1988; reprinted with foreword and afterword by Anna Groundwater. Edinburgh: John Donald, 2017.

Worthington, David. *Rev. James Fraser. 1634–1709: A New Perspective on the Scottish Highlands before Culloden*. Edinburgh: Edinburgh University Press, 2023.

Yellowlees, Michael. *'So Strange a Monster as a Jesuite': The Society of Jesus in Sixteenth-century Scotland*. Argyll: House of Lochar, 2003.

Yeoman, Louise. 'A Godly Possession? Margaret Mitchelson and the performance of Covenanted Identity'. In *The National Covenant in Scotland, 1638–1689*, edited by Chris R. Langley, 105–25. Woodbridge: Boydell, 2020.

Yeoman, Louise. 'Away with the Fairies'. In *Fantastical Imaginations: The Supernatural in Scottish History and Culture*, edited by Lizanne Henderson, 29–46. Edinburgh: Birlinn, 2009.

Yeoman, Louise. 'Heart-work: Emotion, Empowerment and Authority in Covenanting Times'. PhD diss., University of St Andrews, 1991.

Young, Alan. *Robert the Bruce's Rivals: The Comyns, 1212–1314*. East Linton: Tuckwell Press, 1997.

Young, John R. 'The Covenanters and the Scottish Parliament, 1639–1651: The Rule of the Godly and the Second Scottish Reformation'. In *Enforcing Reformation in Ireland and Scotland*, edited by Elizabethanne Boran and Crawford Gribben, 131–58. London: Routledge, 2006.

Young, John R. 'The Scottish Parliament and Witch-hunting in Scotland under the Covenanters'. *Parliaments, Estates & Representation* 26, no. 1 (2006): 53–65.

Youngs, Deborah. *The Life Cycle in Western Europe, c. 1300–c. 1500*. Manchester: Manchester University Press, 2006.

Index

Note: **bold** indicates illustrations

Aberdeen, 141, 148
Abernethy, Alexander, 162, 163–6, **164**, 169, 176, **177**
Abernethy, Hugh, 165
Abernethy, Mary, 171
Abernethy, Patrick, 165
Abernethy, William, 165
Abernethy family, 161–72, 175–6, **177**
adiaphora, 97
adultery, 16, 24, 131, 132
advice, 196–7, 200, 201–4, 205, 218, 221–2
affect, 142, 143, 145–7, 149, 152, 156–7
age, 3, 8, 9, 193–209, 218
age of majority, 199
agency, 4, 8–9, 15, 30, 35–6, 79, 83, 101, 102, 126, 185, 210, 211, 213, 215–16, 222–3
Aiken, Margaret, 92–3
Albany Stewarts, 171
Alexander III, King of Scots, 195
Alison, Isobel, 61, 138
alliances, 16, 20, 21–2, 214–15
altars, 106–8, 109, 111–12, 119, 121
Andrew of Wyntoun, 165, 180, 188–9, 197, 200–2, 203–4
Angus family, 168–73, 178
Annals of the Four Masters, 218
Annand, William, 127
Anning, Mary, 64
anticlericalism, 88, 93–5
Antinomianism, 49

Aodh Eangach, 214
Armenia, 106
Armorial de Berry, 167
Armorial of Gelre, 167, 173
armorial rolls, 167, 173
army *see* military
Arthur's Seat, Edinburgh, 65
assassinations, 13, 27–8, 113, 114–16, 136; *see also* murders
Austria, 167
authority
  and emotion, 142, 147, 151, 154, 155–6
  female, 15, 17, 22, 24, 31, 162, 185, 187, 191, 210
  legal, 31, 34–5, 45
  male, 34–5, 45, 109, 116–17, 118, 121, 139, 190
  royal, 22, 24, 139
  spiritual, 130, 147, 151, 154, 155–6
Ayr, 124, 127

Badenoch, 180, 187
Baillie, Robert, 127–8, 129
Balcanquhall, Walter, 127, 129
Balfour, Sir James, 33, 127, 199
Balfour family, 17
Ballie, Sir William, 30
Balliol, Edward, King of Scots, 180, 183
baptism, 23–4, 91, 95, 203
Barber, George, 55
Barclay, Robert, 141

Bartholomew, St, 106–8, **107**, 110–12, 121
Bavaria, 167
Beaton, David, Archbishop of St Andrews, 17
Beaton, Elizabeth, Lady Innermeath, **14**, 17
Beaton, James, II, Archbishop of Glasgow, 17, 90–1
Beaton, Janet, Lady Buccleuch, **14**, 28
Beaton, John, of Creich, **14**, 17, 28
Beaton, Margaret, Lady Reres, **14**, 15–17, 18, 20–4, 26–7
Beaton, Mary, **14**, 18, 23
Beaton, Robert, 21
Beaufort, Joan, 112–13
Beaumont, Henry, 184
Beaumont, Katherine, Countess of Atholl, 7–8, 9, 168, 179–92
Bell, John, 94
Bellenden, John, 202, 206
Bellenville Roll, 167, 173
Berwick-upon-Tweed, 180, 183, 189
bestiality, 48, 51
Biggar, 130
Black Agnes *see* Randolph, 'Black Agnes', Countess of Dunbar
Black Douglases, 171
Blackfriars, Perth, 112
Blair, Robert, 129
Boece, Hector, 202, 206
Book of Common Prayer, 123, 127, 139
Bothwell *see* Hepburn, James, 4th Earl of Bothwell
Botriphnie, 117
Bower, Walter, 189, 193, 197, 200, 201–2, 203, 204, 206–8
Bowie, Walter, 91
Bowie, William, 91
Brensesin, Margaret, 165
British Civil Wars, 124, 137
British Empire, 225
Brittany, 34
Bruce, Christina, 182, 183, 185, 188–9
Bruce, Robert I, King of Scots, 66, 180
Bruce Scots, 180–4, 186, 191, 192
Buchanan, George, 24, 26, 28, 29, 202, 204
burgh courts, 4, 5, 9, 31–47, 91
Burne, Nicol, 25, 96

Calvin, John, 121
Calvinism, 49, 121, 146, 147
Campbell, Agnes, 8, 210–16, 219–21, 222–3
Campbell, Archibald, 4th Earl of Argyll, 212
Campbell, Archibald, 5th Earl of Argyll, **14**, 212, 213, 215
Campbell, Sir Colin, of Boquhan, 30
Campbell, Colin, 3rd Earl of Argyll, 212
Campbell, Colin, 6th Earl of Argyll, 215
Campbell, Margaret, 16
candlesticks, 114–16, **115**, 117
Carthusian order, 112–13
Casket Letters, 26
catharsis, 145, 150
Catholicism, 6, 9, 87–103, 108, 117, 118, 121, 124, 142, 145
cautioners, 41–2
Cecil, William, 25–6
Chalmers Close, Edinburgh, 63, 69–70, 78, 79; *see also* Trinity Apse
chandelier, 106–8, **107**, 109–10, **110**, **111**, 114, 121
charitable foundations, 73–4, 78–81
Charles I, King of England, Scotland and Ireland, 123, 124, 128, 130
Charles II, King of England, Scotland and Ireland, 130, 137
Charterhouse, Perth, 112–13
chastity, 121, 190
Cheyne, Christian, Lady Seton, 183, 189
childbirth, 4, 9, 15, 18, 23–5, 181, 189–90
children, 8, 15, 16, 23–5, 29, 181, 183, 194–5, 197–9, 203, 213; *see also* childbirth; motherhood; youth
chivalry, 162, 166–8, 174, 176, 179, 188
Christina, Countess of Buchan, 17, 29
Chronicle of Fordun, 189
Chronicle of Lanercost, 165, 188
civility, 221
Clandeboy, 212
clans, 210, 212, 215
class, 3, 105; *see also* social status
co-creation, 76–8, 83–4
Colinton, 128
Collace, Jean, 136
Collace, Katharine, 136

colonialism, 225
commemoration, 74, 76, 120, 163
common law, 34–5, 43–4, 199
communion, 94, 95, 128, 135
Comyn, Alice, Countess of Buchan, 184
Comyn, John, of Badenoch, 180
confessions, 50, 51, 53, 92–3
consent, 31, 34–40, 45–7
continuity, 105, 108, 113, 195
conventicles, 125, 135–7, 138, 139
Cooper, John, 91–4
Coupar Angus Abbey, 181
Court of Session, 36–7, 38–9
courts, 4, 5, 9, 31–47, 50, 53, 91
covenanting movement, 6, 9, 48, 49, 59–61, 123–40, 149
coverture, 34–5, 44
Covid-19 pandemic, 70–2
Cowgate, Edinburgh, 63, 69–70, 72–3, 76; *see also* Magdalen Chapel
Cowper, William, 120
craft guilds, 73, 106–8, 110–12, 121
Craig, Sir Thomas, 33
critical race theory, 225
Cromwellian occupation, 56, 132, 138
cross-cultural theory, 119, 121
crusading, 112, 175
Culblean, Battle of, 179, 182
Cullooney Castle, 216–17
cult of saints practices, 6, 104–22
Cumbernauld Castle, 184
Curthose, Robert, 207
customary law, 35

Dalkeith, 52, 54, 55, 56
Dalrymple, Sir James, Lord Stair, 33
'damsel in distress' narratives, 8, 192
Dante, 205
Darnley, Lord *see* Stewart, Henry, Lord Darnley
David II, King of Scots, 174, 180, 193, 198, 200–4, 207
David, Duke of Rothesay, 201, 202, 203, 205
de Braose, Matilda, 191
de Menteith, Margaret, 169
de Menteith, Mary, 176
de Monthermer, Mary, Countess of Fife, 184

debt, 35, 38–9, 40–2
Deidis of Armorie, 166
Devil, 49, 52–4, 57, 133
Dewars, 113–14, 117
diabolism, 49, 52–4, 57, 133
diaspora, 225
diplomacy, 20
discipline, 87, 92–7, 124, 125–6, 131–4, 139, 151, 152–3
Disinherited, The, 180–4, 189, 192
display, 19–20, 58, 78
dissent, 125, 127, 130, 135, 137–9, 141
dittays, 52, 54–5
Dominican Order, 112
Donald, Lord of the Isles, 175
doublets, 113, 121
Douglas, George, 1st Earl of Angus, 170
Douglas, George, 4th Earl of Angus, 171
Douglas, Robert, of Lochleven, **14**, 16, 29
Douglas, William, Lord of Liddesdale, 182
Douglas, William, of Lochleven, **14**, 17, 25, 29
Douglas, William, 2nd Earl of Angus, 170
dowry, 18, 68, 211, 213
dream allegories, 146, 155
Dublin, 218
Dunbar Castle, 62, 183–4, 189
Duncan, Earl of Fife, 165
Dundarg Castle, 184
Dundee, 41
Dunning Riot, 130
Dupplin Moor, Battle of, 180

eagle iconography, 161–78, **164**, **168**, **170–3**, **175–6**
economic power, xviii–xix, 2, 8, 41–2, 46, 210
Edinburgh, 5, 23, 40–1, 48–51, 54–8, 62–84, 112, 116, 118, 123, 127, 128, 129, 135, 137, 140
Edinburgh Brass Rubbing Centre, 72
Edinburgh Castle, 28, 66–7
education, 18, 33, 54, 69, 212, 220
Edward I, King of England, 163
Edward III, King of England, 179, 180, 183, 185, 187–91, 192
elegy, 144, 145, 149–50
Elizabeth I, Queen of England, 20, 28–9

Elizabeth, Princess Palatinate, 141
emotion, 6, 128, 142–57
England, 8, 20, 21–2, 25–9, 34–7, 43–5, 58, 97, 187–8, 206–7, 211, 214, 218–22
English Revolution, 131, 137
episcopacy, 56, 57, 60, 100, 123, 125, 134, 135, 137, 138
Erastianism, 134, 138
Erskine, Arthur, 19
Erskine, George, 25, 29
Erskine, John, 1st Earl of Mar, 29
Erskine, John, 5th Lord, 16
Erskine, Margaret, Lady Lochleven, **14**, 15–17, 20–6, 28, 29, 30
estate management, 17, 20, 22
Ethiopia, 106
Eworth, Hans, 20
excommunication, 93, 102
executions, 4–5, 48–9, 57–61, 88, 92, 133, 134, 138, 171, 207
exhibitions, 64, 66–7
exile, 22, 29, 90–1

Falkland Palace, 1, 17, 21, 23
family
    connections and networks, 7, 8, 16–21, 30, 87, 89–90, 93
    family seals, 7, 8, 9, 161–78, **164**, **168**, **170-3**, **175-6**
    and honour, 14–15, 16, 28
    and identity, 7, 161–6, 173–4, 175, 178
    and incest, 4, 48–58
    and inheritance, 8, 17, 29, 31, 38, 190, 212, 220–1, 222–3
    and legitimacy, 14–15, 178
    lineage, 7, 29–30, 161–78, 190
    memories and traditions, 117, 163
    and power, 7, 8, 14–21, 163, 166–7, 168, 178, 210–23
    protection of, 7–8, 182–3, 189
    and reputation, 52, 161–6, 168, 174–6, 178, 190
    succession, 21–4, 25, 29, 213–14, 217, 220–1
    see also children; marriage; marital economy feminism, 3, 64, 83
Fife, 4, 13–30, 59, 92, 118, 171

Fitzwilliam, Sir William, 216
Flannan, St, 113
Fleming, Margaret, Countess of Atholl, 23
folklore, 54
Forbes, Arthur, of Reres, **14**, 17, 22, 28
Forbes, John, of Reres, 13, **14**, 17
Fordun, John, 189
Fox, George, 157
France, 16, 18, 22, 29, 34, 90, 167, 200, 203
Francis II, King of France, 18, 144
Fraser, James, 56–60, 61
Frederick the Wise, Elector of Saxony, 119–20
Fumac, St, 117

Gaelic poetry, 142, 145
Gaelic traditions, 114, 117
gate-keeping roles, 106, 117
Geddes, Jenny, 9, 123, 140
gender roles, 2–3, 9, 45, 90, 106, 117, 141
gender stereotypes, 63
gendered identity, 6, 10, 194
Germany, 34, 35, 53, 101–2, 106, 109, 167
Gladstone's Land, Edinburgh, 83
Glasgow, 6, 40, 42–3, 45, 69, 87–103, 127, 131
Glasgow Women's Library, 69
Glen Vale, 118
Glens of Antrim, 212, 215, 220
Glover Incorporation, 106–8, 110–12
Glover Incorporation altar, 106, 111–12
Glover Incorporation portrait, 106–8, **107**, 110–12, 121
Godlie Dreame, Ane (Melville), 146–7, 154, 155, 157
Grassmarket, Edinburgh, 48, 58, 70
Gray, Thomas, 187
grief, 24, 120, 142–54, 157
griefwork, 142–3, 146–9, 157
Grote, Gilbert, 45–6
guidebooks, 67, 117
Guthrie, Charles J., 116

Haddington, 41
Haddington, Thomas, 36–7
Halidon Hill, Battle of, 180

Hamilton, Dame Grissell, 130
Hamilton, James, Duke of Châtelherault, 17
Hamilton, James, of Bothwellhaugh, 27
Hammermen Incorporation, 73–4, 108
Hannay, James, 123
Harvie, Marion, 61, 138
Hay, Janet, **14**, 17
healing, 142–3, 146, 151, 154, 157
Hegate, Archibald, 100
Hegate, James, 100
Hegate, Robert, 100
heirlooms, 117, 118
Henry IV, King of England, 206, 207
Henry V, King of England, 207
Henryson, Robert, 144
Hepburn, James, 4th Earl of Bothwell, 24, 26
heraldry, 161–78
Herbertson, George, 96
heritage, xix, 5, 9, 62–84
heroism, 6, 8, 105, 108, 109, 113, 116, 118, 119, 121–2, 188
Highlands and Islands, 179, 210–11, 215, 225
Hill, J. Michael, 216
Historic Environment Scotland, 64–5, 66
Hog, James, 136
Holy Land, 112
Holy Roman Empire, 166
Holyrood Abbey, Edinburgh, 19–20
Holyrood Palace, Edinburgh, 66, 67
homosocial bonding, 200, 203
honour, 14–15, 16, 24–8
Hope, Sir Thomas, 33
hospitals, 73, 75, 78
Hundred Years War, 187
husbands' consent, 31, 34–40, 45–7

iconography, 96, 106–12, 161–78
identity, 6, 7, 10, 78–9, 104, 134, 138, 142, 154, 161–6, 173–5, 178, 193–4, 198, 203, 209
illegitimate children, 16, 18, 204
imprisonment, 9, 24, 50–1, 57, 137, 141, 148, 149, 154, 207, 218
incest, 4, 48–58
India, 106
infirmity, 116, 205, 206, 208

inheritance, 8, 17, 29, 31, 38, 190, 212, 220–1, 222–3
inner light, 143, 150–1, 152, 157
institutional power, 132, 138–9
interdisciplinarity, xix, 81, 84, 104, 224
intersectionality, 3, 8, 100, 221–2
Inveraray Castle, 21
Inverness, 46
Ireland, 7, 8, 55, 210–23, 224
Italy, 106, 167

James I and VI, King of England, Scotland and Ireland, **14**, 23–4, 25, 29, 67, 112–13, 193, 203, 204, 206
James I, King of Scots, 113, 121
James II and VII, King of England, Scotland and Ireland, 78, 81, 203
James III, King of Scots, 208
James V, King of Scots, **14**, 16, 17, 18, 25
Jerusalem, 112, 191
John, Earl of Carrick, 207–8
John Knox's House, Edinburgh, 116, 118
John Knox's Pulpit, Glen Vale, 118
Johnston, Archibald, of Wariston, 128
jus mariti, 38
Justiciary Court, Edinburgh, 53

Keith, Annas, Countess of Moray, **14**, 15, 18–30
Keith, Margaret, 18
Keith, William, 3rd Earl Marischal, 18
Ker, Lady Ann, 144
Ker, Anna, 50
Kilconquhar, 17
Kildrummy Castle, 182, 183, 185, 188
King, Mary, 67–8
Kinghorn, 127–8, 129
King's Covenant, 128
kingship, 6–7, 8, 9, 128, 193–209
Kinloss Abbey, 181
Kinnear, 13–14, 28, 30
kirk courts, 9, 29, 96, 132–3
Kirkintilloch, 113
Kirkton, James, 134–5
Knights Hospitaller, 112
Knox, John, 6, 20, 21, 25, 67, 87, 101, 110, 113–19, 121
Knox candlestick, 114–16, **115**, 117
Knox walking stick, 114–17, **115**

'Lady Laudian's Lament' (Ker), 144
'Ladyis Lamentatione, A' (Montgomerie), 144
Lamington, 130
Lamont, John, 58–60
land grants, 111, 174, 182, 213, 220
Langside, Battle of, 25
Lauder, John, of Fountainhall, 59
law, 4, 9, 31–47, 48–54, 99, 131–2, 134, 199
law of agency, 35–6
law of necessaries, 35–6
lawyers, 44–5
Leat, Trevor, 1
leatherworking, 106–8
legal agency, 35–6
legal authority, 31, 34–5, 45
legal capacity, 33–4
legal handbooks, 33–4, 37
legal status, 31–47, 105–6
legitimacy, 9, 14–15, 178
Leonardo Royal Hotel, Edinburgh, 70, **71**, 78
Leslie, Euphemia, Countess of Ross, 171–5, **172**
Leslie, Henry, 129
Leslie, John, Earl of Rothes, 137
Leslie, Mary, Countess of Ross and Lady of the Isles, 175–6
Leslie, Walter, 171–5, **172**, **173**
Leuchars, 17, 20
Liberton, 135
Licoricia of Winchester, 64
life-writing, 136, 138, 148
life stages, 193–4, 197, 198–9, 205, 209
Lindsay, Robert, of Pitscottie, 13–14, 20
lineage, 7, 29–30, 161–78, 190
Linlithgow, 27
listed buildings, 69
Lister, Anne, 64
Literary and Antiquarian Society of Perth (LASP), 106, 109, 114, 116–17
Livingstone, Magdalen, 19
Lochaber, 180, 181
Lochindorb Castle, 179, 181, 182–92
Lochleven, 16, 21, 22, 23, 24–5, 27
London, 23, 25, 44, 58, 116
Low Countries, 106, 109
Lowlands, 210, 225

Luther, Martin, 97, 113, 119–20
Lutheran Church, 97
Lyndsay, Sir David, 16

MacDonald, Angus, 213, 215, 220
MacDonald, Archibald, 213
MacDonald, Donald Gorm, 213
MacDonald, Finola, 8, 210–19, 220–23
MacDonald, James, of Dunivaig and the Glens, 212–13, 220
MacDonald, Katherine, 213
MacDonald, Sorley Boy, 212, 215, 220
MacDonald family, 168, 171, 175–6
McGrie, Andrew, 130
Mackenzie, Sir George, 33
McQueen, Michael, 73–4
Madeleine, Princess of France, 16
Magdalen Chapel, Edinburgh, 5, 63, 69–78, **71**, **75–7**, 82–4
magic, 54, 56–8, 61, 105, 108
Mair, John, 204, 207, 208
manhood, 193–209; *see also* masculinity
Margaret of Beverley, 191
marginalisation, 6, 9, 63, 64, 65, 93, 145, 210
Marian chandelier, 106–8, **107**, 109–10, **110**, **111**, 121
Marian civil war, 14, 27
Marian devotion, 105–6
marital economies, 35–6, 40–1, 45–6, 47
markets, 72–3
marriage, 15, 16–22, 29–30, 31–40, 42–7, 54–5, 100, 102, 162–6, 169, 171–4, 178, 210–15, 221
martyrdom, 106–8
Mary, Countess of Strathearn, 165
Mary, Queen of Scots, 1, 5, 9, 13–16, **14**, 18–30, 67, 69, 73, 144, 145
Mary, Virgin, 105–6, 181
Mary of Guelders, 78–81, 83–4
Mary of Guise, **14**, 16, 18
masculinity, xix, 2–3, 6, 7, 8, 63–4, 66–7, 105, 112, 116, 121–2, 125–6, 151, 167, 173–4, 193–209, 225
material culture, 6, 9, 88, 96–9, 104–22
media *see* press
Mein, Isobel, 55
Meldrum, George, 149

Melville, Elizabeth, 145–7, 154, 155, 157
Melville, James, of Halhill, 23
Melville family, 17
memorabilia, 118
men of law, 33–4, 36–40, 46
Menteith family, 161–9, 176
mercenaries, 211, 213, 215–23
military, 8, 55, 56, 66–7, 112, 132, 151, 200, 211, 213, 215–23
miscarriage, 24–5
mistresses, 16, 17
Mitchelson, Margaret, 128–9, 131
Montgomerie, Alexander, 144
monuments, 64–5, 66, 67, 130; *see also* plaques; statues; tombs
morality, 49, 124, 131–4, 139
Moray, Regent *see* Stewart, James, 1st Earl of Moray
motherhood, 30, 67, 181–3, 189–90, 210, 214, 222; *see also* childbirth; children; family
Mowbray, Eve, 184
Mowbray, Margaret, 184
Mowbray, Philippa, 184
Murdach, Earl of Menteith, 167
murders, 1, 4, 13–15, 27–30, 68, 165, 202, 207, 208, 217, 219, 221, 222; *see also* assassinations
Mure, Archibald, 90
Mure, John, 90
Mure, Margaret, 96–7
Murray, Andrew, 179, 182, 187, 188
Murray, Annabella, Countess of Mar, 23
museums, 63, 65, 109, 118
Muses Threnodie, 113

na Ceapaisch, Sìleas, 142,145
National Covenant, 123–4, 128, 129–30; *see also* covenanting movement
negotiation, 19, 29, 101, 102, 103, 182, 212, 214, 219–20, 221
Neville's Cross, Battle of, 201–2
New Inns, St Andrews, 21
New Town, Edinburgh, 66, 70
Newry, 219
Niddry's Wynd, Edinburgh, 73, 74
Nine Years War, 214, 221
Ninety-Five Theses (Luther), 120
Nisbet, Sir John, of Dirleton, 51

Normandy, 167
norms, 1, 6, 8, 126, 129, 137, 214–15, 219
North Channel, 8, 9, 210–23, 224
notaries, 33, 35, 45–6, 100

Oath of Allegiance, 134
Oath of Supremacy, 136
O'Clery, Lughaidh, 217, 218
O'Connor, Donogh, 216–17
O'Donnell, Donnell, 217
O'Donnell, Hugh McManus, 213–14, 216–18
O'Donnell, Red Hugh (Hugh Roe), 214, 216–19, 220–1
O'Donnells of Tyrconnell, 211, 213–14, 216–19, 220–2
O'Gallagher, Hugh, 217, 219
Ogilvie, John, 88–9, 90, 91, 95, 100, 102, 103
old age, 8, 9, 195, 197, 198, 204–9, 218
Old Town, Edinburgh, 62–3, 66–84
O'Neill, Turlough Luineach, 213, 215, 219–20, 222
O'Neills of Tyrone, 211, 213, 215, 216–17, 219–20, 222
Original Chronicle of Scotland, 165
othering, 221, 222
Otterburn, Battle of, 208
Ottoman Empire, 112

parish visitation records, 95
Paterson, Ninian, 135
patriarchal equilibrium, 6, 126, 139, 190
patriarchy, 6, 8, 9, 30, 31, 35, 38, 45–6, 49, 125–6, 130, 132, 139
Patrick, Earl of March, 182
patronage, 73–4, 78–81, 83
Percy, Walter, 165
Perrot, Sir John, 216
Perth, 6, 104–22, 124, 184, 200–1
Perth Hand-book, 117
Perth Museum, 109
petitions, 124, 125, 129, 130, 135, 137
pilgrimage, 98, 104–5, 112
Pitlethie hunting lodge, 17, 21
place names, 64–5
plaques, xx, 64, 74, **75**
poetry, 6, 9, 141–57, 196–7

political activism, 9, 123–40, 141–2, 146, 148–9; *see also* agency
political participation, 9, 18, 78–9, 125, 137–8, 141, 162 n. 4
political power, 2, 6, 7–8, 16 n.10, 19, 203, 210–23, 224, 225
power *see also* economic power; political power and age, 8, 9, 193–209
   association with masculinity, 63
   and the Church, 17, 89–90, 126, 131
   display of, 19–20, 58
   and family, 7, 8, 14–21, 163, 166–7, 168, 178, 210–23
   iconographies of, 163, 166–7, 168, 178
   institutional power, 132, 138–9
   limits of, 8
   soft power, 19–20
   of the state, 58, 126, 136
Practicks, 33–4, 199
Practicks of Sir James Balfour of Pittendreich, 199
praeposituras, 35, 38–9
prayerbook riots, 123, 127, 139
presbyterianism, 56, 57, 60, 123–40
press, 64, 128, 131, 144
print culture *see* press
private spaces, 4–5, 9, 48, 67, 184–5
Privy Council, 51, 53, 61, 125, 135, 137, 149
propaganda, 25–6, 188, 190, 222
property rights, 31–4, 37–8, 46, 47
prophecy, 120, 124, 128, 130, 135, 214
Protestantism, 18, 20, 22, 88, 101–2, 103, 108, 113–14, 118–21, 145; *see also* episcopacy; presbyterianism; Reformation
public spaces, 4–5, 48, 185–6, 189
punishment *see* discipline purchase of goods, 35, 38–9, 43

Quakerism, 6, 141–3, 148–51, 154, 156–7
Queen, The (Leat), 1
queenship, 6–7, 79

Ramsay family, 167
Randolph, 'Black Agnes', Countess of Dunbar, xviii, 62, 183–4, 188, 189, 191

Randolph, John, Earl of Moray, 181
rape, 24, 188, 190; *see also* sexual abuse
'Ratis Raving', 196–7, 199–200, 202, 205, 207
Real Mary King's Close, Edinburgh, xx, 62, 67–9
rebellions, 18, 22, 55, 211, 221–2
recusancy, 88, 93, 100–2
Red Douglases, 171
Reformation, 6, 87–8, 90, 94, 97–102, 105, 108–22, 124, 127, 131
relics, 106, 108, 113–22
religious activism, 9, 61, 90, 123–40, 141–2, 146, 148–9; *see also* agency
Religious Society of Friends *see* Quakerism
religious tolerance, 89, 100
reliquary altars, 119
reputation, 15, 24–8, 48, 52, 92, 129, 133, 161–6, 168, 174–6, 178, 190
resistance, 6, 87–9, 93, 108, 118, 134, 138–9, 140, 141, 148–9
Restoration, 126, 134, 138
retreat, 143, 151, 154–6
'Reviving the Trinity' network, 81, 83
Rhind, Jonet *see* Rynd, Jonet
rioting, 9, 123, 124, 127, 130, 139
ritual, 99, 101–2, 105, 108, 118–19, 120, 122
Rizzio, David, 67
Robert I, King of Scots, 66, 180, 189
Robert II, King of Scots, 174, 204–5, 207–9
Robert III, King of Scots, 201, 204, 205–6, 207
Robert, Earl of Fife and Duke of Albany, 202, 203, 205–6, 208
Robert the Steward, 200–1, 207
Roman Empire, 166
Ross, Hugh, 174
Ross family, 168, 171–6
Rothes *see* Leslie, John, Earl of Rothes, 137
Rough, Alison, xviii, 62, 67–9
Route, the, 212, 215, 220
Row, William, 127, 135
Royal Mile, Edinburgh, 62, 66, 67, 69–70, 83, 118
royal progresses, 21, 23

rumours, 23, 25–6
Rutherford, Samuel, 129
Ruthven, George, 113
Rynd, Jonet, 72–8, **77**, 83–4

sacraments, 90, 91, 95, 100; *see also* baptism; communion
St Andrews, 16, 20–1, 22, 27, 29, 60, 102
St Giles' Cathedral, Edinburgh, 20, 66, 67, 123, 127, 129, 140
St John's parish kirk, Perth, 106–8, 109–12
sale of goods, 31, 35, 38–9, 43
Sandilands, Barbara, 17
Satan *see* Devil
Savoy, 167
Scalacronica, 187
Scotichronicon, 197, 200, 201–2, 203, 204, 206–8
Scots Roll, 167
Scottish Reformation Society, 72, 76–8
Scottish Reformers, The (anon.), 117
sculpture, 1, 140; *see also* statues
seals, 7, 8, 9, 79, 161–78, **164**, **168**, **170–3**, **175–6**
self-writing, 136, 138, 148
sermons, 120, 122, 134
sexual abuse, 48–58; *see also* incest; rape
sexuality, 15, 24, 132–3, 139, 200
Sharp, James, Archbishop of St Andrews, 60, 134, 136, 137
Shoemaker Incorporation, 106–8
Shoemaker Incorporation altar, 106
Sidney, Sir Henry, 213
sieges, 28, 179, 180, 182–92
sin, 49, 59, 125, 126, 131–4, 136, 139, 150
Sinclair, George, 59
1641 rebellion, 55
Skene, Sir John, 33
Skene, Lilias, 6, 9, 141–57
Smith, Merilyn, 140
social class *see* class
social norms, 1, 6, 8, 126, 129, 137, 214–15, 219
social status, 3, 8, 9, 15, 19, 55, 73, 74, 79, 93, 99, 100, 127, 161–4, 168, 173–4, 178
soft anticlericalism, 93–4

soft power, 19–20
Solemn League and Covenant, 124
Spain, 186
speech, 6, 87–8, 92–3, 96–102, 151–2, 188, 191
spirituality, 5–6, 9, 105, 139, 142–57
splinters, 120
Spottiswoode, John, 92, 100
stained glass, 74
state power, 58, 126, 136
statues, 64, 66, 67, 113
status *see* legal status; social status
Stewart, Alexander, Duke of Rothesay, 203
Stewart, Alexander, Earl of Mar, 204
Stewart, Esme, 204
Stewart, Henry, Lord Darnley, **14**, 22, 67
Stewart, James, 1st Earl of Moray, 13, **14**, 16–17, 18–22, 25–8
Stewart, James, of Bute, 212
Stewart, Jean, Countess of Argyll, **14**, 17, 18, 21, 23, 28
Stewart, John, of Bunkle, Earl of Angus, 169
Stewart, Margaret, Countess of Angus, 162, 165, 169–71
Stewart, Margaret, Countess of Angus and Mar, 170–1, **170**
Stewart, Thomas, 169
Stewart, Walter, Earl of Atholl, 205, 206–7
Stewarts of Bunkle, 169, 170
Stewarts of Menteith and Abernethy, 161–78
Stirling, 23
Strathbogie, David (IV), Earl of Atholl, 179, 180–3, 189
Strathbogie, David (V), 180, 185, 189, 192
succession, 21–4, 25, 29, 213–14, 217, 220–1
supernatural, 56, 102, 104, 113, 118, 119, 120
superstition, 97, 104, 119
Sweden, 34
Sybil, wife of Robert Bordet, 186
sympathetic magic, 108, 119

Tarragona, 186
Testament of Cresseid (Henryson), 144

tombs, 29, 74, 75–6, **77**, 112–13, 163
torture, 53
tourism, 62–3, 66–72, 84
town baillies, 33, 41, 45
Trinity Altarpiece, 79–81
Trinity Apse, Edinburgh, 5, 63, 69–72, **71**, 78–84, **80**, **82**
Trinity Collegiate Church, Edinburgh, 70, 78–9
TripAdvisor reviews, 67–9, 70, 72, 75–6

Ulster, 8, 210–23, 224
UNESCO World Heritage Sites, 63, 66
Urban VIII, Pope, 100
urban heritage, 62–84

vernacular poetry, 145, 197
victimhood, 8, 48–9, 55–6, 61
vulnerability, 15, 143, 149–50, 157

Wales, 44–5, 172
Walker, Marion, 6, 9, 87–103
Walker, William, 90–1
walking sticks, 114–17, **115**
Wallace, William, 66
Walsingham, Sir Francis, 219
war, 66–7, 131, 132, 138, 151, 179–84, 200–1; *see also* military
wardship, 17, 162, 165–6
Wars of Independence, 9, 66, 179–84

Wars of the Three Kingdoms, 56, 132
Waverley station, Edinburgh, 78
weddings, 15, 19–20, 22; *see also* marriage
Weir, Jean, 4–5, 8, 48–61
Weir, Jean (mother of Jean, Thomas and Margaret), 50, 51, 54, 57
Weir, Margaret, 49, 50–1, 54–5
Weir, Thomas, 48–61
Weir, Thomas, of Kirkton (father of Jean, Thomas and Margaret), 50, 55
Welwood, James, 136
Wemyss, David, 94
Wemyss, Sir John, 202
West Bow, Edinburgh, 58
Westminster Abbey, 29
widowhood, 16–17, 35, 42, 73, 74, 78–9, 137, 179, 185, 210
William I, 'the Conqueror', King of England, 207
Winram, John, 20
wisdom, 205, 206
witchcraft, 2, 4–5, 8, 48, 52–4, 56–8, 92–3, 131, 133, 139
'Women and Materiality in Medieval and Early Modern Scotland' symposium, 69
Women's Petition, 135, 137
Wood, John, 13, 24, 25–9

youth, 8, 9, 194–5, 197, 198–204, 209

EU Authorised Representative:
Easy Access System Europe Mustamäe tee 50, 10621 Tallinn, Estonia
gpsr.requests@easproject.com

Printed and bound by CPI Group (UK) Ltd, Croydon, CR0 4YY
10/03/2026
02068804-0006